GW01367234

EUREKA!

Activity Pack 1

*Carol Chapman, Rob Musker,
Daniel Nicholson, Moira Sheehan*

Heinemann Educational Publishers
Halley Court, Jordan Hill, Oxford, OX2 8EJ
a division of Reed Educational & Professional Publishing Ltd
Heinemann is a registered trademark of Reed Educational & Professional Publishing Ltd

OXFORD MELBOURNE AUCKLAND
JOHANNESBURG BLANTYRE GABARONE
IBADAN PORTSMOUTH NH (USA) CHICAGO

First published 2000

ISBN 0 435 57611 9

04 03 02 01 00
10 9 8 7 6 5 4 3 2

Edited by Sarah Ware

Designed and typeset by Ken Vail Graphic Design, Cambridge

Illustrated by Barry Atkinson, Graham-Cameron Illustration (Darin Mount and Sarah Wimperis), Nick Hawken, B.L. Kearley Ltd. (Jeremy Gower and Pat Tourett), David Lock, Joseph McEwan, Sylvie Poggio Artists Agency (Rhiannon Powell and Sean Victory) and Linda Rogers Associates (Keith Howard).

Printed and bound in Great Britain by Athanaeum Press Ltd, Gateshead.

Acknowledgments

Cover photos: **Tower arch**, Tony Stone Images. **Blue spotted coral trout**, Oxford Scientific Films/Mark Webster. **Radio telescope at night,** Science Photo Library/David Nunuk.

The publishers have made every effort to trace the copyright holders, but if they have inadvertently overlooked any, they will be pleased to make the necessary arrangements at the first opportunity.

Introduction to the Eureka! course

Eureka! is designed so you can give top priority to your pupils' learning and success in science. All the components of Eureka can be used together to ensure that all your pupils' and your needs are met.

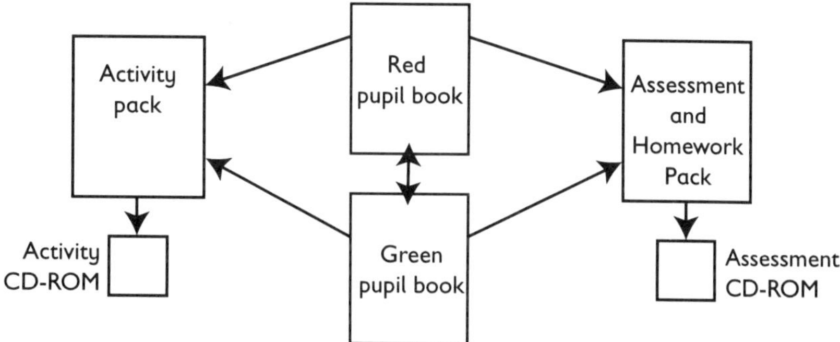

Lift-off!

Each unit starts with an exercise in the *Assessment and Homework Pack* to help you elicit information about what your pupils already know about the topic that they are to study. This helps you to ensure pupil progress by avoiding repetition.

Setting the scene pages

Each unit in the pupil book opens with a double-page spread that introduces the key concepts of the unit within an exciting context. It also reminds pupils of the material that they have already met at Key Stage 2. These spreads also meet some Sc 1 requirements using historical, social and environmental contexts and looking at innovations and investigations.

Unit maps

These are provided for each unit in the *Activity Pack*. They can be used either at the beginning of a unit to reactivate pupils' knowledge through brainstorming and word work, or at the end of the unit to consolidate pupils' learning for the *End of unit test.*

Learn about pages and activities

The pages explain new concepts. Each double-page spread starts with the learning objectives in the *Learn about* box and finishes with a summary of key points in the *For your notes* box. Icons indicate for the teacher where activities are provided in the *Activity Pack*.

Think about pages

Each unit has an opportunity to develop thinking skills within the context of science in *Think about* pages. For more details on how to use these pages, see page vii.

Homework sheets

Stand-alone photocopiable sheets for each unit are provided in the *Assessment and Homework Pack*. Each unit usually has two homework exercises focussing on literacy and numeracy. Sometimes there is a third exercise on science skills. All homework has been developed at two levels to support pupils working on either the *Red* or *Green* books.

Self-assessment quiz and revision sheets

Having completed the unit pupils can consolidate their learning and diagnose their own misconceptions using the quiz from the *Assessment and Homework Pack*. Pupils mark the multiple-choice quiz themselves and record their scores on a *Progress record*. This shows which topics in a unit they need to do more work on and directs them to a *Revision sheet* which helps them to revisit the concepts with which they have most difficulty.

End of unit tests

Each *End of unit test* tests all the required National Curriculum points and gives a summative assessment of the pupil's current NC level. The combined scores from a number of tests will give an accurate measure of performance.

Contents

Activity sheets

1 Energy

2 Changing state

3 Living things

4 Burning

5 Electricity

Using the Activity Pack

This pack provides all the resources you need to carry out the activities in the *Eureka!* course. Each activity usually consists of photocopiable worksheets to lead the pupil through the activity. The activities are often differentiated to two or three levels so that you can choose the most suitable level of support for each pupil.

The *Book notes* and *Activity notes* provide guidance for using double-page spreads in the books and activities in the pack. These are arranged so that the notes for each double-page spread and its associated activities are together. There are separate *Technician's notes* giving equipment lists and set-ups for the technician.

The activities are linked to specific pages in the books. Icons on the book pages signal to you that activities are available for you to use. There are four types of activity shown by these icons on the book pages:

Practical activities

These are practical activities that reinforce the main concepts illustrated in the text. Each activity has been tried in the classroom and checked for safety.

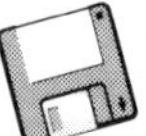

ICT activities

These include datalogging, database activities, spreadsheets, web searches, and presentation activities. Each activity has suggestions for software and equipment that may be used.

Writing activities

These include writing frames and opportunities for extended writing. These activities have been designed with a literacy focus and to support students with English as a second language.

Discussion activities

These activities encourage pupils to talk around or debate some of the issues covered within a topic. They also develop key-skills in communications.

Book notes

These notes provide all the information you need to teach from both the red and green books.

- an introduction to the spread and some supporting information for the lesson
- key ideas covered in each double-page spread from the book together with their National Curriculum reference
- list of the concepts the pupils will need to have from Key Stage 2 or previous units
- the answers to all the questions from the relevant spread in both the *Red* and *Green* books
- references to the *Activity sheets* available
- opportunities for further study not covered in the *Activity sheets*.

Activity notes

These notes provide a path through the activities by:

- indicating the purpose of the activity
- suggesting possible ways of running and differentiating the activity
- flagging the expected outcomes
- pointing out the pitfalls
- safety note to aid with COSHH assessment
- the answers to the questions on all the sheets

Technician's notes

These are a complete guide for technicians providing them with all the information they need to resource each activity.

Using the Assessment and Homework Pack

Here you will find all the resources that you will need to track the progress of all your pupils through **Eureka!** For more detail on how to use this pack see *How to use this pack* in the *Assessment and Homework Pack*.

Lift-off!

These exercises can be used as write-on sheets. There is an answer sheet with the answers written in. They are designed to be marked quickly by the pupils, either by the teacher reading out the answers or by photocopying the answer sheet onto an OHP. You can get an impression of who got the answers right either by a show of hands or by walking round the class.

Self-assessment quiz

Each quiz has a *Progress record* for the pupils to mark their answers on from the multiple-choice questions. They can then mark their own work from the answer sheet which you can read out or photocopy on to an OHP. The *Progress record* then guides each pupil to the most appropriate *Revision sheet* for their individual needs.

Revision sheets

These are write-on sheets and pupils can mark their own work using the answer sheets with the answers written in.

End of unit test

These are structured questions in a write-on format. Alternatively, question-only and answer-only versions of the questions are provided on the CD-ROM if you prefer pupils to write in their own books or to reuse the question papers and only need to photocopy the answer papers.

Teacher CD-ROMs

Activity Pack CD ROM

This contains:

- All the Activity sheets and Skills sheets from the pack in fully customisable Word format including artwork. This means that you can easily adapt them to the particular needs of your pupils.
- All the Activity sheets and Skills sheets exactly as they appear in the pack. These are intended as a reference to the printed sheets if you are using the CD-ROM alone to prepare lessons.
- All the Outline schemes of work in a customisable form to allow you to adapt them as required
- All curriculum matching charts as they appear in the pack
- The spreadsheets and databases used in some activities
- All the artwork from the pack provided as a resource bank for your own worksheets

Assessment Pack CD-ROMs

This contains:

- All the tests (Lift-off, Self assessment quiz and End-of-unit), together with answers and mark schemes, in fully customisable Word format so that you can adapt them to meet the needs of your pupils.
- All the Revision sheets and Homework sheets in customisable form.
- All the above material exactly as it appears in the pack for your reference if using the CD-ROM alone to prepare.

Both CD-ROMs are provided as single copies and in packs of five. The five packs are available with a ten-user license which means that members of the department can take CD-ROMs home for lesson preparation rather than the packs and still have access to the full range of resources.

A site licence (with 5 free CD-ROMs) is also available for unlimited use of the CD-ROM by anyone within the school.

Using the Think about **pages**

Thinking skills

These spreads are designed to encourage pupils to develop the skills they will need to be successful in science. They help pupils move towards higher order thinking which enables them to develop skills in application, analysis, synthesis and evaluation. These skills will help pupils to be successful in:

- completing science investigations
- working like scientists and using scientific models
- problem-solving using group work and discussion.

CASE

Many schools have incorporated CASE (Cognitive Acceleration in Science Education) into their science teaching. CASE was developed in response to research that indicated that pupils struggled with science because they could not cope with the demanding scientific concepts such as variables, probability and correlation. CASE activities encourage pupils to think scientifically, so that they develop the skills they need.

Think about spreads bridge to CASE

The *Think about* spreads offer unique opportunities to bridge to CASE activities. They develop similar skills to CASE and do this in the context of one or more of the main *Learn about* spreads of the unit. They do not take the place of CASE but bridge to it. CASE activities can still be used as intervention lessons running parallel with the school's science course.

Getting discussion going

The *Think about* spreads are designed to stimulate discussion in pairs, small groups, or as a whole class. The pupils should be encouraged to discuss the questions rather than write down individual answers. The teacher should act as a mediator, questioning pupils' thinking and giving credit to all the pupils' responses, as many of the questions are open-ended and do not have right or wrong answers. Almost any answer can be met with a further question that moves the pupil's thinking forward.

Think about spreads have five stages

A lesson using the *Think about* spread will usually fall into five parts:

1 A context is given which pupils are familiar with and they are introduced to any new terminology or apparatus that will be used.

2 The pupils are then lead to make an observation which may surprise them because it conflicts with their current understanding or way of thinking.

3 Pupils work in groups to find a way to resolve the conflict and thus develop new thinking patterns.

4 Pupils are encouraged to reflect on how they thought through the problem and compare their way of thinking with others in the group. They then feedback their ideas to the class to reinforce the new thinking patterns. This can be encouraged by asking open questions such as:

- What did you do?
- How do you explain…?
- What would happen if…?
- What does … tell you?
- What did you do next?
- What do you think they should do next?
- Explain why/how…
- Why do you think that…?

5 There may be opportunities to remind pupils of similar occasions where they can use their new thinking skills.

A number of the pupils using the *Green* book will be working at NC level 4 or below so these spreads will allow fewer opportunities to develop higher order thinking patterns than the *Red* book. But its structured approach will help these pupils to access these opportunities more easily, if they meet them either in the *Red* book or in CASE lessons.

Safety information

The following symbols are used in the pupil activity sheets to help pupils work safely:

> Wear eye protection.
>
> ⚠ This warning is accompanied by suitable explanatory text.

We have attempted to identify any activities that might present some hazard, and suggest the appropriate strategies to reduce the risk to acceptable levels (see *Safety notes* sections in both the *Activity notes* and *Technician's notes* of this pack). Most educational employers have adapted various national publications such as:

- *Safety in Science Education* (DFEE 1996)
- *Topics in Safety* (ASE, 2nd edition 1988)
- *Hazcards* (CLEAPSS School Science Service 1997), or in Scotland, SSERC *Hazardous Chemicals Manual 1997*
- *Safeguards in the School Laboratory* (ASE 10th edition 1996)

as the basis for their general risk assessments, and proposed activities should be compatible with advice contained in these publications. In all cases, however, teachers must follow the guidance or local rules produced by their employer.

It is assumed that a good laboratory policy and practice is observed throughout, for example:

- Eye protection is worn by both pupils and teacher whenever the risk assessment requires it. (This is indicated on the pupil activity sheets and in the *Safety notes* sections of the *Activity notes* and *Technician's notes*.)
- Other protective control equipment (e.g. safety screens, efficient fume cupboards) is similarly used when the risk assessment requires it.
- Long hair is tied back, pupils do not wear 'wet-look' hair preparations, and ties, scarves,and cardigans are not allowed to hang freely.
- Pupils are trained in how to heat chemicals safely, and reminded frequently of the technique.
- Pupils are taught how to smell gases safely.
- Containers of chemicals are clearly labelled with an appropriate name and any hazards.
- Eating, drinking and chewing are not permitted.
- Electrical and other equipment is well maintained and subject to regular checks.
- Pupils at particular risk (e.g. asthmatics, those with allergies and those with known disabilities) are identified and catered for.
- The size of the class and behaviour of pupils within it may be considered inappropriate for certain activities.
- Science staff have received appropriate training in the activities, including hazard identification and risk assessment.

For detailed information on IT safety an article in *School Science Review* may be useful: 'Safety aspects of IT' by Joe Jefferies, *SSR*. December 1997. 79(287).

Opportunities for covering Sc1 with Eureka! 1

This table shows the opportunities for teaching the skills needed in Sc1 investigations. Other activities in the course may give opportunities for only partial coverage of a statement.

There are some activities in the pack that also give opportunities for practising full Sc1 investigations. These are 2.5, 3.6B, 5.8 and 7.7A.

Ideas and evidence in science

PoS	*Book spread*	*Activity*
1a	5.1	4.6, 5.1
1b		5.3B, 5.4B, 5.8
1c	3.7, 4.3, 5.1, 5.5, 6.1, 7.1	4.6, 5.1, 5.5, 6.1B, 6.2C

Investigative skills

PoS	*Book spread*	*Activity*
2a		7.7A
2b		
2c		1.2AB, 1.4B, 2.3, 4.7, 5.3B, 5.4B, 7.7A
2d	1.9, 8.7	3.6B(Ext), 5.8, 7.7A
2e	3.7	3.6B(Ext), 5.8, 7.7A
2f		3.2, 4.2, 4.3, 4.4AB, 4.5, 5.8
2g		1.5A, 1.6B, 2.3, 3.2, 3.5, 4.2, 4.3, 4.4AB, 4.7, 5.3B, 5.4B, 5.8, 6.2AB, 6.3AB, 6.4, 6.5AB, 6.6B, 7.6A, 7.7A, 8.1A, 8.3A, 8.5A, 8.6A
2h		
2i	1.9, 8.7, 9.6	3.7, 4.7, 5.3B, 5.4B, 5.8, 6.2AB, 6.3C, 6.4, 6.5AB, 6.6B, 7.7A, 8.1A, 8.3A, 8.6A
2j	1.9, 4.7, 8.7, 9.6	3.2, 3.5, 4.3, 4.4AB, 4.7, 5.3B, 5.4B, 5.8, 8.3A, 8.5B, 8.6A, 9.3B, 9.5
2k	1.9, 2.7, 3.7, 4.7, 5.8, 8.7, 9.6	1.5A, 1.6B, 3.2, 3.3B, 3.4, 3.5, 4.2, 4.3, 4.4AB, 4.5, 4.7, 5.3B, 5.4B, 5.6AB, 6.3ABC, 7.3AB, 7.4AB, 7.7A
2l		2.3, 4.7, 5.3B, 5.4B, 5.8, 7.7A, 8.5
2m		1.4B, 2.3, 3.7, 4.7, 8.5AB, 9.3B, 9.5
2n		3.6B, 5.8
2o		3.7, 5.8
2p		1.4B, 4.7, 5.8, 6.3C, 7.7A, 8.3A, 8.5AB, 8.6A

Eureka! 1 National Curriculum match by unit

Sc 2	*Sc 3*	*Sc 4*
3 Living things Plants, animals, microbes Classify animals Variation in species, adaptation 4a, 4b, 5b, 5c	**2 Changing state** Solids, liquids and gases Particle theory Separating mixtures 1a, 1b, 1g, 1h, 2b	**1 Energy** Definition, transfers, conservation Sound and hearing 3g, 3h, 3j, 3k, 5b, 5d, 5e, 5g
6 Plant power Plant and animals cells Photosynthesis, reproduction 1b, 1d, 3a, 3b, 3d	**4 Burning** Combustion, oxidation, simple reactions Food and fuel Word equations 1e, 1f, 2g, 2h, 2i, 3a	**5 Electricity** Circuit components, current, voltage Series and parallel Magnets Electromagnets 1a, 1b, 1c, 1d, 1e, 1f
9 Life story Human reproduction, variation, cells Pregnancy Adolescence 1d, 2f, 2g, 2h	**7 Metals** Metals and non-metals, properties Elements, periodic table, simple reactions Rusting 1a, 1b, 1c, 1d,1e, 1g, 3a	**8 Forces** Weight, mass, gravity, friction Unbalanced and balanced Speed 2a, 2b, 2c, 2d

Eureka! 2 National Curriculum match by unit

Sc 2	Sc 3	Sc 4
2 Vital organs Cells, tissues, organs and systems Specialised cells Skeleton, joints, movement 1a, 1c, 1e, 2e, 2l	**1 Acids and bases** Acids, bases, pH, litmus, UI Neutralisations form salts With metals, carbonates Acids in the environment 2i, 3d, 3e, 3f, 3g, 3h	**3 Space** Solar system, Moon phases Day/night, seasons, eclipses Satellites, natural and unnatural, orbit 3a, 3b, 4a, 4b, 4c, 4d, 4e
5 Using food Animal nutrition, balanced diet Digestion, enzymes Respiration Breathing and circulation systems 2a, 2b, 2c, 2d, 2j, 2k, 2l	**4 Matter** Physical changes, kinetic theory Diffusion. expansion, contraction Gas pressure Dissolving, solvents 1b, 1c, 1f, 2a, 2b, 2c	**6 Energy resources** Fossil fuels Generating electricity Renewables Fuels for the future 5a, 5b, 5c, 5e, 5g, 3.2h, 3.2i
8 Environment Classify plants Plant respiration and nutrition, biomass Food chains and webs and pyramids 3a, 3b, 3c, 3e, 4b, 5a, 5b, 5e, 5f	**7 Rocks** Physical and chemical weathering Types of rocks, properties, uses Rock cycle 1g, 2d, 2e, 2f, 2i	**9 Light and sound** Light and luminous/non-luminous Reflection, refraction Colour and filters Sound, how different/same as light 3a, 3b, 3c, 3d, 3e, 3f

Eureka! 3 National Curriculum match by unit

Sc 2	*Sc 3*	*Sc 4*
2 Being healthy Drugs and smoking, breathing air exchange Effect of drugs on pregnancy Recap cells, cell division Growth of bacteria and viruses Body's immune system 2i, 2m, 2n	**1 Chemical reactions** Chemical changes, quantitative Recap symbols, word equations Chemical reactions in everyday situations – useful and unuseful including acids 1c, 1e, 1f, 2g, 2h, 3d, 3e, 3f	**3 Balanced forces** Recap balanced/unbalanced, density Pivots and moments Pressure and applications 2c, 2e, 2f, 2g
5 Competition Causes of variation in species Selective breeding Protecting living things and environment Predation, competition, population 4a, 4c, 5a, 5d	**4 Chemical patterns** Metals recap on reactivity Displacement reactions Reactivity series and periodic table Using patterns of reactions, e.g. with acid 1f, 3a, 3b, 3c, 3g, 3h	**6 Moving energy** Recap energy transfer Different temperatures give energy transfer Conduction, convection, evaporation radiation Energy conserved but dissipated 1c, 5a, 5b, 5c, 5d, 5e, 5f, 5g
8 Biology revision Human reproduction Respiration Cell types and organ systems Nutrition in plants and animals Variation/classification/adaptation	**7 Chemistry revision** Physical changes – changing state Physical changes – separation Kinetic theory and molecules Rocks	**9 Physics revision** Energy and resources Electricity Light and sound Speed Earth and space

Opportunities for covering ICT PoS with Eureka! 1

The ICT activities in this pack provide opportunities to cover some of the ICT PoS.

ICT PoS	*Activity*
1c (databases)	1.5, 3.7, 7.3B, 7.4B
2a (information)	3.3A, 3.4, 3.6A
2b (datalogging)	3.6B, 4.4A, 4.7, 6.3C, 8.6A
4a (reflect critically)	3.7

Further suggestions in the teacher's notes under the heading "ICT opportunities" provide ideas for covering some of the ICT PoS. These ideas are related to the following book spreads.

ICT PoS	*Book spread*
1a	
1b (information search)	1.3, 2.2, 2.3, 2.4, 2.7, 3.1, 4.7, 5.1, 5.6, 5.8, 6.1, 6.2, 7.1, 7.3, 7.4, 8.2, 9.1
1c (databases and spreadsheets)	8.3, 8.4, 9.6
2a	
2b	
2c (models)	5.2, 5.6, 6.3
2d	
3a	
3b (presentations)	6.2, 8.1, 8.5
3c	
4a	
4b	
4c	
4d	
5a	
5b	
5c	
5d	

Further ICT PoS statements can be covered depending on the emphasis given to ICT in the class room.

Opportunities for covering Literacy skills with Eureka! 1

Key:

Bold = Green and Red books, Core activity, Green and Red homework

Normal = Green book only, Help activity only, Green homework only

Italics = Red book only, Extension activity only, Red homework only

[ ] = Also covered under another skill

Literacy Skills	*Book Spread*	*Activity*	*Homework*
Words and meanings/ definitions	1.7A (q1), 2.1B (q2), **2.3A (q1)**, 2.5 (q1), **2.6A (q1)**, 3.1 (q1), 3.4 (q1), 3.5 (q1), **4.1A (q1)**, **4.2 (q1)**, 4.4 (q1), 4.5 (q1), 4.6 (q1), **6.1A (q1)**, 6.4 (q1) 6.6B (q3), **8.2 (q.1)**, 8.3A (q.1) **8.7A (q1)**, **9.2 (q1)**, **9.5 (q1)**	**2.4A**, 2.6A, **6.1A**, **6.6A**, **9.2A**, 9.2A, **9.2B**, 9.2B, **9.4**, 9.4	**2A**, **5B**
Brainstorming specific vocabulary using the Unit map	**1.1**, **2.1**, **3.1**, **4.1**, **5.1**, **6.1**, **7.1**, **8.1**, **9.1**	**4.1**	
Reading comprehension (analysing and synthesising information)	*5.2 (q3)*, *6.4 (q2)*, **7.7** *(q1/2)*, (q2/3), *8.2 (q4)*, *8.4 (q1)*	**5.7A**, *6.6C*, *7.1A*, **7.7B**, 7.7B, *7.7B*	**1A**, **3B**, **4A**, **7A**, **9A**
Cloze	1.3 (q1), 1.7 (q1) [2.1 (q2)], **2.2 (q1)**, [2.3 (q1)], **2.5 (q1)**, **[2.6 (q1)]**, 3.2 (q1), [3.5 (q1)] 3.6 (q1), 3.7 (q1), [4.2 (q1)]. [4.4 (q1)], [4.5 (q1)], [4.6 q1)], 5.3 (q1), **6.3 (q1)**, 6.4 (q1), 6.5 (q1), [6.6 (q3)], 8.1 (q1), [8.2 (q1)], [8.3 (q1)],8.4 (q1), 8.5 (q1), 8.6 (q1), [8.7 (q1)], [9.2 (q1)], 9.4 (q2)	3.2, 3.5, 4.2, 4.4, 4.7	
Sequencing	7.1 (q1), **7.2** *(q1)*, (q.5), 9.1 (q1)	*6.6C*, **9.1**, **9.3A**	**2A**, **4A**
Recording information	**2.1 (q1)**, **2.2 (q2)**, 3.2 (q2), 3.3 (q1), **5.2 (q2)**, **5.6 (q1)**, **6.7**, **8.6**	**1.2A**, **1.3B**, 1.3B, *1.3B*, **1.4A**, **2.2**, 2.3, **2.4A**, **2.5**, 2.5, *2.5*, **3.2**, 3.2, 3.5, **4.3**, 4.3, 4.4B, 5.8, *5.8*, **6.3A**, 6.3A, **6.3B**, **6.6B**, **7.2A**, **7.7A**, 7.7A, 9.4	
Extended writing supported by writing frames	**6.1 (q3)**, **7.1 (q2)**, **8.1**, **8.3 (q2)**, **9.3**	**4.6**, 4.6, **6.1B**, **7.1B**, **8.1B**, **8.3B**, **9.3C**	
Extended writing unsupported	1.5 (q2), **2.1 (q3)**, **5.1**, *6.4 (q3)*, **9.1**	*5.1*	
Poem/slogan writing	**2.4**, 6.5 (q4), 8.6 (q2)	**4.1**	
Discussion		**1.8A**, **2.4B**, **3.1**, **3.3B**, **4.1**, **5.8**, *5.8*	
Writing conclusions	*1.6 (q4)*, **1.9**, *2.3 (q4)*, *5.5 (q1)*, *5.8 (q2)*, *8.7 (.2c)*	**1.4B**, 1.4B, **1.6B**, **2.3**, **2.5**, *3.6B*, **4.3**, **5.8**, 5.8, *5.8*	**5A**, **7A**
Predicting [and planning]	*2.6 (q3)*, *4.7 (q3/4)*, *7.6 (q3)*, *9.6 (qf)*	**1.8A**, **2.5**, 2.5, 2.5, **3.6B**, 3.6, *3.6B*, **4.4A**, **5.3B**, *5.3B*, **5.4B**, *5.4B*, **5.8**, 5.8, *5.8*, **6.3B**, **6.3C**, **7.7A**, 7.7A	**6C**
Summarising	1.7 (q2), *6.6 (q2)*, **7.3**, *7.8 (q7)*, *8.3 (q1)*, 8.5 (q3), **9.2**, *9.3 (q4)*	2.5, **3.1**, *3.6B*, **5.8**, *5.8*, **6.4**, **6.5B**, **7.7B**, 7.7B, *7.7B*, 9.4	**2A**, **4A**, **6B**, **6C**
Evaluating arguments	**7.3**, **9.1**, 9.6 (qf)	**8.2**	
Presenting information	*6.2 (q.3)*, **9.4**	**1.8A**, **4.1**	

Opportunities for covering Numeracy skills with Eureka! 1

Key:

Bold = Green and Red books, Core activity, Green and Red homework

Normal = Green book only, Help activity only, Green homework only

Italic = Red book only, Extension activity only, red homework only

Numeracy Skills	*Book Spread*	*Activity*	*Homework*
Numbers and number system	**6.7**		**3B**
Calculating	**6.1**, **6.7**, **8.2**, *8.4*, **8.6**	**8.2**, *8.4*, **8.6B**	**1B**, **4B**, **6A**, **8B**, **9B**
Solving problems	**5.2**, **5.3**, **5.4**, **5.6**, **7.5**	**5.6A**	**5C**, **7B**
Using data	**1.5**, **1.7**, **1.9**, **3.7**, **4.7**, **5.8**, **7.2**, **8.6**, **8.7**, **9.6**	**2.6B**, **3.6B**, **3.7**, **4.4A**, **4.7**, **5.3B**, **5.4B**, **5.8**, **6.3C**, **7.2B**, **8.3A**, **8.5B**, **8.6A**, **9.5**	**1B**, **6C**, **9A**, **9B**
Measuring		**8.1A**	
Using equations	**8.6**	**8.6B**	**8C**

Outline Scheme of Work for Eureka! 1

1 Energy

Expected outcomes

Recognising energy is present	Knowing types of energy	Understanding energy transfers	Understanding sound

Unit content

Spread	PoS	Learning objectives Pupils should know:	Teaching activities	ICT PoS	Specific literacy objectives	Specific numeracy objectives
1.1 S	Not in KS2	Energy is present	Lift–off! and Unit map goggles – Energy circus – C			
1.2	4.5e 1.2c	Things that move have movement energy Energy given out as light is light energy Energy given out as sound is sound energy Energy that warms is heat energy	goggles – A: Energy out! – C pen – B: Energy everywhere! – C		Recording information	
1.3	4.5e	Energy is transferred Energy transfers are shown as energy diagrams Energy carried by electricity is electrical energy	goggles – A: Energy in, energy out – C pen – B: Move it! (transfer diagrams) – C H E		Recording information	
1.4	4.5e 1.2cmp	Energy can be stored as strain energy Energy can be stored as chemical energy Energy can be stored as gravitational energy	goggles – A: Stored energy – C goggles – B: Cotton reel racers – C H			
1.5	1.2gik 4.5ae	Energy is stored in food as chemical energy	goggles – A: Energy in food – C ICT – B: How much energy? – C			
1.6	4.3gi 1.2gk	Sound is made by vibrations The eardrum vibrates when sound enters the ear Sound needs a material to travel through	goggles – A: Bell in a vacuum demonstration – C goggles – B: Investigating sound – C			
1.7	4.3ghjk	Loud sounds can damage hearing The larger the amplitude of vibration, the louder the sound The larger the frequency of vibration, the higher the pitch of the sound Some people can hear higher pitch sounds than others	goggles – CRO demonstrations – C			
1.8	4.5bg	Energy is conserved Most energy can be traced to the sun When energy is transferred, only some of it is useful	speech – A: Energy trails – C pen – B: 'Wasted' energy – C		Presenting information	
1.9 T	1.2d	Things that change during an investigation are variables In a fair test most variables are kept the same One variable, the input variable, is changed One variable, the output variable, is measured to get the results	goggles – The best fuel? – C			

Homework and assessment

Unit map for summarising key ideas of unit	Assessment
Homework	Quiz
1A Types of energy: Literacy	Revision sheets 1–4
1B Using energy: Numeracy	End of unit test
1C Energy transfer: Science skills	

2 Changing state

Expected outcomes

Properties of matter	Particles	Separations	

Unit content

Spread	PoS	Learning objectives Pupils should know:	Teaching activities	ICT PoS	Specific literacy objectives	Specific numeracy objectives
2.1 S	KS2 3.1e	Differences between solids liquids and gases	Lift-off! and Unit map pen – The birthday party – C			
2.2	1.2cglm 3.1b	Solids are hard and have a fixed shape and volume Liquids have a fixed volume but are runny and can be poured Gases do not have a fixed shape or volume Gases take the shape of their container, and can be squashed easily	pen – Classifying materials – C		Recording information	
2.3	3.1ab	Everything is made of particles In solids, particles are close together and have a neat pattern In liquids, particles are less regularly arranged and not all joined In gases, particles are far apart, and there is no pattern Solids and liquids are more dense than gases	goggles – A tight squeeze – C H		Recording information	
2.4	3.1b 3.2c	Particles move fast when heated, and slow down as they cool A solid melts because the particles stop being strongly attached to each other. A liquid evaporates because the particles are no longer attracted to each other and move on their own These changes are called changes of state	goggles – A: Moving particles – C speech – B: Role play – Particles – C		Recording information Discussion	
2.5	2.1a–p 3.2b	A solute dissolves in a solvent The solute particles fits in amongst the solvent particles The mixture of a solute dissolved in a solvent is called a solution	goggles – Investigating dissolving – C H E			
2.6	3.1gh	Distillation is used to separate a pure liquid from a solution Chromatography is a way of separating a mixture of dyes	goggles – A: Distillation – H pen – B: Looking at mixtures – C			Using data
2.7T	1.2klo 3.1h	Analysing results scientifically Applications of chromatography				

Homework and assessment

Unit map for summarising key ideas of unit	**Assessment**
Homework	Quiz
2A Particles: Literacy	Revision sheets 1–3
2B Marbles: Literacy	End of unit test

3 Living things

Expected outcomes

Life processes/plants and animals	Vertebrate classification	Invertebrate classification	Variation and adaptation

Unit content

Spread	PoS	Learning objectives Pupils should know:	Teaching activities	ICT PoS	Specific literacy objectives	Specific numeracy objectives
3.1 S	KS2 2.1ab	That there are life processes common to plants and animals These include nutrition, movement, growth and reproduction	Lift–off! and Unit map speech – Survival – C		Discussion	
3.2	1.2fgjk 2.4b	Living things with similar features are classified into groups Vertebrates are animals with a backbone Invertebrates are animals without a backbone	goggles – Pond survey – C H		Recording information	
3.3	1.2k 1.4b	Vertebrates are classified into 5 groups which have different features The groups are mammals, birds, reptiles, amphibians and fish	ICT – A: All backbone! – C E speech – B: Vertebrates games – C	2a	Discussion	
3.4	1.2k 2.4b	Invertebrates are divided into 7 groups The groups are jellyfish, starfish, flatworms, roundworms, segmented worms, molluscs and arthropods The arthropods are split into crustaceans, centipedes, millipedes, spiders and insects	ICT – Suits of armour – C	2a		
3.5	1.2gjk 2.4a	Differences between living things are called variations Organisms that differ sufficiently are classified as different species Some variation within species is inherited and some is environmental Discontinuous variation means having one feature or another. In continuous variation there are lots of inbetweens. (Red only)	goggles – Spot the species! – C H		Recording information	
3.6	1.2a–p 2.5bc	Many animals are adapted to survive in a particular habitat Animals adapted to live in the cold have fur or fat as insulation Some animals are camouflaged to hide from other animals Some animals change their behaviour to cope with temperature change	ICT – A: Bear necessities – C ICT – B: A winter coat – C H E	2a 2b		Using data
3.7T	2.4a 1.2gimo	Sampling Displaying data	ICT – Class heights – C H	1c 4a		Using data

Homework and assessment

Unit map for summarising key ideas of unit	Assessment
Homework	Quiz
3A Identifying animals: Science skills	Revision sheets 1–4
3B Turtle breeding: Literacy/Numeracy	End of unit test

Outline Scheme of Work for Eureka! 1

4 Burning

Expected outcomes

Burning, fuels and energy	Metals reacting with oxygen	Word equations for reactions	

Unit content

Spread	PoS	Learning objectives Pupils should know:	Teaching activities	ICT PoS	Specific literacy objectives	Specific numeracy objectives
4.1 S	KS2 3.2g	When materials are burned, new materials are formed Burning is an irreversible change	Lift–off! and Unit map speech – The burning question – C		Brainstorming	
4.2	1.2fgk 3.2h	Oxygen from the air is needed for burning, and also for life Flammable materials burn more easily than others Fires need fuel, oxygen and heat to burn	goggles – Putting fires out – C H			
4.3	1.2fgjk 3.1ef 3.3a	Substances join with oxygen to make oxides. This is a chemical change Some metals burn in air to make oxides (Red only) Word equations	goggles – Burning metals – C (H) E		Recording information	
4.4	1.2fgijk 3.2h 4.5ae	Fuels store energy, which is released when fuels burn There are many different fuels The body uses food as fuel Energy is measured in joules, J	ICT – A: How much energy? – C (H) goggles – B: A good fuel? – C H	2b	Recording information	Using data
4.5	1.2fgk 3.1e 3.2h	Fuels, including food, contain carbon When carbon burns it combines with oxygen in the air to make carbon dioxide Carbon dioxide is a gas that turns lime water milky	goggles – What happens when a fuel burns? – C H			
4.6	1.1ac 3.1f 3.2gh	When fuels burn a chemical reaction, called combustion, takes place A word equation shows what happens in a chemical reaction Equations must balance (Red only) Hydrocarbons are fuels that contain carbon and hydrogen	pen – The day we discovered oxygen – C H		Extended writing with frame	
4.7T	1.2cgijklmp 3.2i	The word "relationship" describes how an outcome variable changes when the input variable is changed A straight line graph shows that there is a relationship between the variables Scientists use a model to represent a real situation that is difficult to test The greenhouse effect	ICT – Grow your own greenhouse effect – C H	2b		Using data

Homework and assessment

Unit map for summarising key ideas of unit	Assessment
Homework	Quiz
4A Fire safety: Literacy	Revision sheets 1–3
4B Burning peanuts: Numeracy/data handling	End of unit test
4C Word equations: Science skills (Red only)	

5 Electricity

Expected outcomes

Basic electricity	Voltage, current and energy	Magnets and electromagnets	

Unit content

Spread	PoS	Learning objectives Pupils should know:	Teaching activities	ICT PoS	Specific literacy objectives	Specific numeracy objectives
5.1 S	KS2 1.1a 1.1ac 4.1a	The discovery of the electric light bulb	Lift–off! and Unit map pen – Developing the lightbulb –E		Extended writing	
5.2	4.1c	Electricity provides energy to make things work A complete circuit is needed for the energy to be transferred	goggles – A: Find the fault – (C) pen – B: Switch on! – C E			
5.3	1.1b 1.2cgijkl 4.1ab	Current is measured in amps, A, using an ammeter The current is the same on both sides of a lamp Increasing the number of lamps in a circuit decreases the current Increasing the number of batteries in a circuit increases the current	goggles – A: Demonstration: the current either side of a lamp – (C) goggles – B: Investigating current – C E		Predicting	Using data
5.4	4.1ac 1.1b 1.2gijkl	Voltage is measured across parts of a circuit Voltage is measured in volts, V, using a voltmeter There is a voltage wherever energy is entering or exiting the circuit	goggles – A: Demonstration: the voltage across different parts of a circuit – (C) goggles – B: Investigating voltage: batteries – C E		Predicting	Using data
5.5T	1.1c	Models of electricity	goggles – Demonstration: 'class and matches' model – (C)			
5.6	4.1a	Series and parallel circuits Lamps in parallel are brighter than lamps in series In series, the current is the same at all points and the voltage is shared between the lamps In parallel, the current is shared between the loops of the circuit, and the voltage is the same across the battery and each lamp	goggles – A: Series and parallel circuits: current – C E goggles – B: Series and parallel circuits: voltage – C			
5.7	4.1de	A coil of wire connected to a battery becomes a magnet Magnets make magnetic fields, which have magnetic field lines Like magnetic poles repel, and opposites attract Iron, nickel and cobalt are magnetic metals	goggles – A: What do magnets do? – C (H) goggles – B: Demonstration: the magnet field around a bar magnet and a coil – (C) goggles – C: Demonstration: how a coil behaves like a magnet			
5.8	4.1f 1.1b 1.2cefgijkln op	An electromagnet is a coil of wire with a current running through it and a core inside. If the core is iron, the electromagnet can be switched off. Increasing the current makes the electromagnet stronger Increasing the number of turns in the coil makes the electromagnet stronger	goggles – Electromagnets – C H E		Predicting Recording Summarising	Using data

Homework and assessment

Unit map for summarising key ideas of unit	Assessment
Homework	Quiz
5A Circuits and switches: Science skills	Revision sheets 1–3
5B Flowing current: Literacy	End of unit test
5C Circuit components: Numeracy	

6 Plant power

Expected outcomes

Cells (building blocks)	Photosynthesis	Plant structure	Plant reproduction

Unit content

Spread	PoS	Learning objectives Pupils should know:	Teaching activities	ICT PoS	Specific literacy objectives	Specific numeracy objectives
6.1 S	1.1c	How microscopes were discovered The concept of cells	Lift–off! and Unit map pen – A: The parts of a microscope – C (E) pen – B: A letter from Robert Hooke – C		Extended writing with frame	
6.2	1.1a, 1.2gi 2.1b	All living things are made of cells There are 2 types of cell: animal cells and plant cells Both types of cell have a cell membrane, cytoplasm and a nucleus Plant cells also have a cell wall, chloroplasts and a vacuole. They have a regular shape.	goggles – A: Looking at plant cells – C goggles – B: Looking at animal cells – C goggles – C: Making a model cell – C E			
6.3	1.2gikp 2.3ab	Plants make food by photosynthesis In photosynthesis plants use light energy, carbon dioxide and water to make sugars and oxygen	goggles – A: What do plants need for photosynthesis? – C H goggles – B: What gas is made in photosynthesis? – C ICT – C: When do plants grow the fastest? – C	2b	Recording information	
6.4	1.2gi 2.3ab	Photosynthesis occurs in the leaves Leaves have a large surface area to trap sunlight Leaves have air holes so carbon dioxide can move in and oxygen can move out	goggles – Looking at leaves – C			
6.5	1.2gi 2.3d	Plant roots anchor the plant and absorb water and minerals Root hairs are tiny parts with a large surface area to absorb water Water is transported around the plant through the veins	goggles – A: Looking at root hairs – C goggles – B: Water transport in celery – C		Summarising	
6.6	1.2gi 2.1d	Flowers contain the sex parts of plants The male cells are the pollen grains The female cells are the egg cells Pollination is the transfer of pollen from anther to stigma Fertilisation happens when the nuclei of the pollen and egg join	pen – A: Flower structure – C (E) goggles – B: Growing pollen tubes – C (E) pen – C: How pollination happens – E		Recording Reading comprehension	
6.7T	–	Concept of scale diagrams – scaling up and down	–			

Homework and assessment

Unit map for summarising key ideas of unit	Assessment
Homework	Quiz
6A Using microscopes: Numeracy	Revision sheets 1–4
6B Photosynthesis: Literacy	End of unit test
6C Investigating photosynthesis: Numeracy/Data handling	

Outline Scheme of Work for Eureka! 1

7 Metals

Expected outcomes

Properties of metals and non-metals	Elements and compounds	Reactions of elements	

Unit content

Spread	PoS	Learning objectives Pupils should know:	Teaching activities	ICT PoS	Specific literacy objectives	Specific numeracy objectives
7.1 S	1.1c, 3.2h KS2 3.1a	Metals through history Metals have different uses depending on their different properties	Lift-off! and Unit map pen – A: Making iron and steel – E pen – B: A better knife – C		Reading comprehension Extended writing	
7.2	1.2e 3.1ad	Metals are shiny. Most are solids at room temperature Metals conduct electricity and thermal energy A few metals, including iron, are magnetic	goggles – A: Properties of metals – C pen – B: Sold, liquid or gas? – C H E		Recording information	Using data
7.3	1.2k 3.1cd	An atom is the simplest type of particle Elements are made up of only one type of atom. Many metals are elements Each element has a symbol Elements are arranged in the periodic table. The periodic table has groups (columns) and periods (rows)	goggles – A: Display of metallic elements – (C) ICT – B: Metallic elements – C	1c		
7.4	1.2k 3.1d	Some elements are non-metals Most non-metals are not shiny and do not conduct electricity or heat At room temperature some non-metals are solids, some are liquids and some are gases	goggles – A: Display of non-metallic elements – (C) ICT – B: Non-metallic elements – C	1c		
7.5T	3.1d	Classifying elements according to physical properties	pen – Grouping metals – C H			
7.6	1.2g 3.1e 3.3a	New substances are made during chemical reactions, but not during physical changes When metal reacts with oxygen, an oxide is made When metal reacts with chlorine a chloride is made When metal reacts with sulphur a sulphide is made	goggles – A: Making iron sulphide – C pen – B: Recording reactions – C H E			
7.7	1.2acdgiklp 3.2h	Iron rusts when exposed to water and oxygen Rusting turns iron into iron oxide Rusting is a type of corrosion. Corrosion destroys metals	goggles – A: Will it rust? – C H pen – B: Rusty screws – C H E		Reading comprehension	
7.8	3.1efg 3.2g	A compound contains more than one type of atom joined together A pure substance contains only one element or compound A molecule is a group of atoms joined together	pen – A: Which particles are present? – C pen – B: Formulae – E			

Homework and assessment

Unit map for summarising key ideas of unit	Assessment
Homework	Quiz
7A Sulphur and copper: Literacy	Revision sheets 1–3
7B Periodic table: Literacy	End of unit test

8 Forces

Expected outcomes

Types of force	Balanced and unbalanced forces	Speeds	Variables and relationships

Unit content

Spread	PoS	Learning objectives Pupils should know:	Teaching activities	ICT PoS	Specific literacy objectives	Specific numeracy objectives
8.1 S	KS2 4.2bce 1.2gi	Objects are pulled downwards because of the gravitational attraction between the object and the earth Forces act in particular directions and can be measured	Lift–off! and Unit map goggles – A: Measuring forces – C pen – B: Forces in everyday life – C		Extended writing with frame	
8.2	4.2b	Gravity is the force that pulls everything towards the centre of the earth Weight is measured in newtons, N, and is the force of gravity on an object Mass is measured in kilograms, kg, and is a measure of how much matter an object is made of	pen – Mass and weight – C			Calculating
8.3	1.2gikp (Ext.1.2a–e) 4.2d	Friction is a force exerted wen things rub against each other Air resistance is a form of friction Friction can be increased or reduced	goggles – A: Shoe soles – C (E) pen – B: A world without friction – C		Extended writing with frame	
8.4	4.2c	Unbalanced forces on a stationary object make the object move in the direction of the force. Unbalanced forces on a moving object make the object speed up or slow down	pen – Unbalanced forces – C E			Calculating
8.5	1.2gikmp 4.2c	If two forces of the same size act in opposite directions, they are called balanced forces The reaction force stops something falling through a solid object. The reaction force balances the weight When an object floats, the forces of weight and upthrust are equal	goggles – A: Making bridges – C goggles – B: Stretching – C pen – C: Balanced forces – H			Using data Calculating
8.6	1.2gikp 4.2a	Speed is the distanced an object travels in a certain time Speed = distance travelled in metres, divided by time taken, in seconds Speed is measured in metres per second, m/s, or kilometres per hour, km/h	ICT – A: Speeding trolleys – C pen – B: Speed freak – C	2b		Using data Calculating Using equations
8.7T	1.2j 4.2a	Relationships between variables How to determine the speed of a moving object Quantitative relationship between speed, distance and time	–			

Homework and assessment

Unit map for summarising key ideas of unit	Assessment
Homework	Quiz
8A Friction: Literacy	Revision sheets 1–4
8B Opposing forces: Numeracy	End of unit test
8C The speed triangle: Science skills/Numeracy	

9 Life story

Expected outcomes

Male and female reproductive systems	Fertilisation	Pregnancy and birth	Adolescence

Unit content

Spread	PoS	Learning objectives Pupils should know:	Teaching activities	ICT PoS	Specific literacy objectives	Specific numeracy objectives
9.1 S	KS2 2.1a KS2 2.2f	The main stages of the human life cycle Reproduction is a life process common to animals and humans	Lift-off! and Unit map pen – Life cycles – C			
9.2	2.2g	Sperm are made in the testes. They pass down the sperm duct and out of the penis Eggs are made in the ovaries. They pass down the oviduct to the uterus	pen – A: Male parts – C H pen – B: Female parts – C H		Words and meanings	
9.3	1.2jm 2.1e 2.2g	Sexual intercourse releases millions of sperm into the woman's vagina Most of the sperm die, but one may make it to the egg Fertilisation occurs when the nuclei of the egg and sperm join together	pen – A: Fertilisation – C (H) pen – B: Sperm meets egg – C pen – C: The sperm's story – C		Sequencing Extended writing with frame	
9.4	2.2h	It takes 9 months for a human baby to develop fully. This 9 months is called pregnancy	pen – The fetus – C H E		Words and meanings	
9.5	1.2jm 2.2fg	Adolescence is a time when physical and emotional changes happen Puberty is the first part of adolescence Most physical changes happen during puberty	pen – Growth spurts – C			Using data
9.6T	2.2h	Drawing and interpreting graphs and bar charts Different animals have different gestation periods Relationship between adult mass of an animal and its gestation period	–			

Homework and assessment

Unit map for summarising key ideas of unit	Assessment
Homework	Quiz
9A Breast feeding: Literacy/Numeracy	Revision sheets 1–4
9B Pregnancy: Numeracy	End of unit test

Eureka! to QCA Schemes of Work match

Eureka! unit	*Scheme of Work unit*
Book 1	
1 Energy	Energy Resources, Sound and Hearing
2 Changing state	Particle Model, Solutions, Using Chemistry
3 Living things	Environments and Feeding, Variation and Classification
4 Burning	Simple Chemical Reactions, Environmental Chemistry, Using Chemistry
5 Electricity	Electric Circuits, Magnets and Electromagnets
6 Plant power	Cells, Plants and Photosynthesis
7 Metals	Simple Chemical Reactions, Particle Explanation of Changes, Atoms and Elements, Patterns of Reactivity, Reactions of Metals and Metal Compounds
8 Forces	Forces and their Effects, Gravity and Space, Speeding Up
9 Life story	Reproduction
Book 2	
1 Acids and bases	Acids and Alkalis, Chemical Reactions, Materials, Compounds and Mixtures, Environmental Chemistry, Reactions of Metals and Acids
1 Vital organs	Cells, Respiration
3 Earth in Space	The Solar System and Beyond, Gravity and Space
4 Matter	Particle Explanation of Material, Particle Explanation of Changes, Compounds and Mixtures
5 Nutrition	Cells, Food and Digestion, Respiration
6 Energy resources	Energy Resources
7 Rocks	Rocks and Weathering, The Rock Cycle, Environmental Chemistry
8 Environment	Environment and Feeding, Ecological relationships, Respiration, Plants and Photosynthesis, Plants for Food,
9 Light and sound	Light, Sound and Hearing
Book 3	
1 Chemical reactions	Using Chemistry
2 Being healthy	Respiration, Fit and Healthy, Microbes and Disease
3 Balanced forces	Pressure and Moments
4 Chemical patterns	Patterns of Reactivity, Using Chemistry
5 Competition	Inheritance and Selection, Plants for Food
6 Moving energy	Heating and Cooling, Energy and Electricity

QCA Schemes of Work to Eureka! match

Scheme of Work unit	*Eureka! unit*
Year 7	
Cells	Bk1: 3 Living things; 6 Plant power; Bk2: 2 Vital organs; Bk3: Being healthy
Reproduction	Bk1: 9 Life story; Bk3: 2 Being healthy
Environments and Feeding	Bk1: Living things; Bk2: 8 Environment
Variation and Classification	Bk1: 3 Living things
Acids and Alkalis	Bk2: 1 Acids and bases
Simple Chemical Reactions	Bk1: 4 Burning; Bk2: 1 Acids and bases
Particle Model	Bk1: 2 Changing state; Bk2: 4 Matter
Solutions	Bk1: 2 Changing state; 7 Metals; Bk2: 4 Matter
Energy Resources	Bk1: 1 Energy; 4 Burning; Bk2: 6 Energy resources
Electric Circuits	Bk1: 5 Electricity
Forces and their Effects	Bk1: 8 Forces
The Solar System and Beyond	Bk2: 3 Earth in space
Year 8	
Food and Digestion	Bk2: 2 Vital organs; 5 Nutrition
Respiration	Bk2: 5 Nutrition; 8 Environment
Microbes and Disease	Bk3: 2 Being healthy
Ecological Relationships	Bk1: 3 Living things; Bk2: 8 Environment
Atoms and Elements	Bk1: 7 Metals
Compounds and Mixtures	Bk1: 7 Metals; Bk2: 1 Acids and bases
Rocks and Weathering	Bk2: 7 Rocks
The Rock Cycle	Bk2: 7 Rocks
Heating and Cooling	Bk3: 6 Moving energy
Magnets and Electromagnets	Bk1: 5 Electricity
Light	Bk2: 9 Light and sound
Sound and Hearing	Bk1: 1 Energy; Bk2: 9 Light and sound
Year 9	
Inheritance and Selection	Bk3: 5 Competition
Fit and Healthy	Bk2: 5 Nutrition; Bk3: 2 Being healthy
Plants and Photosynthesis	Bk1: 6 Plant power; Bk2: 8 Environment
Plants for Food	Bk2: 8 Environment
Reactions of Metals and Metal Compounds	Bk1: 7 Metals; Bk2: 1 Acids and bases
Patterns of Reactivity	Bk1: 4 Burning; 7 Metals; Bk3: 4 Chemical patterns
Environmental Chemistry	Bk1: 4 Burning; Bk2: 1 Acids and bases; 7 Rocks
Using Chemistry	Bk1: 2 Changing state; 4 Burning; Bk2: 4 Matter; 1 Acids and bases; Bk3 Chemical reactions
Energy and Electricity	Bk2: Energy resources; Bk3: Moving energy
Gravity and Space	Bk1: 8 Forces; Bk2: Earth in space
Speeding up	Bk1: 8 Forces
Pressure and moments	Bk3: 3 Balanced forces

1 Energy

Unit map

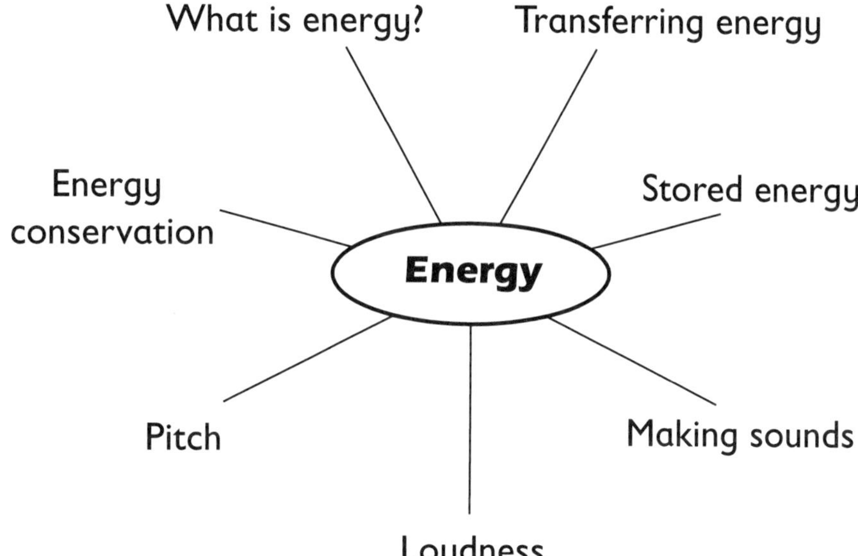

1 Energy

Unit map

Use these words to help you copy and complete your unit map.

movement energy	strain energy	decibels
light energy	chemical energy	amplitude
sound energy	gravitational energy	frequency
heat energy	joules	hertz
electrical energy	kilojoules	Sun
transfer	eardrum	useful
energy transfer diagram	vibrations	

Energy circus

Activity 1.1
Core

You are going to start investigating energy with a series of short activities.

⚠ Do not eat the food.

A Energy from food

1 Look at the foods in front of you. Discuss which are high energy foods. Discuss which are low energy foods.

2 Sort the foods into two groups:
- High energy foods
- Low energy foods

Wear eye protection.

⚠ Beware of hot objects.

B Energy in fuel

1 You are going to heat water in a boiling tube for 1 minute and measure the temperature rise. Use the apparatus shown here.

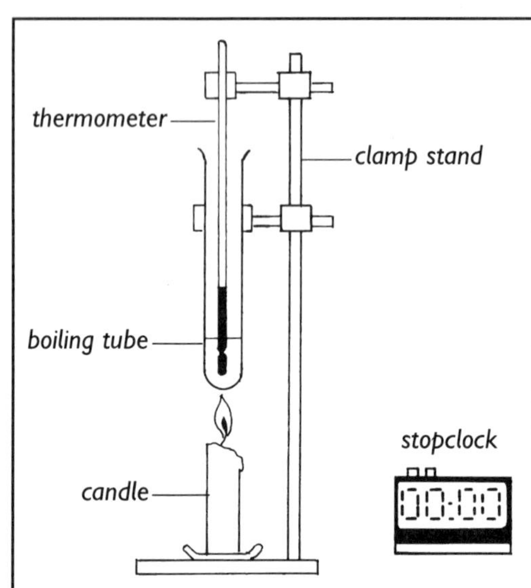

- Put 10 cm^3 of cold water in a boiling tube.
- Take the temperature of the water (start temperature).
- Light the candle and start the stopclock.
- Heat the boiling tube with the candle for 1 minute.
- Take the temperature of the water in the test tube after 1 minute (end temperature).

2 Work out the rise in temperature.
rise = end temperature – start temperature

3 What caused the rise in temperature?

C Energy to run

⚠ Run on the spot, not around the room.

1 One person runs on the spot as fast as possible. Another person walks slowly on the spot. They will do this for 1 minute.

2 Ask them how they feel after 1 minute.

3 Which person used the most energy?

D Energy to lift

1 One person lifts as many sandbags as possible in 1 minute. Another person lifts one sandbag every 5 seconds for 1 minute.

2 Ask the speedy lifter and the lazy lifter how they feel after 1 minute.

3 Which lifter used the most energy?

Energy out!

Activity 1.2A
Core

⚠ Beware of hot objects.

You are going to look at lots of objects. Decide if the object moves. Decide if the object gives out sound, light or heat energy.

1 Make a table like the one below.

2 Read an instruction card and do what it says.

3 Write the name of the object under the correct heading in your table.

4 Repeat steps **2** and **3** for each object.

Gives out sound energy	Gives out light energy	Gives out heat energy	Shows movement energy

Energy out!

Activity 1.2A
Core

⚠ Beware of hot objects.

You are going to look at lots of objects. Decide if the object moves. Decide if the object gives out sound, light or heat energy.

1 Make a table like the one below.

2 Read an instruction card and do what it says.

3 Write the name of the object under the correct heading in your table.

4 Repeat steps **2** and **3** for each object.

Gives out sound energy	Gives out light energy	Gives out heat energy	Shows movement energy

Energy everywhere!

Activity 1.2B
Core

Many objects in the picture are moving, or giving out light, sound or heat energy. Can you spot them?

1 Look at this picture. Imagine you are there.

2 Write a list to answer each of these questions:

1. What things would be giving out light energy?
2. What things would be giving out sound energy?
3. What things would be giving out heat energy?
4. What things would be moving? These things have movement energy.

Energy in, energy out

Activity 1.3A
Core

You are going to look at some electrical devices. Electricity goes into each one.

1. Make a table like the one below.
2. Look at the devices. What energy is going in to each device? What energy is each device giving out?
3. Write in the table the name of each device, the energy that goes in and the energy it gives out. One has been done for you.

Energy in	Device	Energy out
electrical energy	*food mixer*	*movement energy* *sound energy* *heat energy*

1.3 A

Energy in, energy out

Activity 1.3A
Core

You are going to look at some electrical devices. Electricity goes into each one.

1. Make a table like the one below.
2. Look at the devices. What energy is going in to each device? What energy is each device giving out?
3. Write in the table the name of each device, the energy that goes in and the energy it gives out. One has been done for you.

Energy in	Device	Energy out
electrical energy	*food mixer*	*movement energy* *sound energy* *heat energy*

Move it!

Activity 1.3B
Core

You can use simple diagrams to show how energy is moved or transferred in different devices.

❶ Copy and complete these energy transfer diagrams.

a

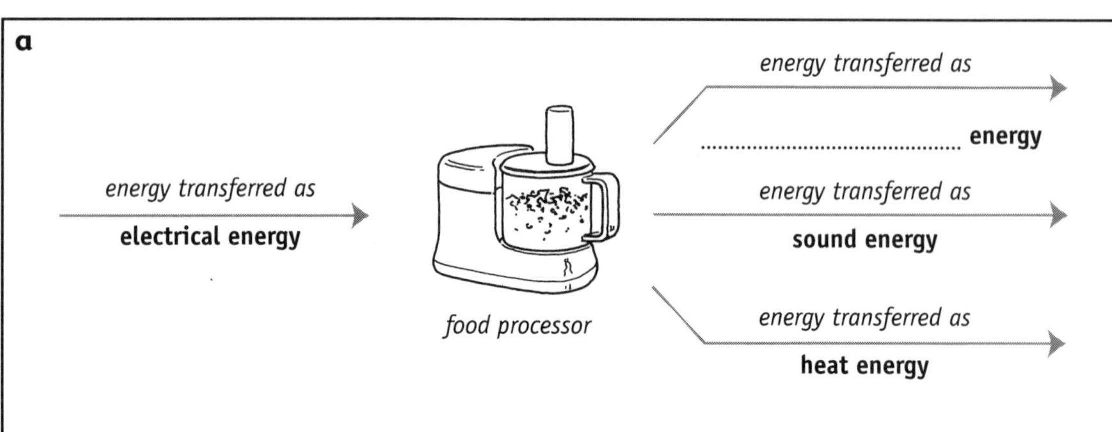

food processor

b

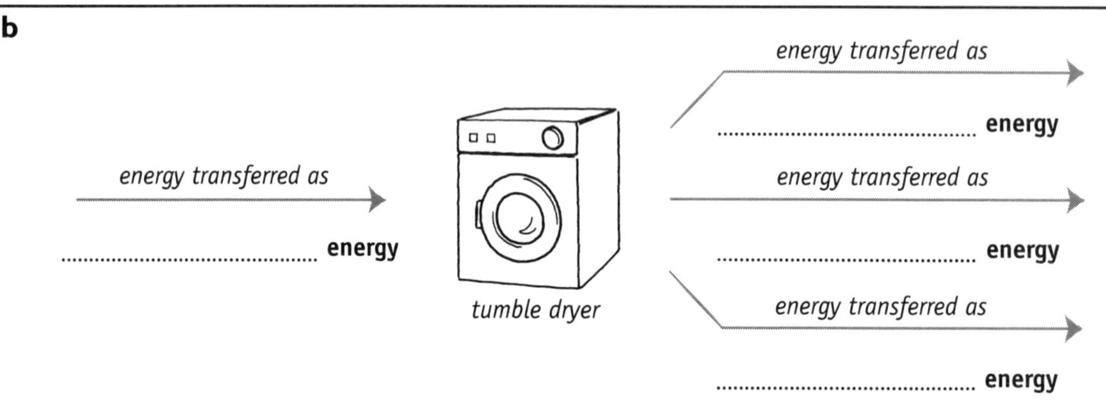

tumble dryer

c

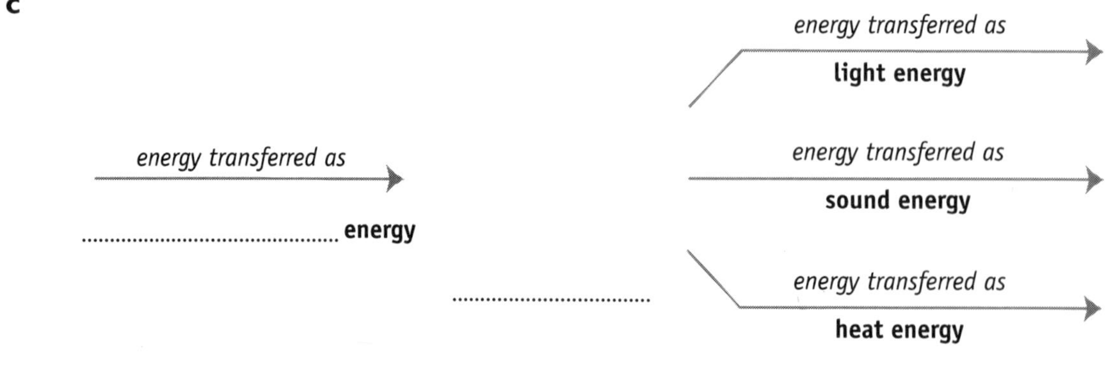

d

energy transferred as

.... **energy**

kettle

Move it!

Activity 1.3B
Help

You can use simple diagrams to show how energy is moved or transferred in different devices.

1 Complete these energy transfer diagrams.

a

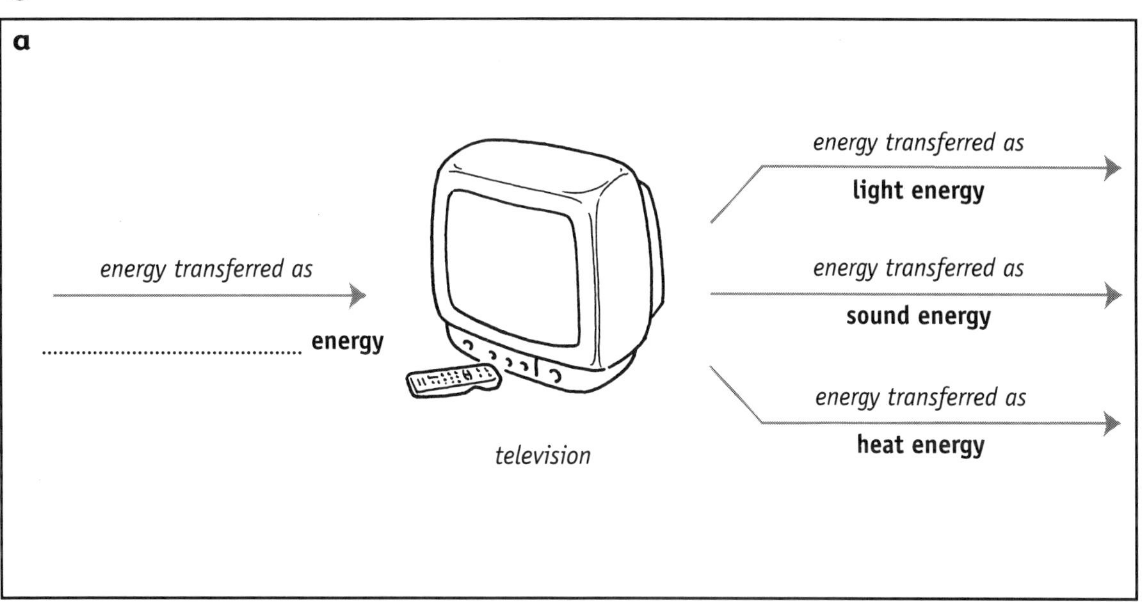

television

b

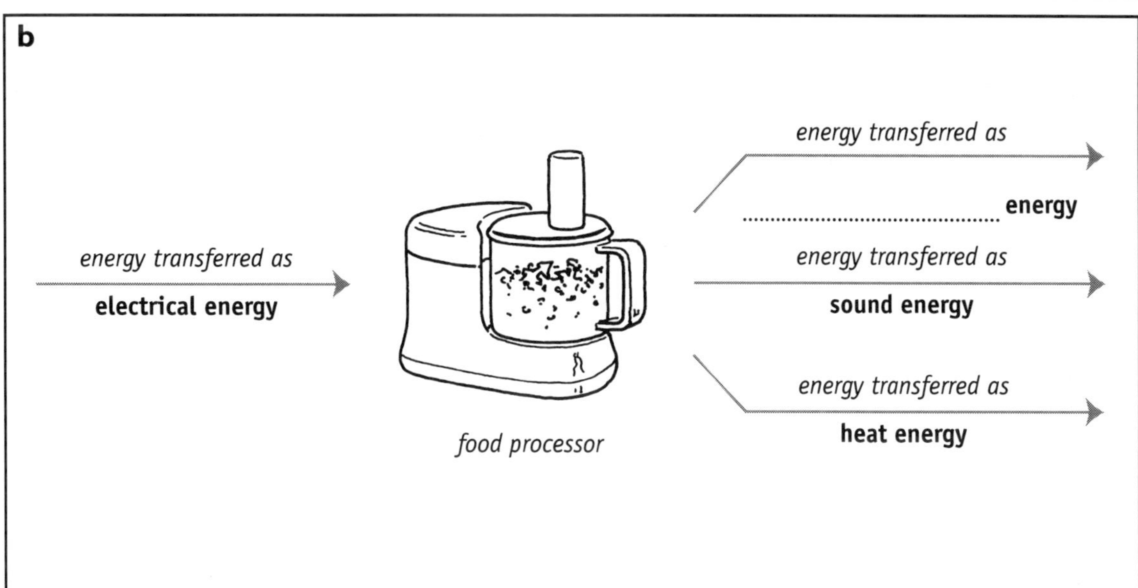

food processor

c

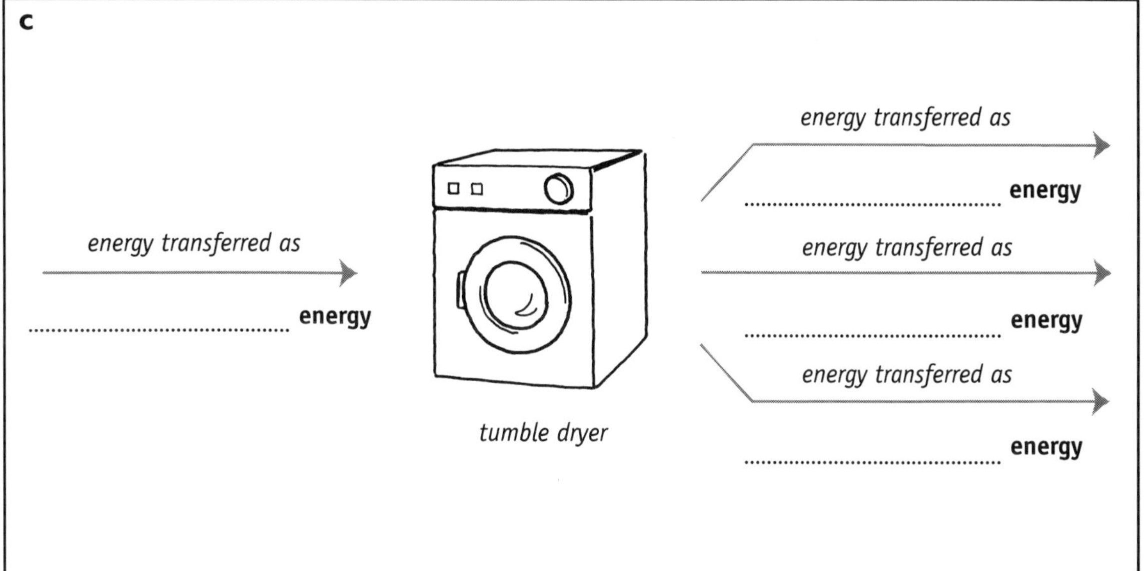

tumble dryer

Move it!

Activity 1.3B
Extension

You can use simple diagrams to show how energy is moved or transferred in different devices.

1 Copy and complete these energy transfer diagrams.

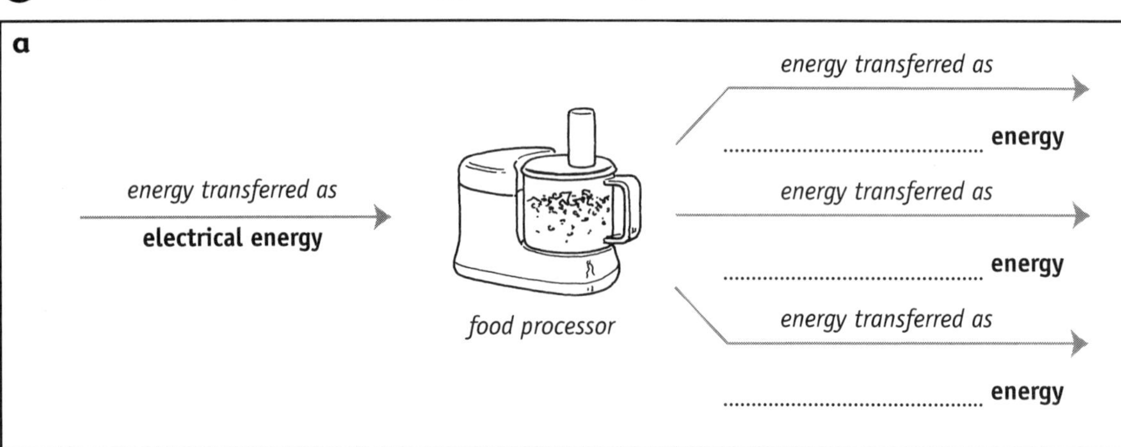

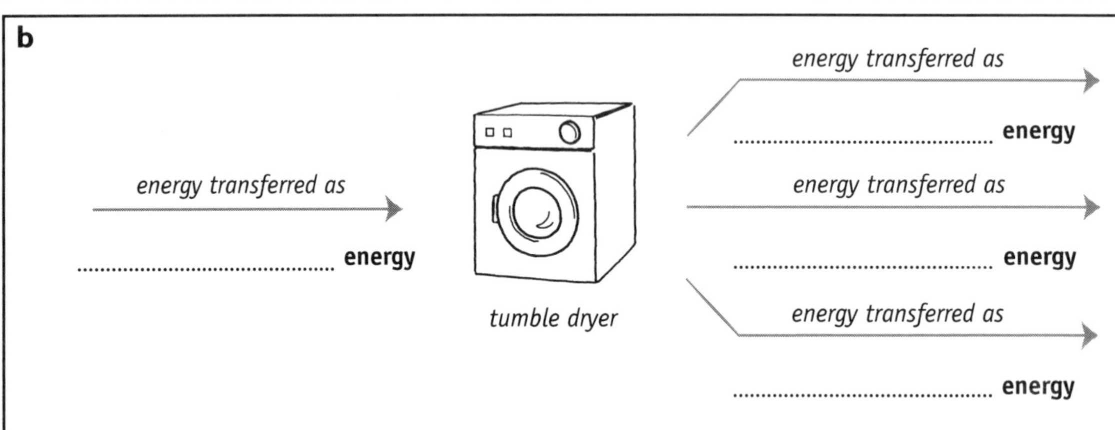

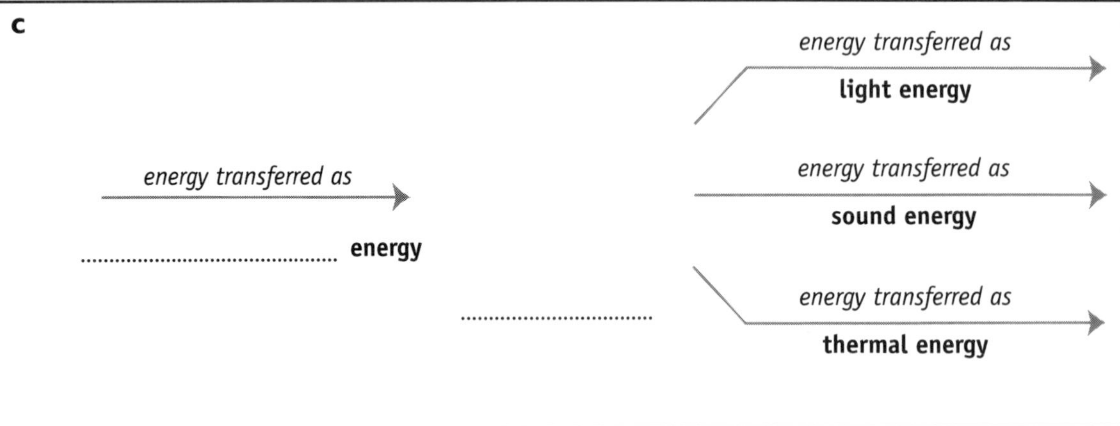

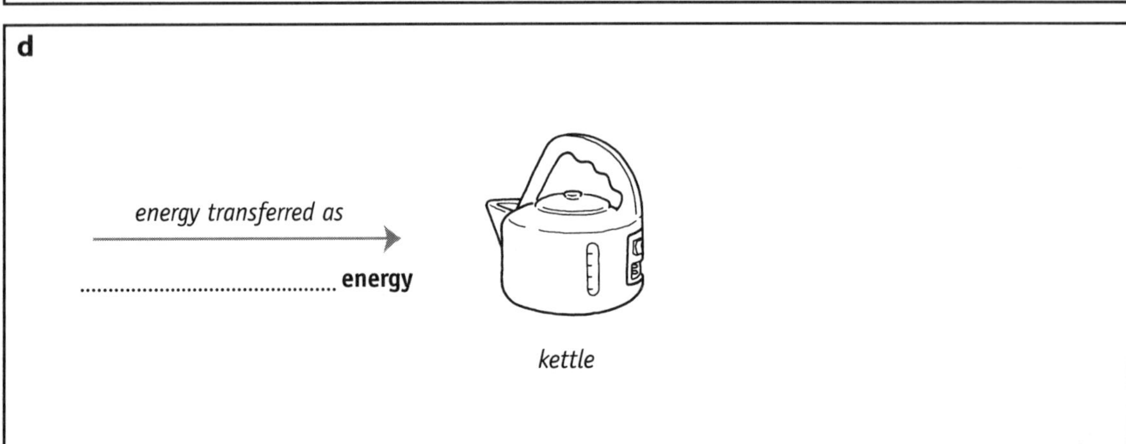

Stored energy

Activity 1.4A
Core

You are going to look at how energy is stored in different things.

Energy can be stored in three ways:

- chemical energy (like in food, fuel or batteries)
- strain energy (when something is stretched or squashed)
- gravitational energy (when something has been lifted up).

Wear eye protection.

1 Make a table like the one below.

2 Look at each object. Decide how the energy is stored in it.

3 Record your decision in your table. Tick the correct type of energy.

Object	Chemical energy	Strain energy	Gravitational energy

1.4
A

Stored energy

Activity 1.4A
Core

You are going to look at how energy is stored in different things.

Energy can be stored in three ways:

- chemical energy (like in food, fuel or batteries)
- strain energy (when something is stretched or squashed)
- gravitational energy (when something has been lifted up).

Wear eye protection.

1 Make a table like the one below.

2 Look at each object. Decide how the energy is stored in it.

3 Record your decision in your table. Tick the correct type of energy.

Object	Chemical energy	Strain energy	Gravitational energy

Cotton reel racers

Activity 1.4B
Core

Cotton reel racers store energy in the rubber band. In this investigation, you will find out how much movement energy you can get out of a cotton reel racer.

Wear eye protection.

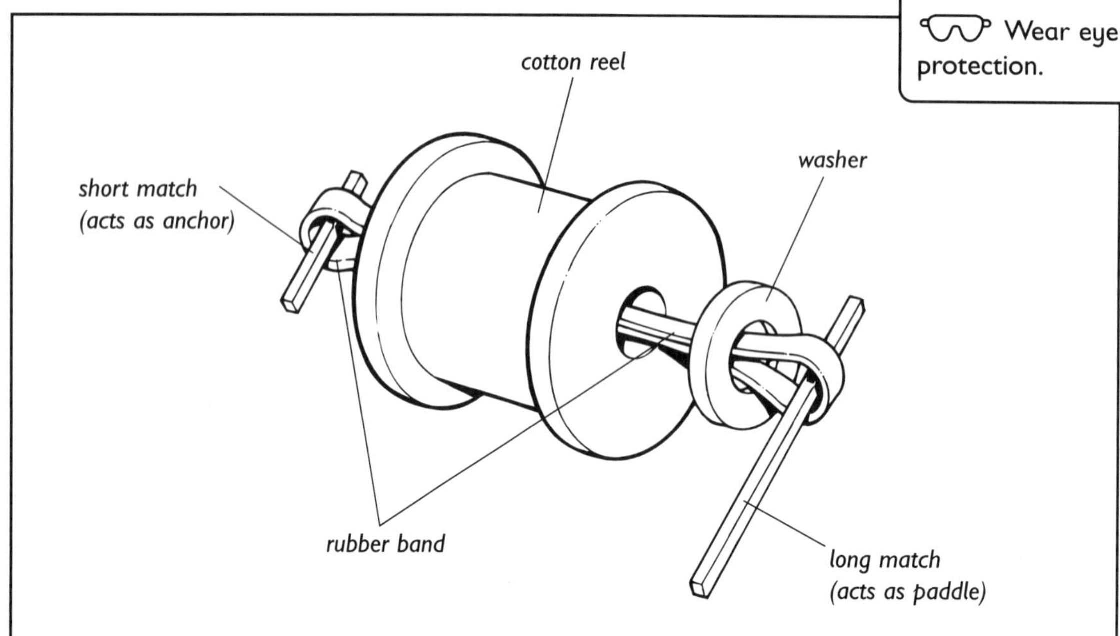

Plan

1 Design and make your cotton reel racer.

2 Do some trial runs.

Do

3 Take your racer to the Derby and compete.

Record

4 Make sure you write down:

- the number of rubber bands you used
- the number of turns you put into the rubber band(s)
- the distance your racer moved
- the time your racer kept moving.

Analyse and conclude

❶ Explain how you stored lots of energy in your racer.

Evaluate

❷ How could you improve your cotton reel racer?

Cotton reel racers

Activity 1.4B
Help

Cotton reel racers store energy in the rubber band. In this investigation, you are will find out how much movement energy you can get out of a cotton reel racer.

Wear eye protection.

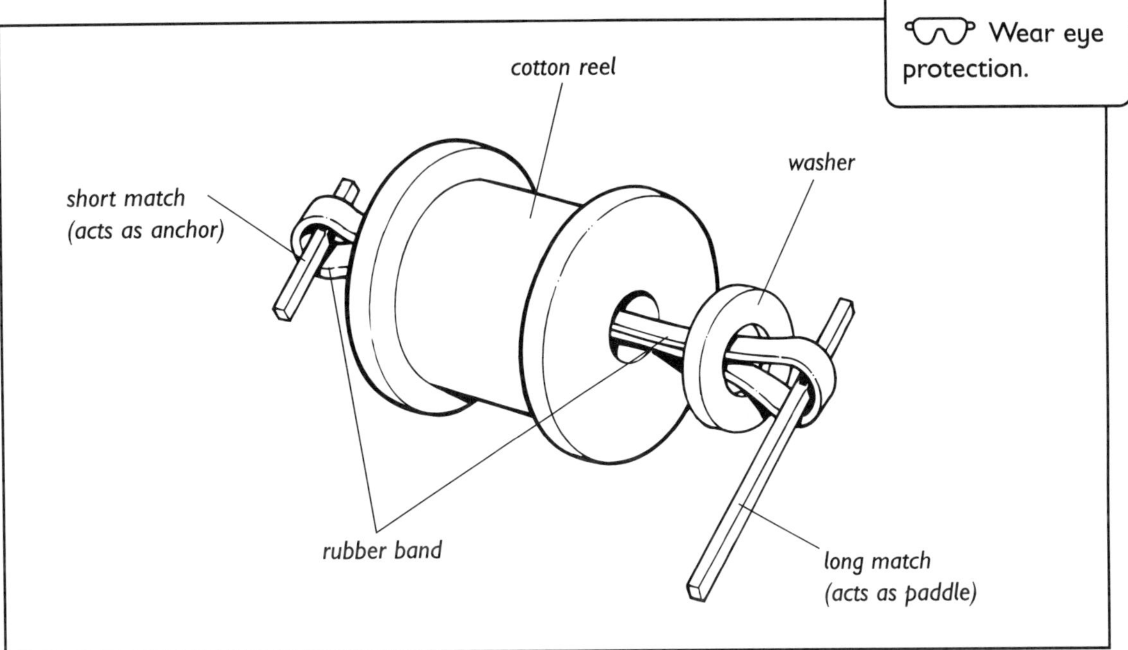

Plan

1 Make a cotton reel racer as in the diagram above.

2 Do some trial runs.

3 Decide how many rubber bands you are going to use.

4 Decide how many times you will wind the rubber band.

Do

5 Compete in the cotton reel racers Derby. Measure the distance your racer went and the time it took.

Record

❶ Complete these sentences to record your results.

We used .... rubber band(s). We wound the rubber band(s) .... times.

Our racer went .... metres. It ran for .... seconds.

Analyse and conclude

❷ Explain how you stored lots of energy in your racer.

Evaluate

❸ How could you improve your cotton reel racer?

Energy in food

Activity 1.5A
Core

You are going to burn a pea and a raisin. The energy stored in them will be released as heat energy. You are going to use the heat energy to heat water.

Wear eye protection.

Equipment available

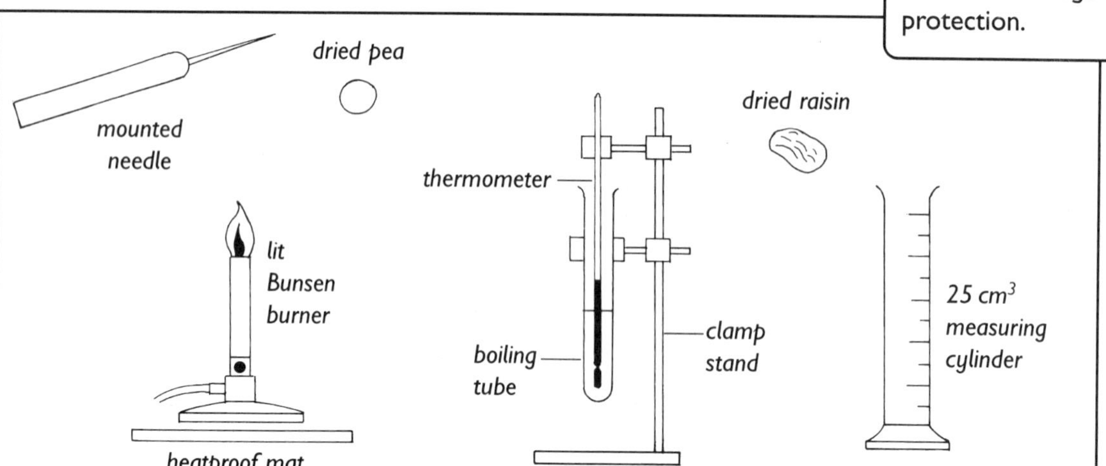

Do

1 Put 20 cm^3 of water into a boiling tube.

2 Take the temperature of the water.

3 Set up the apparatus as shown in the diagram.

4 Put the pea onto the mounted needle. Use the hole that is already there.

5 Light the pea in the Bunsen flame.

6 Use the burning pea to heat the water.

7 Take the highest temperature of the water.

8 Repeat steps **1** to **7** for the raisin. Remember to use fresh, cold water.

Record

9 Make a table like the one below. Record your results.

	Temperature of water at start	**Temperature of water at end**	**Temperature rise**
pea	°C	°C	°C
raisin	°C	°C	°C

Analyse and conclude

1 Calculate the energy rise. Fill in the last column of your table.

2 Which gave out more heat energy, the pea or the raisin?

3 Draw an energy transfer diagram for the pea and the raisin to show what happened during your experiment.

How much energy?

You are going to use a computer to calculate the amount of energy in a meal.

- Use the database to look up information.
- Use the spreadsheet to do calculations.

Leroy eats the meal shown in the picture.

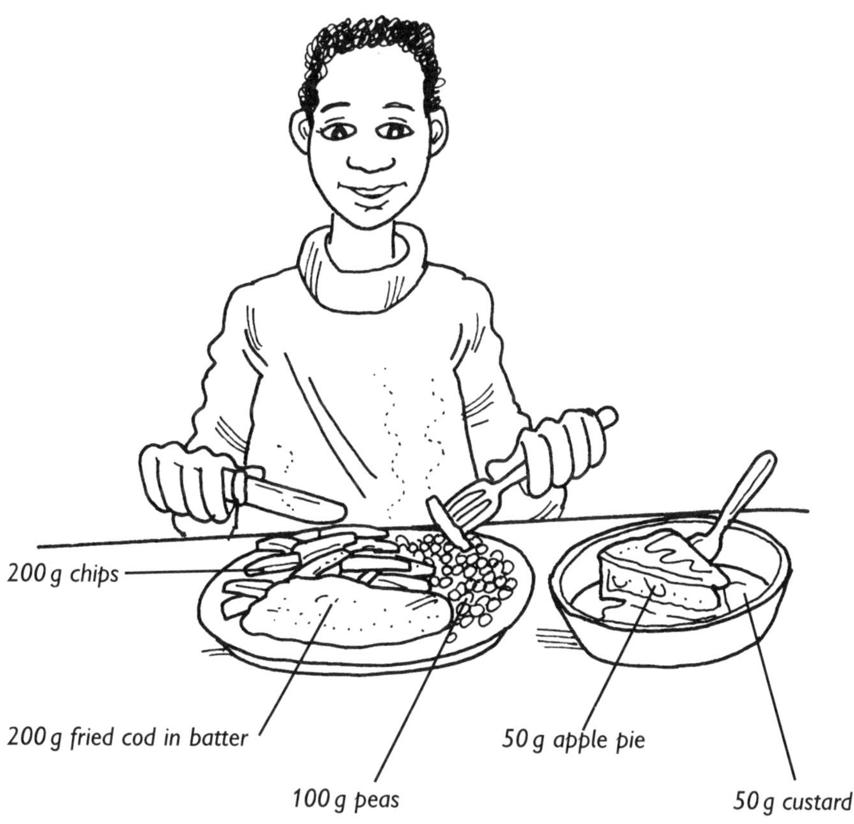

The database lists many foods and the energy they contain in each 100 g.

1 Find 'fried cod in batter' in the first column.
   - Click on A at the top of column A.
   - Go to *Edit* and select *Find*. The *Find* window will appear.
   - Type 'fried cod in batter'. Click on *Find next*.
   - Close the *Find* window.

2 Type the size of Leroy's portion (200 g) into column C. Press the return key to enter the information.

   The computer will now calculate the energy in Leroy's portion of fried cod in batter. The answer will appear in column D.

3 Repeat for all other parts of Leroy's meal.

4 Scroll down to the bottom of column D to find the total energy.

   The computer will have added up the energy in all the food.

❶ How much energy was in Leroy's meal?

Investigating sound

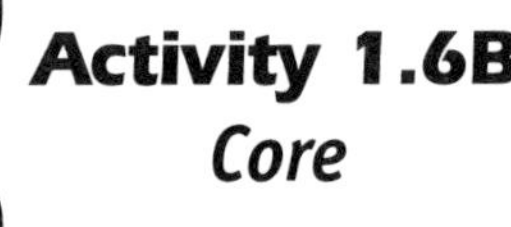

You are going to find out what materials sound can travel through.

1 Can you hear other people in the room?

❶ What material is between you and the other people?

2 Whales use sound to communicate with each other over long distances.

❷ What material is between the whales?

3 One person taps the table very softly, while you listen with your ear to the table.

❸ What material is between you and the person tapping the table?

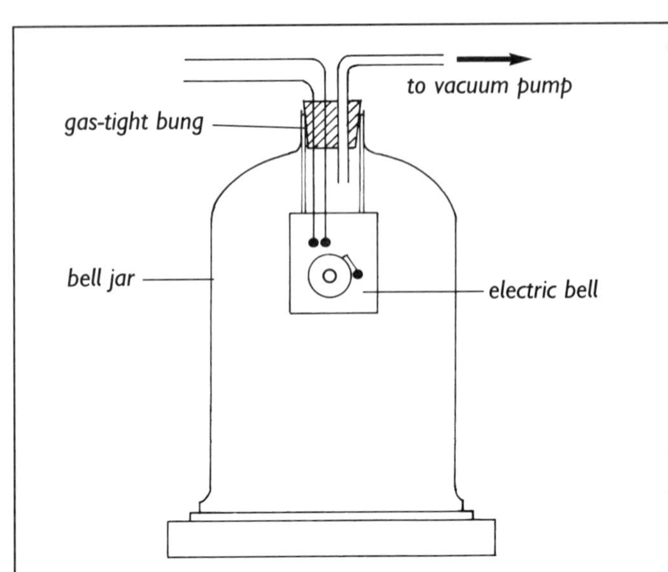

4 Remember the experiment with the bell in the jar. All the air was pumped out of the jar.

❹ Could you hear the sound when the air was pumped out?

❺ What was between the bell and the sides of the jar?

❻ What does sound need to travel? Explain how you came to this conclusion.

Energy trails

Activity 1.8A
Core

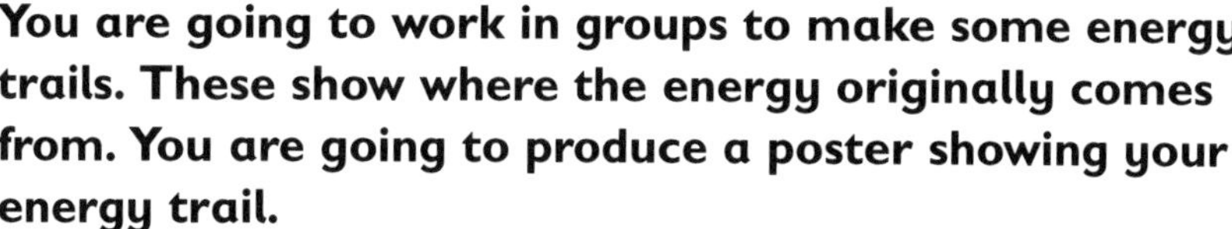

You are going to work in groups to make some energy trails. These show where the energy originally comes from. You are going to produce a poster showing your energy trail.

Remember these things when making your energy trail.

- Show where the energy is stored using boxes like this:

Energy stored in a firework *as* ***chemical energy***

- Show energy transfers using arrows like this:

  energy transferred as → **light energy**

1 Choose your starting point. You could use one of these suggestions, or think of one of your own.

a burger   a cyclist   a barbecue   an aeroplane   a bungee jumper

2 Discuss in your group where the energy came from. Trace the energy back to its source.

3 Make a rough sketch of where the energy was stored, and what energy transfers happened.

4 Check your rough sketch against other energy trails (maybe in your textbook). Is everyone in the group satisfied with it?

5 Show your rough sketch to your teacher.

6 Plan your poster. Look at the resource sheet. Are there any boxes you would like to use in your poster? Decide if you are going to use the boxes given or draw your own.

7 Decide who is going to do what, then build your energy trail!

Energy trails

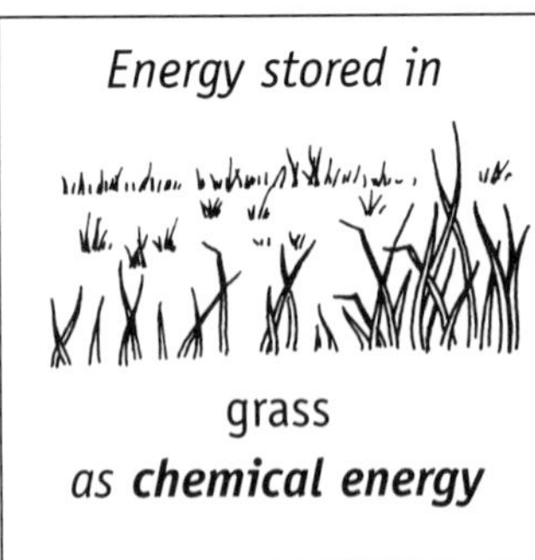

Energy stored in grass *as* ***chemical energy***

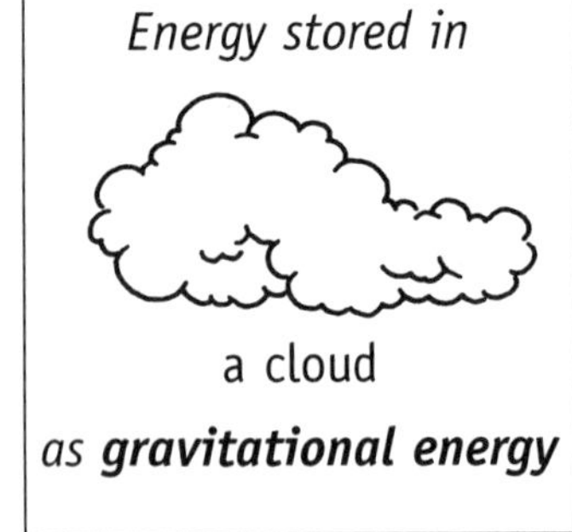

Energy stored in a cloud *as* ***gravitational energy***

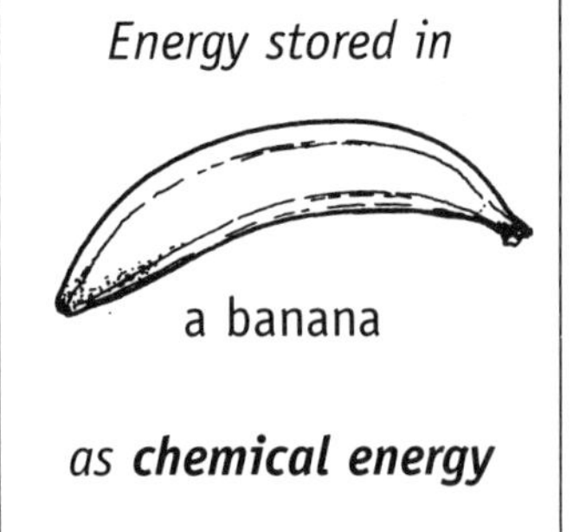

Energy stored in a banana *as* ***chemical energy***

Energy stored in a battery *as* ***chemical energy***

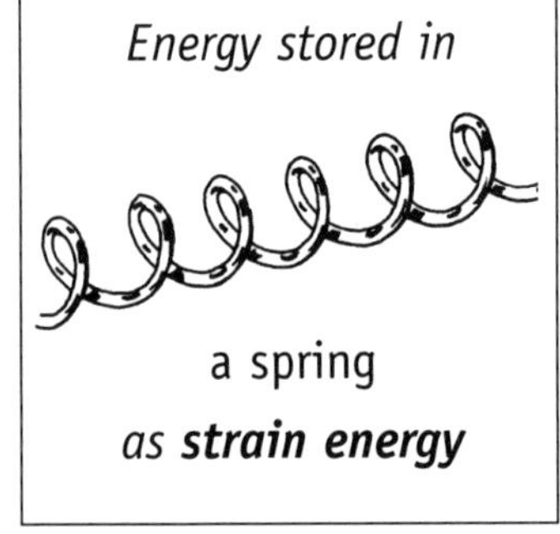

Energy stored in a spring *as* ***strain energy***

Energy stored in a cow *as* ***chemical energy***

Energy stored in weights *as* ***gravitational energy***

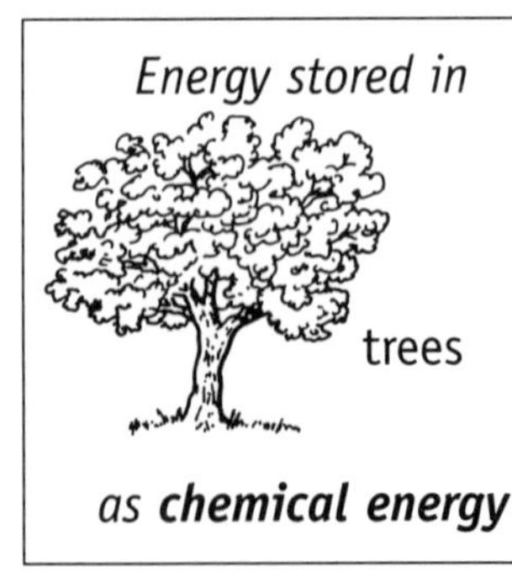

Energy stored in trees *as* ***chemical energy***

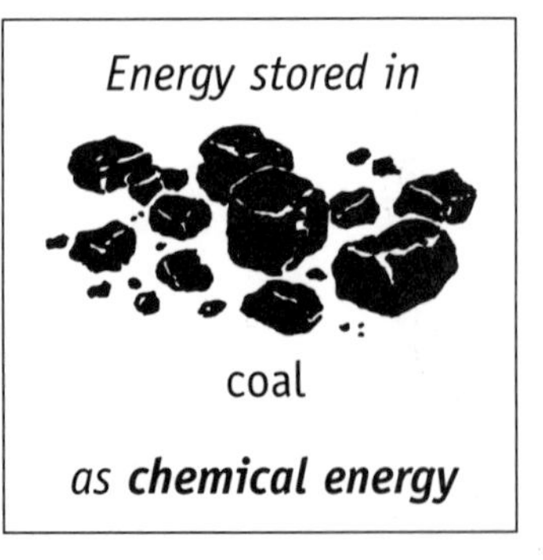

Energy stored in coal *as* ***chemical energy***

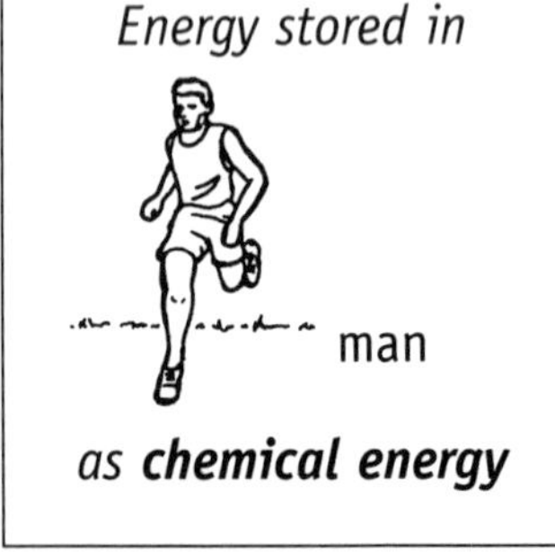

Energy stored in man *as* ***chemical energy***

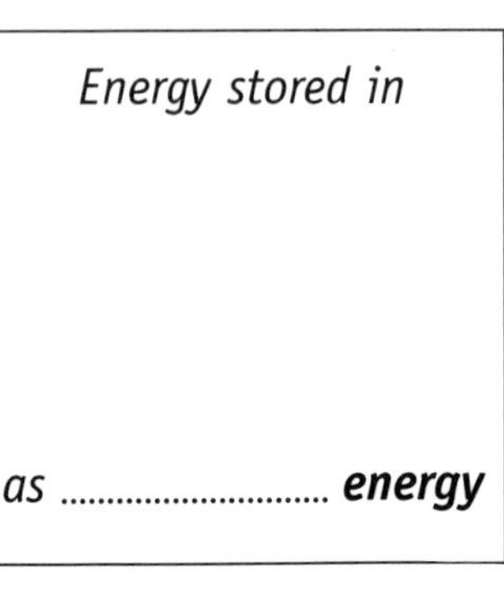

Energy stored in

as .... ***energy***

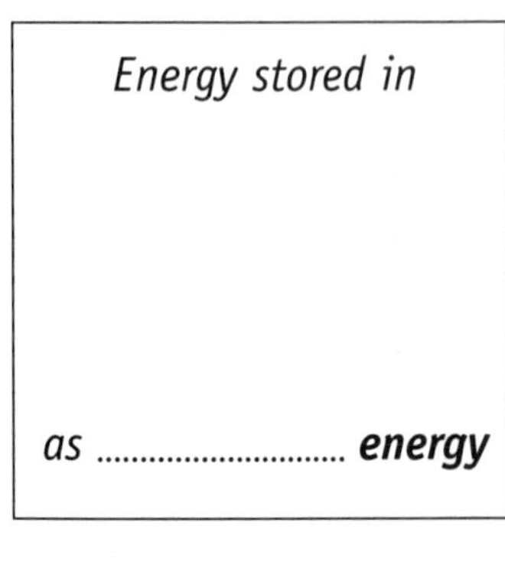

Energy stored in

as .... ***energy***

'Wasted' energy

When energy is transferred, where does it all go? You are going to think about some everyday devices.

1. What type of energy goes into a hairdryer?
2. What three types of energy come out of a hairdryer?
3. Draw an energy transfer diagram for a hairdryer.
4. What do you use a hairdryer for?
5. What types of energy do you want from a hairdryer?
6. What unwanted energy comes out of a hairdryer?

7. What type of energy goes into a car?
8. What types of energy come out of a car?
9. Draw an energy transfer diagram for a car.
10. What does a car do?
11. What type of energy do you want from a car?
12. What unwanted energy comes from a car?

Changing state

Unit map

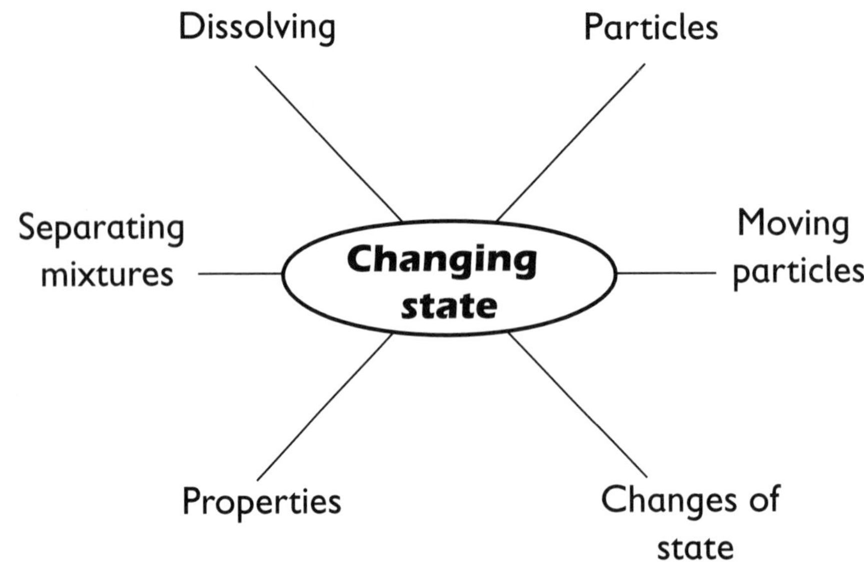

Changing state
2

Changing state

Unit map

Use these words to help you copy and complete your unit map.

gas	vibrate	hotter	can move
chromatography	always moving	hard	condensing
solution	fixed volume	far apart	can be poured
faster	boiling	liquid	fixed shape
distillation	kinetic energy	soluble	close together
change shape	can't be poured	not ordered	solid
dissolve	colder	solvent	freezing
solute	insoluble	runny	ordered
random	slower	evaporating	melting

The birthday party

Activity 2.1
Core

Here is a picture of Matthew's birthday party. There are lots of different solids, liquids and gases in this picture.

1. Make a list of all the liquids.
2. Make a list of all the solids.
3. Make a list of all the gases. 
4. What is happening to the ice cream now it is not in the freezer?
5. What will happen to the ice cream if it is put back in the freezer?
6. What is happening to the candle wax?
7. What is happening to some of the water as it boils in the kettle?

Classifying materials

Activity 2.2
Core

Different materials have different properties. You are going to decide if some materials are solid, liquid or gas.

1 Make a table like the one below.

Solid	Liquid	Gas

❶ Here is a list of different materials. Write the name of each material under the correct heading in your table.

gold iron air glass oil plastic mercury carbon dioxide lemonade oxygen water brick

❷ List three properties which helped you decide which things are solids.

❸ List three properties which helped you decide which things are liquids.

❹ List four properties which helped you decide which things are gases.

Changing state
2.2

Classifying materials

Activity 2.2
Core

Different materials have different properties. You are going to decide if some materials are solid, liquid or gas.

1 Make a table like the one below.

Solid	Liquid	Gas

❶ Here is a list of different materials. Write the name of each material under the correct heading in your table.

gold iron air glass oil plastic mercury carbon dioxide lemonade oxygen water brick

❷ List three properties which helped you decide which things are solids.

❸ List three properties which helped you decide which things are liquids.

❹ List four properties which helped you decide which things are gases.

2.3 A tight squeeze

Activity 2.3
Core

You are going to investigate how easy it is to squash a solid, a liquid and a gas.

Equipment available

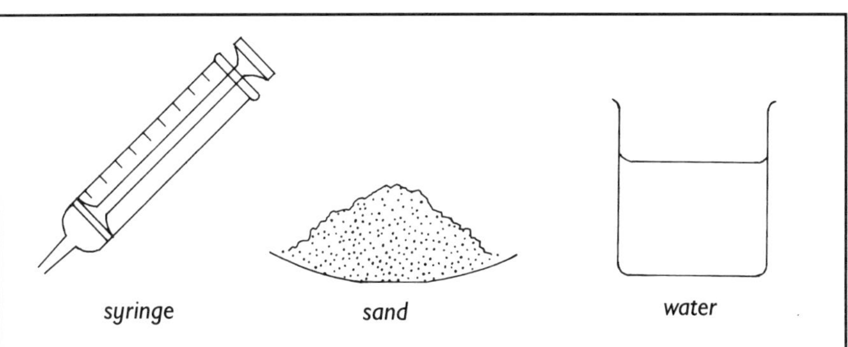

Predict

1. Which do you think can be squashed the most – air, water or sand?
2. Why do you think this?

Do

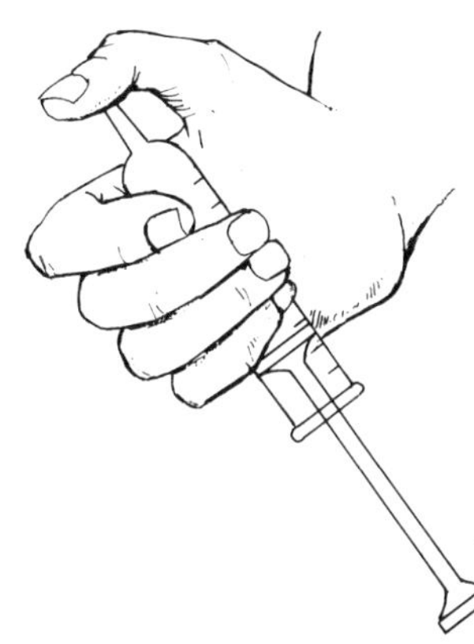

1 Draw the plunger back on the syringe until it is at its highest reading. Record the reading.

2 Place your thumb tightly over the end of the syringe, as shown.

3 Push the plunger in as hard as you can. Remember to keep your thumb over the end.

4 Record how far in the plunger went.

5 Fill the syringe with sand. Put your thumb over the end.

6 Push the plunger in as hard as you can.

7 Record how far in the plunger went.

8 Fill the syringe with water. Make sure there are no air bubbles in it. Put your thumb over the end. Repeat steps **6** and **7**.

9 Calculate how far the plunger moved for air, sand and water.

Analyse and conclude

3. Did the results match your prediction?
4. Which could be squashed the most – the solid, the liquid or the gas?
5. Use your knowledge of particles to explain your answer.

A tight squeeze

You are going to investigate how easy it is to squash a solid, a liquid and a gas.

Equipment available

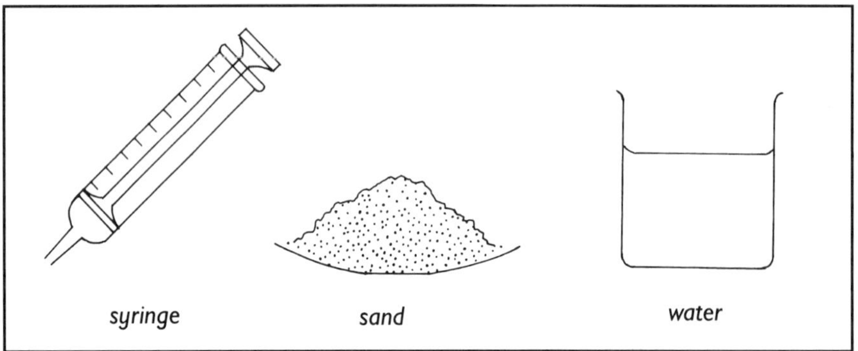

Predict

1 Which do you think can be squashed the most – **air**, **water** or **sand**? Complete these sentences:

I think that .... can be squashed the most.

I think this because ....

....

Do

1 Carry out your investigation. Your teacher will show you what to do.

2 Fill in the results in this table.

	Air (gas)	Sand (solid)	Water (liquid)
start reading			
end reading			
change			

Analyse and conclude

2 Did the results match your prediction?

3 Complete these sentences:

I found out that the .... could be squashed the most.

This happens because the particles in a .... are

.... and so can be ....

Moving particles

You are going to use peas in a box to show what happens to the particles when a solid, such as ice, is heated.

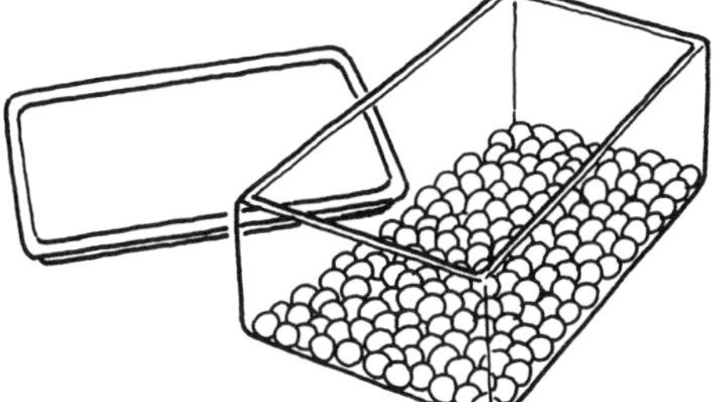

Take care! Spilt peas will make the floor slippery.

1 Put a handful of dried peas into a plastic box.

2 Arrange them so that they make a single layer.

3 Now follow steps **4**, **5** and **6**. As you do so, think about how the peas are moving.

4 Shake the box as gently as you can so that the peas jiggle about a little. Make sure that you do not shake them too much.

5 Shake a bit harder so that the peas start to move around a little and change position.

6 Put the lid on the box and shake really hard.

1 When you heat up a solid it goes through three states – solid, liquid and gas. Decide which steps **4**, **5** or **6** above show the peas behaving like a solid, a liquid and a gas (vapour).

Put your answers in a table like the one below.

State	Step 4, 5 or 6
solid ice	
liquid water	
water vapour (steam)	

2 When you heat ice to melt it and then boil the water, you give the particles energy. How were you giving the peas energy?

3 Copy and complete the flow diagram. It shows how a solid turns into a gas and back to a solid. Use these words to fill in the gaps:

melting **condensing** **freezing** **evaporating**

solid	............→ / ←............	liquid	............→ / ←............	gas

Role play – particles

In this activity you are going to pretend that you are a particle in different substances.

Solid

1 Get together with a few of your classmates.

Put your left hand on the shoulder of the person to your left.

Put your right hand on the shoulder of the person in front.

Stand in neat rows and jiggle very slightly.

Liquid

2 Start to move a little more.

Drop your hands.

Stay close to the other pupils.

Gas

3 Spread out so that you are far apart.

Move around the room in different directions.

1. When you were a solid, how did you move? How close were the other particles?
2. When you were a gas, how did you move? How close were the other particles?
3. What were the two main differences between being a solid and a liquid?
4. When did you have the most energy?
5. Draw a flow diagram for the three stages. This is called **changes of state**.

2.5 Investigating dissolving

Activity 2.5
Core

⚠ Take care when handling hot water.

Do not eat the sugar.

Felicity and Lisa were having an argument. They wanted a sugar that dissolved very quickly in their tea, but could not decide what was the best sugar to choose – lumps, granules or caster sugar.

You are going to carry out an investigation to help them find out.

Equipment available

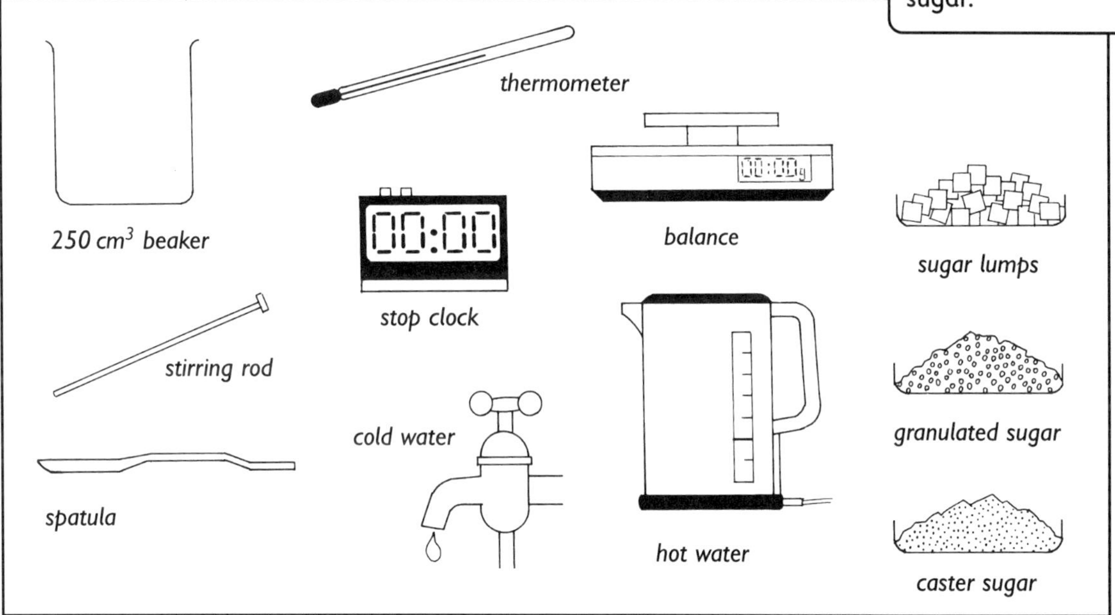

Predict

❶ Make a prediction. Which sugar do you think will dissolve fastest? Which will dissolve slowest?

❷ Explain why you think this will happen.

Plan

❸ Think about other things which could affect how quickly the sugar dissolves. Write them down.

1 Plan how you will make your investigation a fair test. Use your answer to ❸ to help you.

2 Get your plan approved.

Do

3 Carry out your investigation.

4 Record your results in a table.

Analyse and conclude

❹ Was your prediction correct?

Evaluate

❺ How could you improve your investigation?

Investigating dissolving

Activity 2.5
Help

Use this sheet to help you plan and record your investigation into how fast different sugars dissolve.

⚠ Take care when handling hot water.

Do not eat the sugar.

Predict

1 Make a prediction. Put a tick next to the sugar that you think will dissolve the fastest.

sugar lumps ☐ **sugar granules** ☐ **caster sugar** ☐

2 Complete this sentence:

I think this will happen because ....

....

....

Plan

1 Plan what you could do to see how quickly each type of sugar dissolves.

2 You must make sure that each test is fair. What things would you keep the same in each test?

....

3 Write your plan on a clean sheet of paper. Get it approved by your teacher.

Do

4 Carry out your investigation.

5 Fill in your results in this table.

Type of sugar	Time to dissolve in seconds
lump	
granulated	
caster	

Analyse and conclude

3 Which type of sugar dissolved the fastest? ....

4 Was your prediction correct? ....

5 Complete these sentences:

I found out that the ....
dissolved the fastest.

I think this happened because ....

....

Investigating dissolving

Activity 2.5
Extension

If you put sugar into a cup of tea it dissolves. You are going to carry out an investigation into how fast sugar will dissolve in different conditions.

⚠ Take care when handling hot water.

Do not eat the sugar.

Equipment available

- 250 cm^3 beaker
- stirring rod
- spatula
- thermometer
- balance
- stopclock
- sugar lumps
- granulated sugar
- caster sugar
- cold water
- hot water

1 Make a list of the variables that might affect how quickly sugar will dissolve.

2 Choose one of these variables to investigate.

Predict

❶ Make a prediction. What do you think will happen as you change this variable? Explain why you think this.

Plan

3 Plan your investigation to see what effect changing this variable will have.

- Remember to make it a fair test.
- What other variables will you need to keep constant?
- How will you vary your chosen variable?
- How will you measure the time for the sugar to dissolve?
- How will you record your results?

Do

4 Once your plan has been approved, carry out your investigation.

5 Record your results.

Analyse and conclude

❷ Does your prediction match your result?

❸ Write a paragraph explaining what you found out about dissolving.

Evaluate

❹ How would you improve your investigation?

Distillation

Activity 2.6A
Help

Some solutions can be separated by distillation. You are going to watch a demonstration and complete a diagram.

Your teacher will demonstrate how to use distillation to separate salt and water.

Watch closely, then complete the labels on the diagram below to explain what is happening. Use the words at the bottom of the sheet to help you.

❷ The water turns into a .... and .... up the flask. It is called water ....

❸ The gas is cooled down until it turns into a .... This process is called ....

condenser

cold water in

❶ Here the .... is heated until it ....

❹ The liquid drips out of the tube into a test tube. It is called .... water.

gas **vapour** **boils** **condensation**
salty water **moves** **liquid** **distilled**

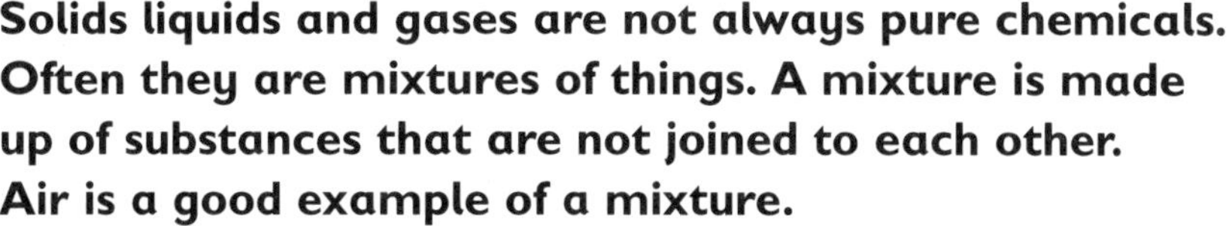

Looking at mixtures

Activity 2.6B
Core

Solids liquids and gases are not always pure chemicals. Often they are mixtures of things. A mixture is made up of substances that are not joined to each other. Air is a good example of a mixture.

The air around you is not just made up from one gas. It is made from lots of different gases all mixed up. The gases are not joined together.

Look at this pie chart. It shows the different gases in the air you breathe.

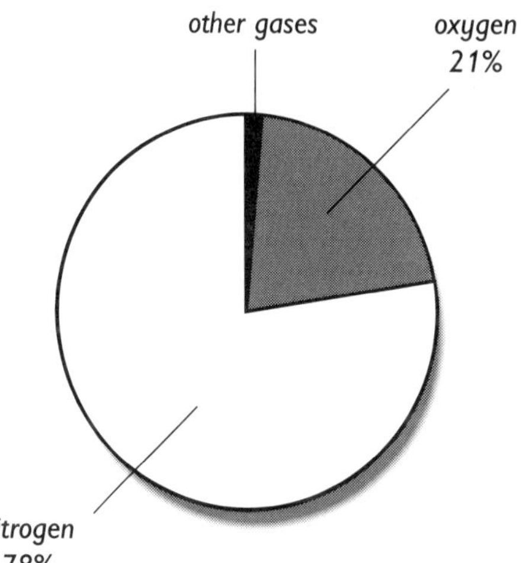

1. What gas makes up most of the air?
2. How much of the air is made up of oxygen?
3. What percentage of the air is made up by 'other gases'?
4. Name three gases that you think you might find in 'other gases'.

Changing state
2.6
B

Looking at mixtures

Activity 2.6B
Core

Solids liquids and gases are not always pure chemicals. Often they are mixtures of things. A mixture is made up of substances that are not joined to each other. Air is a good example of a mixture.

The air around you is not just made up from one gas. It is made from lots of different gases all mixed up. The gases are not joined together.

Look at this pie chart. It shows the different gases in the air you breathe.

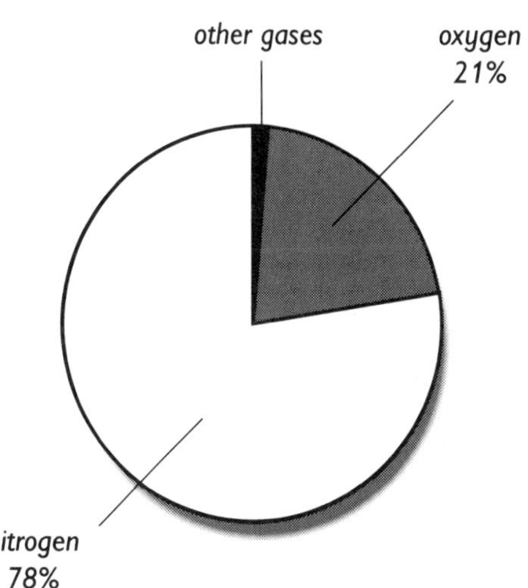

1. What gas makes up most of the air?
2. How much of the air is made up of oxygen?
3. What percentage of the air is made up by 'other gases'?
4. Name three gases that you think you might find in 'other gases'.

Living things

Unit map

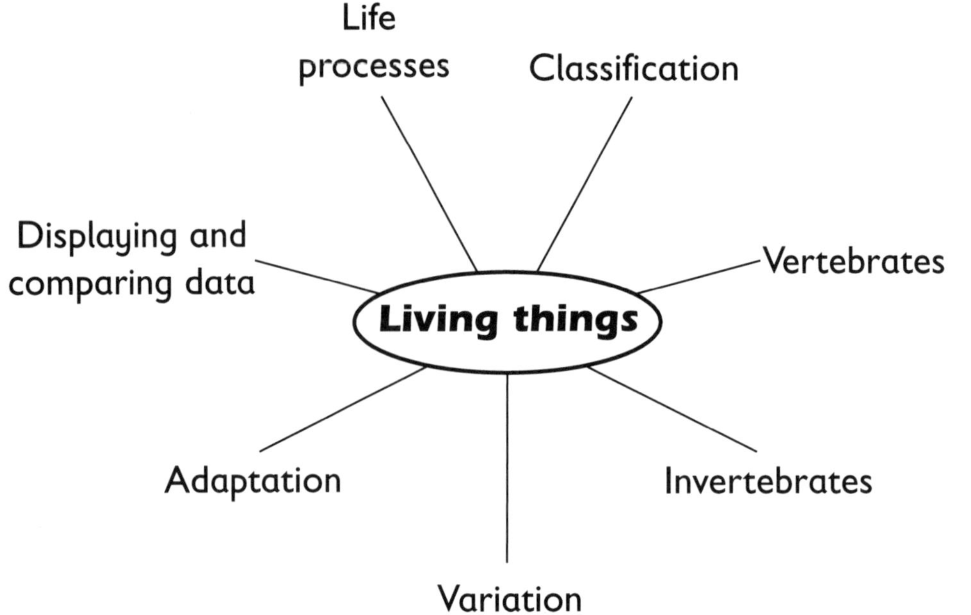

3 Living things

Unit map

Use these words to help you copy and complete your unit map.

movement
reproduction
species
insects
amphibians
animals
starfish
range
fungi
adapted
molluscs

flatworms
vertebrates
roundworms
comparison
crustaceans
birds
habitat
variation
nutrition
reptiles
respiration

plants
insulate
centipede
spiders
desert
sensitivity
jellyfish
arthropods
differences
growth
segmented worms

microorganisms
invertebrates
arthropods
camouflage
mammals
excretion
millipedes
fish
Arctic

Survival

Activity 3.1
Core

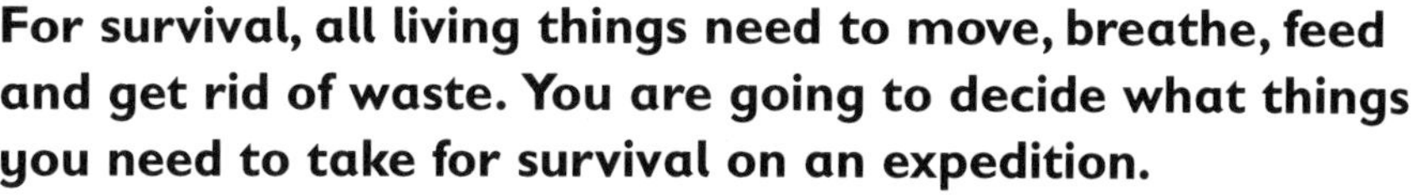

For survival, all living things need to move, breathe, feed and get rid of waste. You are going to decide what things you need to take for survival on an expedition.

You are an explorer. Your team is preparing to walk across the North Polar ice cap. The purpose of the trip is make people more aware that because of pollution the Earth is warming up and the ice caps are melting.

1. On the walk, between camps, you will have a small rucksack. You can pack only five items to help you survive.

   Choose five of the items shown below. Put them in order of importance for survival.

2. Explain your choice to your group.
3. Agree on a list of items for the team to take.

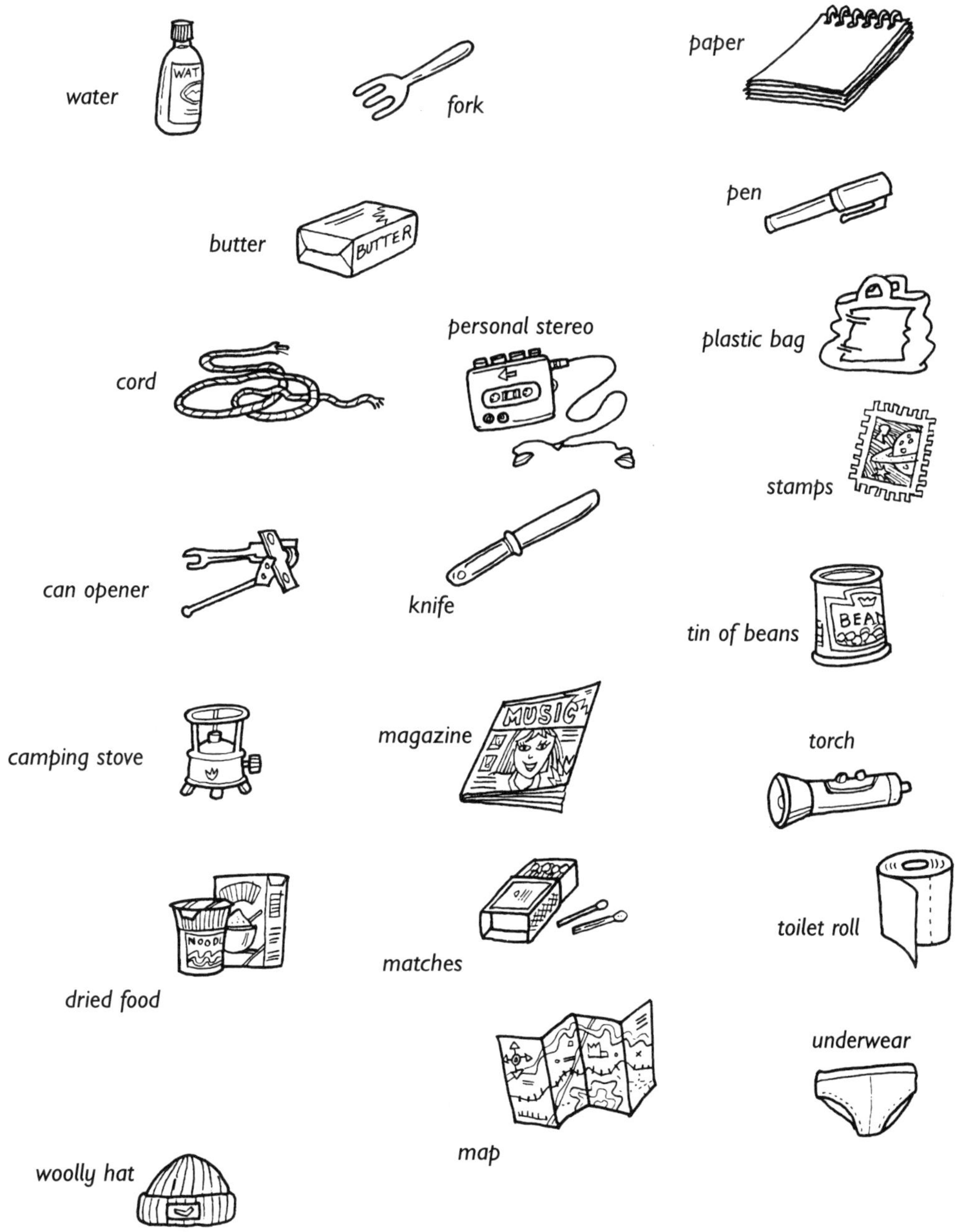

water *fork* *paper*
pen
butter
personal stereo *plastic bag*
cord
stamps
can opener *knife* *tin of beans*
camping stove *magazine* *torch*
matches *toilet roll*
dried food
underwear
map
woolly hat

Pond survey

Core

In and around a pond you will find many examples of plants, animals, microorganisms and even fungi. You are going to visit a pond to look for living things. You will bring back samples of the pond water to look at under a microscope.

⚠ Take care! Wear plastic gloves to handle pond plants.

Do not pick the plants.

Handle all living things with care.

Wash your hands afterwards.

Do

1 Draw all the living things you see in and around the pond.

2 Bring back a sample of pond water in the sample bottle.

3 Back in the laboratory, look at a drop of pond water under the microscope.

4 Draw all of the living things that you see.

⚠ Never use a microscope where the Sun's rays might reflect off the mirror into it. You could permanently damage your eyes.

Analyse and conclude

5 Find out the names of all of the living things you have drawn.

6 Sort the living things you have drawn into plants, animals, microorganisms and fungi. Put your results in a table.

7 Sort the animals into invertebrates and vertebrates. (Hint: you will need to draw a second table.)

❶ Think about food chains. Why do you think there are more invertebrates than vertebrates in the pond?

3.2 Pond survey

Activity 3.2
Help

Analyse and conclude

5 Find out the names of all the living things you have drawn.

6 Sort them into plants, animals, microorganisms and fungi. Write their names in the table below.

Plants	Animals	Microorganisms	Fungi

7 Sort the animals into invertebrates and vertebrates. Write their names in the table below.

Invertebrates	Vertebrates

1 Complete the sentences. Use **invertebrates** or **vertebrates** to fill the gaps.

The group which had the most living things in it was ....

There are more .... than .... in the pond because .... feed on ....

Pond survey

Invertebrates

(not drawn to scale)

Microscopic invertebrates

(not drawn to scale)

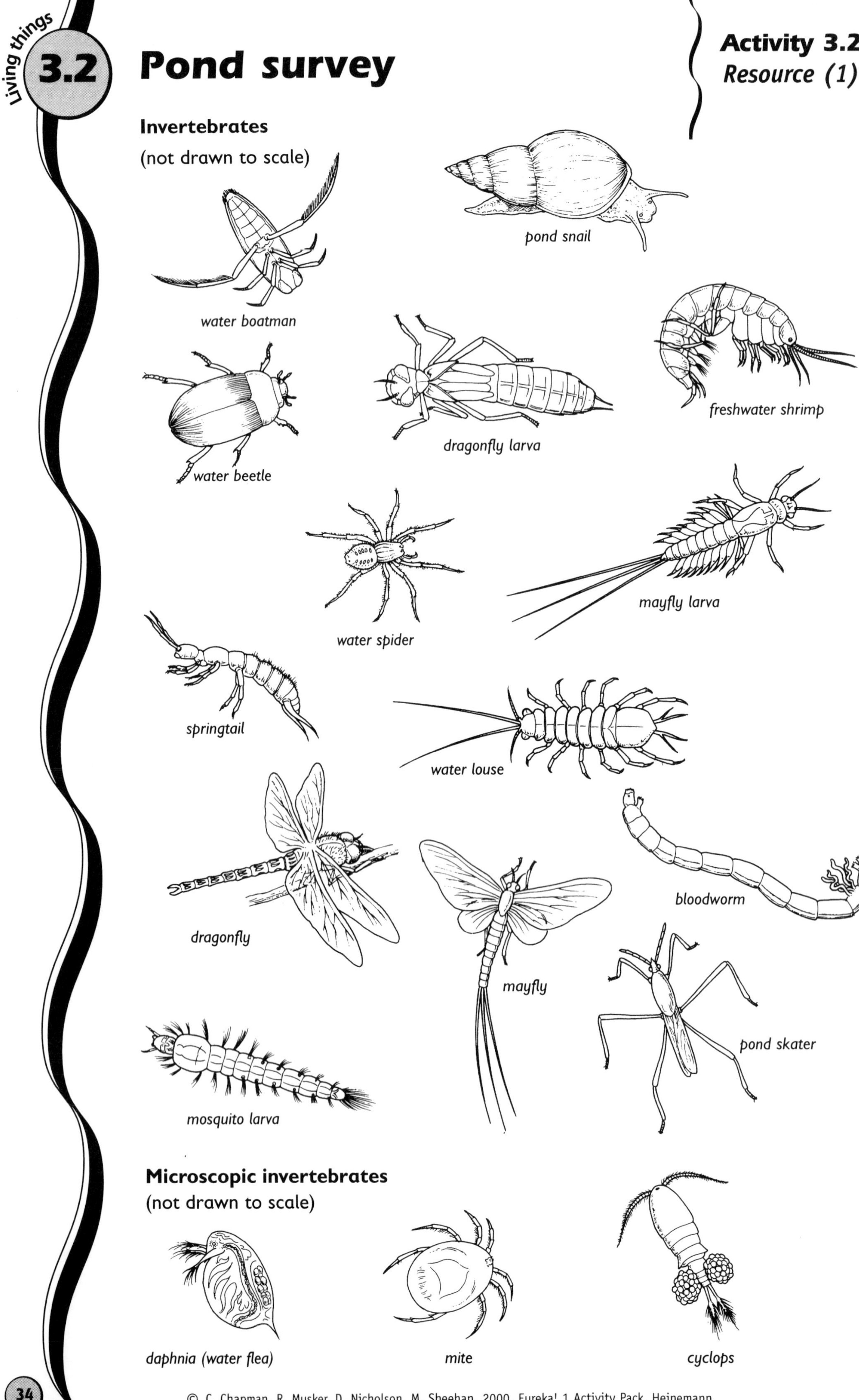

Pond survey

Vertebrates

(not drawn to scale)

stickleback

common frog and tadpole

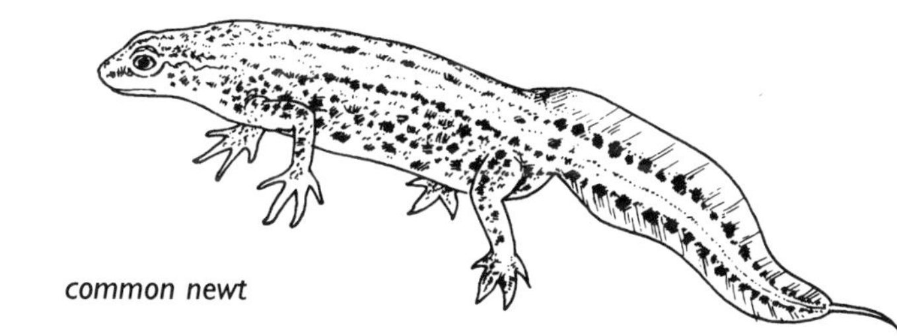

common newt

Plants

(not drawn to scale)

elodea (Canadian pondweed)

water crowfoot

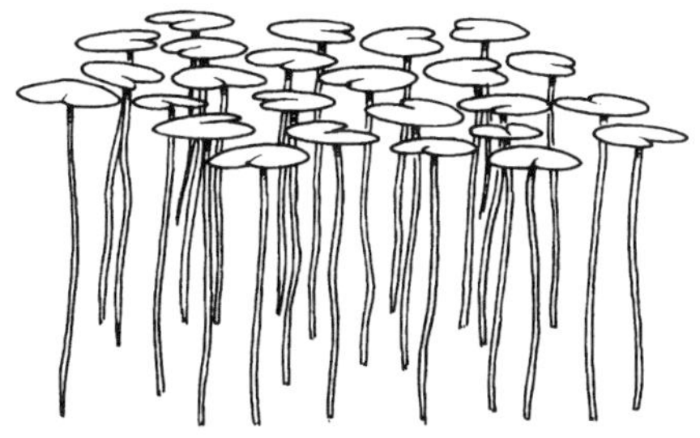

duckweed

All backbone!

Activity 3.3A
Core

There are many different vertebrate animals in Europe and many more in other continents. You are going to find information about vertebrates from the CD-ROM *Dangerous Creatures*.

Follow the instructions to find the answers to the questions.

1
- Click on *Atlas*.
- Click on *Europe*.
- Click on *Wolf*. The wolf is a mammal.
- Click on *Making tracks* to play the video.

❶ How does the wolf communicate?

2
- Click on *Atlas*.
- Click on *Europe*.
- Click on *Vulture*. The vulture is a bird.
- Click on *Predator or scavenger*.
- Click on ☒ to close the window.
- Click on *I saw it first!* to play the video.

❷ How does the vulture feed?

3
- Click on *Atlas*.
- Click on *Europe*.
- Click on *European Adder*. An adder is a reptile.
- Click on *Come a little closer* to play the video.

❸ How does the Australian death adder trap its prey?

4
- Click on *Atlas*.
- Click on *Europe*.
- Click on *Fire Salamander*. A salamander is an amphibian.
- Click on *Salamander variety* to play the video.

❹ Why do you think salamanders have different colours and patterns?

Time left?

See the next sheet.

To finish

- Click on ☒ to close the window.
- Click on *Back*.

All backbone!

Activity 3.3A
Extension

If you have some time left, answer the following questions using the CD-ROM *Dangerous Creatures*.

5 • Click on *Atlas*.
• Click on *North America*.
• Click on any mammal.

5 Write down the name and one interesting fact about the mammal you have chosen.

6 What sort of body covering do mammals have?

7 How do mammals feed their young?

6 • Click on *Atlas*.
• Click on *South America*.
• Click on any bird.

8 Write down the name and one interesting fact about the bird you have chosen.

9 Which parts of its body does a bird use for movement?

10 Describe one feature that a bird has that a mammal does not have.

7 • Click on *Atlas*.
• Click on *Africa*.
• Click on any reptile.

11 Write down the name and one interesting fact about the reptile you have chosen.

12 Where do reptiles lay their eggs?

13 Why do reptiles often sunbathe?

8 • Click on *Atlas*.
• Click on *Australia*.
• Click on any amphibian.

14 Write down the name and one interesting fact about the amphibian you have chosen.

15 Use a dictionary to find the meaning of the word amphibian.

16 What sort of eggs do amphibians lay?

9 • Click on *Atlas*.
• Click on *Asia*.
• Click on any fish.

17 Write down the name and one interesting fact about the fish you have chosen.

18 How do fish breathe under water?

19 What do fish have on the surface of their body?

Vertebrates game

Activity 3.3B
Core

You are going to play a board game that tests what you know about different sorts of vertebrates. Watch out for the forfeits!

The rules

1 Four or six people can play.

2 Each player needs a counter and a score card.

3 You must throw a 6 to start.

4 If you land on a **Q** one of the other players must take a **Q card** from the top of the pile, ask you the question and put the card back at the bottom of the pile.
If you get the question right, tick the box on your score card.
If you get the same question more than once it does not count.

5 If you land on **Can you?** you must play the forfeit on the card.
If the other players are happy with how you do it, tick the box on your score card.

6 The first player to score 10 or the player with the highest score at the end of the game is the winner.

SCORE CARD

Q		**Can you?**	
Mammal	....	Mammal	....
Bird	....	Bird	....
Reptile	....	Reptile	....
Amphibian	....	Amphibian	....
Fish	....	Fish	....

SCORE CARD

Q		**Can you?**	
Mammal	....	Mammal	....
Bird	....	Bird	....
Reptile	....	Reptile	....
Amphibian	....	Amphibian	....
Fish	....	Fish	....

SCORE CARD

Q		**Can you?**	
Mammal	....	Mammal	....
Bird	....	Bird	....
Reptile	....	Reptile	....
Amphibian	....	Amphibian	....
Fish	....	Fish	....

SCORE CARD

Q		**Can you?**	
Mammal	....	Mammal	....
Bird	....	Bird	....
Reptile	....	Reptile	....
Amphibian	....	Amphibian	....
Fish	....	Fish	....

Vertebrates game

Activity 3.3B
Resource (1)

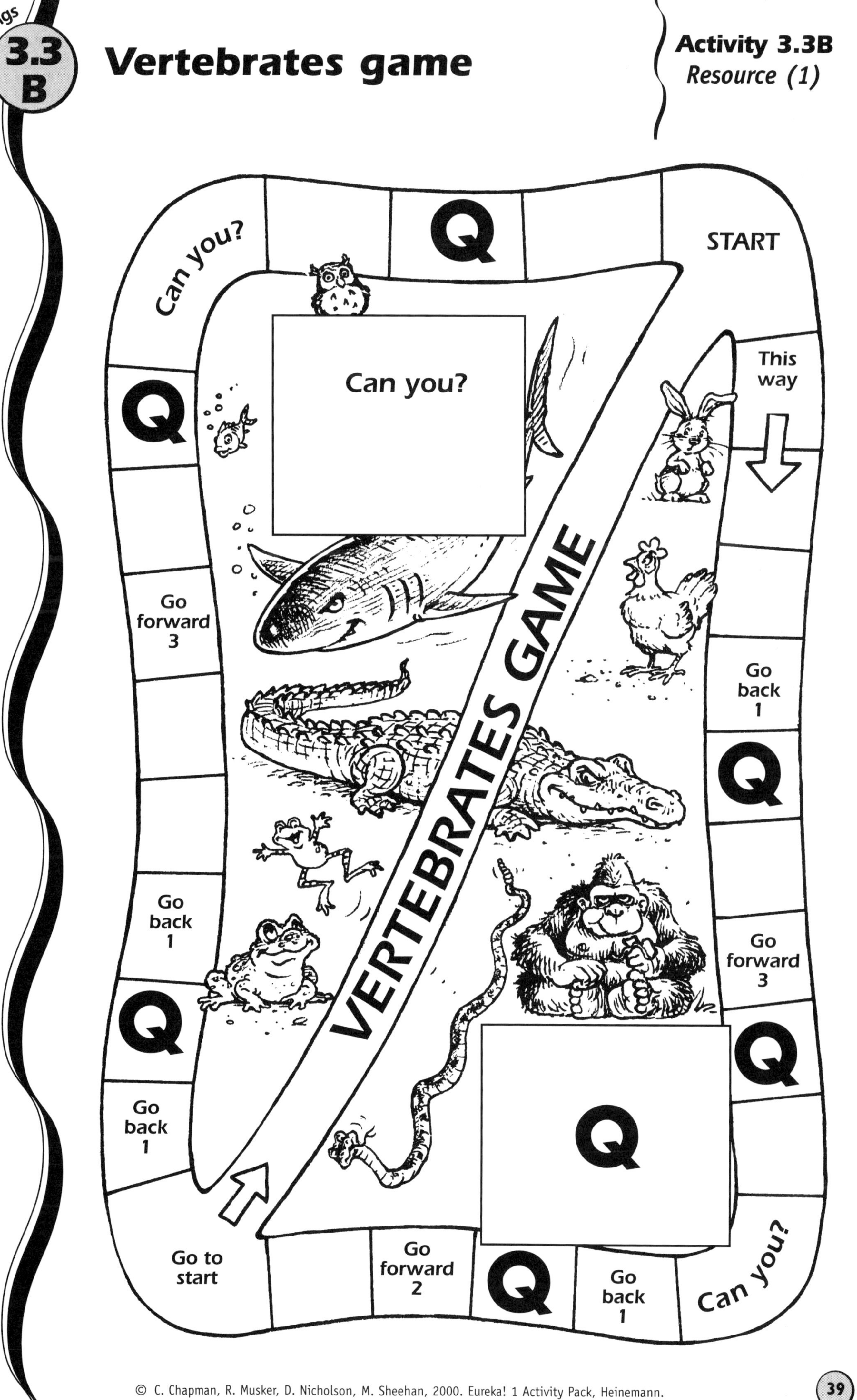

Vertebrates game

Q
I have feathers and wings. I lay eggs with a hard shell.
What group am I in?
A Birds

Q
I have scales and fins. I live in water and breathe through gills.
What group am I in?
A Fish

Can you?
Croak like a frog.
A frog is an **amphibian**.

Can you?
Cluck like a hen.
A hen is a **bird**.

Q
I have dry, scaly skin. I lay eggs with a leathery shell.
What group am I in?
A Reptiles

Q
I am warm blooded and my babies develop inside my body.
What group am I in?
A Mammals

Can you?
Mime a rattlesnake slithering.
A rattlesnake is a **reptile**.

Can you?
Act like a rabbit.
A rabbit is a **mammal**.

Q
I have smooth, moist skin. I can breathe in air. I lay jelly-like eggs in water.
What group am I in?
A Amphibians

Q
I have hairy skin. I feed my babies on milk from mammary glands.
What group am I in?
A Mammals

Can you?
Act like an ape.
An ape is a **mammal**.

Can you?
Mime a killer shark hunting its prey.
A shark is a **fish**.

Vertebrates game

Q

I can fly and I look after my young until they hatch.

What group am I in?

A Birds

Q

I cannot breathe in air. I spend all my life in water.

What group am I in?

A Fish

Can you?

Name six different fish.

Cod, haddock, plaice, salmon, tuna, goldfish, stickleback, perch, trout, etc. are all different types of **fish**.

Can you?

Hoot like an owl.

An owl is a **bird**.

Q

I can breathe on land but I need to move around a lot to keep warm.

What group am I in?

A Reptiles

Q

My blood is warm. I can breathe in air. I do not lay eggs.

What group am I in?

A Mammals.

Can you?

Name three types of cat.

Lions, tigers, cheetahs, leopards and domestic cats are all **mammals**.

Can you?

Make six words out of the word CROCODILE in 30 seconds.

A crocodile is a **reptile**.

Q

I can breathe on land, but I have to go back to water to reproduce.

What group am I in?

A Amphibians

Q

My blood in warm. I can breathe in air. I lay eggs with hard shells.

What group am I in?

A Birds

Can you?

Walk like a penguin.

A penguin is a **bird**.

Can you?

Draw a toad in 30 seconds.

A toad is an **amphibian**.

Suits of armour

Activity 3.4
Core

There are more arthropods than all the other animal groups put together! They all have a skeleton outside their body and jointed legs. You are going to find information about arthropods from the CD-ROM *Dangerous Creatures.*

Follow the instructions to find the answers to the questions.

1
- Click on *Atlas.*
- Click on *Europe.*
- Click on *Crab.*
- Click on *Crazy crustaceans* to play the video.

❶ What does a crab have on the outside of its body?

2
- Click on *Atlas.*
- Click on *North America.*
- Click on *Bad bugs.*
- Click on *Cockroach.*
- Click on *Born to eat* to play the video.
- Click on *Back.*
- Click on *Is it an insect?*

❷ How do we know that the cockroach is an insect?

3
- Click on Atlas.
- Click on *South America.*
- Click on *Tarantula.*
- Click on *Birds for breakfast* to play the video.
- Click on ☒ to close the window.
- Click on *Big and hairy.*
- Click on ☒ to close the window.
- Click on *Hunting spiders.*

❸ The raft spider can walk on water, but how do we know it is a spider?

4
- Click on *Atlas.*
- Click on *Asia.*
- Click on *Centipede.*
- Click on *Millipede or centipede* to play the video.

❹ How can you tell a millipede from a centipede?

To finish

- Click on ☒ to close the window.
- Click on *Back.*

3.5 Spot the species!

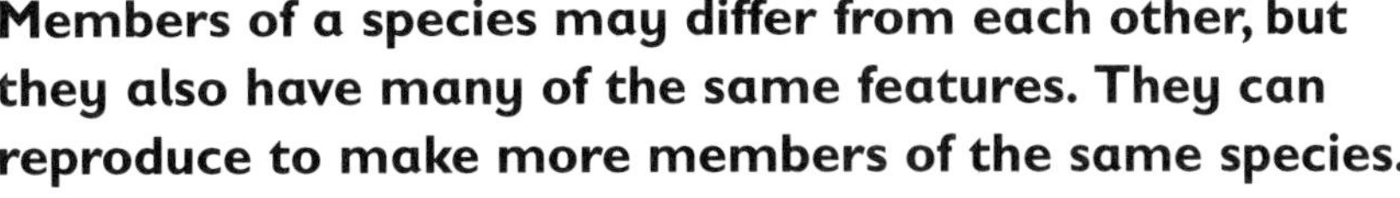

Activity 3.5
Core

⚠ Handle live animals with care.

Wash your hands afterwards.

Members of a species may differ from each other, but they also have many of the same features. They can reproduce to make more members of the same species.

1 Look very carefully at the frog and the toad.

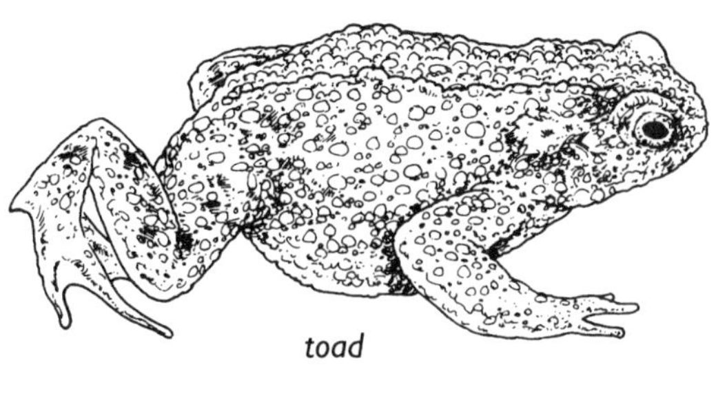

toad

frog

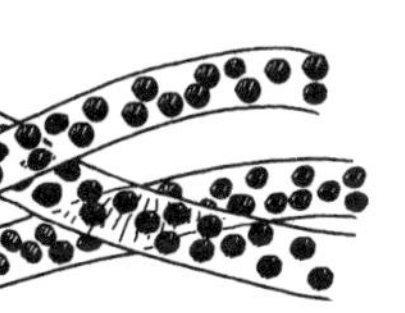

toad spawn

frog spawn

2 Make a list of the features that are the same for both frog and toad. Make a list of the features that are different.

1 Are the frog and the toad members of the same species?

3.5 Spot the species!

Activity 3.5
Core

⚠ Handle live animals with care.

Wash your hands afterwards.

Members of a species may differ from each other, but they also have many of the same features. They can reproduce to make more members of the same species.

1 Look very carefully at the frog and the toad.

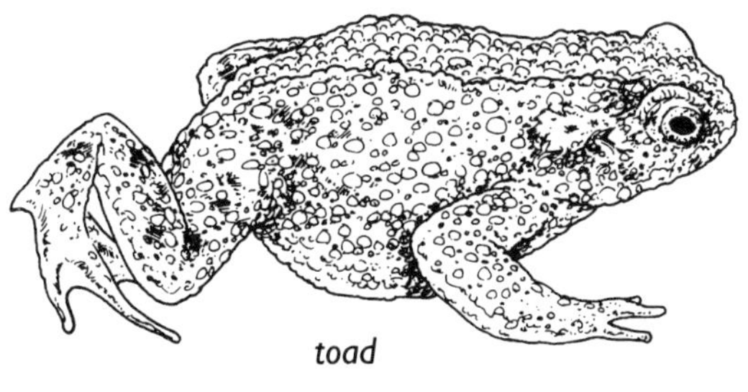

toad

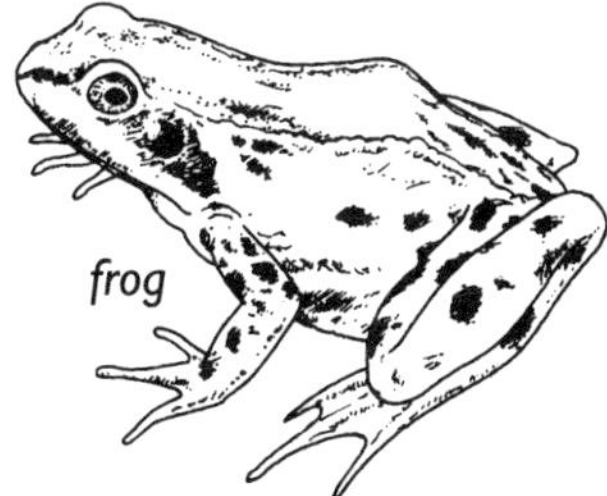

frog

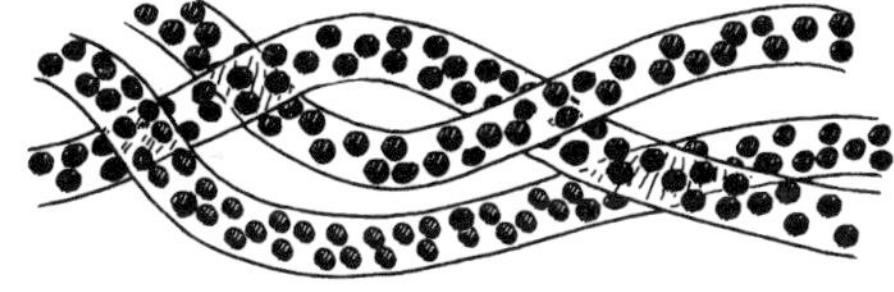

toad spawn

frog spawn

2 Make a list of the features that are the same for both frog and toad. Make a list of the features that are different.

1 Are the frog and the toad members of the same species?

Spot the species!

Activity 3.5
Help

Members of a species may differ from each other, but they also have many of the same features. They can reproduce to make more members of the same species.

⚠ Handle live animals with care.
Wash your hands afterwards.

1 Look very carefully at the frog and the toad.

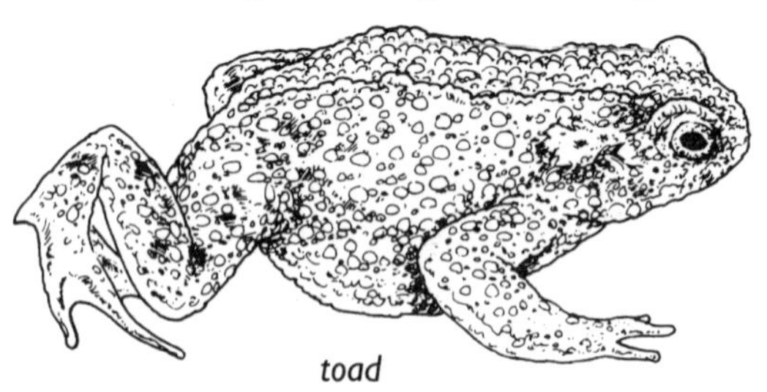

toad

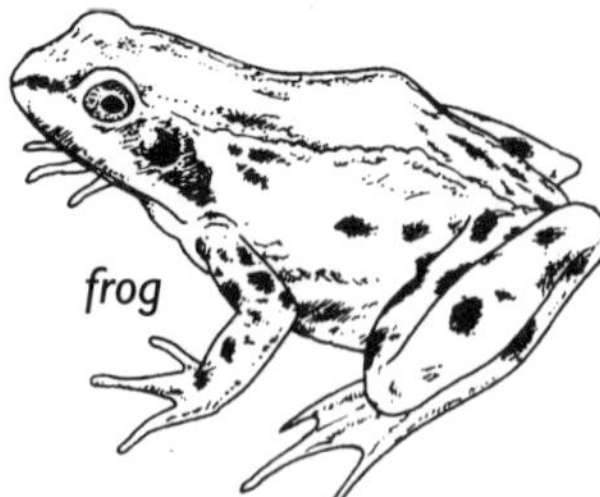

frog

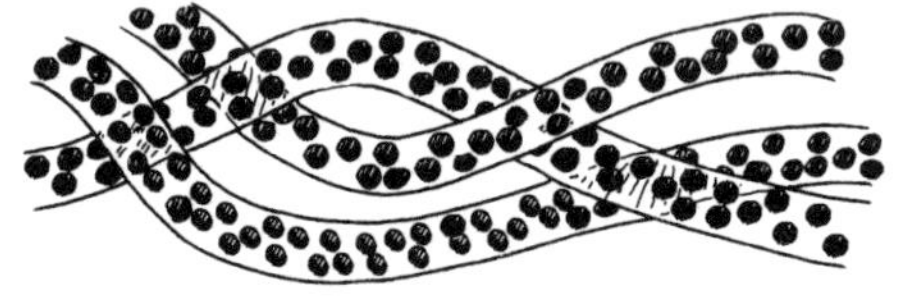

toad spawn

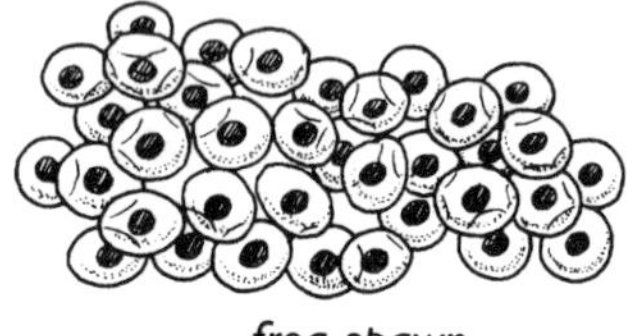

frog spawn

2 Which features are the same in the frog and the toad? Which features are different? Write them in the table below.

Same	Different

❶ Complete this sentence. Use **the same** or **different** to fill in the gap.

The frog and the toad are members of .... species.

Bear necessities

The polar bear is adapted to survive the cold Arctic climate. You are going to find information about the polar bear from the CD-ROM *Dangerous Creatures*.

Follow the instructions to find the answers to the questions.

1 • Click on *Atlas*.
• Click on *North America*.
• Click on *Polar bear*.
• Click on *Facts*.

1 **a** What does the polar bear eat?
b How does it kill its prey?

2 • Click on ☒ to close the window.
• Click on *Begging for trouble*.

2 Some polar bears become town pests. Explain why this is not good for the polar bear.

3 • Click on ☒ to close the window.
• Click on *Check the fridge*.

3 How does the polar bear catch its prey?

4 • Click on *Lands of ice and snow*.
• Click on *Who says it's cold?* to play the video.

4 How are animals that live in the cold adapted to keep warm?

5 • Click on ☒ to close the window.
• Click on *Back*.
• Click on *Polar protection* to play the video.
• Click on ☒ to close the window.
• Click on *Sleeping out*.

5 How do baby polar bears keep warm?

Time left?

6 • Click on *Index*.
• Click on *Find* and search for information about the Arctic fox.
• Click on *OK*.

6 Write down some information about how the Arctic fox is adapted to survive in the Arctic climate.

To finish

• Click on ☒ to close the window.
• Click on *Atlas*.

A winter coat

Activity 3.6B

Core

During the cold winter some animals grow a much thicker layer of fur. You are going to investigate whether a thick layer of fur helps to keep an animal warm.

Wear eye protection.

Take care!
If you scald yourself with boiling water, cool the skin at once with plenty of running water, and keep it in the cold water for 10 minutes.

Equipment available

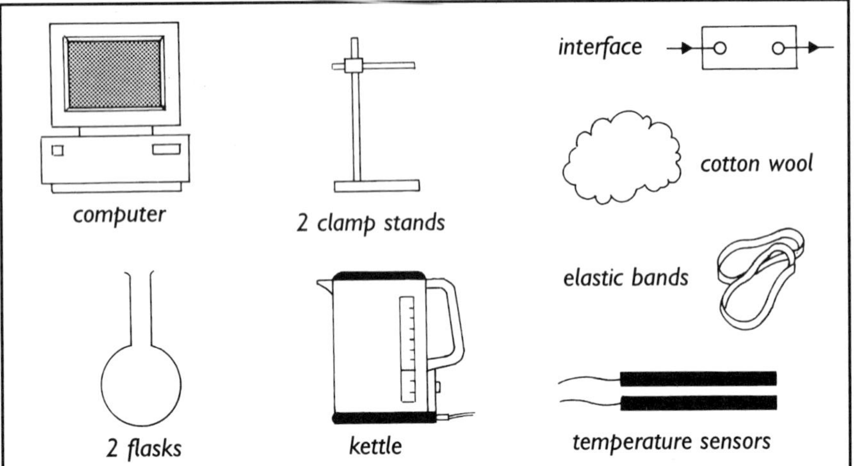

Plan

1 Plan an investigation to see if a thick layer of fur would keep an animal warm. Before you start, think about the following questions.

- What will you keep the same?
- What will you change?
- How will you make sure that your experiment is a fair test?
- What measurements will you take?
- How will you record and display your results? You will need tables and/or graphs. (Printouts from the computer will be useful.)

Predict

❶ Make a prediction. What do you think will happen?

Do

2 Get your plan approved, then carry out your investigation.

3 Sketch or print out a graph of your results.

Analyse and conclude

❷ Was your prediction right?

❸ Did a thick layer of fur help to keep the heat in?

Evaluate

❹ Was your experiment a fair test?

❺ Did any results not fit the pattern?

❻ What improvements could you make?

A winter coat

Activity 3.6B

Help

During the cold winter some animals grow a much thicker layer of fur. You are going to investigate whether a thick layer of fur helps to keep an animal warm.

This is how the experiment will be set up:

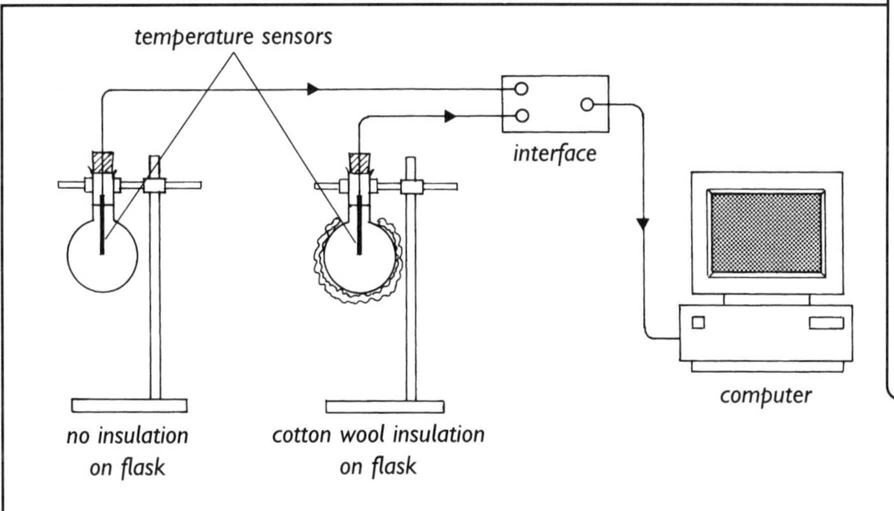

Wear eye protection.

Take care! If you scald yourself with boiling water, cool the skin at once with plenty of running water, and keep it in the cold water for 10 minutes.

Predict

1 Complete this sentence. Use **slower** or **quicker** to fill in the gap.

I think that the flask with insulation will cool down .... than the flask without insulation.

Do

1. Watch your teacher carry out the experiment.
2. Look at the graph displayed by the computer.
3. Draw a sketch of the graph (or your teacher may give you a printout).

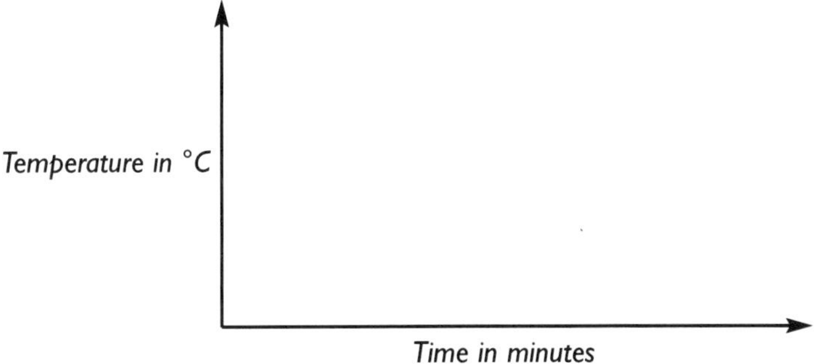

Analyse and conclude

2 Which flask cooled down the quickest?

3 Which flask cooled down the slowest?

4 Is this what you expected?

Living things 3.6 B

A winter coat

Activity 3.6B

Extension

During the cold winter some animals grow a much thicker layer of fur. You are going to investigate whether a thick layer of fur helps to keep an animal warm.

Here are some ideas to think about.

- You could use a round bottomed flask with hot water inside for your model animal.
- You will need to find a material to represent the 'fur'.
- You could compare different thicknesses of fur with no fur.
- You could use temperature sensors and the computer.

> Wear eye protection.
>
> ⚠ Take care! If you scald yourself with boiling water, cool the skin at once with plenty of running water, and keep it in the cold water for 10 minutes.

Investigation

1. Predict what you think will happen. (You could do a trial run.)
2. Plan your investigation and get your plan approved.
3. Carry out your investigation.
4. Record the results. (Printouts from the computer will be useful.)
5. Use your results to write a report. (Remember to include an analysis and evaluation of your results.)

Living things 3.6 B

A winter coat

Activity 3.6B

Extension

During the cold winter some animals grow a much thicker layer of fur. You are going to investigate whether a thick layer of fur helps to keep an animal warm.

Here are some ideas to think about.

- You could use a round bottomed flask with hot water inside for your model animal.
- You will need to find a material to represent the 'fur'.
- You could compare different thicknesses of fur with no fur.
- You could use temperature sensors and the computer.

> Wear eye protection.
>
> ⚠ Take care! If you scald yourself with boiling water, cool the skin at once with plenty of running water, and keep it in the cold water for 10 minutes.

Investigation

1. Predict what you think will happen. (You could do a trial run.)
2. Plan your investigation and get your plan approved.
3. Carry out your investigation.
4. Record the results. (Printouts from the computer will be useful.)
5. Use your results to write a report. (Remember to include an analysis and evaluation of your results.)

3.7 Class heights

⚠ Take care when walking around with metre rules.

Each person in your class is a different height. This is because they have inherited different information from their parents and because they have grown up in different surroundings.

You are going to measure your height and enter it into a spreadsheet of class heights so that you can analyse the data.

Do

1 Measure your height in centimetres.

2 Enter your data in **table 1** of the spreadsheet.

- Fill in your **Name**.
- Fill in your **Height cm**.

Analyse and conclude

3 Sort the data in ascending order from the shortest to the tallest.

❶ What is the range of heights in the class?

❷ Who is the shortest person?

❸ Who is the tallest person?

4 Use the data to fill in **table 2**.

- Find the **Range cm** column.
- Fill in the **Number in range** categories.

5 Produce a bar chart of the data in **table 2**.

❹ Name a person who is in the biggest range category.

Evaluate

❺ What were the advantages of using a computer spreadsheet for this activity?

Class heights

Activity 3.7
Help

Each person in your class is a different height. This is because they have inherited different information from their parents and because they have grown up in different surroundings. You are going to measure your height and enter it into a spreadsheet of class heights so that you can analyse the data.

The spreadsheet will sort your data and display it as a bar chart.

⚠ Take care when walking around with metre rules.

Do: Enter your data

1 First measure your height in centimetres.

2 Then enter your data in **table 1** of the spreadsheet like this:

- Move the mouse until the cursor is in the empty box under **Name**.
- Click on the left mouse button.
- Type in your name.
- Use the mouse until the cursor is in the box under **Height cm.**
- Type in your height.

When everyone has entered their data, you can start your analysis.

Analyse and conclude: Sort your data

3 Use the mouse or the arrow keys to highlight **table 1** (include the headings).

4
- Click on *Data* on the tool bar
- Click on *Sort*
- Choose *Height cm* to sort by
- Click on *Ascending*
- Click on *OK*.

❶ What is the range of heights in the class?

❷ Who is the shortest person?

❸ Who is the tallest person?

5 Use the sorted data to fill in **table 2** of your spreadsheet.

- Find the **Range cm** column.
- Count how many people are in the first category.
- Move the cursor to the empty box under **Number of people in the range**.
- Type in the number.
- Do the same for the other categories.

Analyse and conclude: Draw a bar chart

6
- Use the mouse or the arrow keys to highlight **table 2** (include the headings).
- Click on the Chart Wizard icon on the tool bar.
- Click on *Column graph* from the chart type.
- Click on *Finish*.

❹ Name a person who is in the biggest range category.

Evaluate

❺ What were the advantages of using a computer spreadsheet for this activity?

4 Burning

Unit map

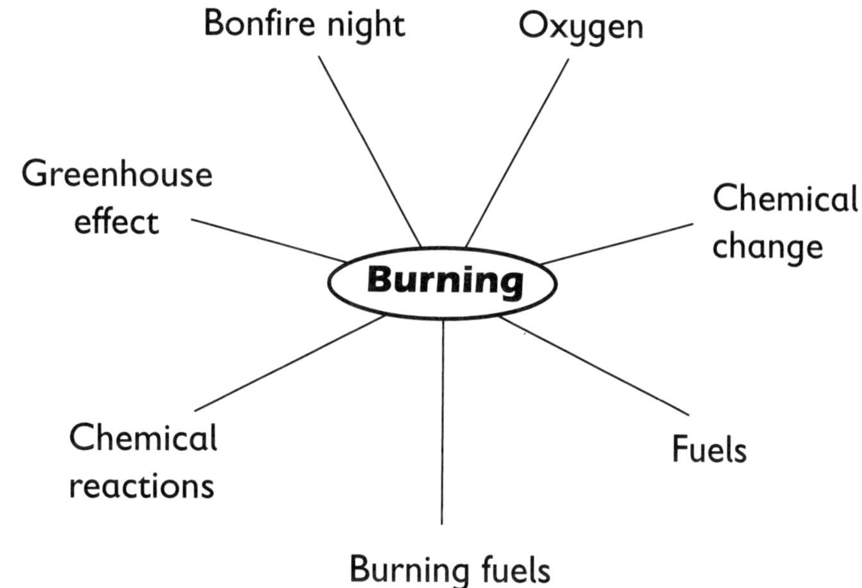

4 Burning

Unit map

Use these words to help you copy and complete your unit map.

burn	variable	limewater	hydrocarbons
oxide	heat	hot	model
metal	energy	iron	carbon
fuel	ash	carbon dioxide	flammable
joules	relationship	word equation	burning
outcome	light	chemical reaction	
particles	copper	air	
input	magnesium	reversible	
combustion	oxygen	material	

The burning question

Activity 4.1
Core

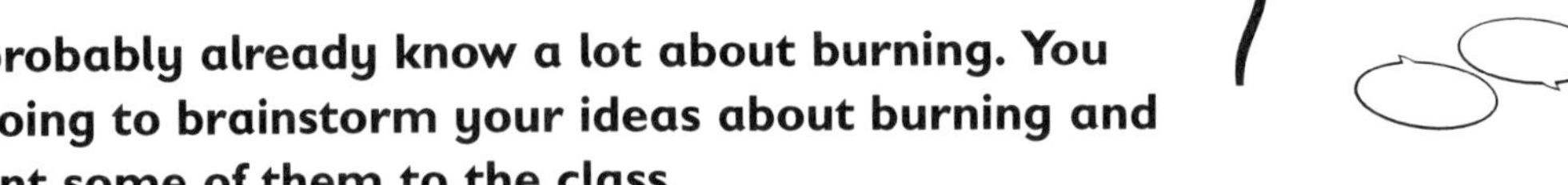

You probably already know a lot about burning. You are going to brainstorm your ideas about burning and present some of them to the class.

Brainstorm

1 Begin this activity by copying the unit map.

2 Add as many words to do with burning as you can think of to your map.

3 Discuss your map with your group. Brainstorm together to find as many words as you can.

4 Draw a big map using all the words from the group.

Plan

5 In your group, choose one word and plan a presentation to explain to the class what it means. You can present your word in any of these ways:

- in a sentence
- as a picture
- a song or rap
- as a mime act.

Present

6 Give your presentation to the class.

4.2 Putting fires out

Activity 4.2
Core

You are going to find out what is the best material for putting out fires – sand, water or foam. Each time, record how long it takes for the fire to go out.

> Wear eye protection.
> ⚠ Keep fires very small.
> Take care not to get acid or foam on anyone's skin or clothes.
> Wash your hands afterwards.

Using sand

1 Take about six wooden splints and a piece of newspaper. Break the splints in half and crumple up the newspaper. Put them in the middle of a heatproof mat to make a fire.

2 Light your fire.

3 Start the stopclock then and carefully pour a beaker of sand on to the fire.

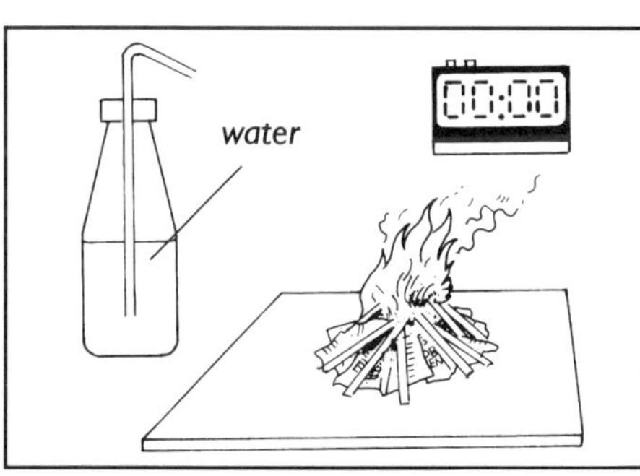

Using water

4 Prepare another small fire and light it.

5 Start the stopclock then squirt the water on to the fire until it goes out.

Using foam

6 Take a conical flask and set it up as shown in the diagram.

7 Prepare a third small fire and light it.

8 Start the stopclock then turn the flask upside down, shake it and point the jet at the fire until it goes out.

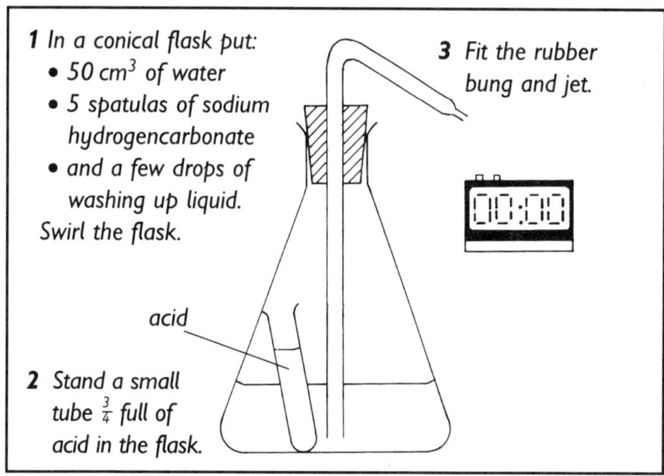

1 In a conical flask put:
• 50 cm³ of water
• 5 spatulas of sodium hydrogencarbonate
• and a few drops of washing up liquid.
Swirl the flask.
3 Fit the rubber bung and jet.
00:00
acid
2 Stand a small tube ¾ full of acid in the flask.

Analyse and conclude

❶ Which method was easiest to use?

❷ Which method put the fire out in the shortest time?

❸ Which method was the easiest to clean up after?

❹ Which method do you think would be most suitable for a large fire?

❺ Write down what each substance does when it puts out the fire:
• sand • water • foam.

Putting fires out

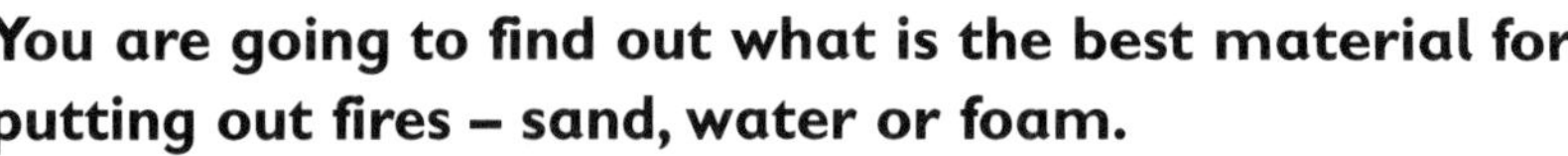

You are going to find out what is the best material for putting out fires – sand, water or foam.

Fill in the gaps to record the results each time.

Wear eye protection.

⚠ Keep fires very small.

Take care not to get acid or foam on anyone's skin or clothes.

Wash your hands afterwards.

Using sand

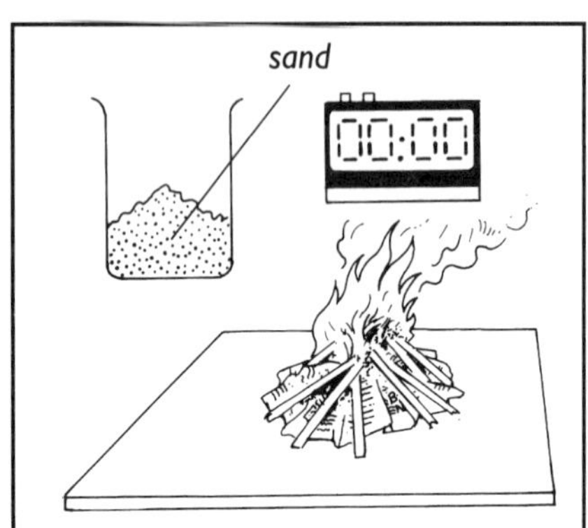

Time to put the fire out:

.... s

Using water

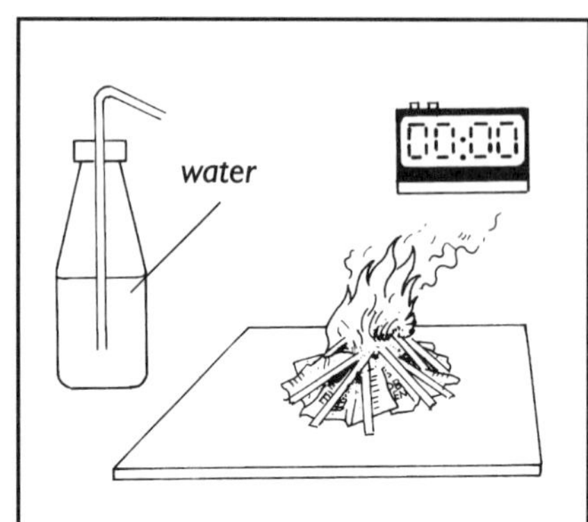

Time to put the fire out:

.... s

Using foam

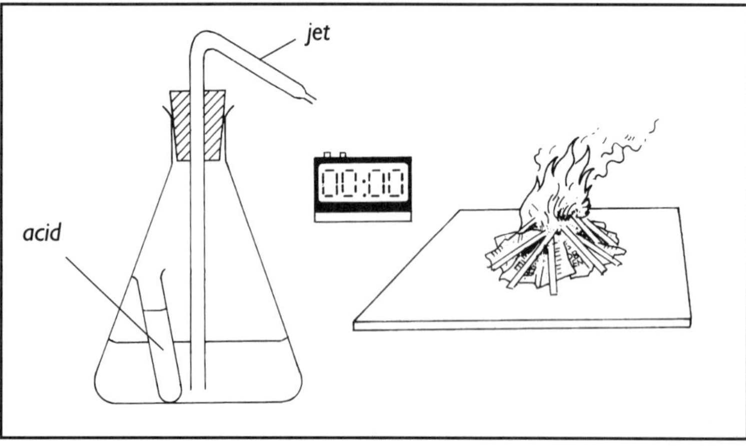

Time to put the fire out:

.... s

Analyse and conclude

1. Complete the sentences. Use these words to fill the gaps.
   acid water foam sand
   - The easiest way to put out the fire was ....
   - The fire was put out fastest by ....
   - The most mess to clear up was left by ....
2. The best method to use on a large fire would be ....
3. When you put out a fire, you break the fire triangle.
   - Using sand, what part of the fire triangle do you break?

     ....
   - Using water, what part of the fire triangle do you break?

     ....
   - Using foam, what part of the fire triangle do you break?

     ....

4.3 Burning metals

Activity 4.3
Core

When metals burn in air, they react with oxygen to make oxides. Some metals release more energy when they burn than other metals do. You are going to see what happens when three different metals are burned in air.

Wear eye protection.

Take care with Bunsen burners.

Copper compounds are harmful.

Do not look directly at burning magnesium. It will hurt your eyes. Look at it through blue glass or look away when you have seen how bright it is.

Wash your hands afterwards.

Magnesium

1 Using tongs, hold a small strip of magnesium ribbon in a Bunsen burner flame until it burns.

2 Record your observations. (Hint: draw a table for the three metals.)

Iron

3 Repeat the experiment with a small piece of iron wool.

Copper

4 Finally, do the experiment with a small square of copper foil.

Analyse and conclude

1 Write down what substance is formed when each metal burns:
- magnesium
- iron
- copper.

2 What else is given out when the metals burn?

3 Which one of these metals would be best for making a distress flare for use at sea? Explain your answer.

Activity 4.3
Extension

4 Copy and complete the word equations.

magnesium + ... → magnesium oxide

iron + oxygen → ....

.... + ... → copper oxide

5 Calcium metal burns in air with a dark red flame. Write a word equation for this reaction.

4.3 Burning metals

Activity 4.3
Help

When metals burn in air, they react with oxygen to make oxides. Some metals release more energy when they burn than other metals do.

You are going to see what happens when three different metals are burned in air:

- magnesium
- iron
- copper.

Wear eye protection.

Take care with Bunsen burners.

Copper compounds are harmful.

Do not look directly at burning magnesium. It will hurt your eyes. Look at it through blue glass or look away when you have seen how bright it is.

Wash your hands afterwards.

Record

Complete the table to record your observations.

Metal	What does the metal look like before heating?	Observations during heating	Observations after heating
magnesium			
iron			
copper			

Analyse and conclude

1. Write down what substance is formed when each metal burns:
   - magnesium ....
   - iron ....
   - copper ....
2. What else is given out when the metals burn? ....
3. Which metal burned the brightest? ....
4. Which of the metals would be best for making a distress flare for use at sea? ....

How much energy?

Activity 4.4A
Core

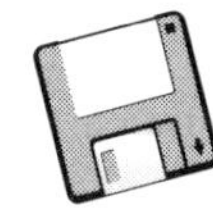

We use the energy from burning fuels for cooking and heating our homes. You are going to see 1 cm^3 of methylated spirits burn to heat 20 cm^3 of water. You will use a temperature sensor to measure how much the water heats up.

Wear eye protection.

This is how the experiment will be set up:

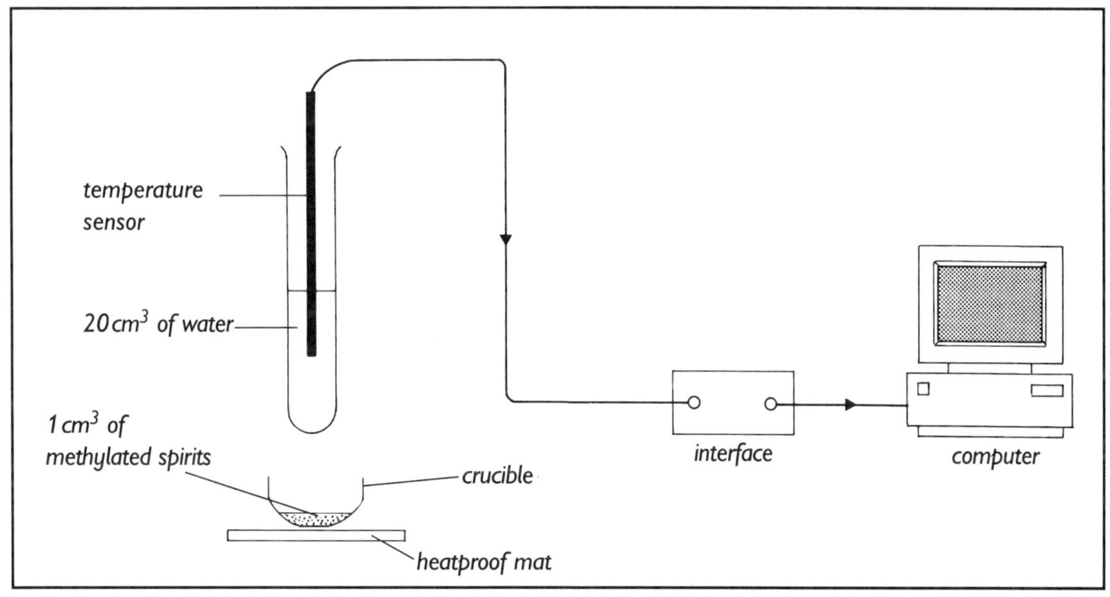

The computer will display a graph of the temperature.

Record

1 Draw a sketch of the graph (or your teacher may give you a printout).

Analyse and conclude

2 Copy and complete the sentences.

- Before heating, the temperature of the water was .... °C.
- After heating, the temperature of the water was .... °C.
- The temperature change was .... °C.

3 Copy and complete the sentences.

- As the fuel burned, the temperature of the water ....
- As the fuel burned, ... was transferred from the fuel to the water.

Plan

4 Jane wants to do this experiment with two fuels to find out which one is better. What should she do to make it a fair test?

A good fuel?

The most important thing we want from a fuel is energy. But there are some other things to consider when choosing a fuel.

Wear eye protection.

Take care with Bunsen burners.

Use small amounts of fuels.

Wash your hands after using fuels.

A good fuel has these features:

- It lights easily.
- It burns for a long time.
- It does not give off a lot of smoke.
- It does not leave a lot of ash.

You are going to test four different fuel samples.

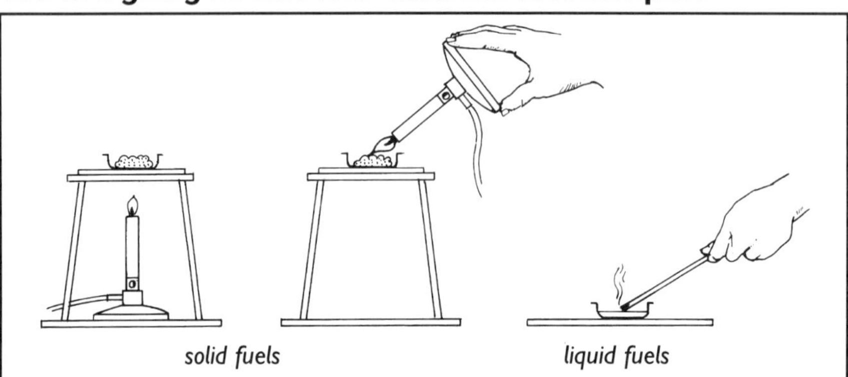

Plan

1 Think what you will need to record. Make a table for your results.

Do: for solid fuels

2 Put a small amount of the fuel on the tin lid and place it on the gauze.

3 Light the Bunsen burner. Use a small flame with the air hole open half-way.

4 Heat the fuel from below for 1 minute.

5 If the fuel has not started to burn, try heating from above.

Do: for liquid fuels

6 Use only two drops of the fuel.

7 Light the fuel from above using a long splint.

8 Time how long each fuel burns.

Analyse and conclude

9 When each fuel has finished burning, record your results. Give each fuel a score out of 3 for each of the features of a good fuel. (3 = good.)

10 Add up the scores to get a total score for each fuel.

1 Which fuel was the best? Which was the worst?

Evaluate

2 Was this experiment a fair test?

3 Are there any other fuels that you would have liked to test?

4 Can you think of any other factors you should take into account when choosing a fuel?

A good fuel?

Activity 4.4B
Help

The most important thing we want from a fuel is energy. But there are some other things to consider when choosing a fuel.

A good fuel has these features:

- It lights easily.
- It burns for a long time.
- It does not give off a lot of smoke.
- It does not leave a lot of ash.

Wear eye protection.

Take care with Bunsen burners.

Use small amounts of fuels.

Wash your hands after using fuels.

You are going to test three different fuel samples.

Analyse and conclude

1 Complete the table by giving each fuel a score for each feature.
3 = good   2 = medium   1 = poor

Fuel	How easy it was to light	How long it burned for	How much smoke it gave off	How much ash was left	Total score

2 Add up the scores to get a total score for each fuel.

1 Which fuel was: • the best? ....

• the worst? ....

2 Complete the following sentences. Choose words from this list to fill the gaps.

shortest easy hard least most longest

An ideal fuel is .... to light. It burns for the .... time. It gives off the .... smoke. It leaves the .... ash.

What happens when a fuel burns?

Activity 4.5
Core

Wear eye protection.

Take care with burning candles.

Do not touch the hot wax.

When a fuel burns, a chemical reaction called combustion takes place. The fuel reacts with oxygen to release energy and make new substances. One of these is carbon dioxide gas.

Limewater is clear, but it turns milky white when carbon dioxide bubbles through it. You are going to use limewater to test the gas given off by a burning candle.

Do

The apparatus will be set up like this:

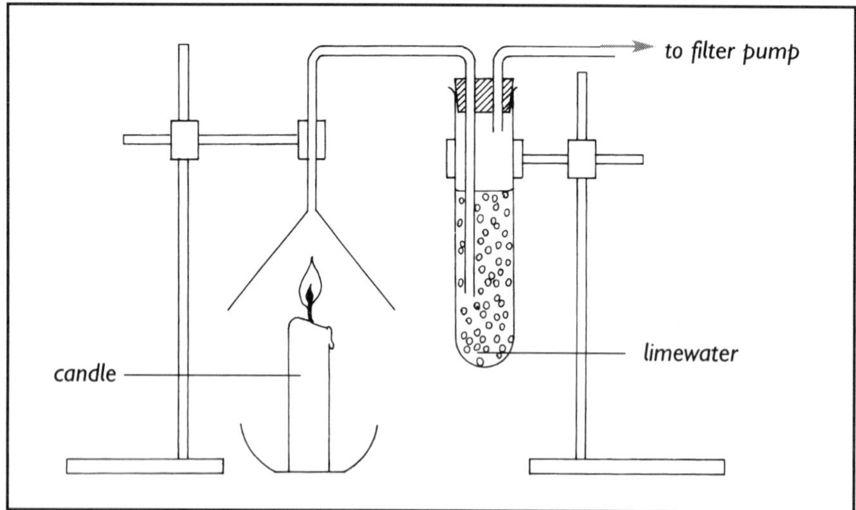

1 Turn on the tap, so that the filter pump starts to draw air through the apparatus.

2 Light the candle.

3 Watch carefully to see if there is any change in the limewater.

4 Put the candle out when you have seen a change, or before it has burned down completely.

5 Turn off the tap.

Analyse and conclude

1. What effect did the gas from the burning candle have on the limewater?
2. What does this experiment show?
3. Which gas is always produced when a fuel burns?
4. Did you notice any other new substance that was made when the candle burned?

What happens when a fuel burns?

Wear eye protection.

Take care with burning candles.

Do not touch the hot wax.

When a fuel burns, a chemical reaction called combustion takes place. The fuel reacts with oxygen to release energy and make new substances. One of these is carbon dioxide gas.

Limewater is clear, but it turns milky white when carbon dioxide bubbles through it. You are going to use limewater to test the gas given off by a burning candle.

Do

The apparatus will be set up like this:

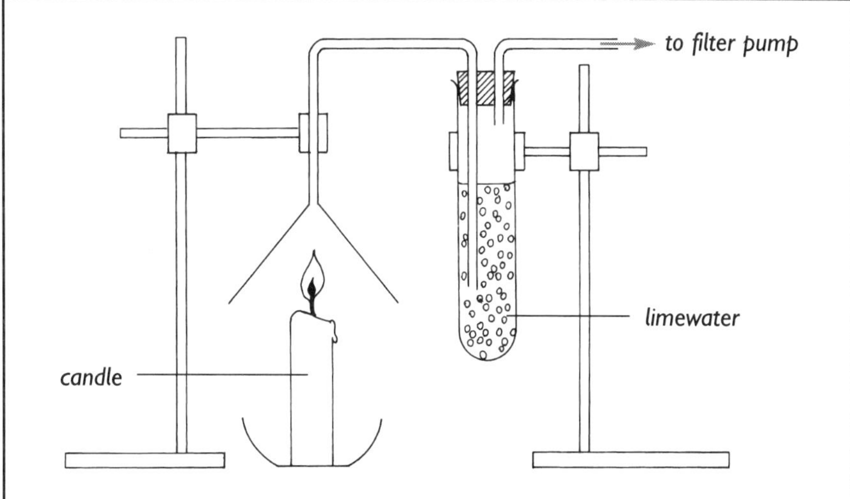

Analyse and conclude

1. Complete these sentences.

   The gas from the burning candle turned the limewater .... This shows that the burning candle produces ....

2. Did you notice any other new substance that was made when the candle burned?

   ....

The day we discovered oxygen

Activity 4.6
Core

In 1772 a scientist called Lavoisier discovered that when substances burn they join with oxygen in the air to make oxides. Laboratories at that time were dark, dingy workshops. The scientists worked by candle-light and they didn't even have Bunsen burners!

You are going to write a diary for the day Lavoisier discovered oxygen.

1 Read *Alchemy Today* about Lavoisier's experiment.

2 Imagine you are Lavoisier's assistant. Use what you have read and the suggestions below to write a diary for the day you discovered oxygen.

My day with Lavoisier

We made an early start. As usual, I walked to work and opened up.
The laboratory seemed ...
Lavoisier wanted me to do an experiment to find out ...
I collected the apparatus. I needed ...
I set everything out on the bench and ...
Much to my surprise, I found that ...
I showed Lavoisier my results, but he said we can't be sure that ...
I have got to repeat my experiment, so I know what I shall be doing tomorrow!

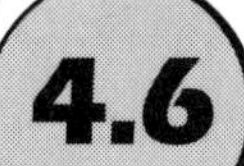

4.6 The day we discovered oxygen

Activity 4.6
Help

In 1772 a scientist called Lavoisier discovered that when substances burn they join with oxygen in the air to make oxides. Laboratories at that time were dark, dingy workshops. The scientists worked by candle-light and they didn't even have Bunsen burners!

You are going to write a diary for the day Lavoisier discovered oxygen.

1. Read *Alchemy Today* about Lavoisier's experiment.
2. Imagine you are Lavoisier's assistant. Complete the sentences below to write a diary for the day you discovered oxygen.

My day with Lavoisier

We made an early start. As usual, I walked to work and opened up. The laboratory seemed ...

Lavoisier wanted me to do an experiment to find out what happens when...

I collected the apparatus. I needed a flask ...

I set everything out on the bench and heated the flask. Then I...

Much to my surprise, I found that the ...

I showed Lavoisier my results, but he said we can't be sure that when substances burn they ...

I have got to repeat my experiment, so I know what I shall be doing tomorrow!

The day we discovered oxygen

Activity 4.6
Resource

Read this page from a very old chemistry textbook to find out about Lavoisier's discovery.

Lavoisier's experiment

Lavoisier set up a flask containing mercury. The flask had a delivery tube going into a bowl, which also had mercury in it. So the air in the flask was sealed off at both ends by mercury.

The mercury in the flask was heated until red mercury oxide

The day we discovered oxygen

Activity 4.6
Resource

Read this page from a very old chemistry textbook to find out about Lavoisier's discovery.

Lavoisier's experiment

Lavoisier set up a flask containing mercury. The flask had a delivery tube going into a bowl, which also had mercury in it. So the air in the flask was sealed off at both ends by mercury.

The mercury in the flask was heated until red mercury oxide

4.7 Grow your own greenhouse effect

Activity 4.7
Core

Does the glass of a greenhouse really help to keep the heat energy inside?

In this activity, a glass jar on a sunny windowsill represents the greenhouse. You are going to use temperature sensors to measure the temperature inside and outside the jar.

The experiment will be set up like this:

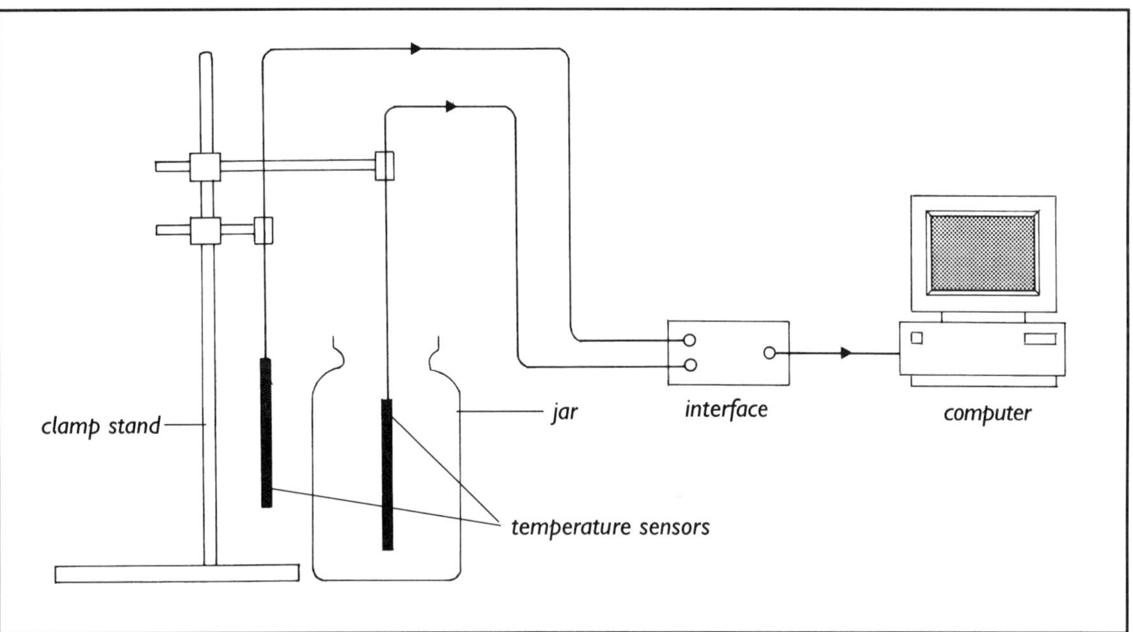

Predict

1 Predict whether it will be hotter or cooler inside the jar, and say why.

Prepare

2 Decide how long you will record for. Make a table for your results.

Record

3 Record and present your results. (You could use a printout from the computer.)

Analyse and conclude

1 Which was hotter, the air inside the jar or the air outside? Explain why.

2 Compare your results with your prediction. Do they show what you expected?

Evaluate

3 Was your experiment a fair test?

4 Can you think of any ways of improving your experiment?

Grow your own greenhouse effect

Activity 4.7
Help

Does the glass of a greenhouse really help to keep the heat energy inside?

In this activity, a glass jar on a sunny windowsill represents the greenhouse. You are going to use temperature sensors to measure the temperature inside and outside the jar.

The experiment will be set up like this:

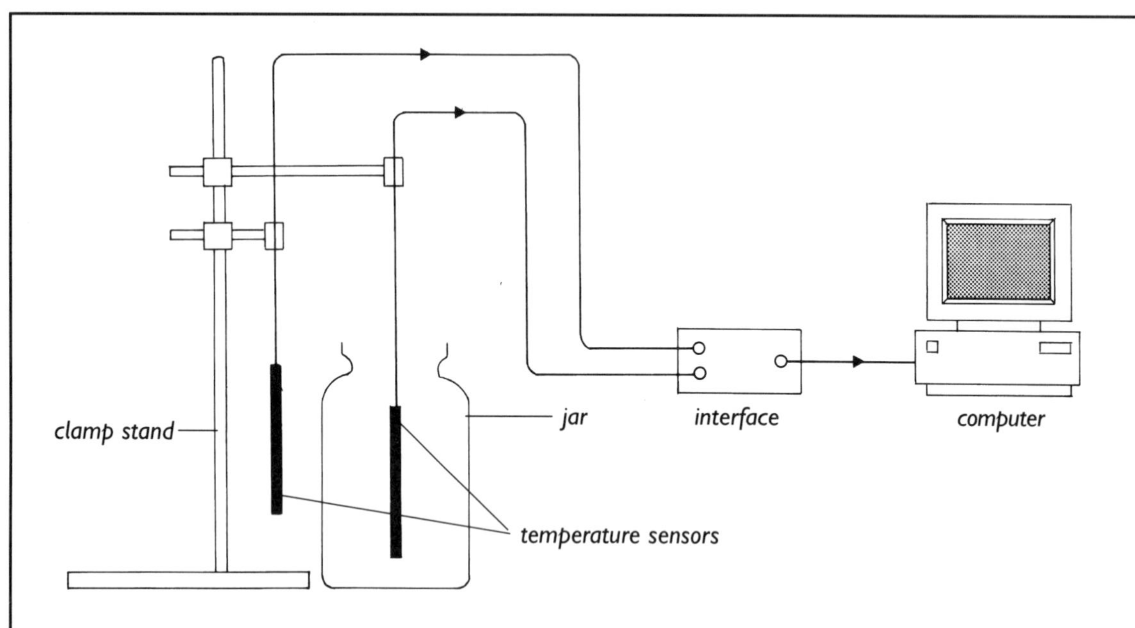

Analyse and conclude

1 Draw a sketch of the graphs shown on the computer (or your teacher may give you a printout).

2 Label your graphs to show which line was for the temperature inside the jar and which line was for outside the jar.

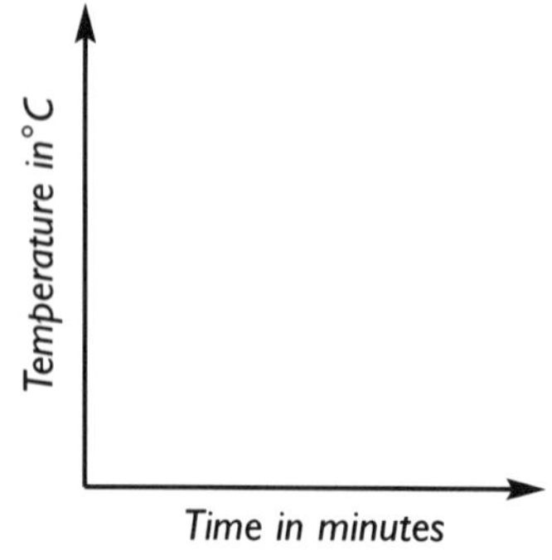

❶ Complete the sentences. Choose words from this list to fill in the gaps.

higher lower escaping entering warm cool

At the end of the experiment, the temperature inside the jar was .... than at the start of the experiment. The glass stops some of the heat energy .... from a greenhouse. The plants stay ....

5 Electricity

Unit map

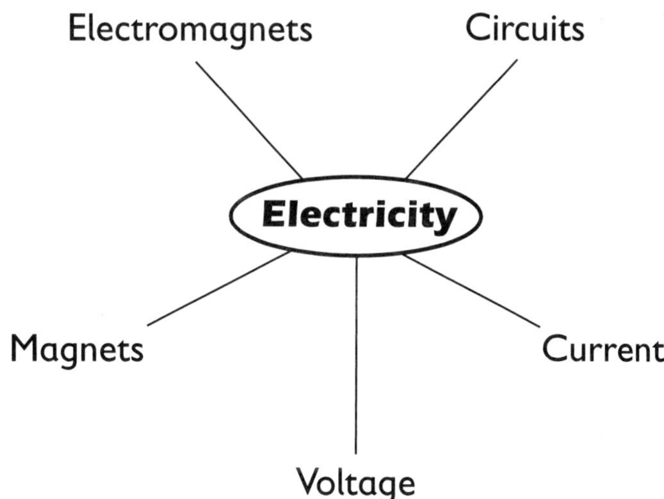

5 Electricity

Unit map

Use these words to help you complete your unit map.

volts	core	lamp
battery	turns	model
switch	magnetic field line	coil
series	magnetic	magnetic field
attract	parallel	repel
magnet	ammeter	voltmeter
electromagnet	filament	amps

Developing the light bulb

Activity 5.1
Extension

You are going to study the biographies of three of the scientists involved in developing the electric filament lamp.

Humphry Davy *was born in Cornwall in 1778. He was a very famous scientist during his lifetime. In 1801, he tried to make an electric filament lamp with strips of platinum, but the platinum strips burned.*

Joseph Swan *was born in Sunderland, England in 1828. He started working on electric filament lamps in 1848, but the filaments burned away in the air. He invented the carbon filament lamp in 1878, soon after the vacuum pump was invented. The pump was needed to take the air out of the bulbs.*

Thomas Edison *was born in America in 1847. Edison was a great inventor, who held a world record of 1093 patents. Edison invented a carbon filament bulb in 1879. He worked independently of Swan, but based his idea on some of Swan's early work.*

Many materials glow when they are heated. When a material is used as a filament in a lamp, it needs to glow but not melt. Carbon melts at 3652 °C and platinum melts at 1772 °C.

1. Based on the information about melting points, which material is more suitable for the filament of an electric lamp? Explain your answer.
2. Based on your general knowledge about carbon and platinum, what other reason is there for using carbon rather than platinum?

Before the invention of the vacuum pump, there was a problem with the filament burning away in the air.

3. What substance would be made when **a** carbon **b** platinum burned?

Inventors patent their inventions. This means the inventor must be paid a fee by people using the invention.

4. Imagine that the inventor of the filament lamp received one farthing for every light bulb sold. Try to estimate how much the patent was worth per year in Britain, using the information opposite. Show how you came to this amount of money.

- How many light bulbs are there in your home?
- There were approximately 5 million households in Britain in the late nineteenth century.
- An early electric filament lamp lasted 6 months.
- There were 240 old pennies in a pound.
- A farthing was one quarter of an old penny.

5. Most people think that Thomas Edison invented the electric filament lamp. Imagine you are a friend of Joseph Swan. You visit America in 1885 and you are very surprised that no one has heard of Joseph Swan, and that everyone thinks that electric filament lamps were invented by Thomas Edison. Write a newspaper article telling the American public about Joseph Swan and his contribution towards the development of the electric filament lamp.

Switch on!

Activity 5.2B
Core

You are going to look at some circuit diagrams and work out what happens when the switches are open and closed.

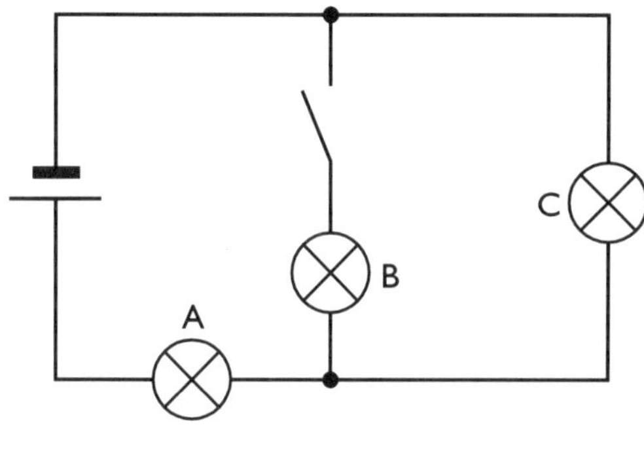

circuit 1

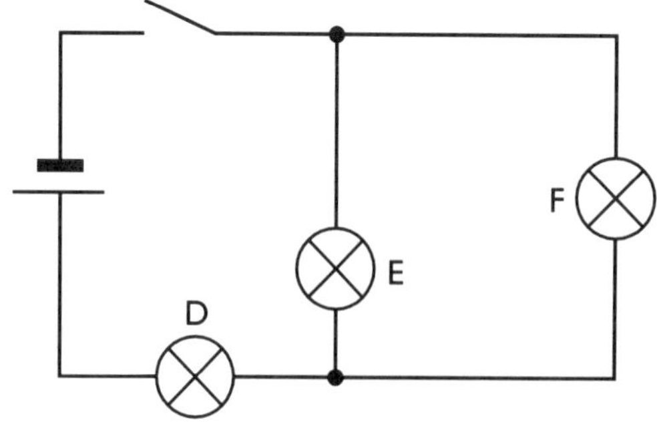

circuit 2

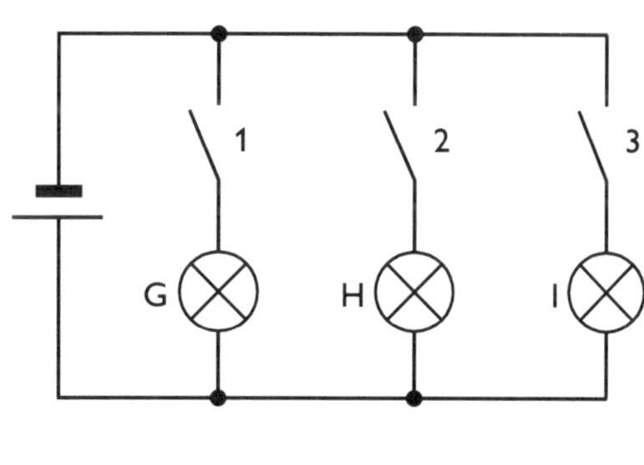

circuit 3

1. Which lamps are lit in **circuit 1**?
2. Which lamps will be lit in **circuit 1** if you close the switch?
3. Which lamps are lit in **circuit 2**?
4. Which lamps will be lit in **circuit 2** if you close the switch?
5. Copy and complete this table for **circuit 3**.

Switches closed	Lamps lit
1	
2	
3	
1, 2	
1, 3	
2, 3	
1, 2, 3	

Switch on!

You are going to look at some circuit diagrams and work out what happens when the switches are open and closed.

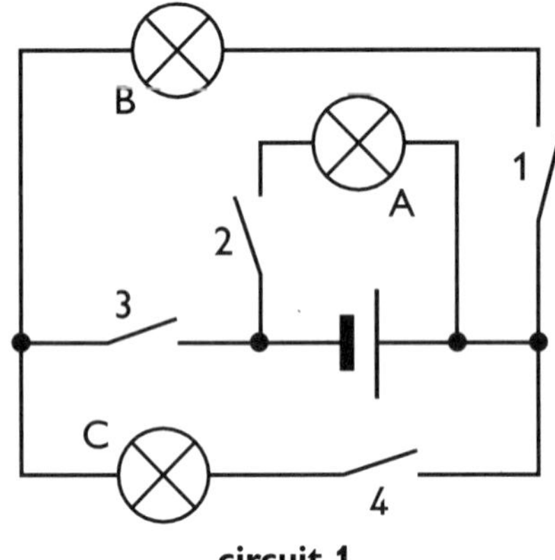

circuit 1

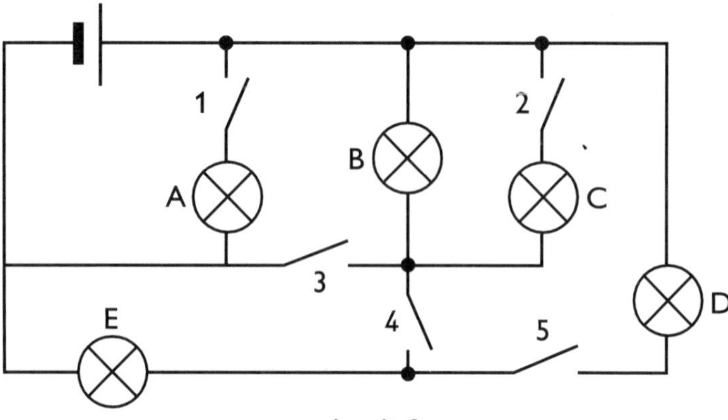

circuit 2

1 Copy and complete the tables.

Circuit 1

Switches closed	Lamps lit
1	
2	
3	
4	
1, 2	
1, 3	
1, 4	
2, 3	
2, 4	
3, 4	
1, 2, 3	
1, 3, 4	
2, 3, 4	
1, 2, 3, 4	

Circuit 2

Switches closed	Lamps lit
1	
2	
3	
4	
5	
1, 2	
1, 3	
1, 4	
1, 5	
2, 3	
2, 4	
2, 5	
3, 5	
4, 5	
1, 2, 3	
1, 4, 5	
2, 4, 5	

Investigating current: batteries

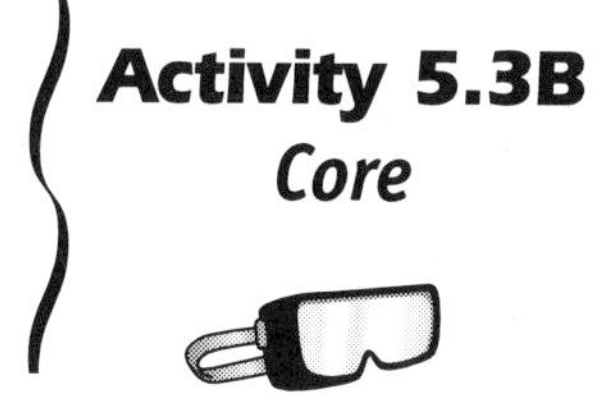

You are going to increase the number of batteries in a circuit and see how this changes the current.

Equipment available

- 5 batteries
- a lamp
- an ammeter
- 7 leads.

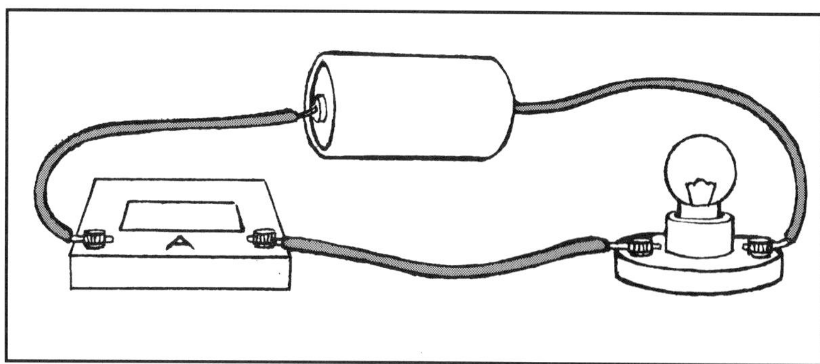

Predict

❶ Look at the circuit above. Make a prediction about how the current will change as you add more batteries to the circuit.

❷ Explain your reasons.

Do

1 Build the circuit shown above. Measure the current.

2 Add another battery to the circuit, as shown. Measure the current.

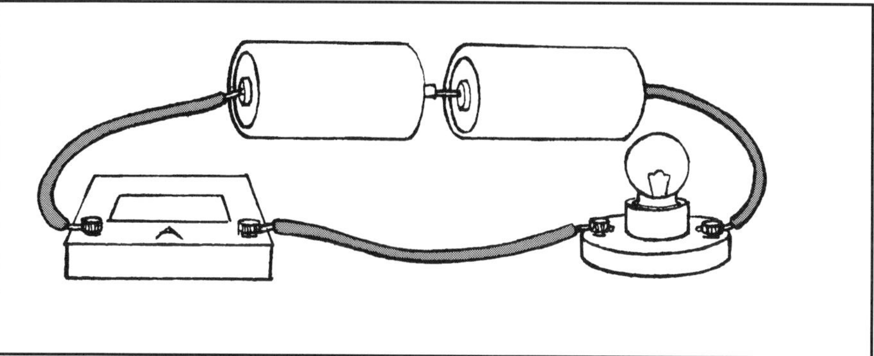

3 Repeat the experiment with 3, 4 and 5 batteries.

Record

4 Make a table like the one below to record your results.

Number of batteries	1	2	3	4	5
Current in amps					

Analyse and conclude

5 Draw a line graph of your results. Put number of batteries along the bottom and current up the side. Draw a line of best fit using a ruler.

❸ How did the current change when you added extra batteries?

❹ Was your prediction correct?

Investigating current: lamps

Activity 5.3B
Extension

You are going to increase the number of lamps in a circuit and see how this changes the current.

Equipment available

- 2 batteries
- 5 lamps
- an ammeter
- 8 leads.

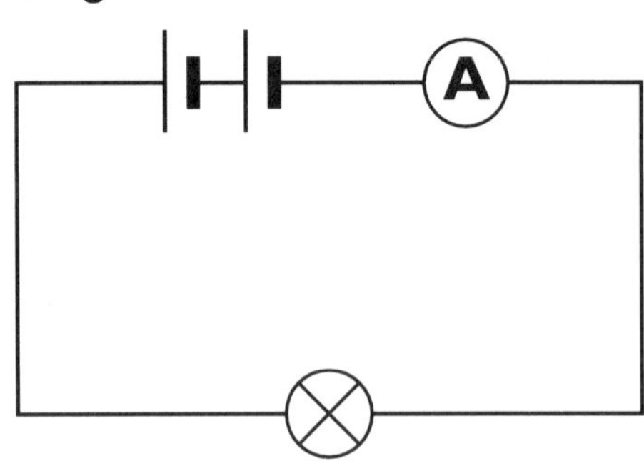

Predict

❶ Look at the circuit above. Make a prediction about how the current will change as you add more lamps to the circuit.

❷ Explain your reasons.

Do

1 Build the circuit shown above. Measure the current.

2 Add another lamp to the circuit, as shown. Measure the current.

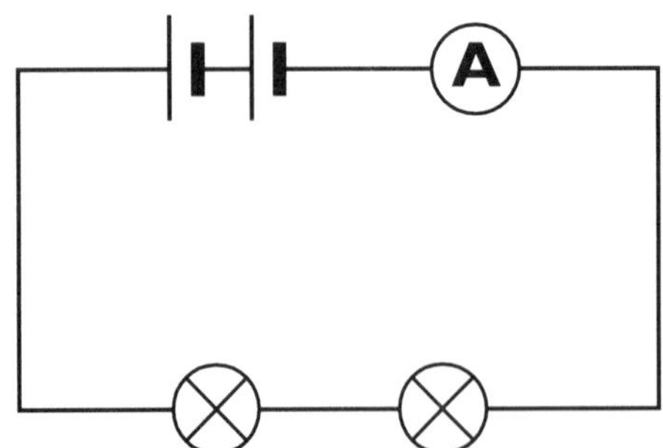

3 Repeat the experiment with 3, 4 and 5 lamps.

Record

4 Make a table like the one below to record your results.

Number of lamps	1	2	3	4	5
Current in amps					

Analyse and conclude

5 Draw a line graph of your results. Put number of lamps along the bottom and current up the side. Draw a line of best fit.

❸ How did the current change when you added extra lamps?

❹ Was your prediction correct?

❺ What current would you have measured if you had used 6 lamps? Use your graph to make an estimate.

Investigating voltage: batteries

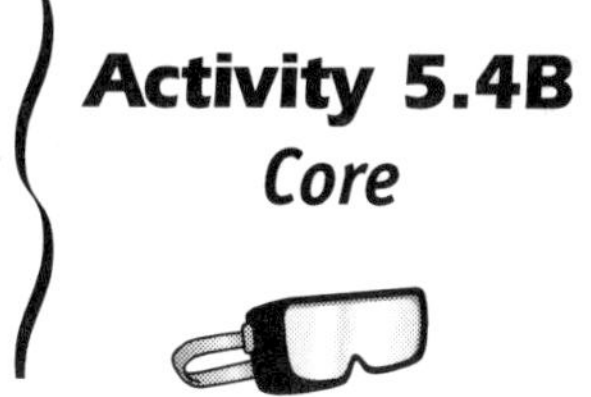

You are going to increase the number of batteries in a circuit and see how this changes the voltage.

Equipment available

- 5 batteries
- a lamp
- a voltmeter
- 8 leads.

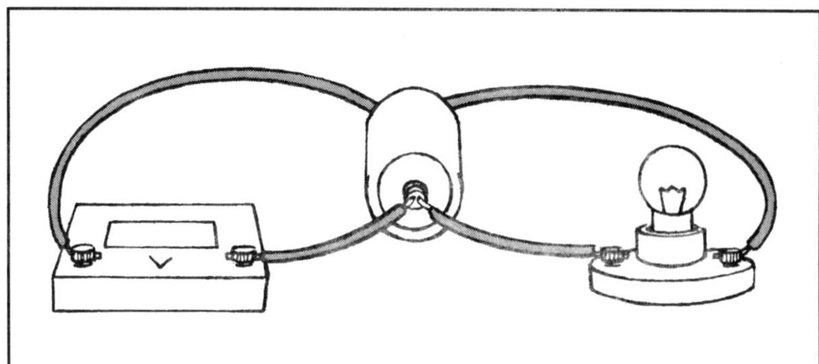

Predict

1 Look at the circuit above. Make a prediction about how the voltage will change as you add more batteries to the circuit.

2 Explain your reasons.

Do

1 Build the circuit shown above. Measure the voltage.

2 Add another battery to the circuit, as shown opposite. Measure the voltage.

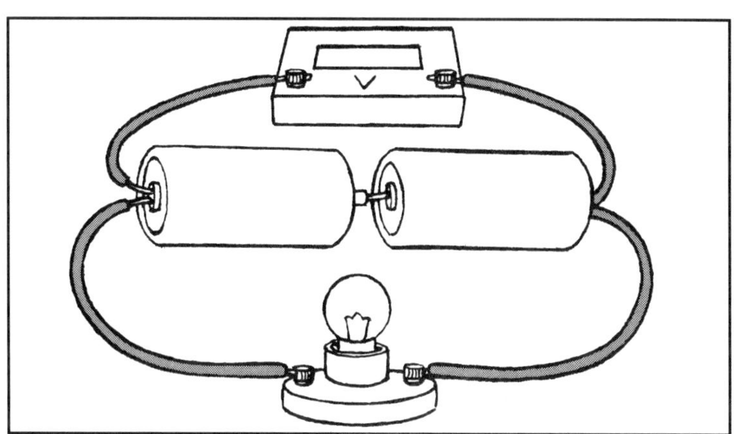

3 Repeat the experiment with 3, 4 and 5 batteries.

Record

4 Make a table like the one below to record your results.

Number of batteries	1	2	3	4	5
Voltage in voltss					

Analyse and conclude

5 Draw a line graph of your results. Put number of batteries along the bottom and voltage up the side. Draw a line of best fit using a ruler.

3 How did the voltage change when you added extra batteries?

4 Was your prediction correct?

Investigating voltage: batteries

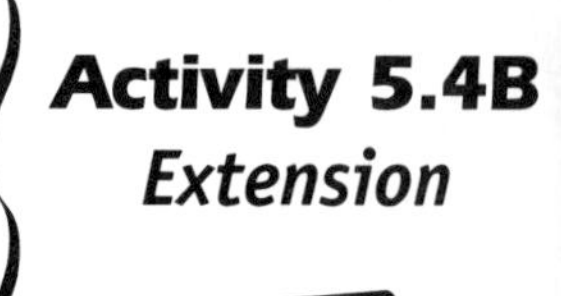

You are going to increase the number of batteries in a circuit and see how this changes the voltage.

Equipment available

- 5 batteries
- a lamp
- a voltmeter
- 8 leads.

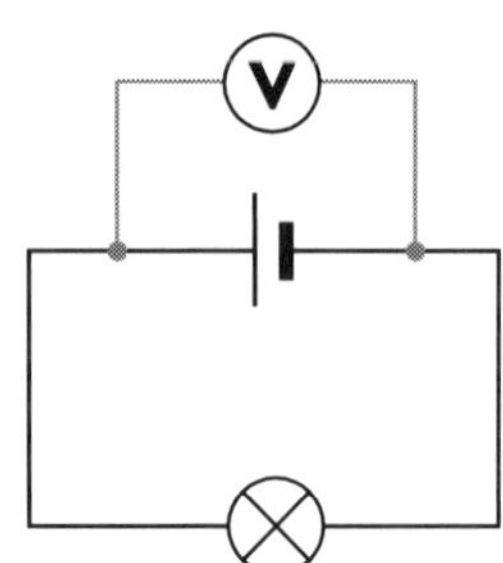

Predict

1. Look at the circuit above. Make a prediction about how the voltage will change as you add more batteries to the circuit.
2. Explain your reasons.

Do

1 Build the circuit shown above. Measure the voltage.

2 Add another battery to the circuit, as shown. Measure the voltage.

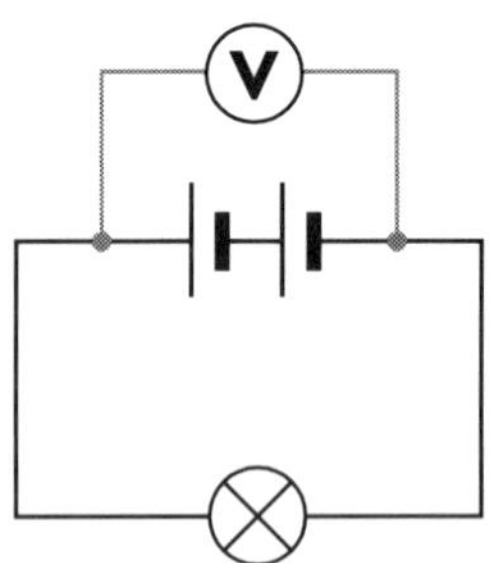

3 Repeat the experiment with 3, 4 and 5 batteries.

Record

4 Make a table like the one below to record your results.

Number of batteries	1	2	3	4	5
Voltage in volts					

Analyse and conclude

5 Draw a line graph of your results. Put number of batteries along the bottom and voltage up the side. Draw in a line of best fit.

3. How did the voltage change when you added extra batteries?
4. Was your prediction correct?
5. Use your graph to suggest the voltage when there are 6 batteries in the circuit.

Series and parallel circuits: current

You are going to build a series circuit and measure the current at three different places.

You are then going to build a parallel circuit and measure the current at three different places.

Equipment available

- a battery
- 2 lamps
- an ammeter
- 5 leads.

Do

1. Build a simple series circuit with two lamps.
2. Measure the current three times by putting the ammeter in the circuit at positions 1, 2, and 3, as shown in the left-hand table below.
3. Build a simple parallel circuit with two lamps.
4. Measure the current three times by putting the ammeter in the circuit at positions 1, 2, and 3, as shown in the right-hand table below.

Record

5. Make tables like the ones below to record your results.

Circuit	Circuit diagram	Current in amps
Series, position 1	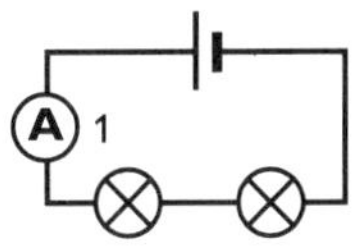	
Series, position 2	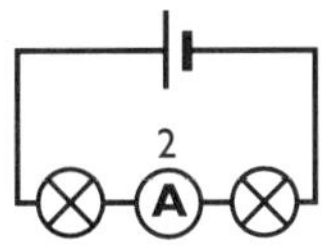	
Series, position 3	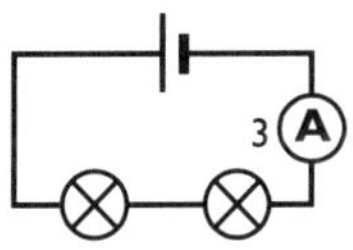	

Circuit	Circuit diagram	Current in amps
Parallel, position 1	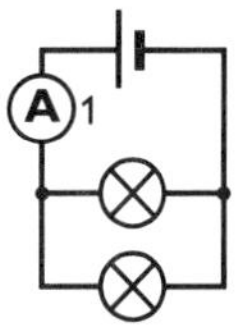	
Parallel, position 2	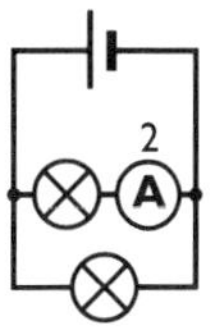	
Parallel, position 3	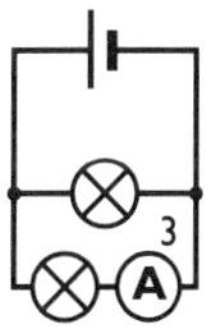	

Analyse and conclude

1. What did you find out about current in a series circuit?
2. What did you find out about current in a parallel circuit?

Series and parallel circuits: current

Activity 5.6A
Extension

You are going to build a series circuit and measure the current at three different places.

You are then going to build a parallel circuit and measure the current at three different places.

Equipment available

- a battery
- 2 lamps
- an ammeter
- 5 leads.

Do

1 Build a simple series circuit with two lamps.

2 Measure the current three times by putting the ammeter in the circuit at position 1, then 2, then 3.

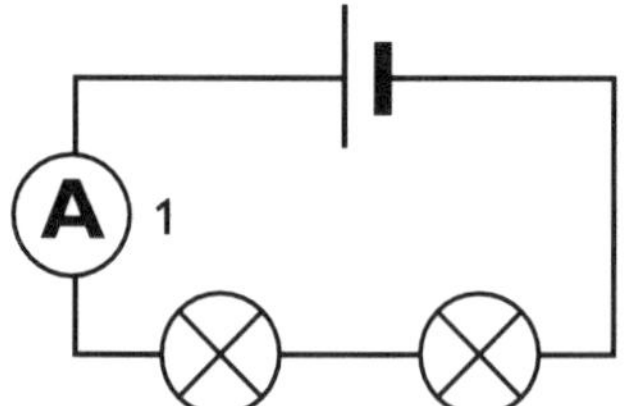

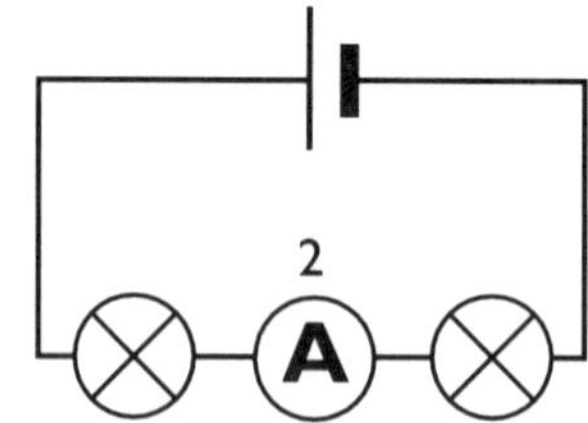

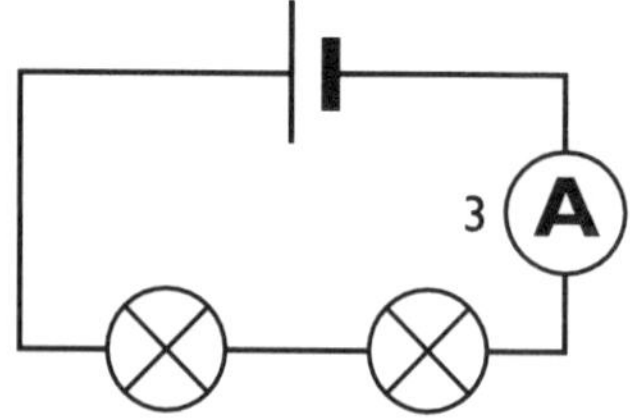

3 Build a simple parallel circuit with two lamps.

4 Measure the current by putting the ammeter in the circuit at position 1,then 2, then 3.

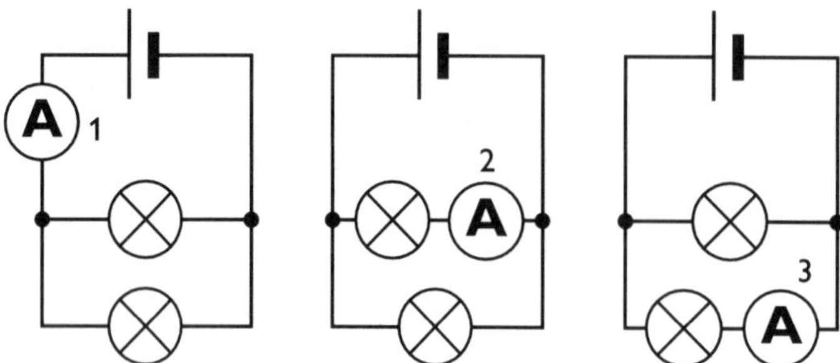

Record

5 Record your results in a table.

Analyse and conclude

❶ What did you find out about current in a series circuit?

❷ Is the current the same at all points in the parallel circuit? Use your results to support your answer.

❸ Can you see a mathematical relationship between the current at positions 1, 2 and 3 in the parallel circuit?

Series and parallel circuits: voltage

Core

You are going to build a series circuit and measure the voltage across three different places.

You are then going to build a parallel circuit and measure the voltage across three different places.

Equipment available

- a battery
- 2 lamps
- a voltmeter
- 6 leads

Do

1 Build a simple series circuit with two lamps.

2 Measure the voltage across the battery.

3 Move the voltmeter and measure the voltage across one lamp.

4 Move the voltmeter and measure the voltage across the other lamp.

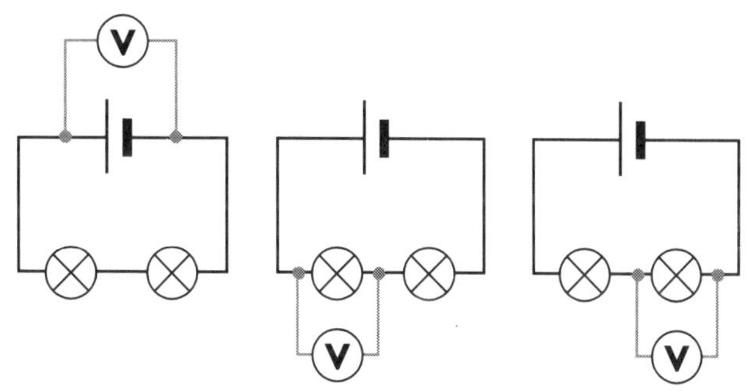

5 Build a simple parallel circuit with two lamps.

6 Measure the voltage across the battery.

7 Move the voltmeter and measure the voltage across one of the lamps.

8 Move the voltmeter and measure the voltage across the other lamp.

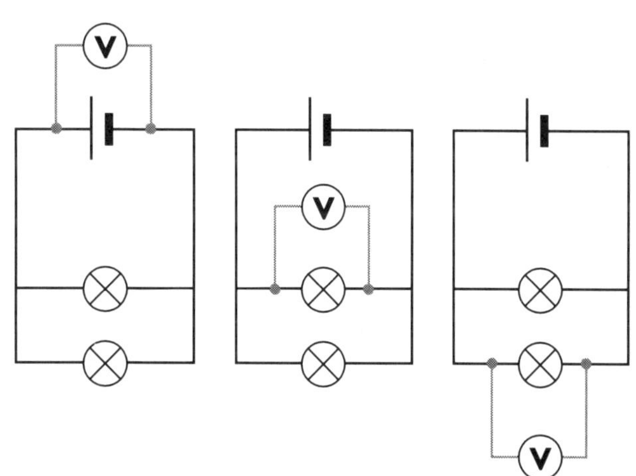

Record

9 Make a table like this to record your results.

Circuit	Voltage in volts
Series, across battery	
Series, across one lamp	
Series, across other lamp	
Parallel, across battery	
Parallel, across one lamp	
Parallel, across other lamp	

Analyse and conclude

❶ What did you find out about voltage in a series circuit?

❷ What did you find out about voltage in a parallel circuit?

What do magnets do?

Activity 5.7A
Core

You are going to see how magnets behave.

Equipment available

- 2 magnets
- small pieces of iron, nickel, copper and aluminium
- a compass.

Do

1 Try picking up each metal with a magnet.

❶ Which metals are **magnetic materials**?

2 Put the compass near a magnet.

❷ What happens?

Magnets have two ends. The ends are called **poles**.

3 Try pushing two magnets together at the ends (the poles).

❸ What happens?

4 Turn one of the magnets around. Try pushing the two magnets together.

❹ What happens?

Analyse and conclude

❺ Look at these statements about magnets. Pick out the correct ones and write them down.

Aluminium sticks to a magnet.

Iron sticks to a magnet.

Nickel sticks to a magnet.

Copper sticks to a magnet.

Iron and nickel are magnetic materials.

Compasses point towards one end (pole) of the magnet.

Compasses always point to the North Pole, even if they are close to a magnet.

Compasses point away from the other end (pole) of the magnet.

Same poles attract.

Same poles repel.

Unlike poles repel.

Unlike poles attract.

Electromagnets

Activity 5.8
Core

You are going to do a class investigation to find out what makes an electromagnet stronger.

⚠ The electromagnet can get hot. Keep it on a heatproof mat. Be careful when you touch it.

Plan and predict

(Ask for a sheet to help you write your plan if you need one.)

1 Write a plan for your part of the investigation. Remember to include:

- a diagram of the circuit
- the three input variables that the class is investigating
- the input variable that your group is investigating
- the safety precautions for your investigation, including the maximum current you can use
- five values for your input variable
- the variable you are measuring (your outcome variable)
- the variables you are going to keep the same and their values.

(Remember that you are going to compare your results with other groups.)

2 Make a prediction for your investigation. Think about these questions:

- What do you think will happen?
- Why will it happen?
- What shape will your graph be?

3 Get your plan approved.

4 Prepare a table for your results.

Do

5 Carry out your investigation and record your results.

Analyse and conclude

6 Draw a line graph using your results. Add a line of best fit.

7 Write a conclusion for your investigation. Remember to mention:

- the shape of your graph
- the relationship between the input variable and the outcome variable
- your prediction.

8 Decide what your group is going to say to the class when you present your results.

Evaluate

9 Write an evaluation of your investigation.

Electromagnets

Activity 5.8
Help

You are going to do a class investigation to find out what makes an electromagnet stronger.

The three input variables that can be changed are:

- the material of the ....
- the .... in the wire
- the number of .... of wire.

> ⚠ The electromagnet can get hot. Keep it on a heatproof mat. Be careful when you touch it.

Plan and predict

1 Plan your investigation and make a prediction.

Our group is going to change the material of the core.

We are going to measure ....

We will keep the .... in the wire the same.

We will use a value of .... A. This lets us compare results with other groups.

We will keep the number of .... of wire the same.

We will use a value of .... turns. This lets us compare results with other groups.

There are .... different materials that we can use.

They are ....

We predict that .... will make good cores.

The electromagnet will pick up paperclips.

We predict that .... will make poor cores.

The electromagnet will not pick up paperclips.

We think this because ....

2 Think about how you will do your investigation.

First we will ....

Then we will ....

Finally we will ....

3 Get your plan approved.

Do

4 Carry out your investigation and record your results in the table.

Analyse and conclude

5 Make a bar chart of your results.

6 Write a conclusion.

7 Decide what your group is going to say to the class when you present your results.

Current used: ..... A	**Number of turns: .....**
Material of core	**Number of paperclips picked up**

Electromagnets

⚠ The electromagnet can get hot. Keep it on a heatproof mat. Be careful when you touch it.

You are going to do a class investigation to find out what makes an electromagnet stronger.

Plan and predict

1 Write a plan for your part of the investigation. Remember:

- Your plan should discuss possible input variables, your input variable and the outcome variable.
- You should state what variables you are keeping the same, and their values.
- You should decide on the values for your input variable (you need enough to draw a line graph).
- You should include enough detail so that someone else could carry out your experiments.
- You must include information about safety.

2 Make a prediction for your investigation. Think about the relationship you expect between the input and outcome variables, and the shape of the graph.

3 Get your plan approved.

4 Prepare a table for your results.

Do

5 Carry out your investigation and record your results.

Analyse and conclude

6 Draw a line graph using your results. Add a line of best fit.

7 Write a conclusion for your investigation. Remember to discuss:

- your graph (see *Skill sheet 6: Interpreting graphs*)
- the relationship between the input variable and the outcome variable
- whether your results fitted with your prediction
- any extra experiments you would have to do to check out your conclusion.

8 Decide what your group is going to say to the class when you present your results.

Evaluate

9 Discuss with the other members of your group what makes a good evaluation.

10 Write an evaluation of your investigation.

Plant power

Unit map

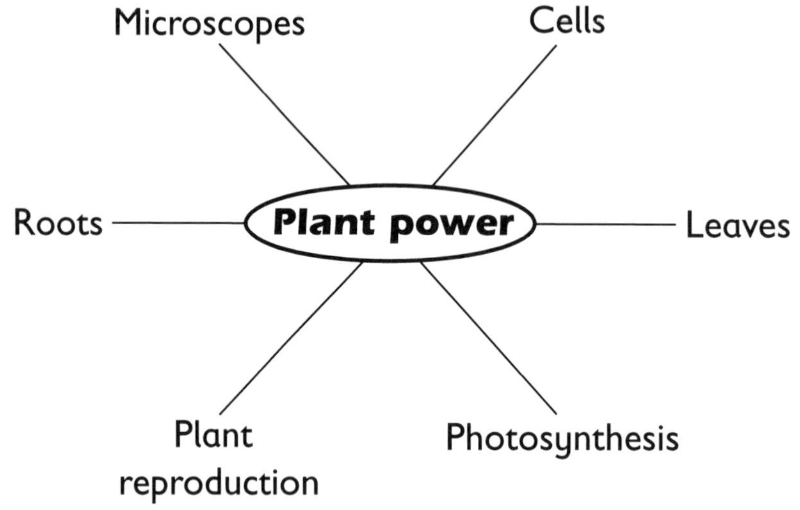

Plant power
6

Plant power

Unit map

Use these words to help you copy and complete your unit map.

carbon dioxide	animal cell	chlorophyll	scale factor
flowers	carpels	egg cell	magnification
cell membrane	palisade	nucleus	scaling down
chloroplast	ovary	shape	veins
plant	cell	water	fruit
sunlight	stamens	cell wall	vacuole
oxygen	air hole	plant cell	pollen grains
water	pollination	scale diagram	
scaling up	seed	electron microscope	
cytoplasm	embryo	compound microscope	
sugars	fertilisation	root hairs	

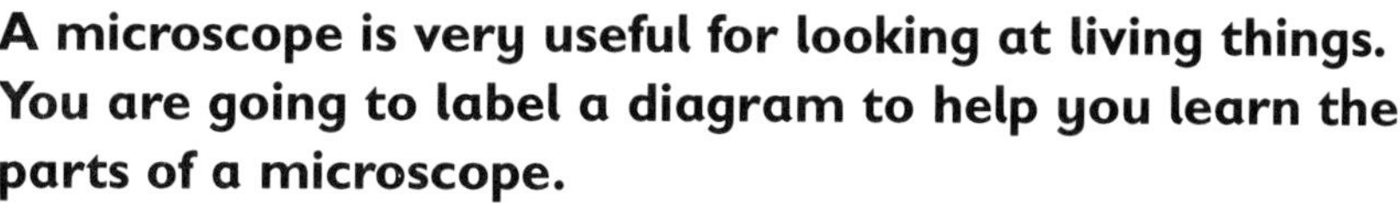

The parts of a microscope

Activity 6.1A
Core

A microscope is very useful for looking at living things. You are going to label a diagram to help you learn the parts of a microscope.

⚠ Never use a microscope where the Sun's rays might reflect off the mirror into it.

You could permanently damage your eyesight.

1 Use the words below to label the parts of the microscope on the diagram.

stage eyepiece lens objective lens tube coarse focus mirror fine focus

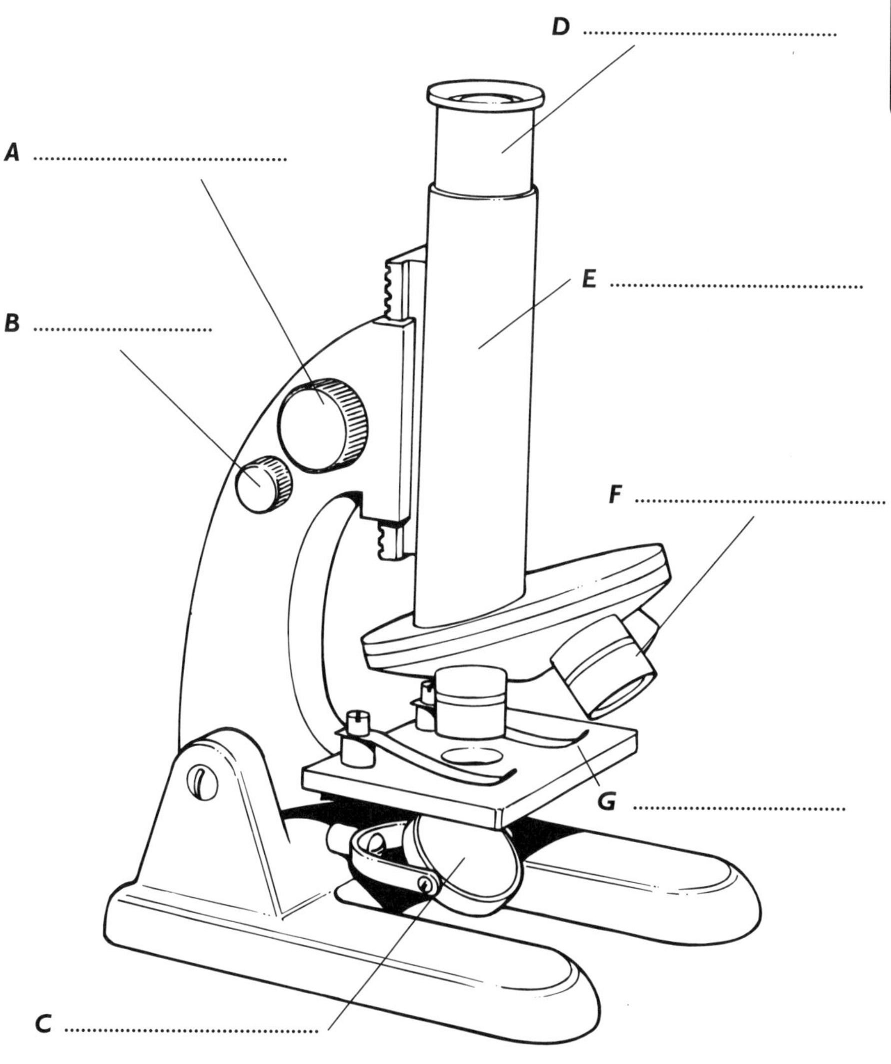

✂ -

Activity 6.1A
Extension

2 Write a short explanation of what each part does.

A letter from Robert Hooke

Activity 6.1B
Core

Robert Hooke invented a new kind of microscope, which allowed him to see many things people had never seen before. As well as slices of cork, he also looked at insects and other small living things. He recorded his observations very carefully.

You are going to write a letter about the new microscope.

1 Imagine you are Robert Hooke, writing to a scientist friend. Describe your new microscope to your friend, who hasn't seen it yet. You can use the suggestions below to help you, or you can use your own ideas.

Robert Hooke
London
England
17 November 1680

Dear ...

I hope you saw my report about my .... microscope.

The invention is different from simple microscopes because it has another .... which ...

My invention is very important because ...

I have used it to look at ...

I hope you will be in London soon so I can show you the microscope.
Yours sincerely

Robert Hooke

Looking at plant cells

Activity 6.2A
Core

Plants are made up of millions of tiny building blocks called cells. You are going to look closely at some plant cells using a microscope.

⚠ Take care with microscopes and slides.

Take care with the knife. It is very sharp.

Iodine solution is harmful. It can stain your skin and your clothes.

Do

1 Cut a small piece of onion. Peel off a piece of the inner surface. This should be very thin and look like tissue paper.

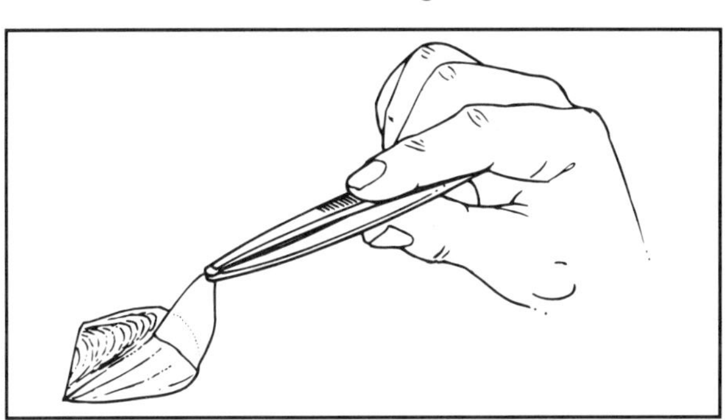

2 Put this thin piece of onion onto a slide.

3 Add two drops of iodine solution to stain the cells.

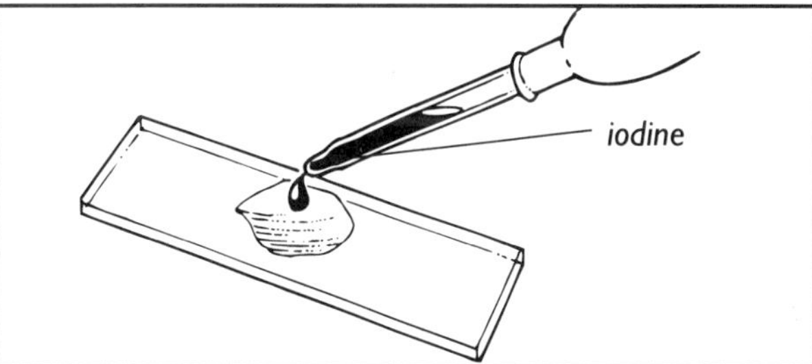

4 Lower a coverslip gently on to the slide using a mounted needle.

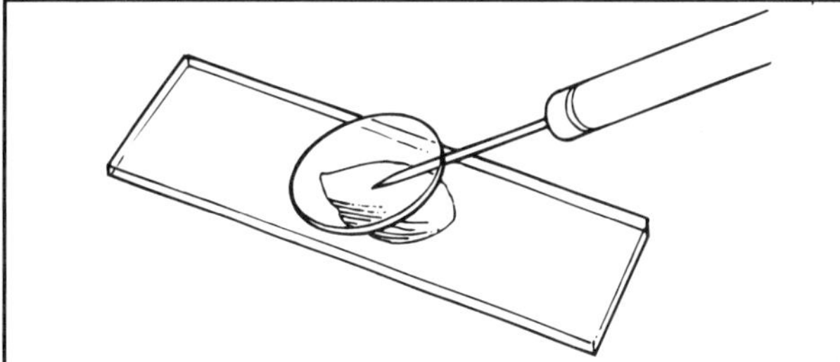

5 Place the slide on a microscope stage.

6 Focus using the low power lens first to find the cells. Then make them look bigger by using the high power lens.

Record

7 Draw a group of three onion cells as accurately as you can.

8 Label the parts of the cell that you can see.

Analyse and conclude

❶ What parts of the onion cell could you see?

❷ Why do you think you could not see much inside the cell?

❸ Why did you think we added the iodine solution? What does it do?

❹ Onion cells do not have any chloroplasts. Suggest why.

Looking at animal cells

⚠ Take care with microscopes and slides.

Like plants, animals are made of tiny building blocks called cells. You are going to look closely at some animal cells using a microscope.

Do

1 Your teacher will give you a slide that has already been set up. Put this slide on your microscope stage.

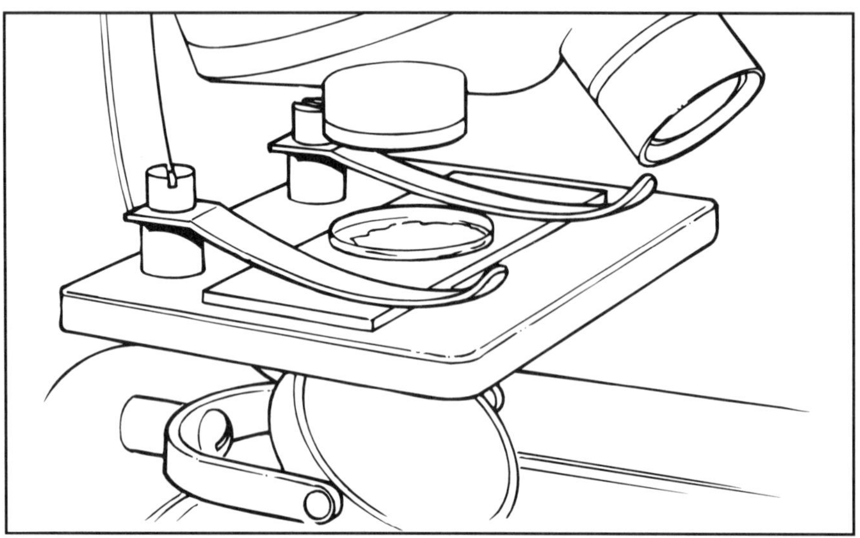

2 Focus using the low power lens to find the cells.

3 Draw a diagram of one of the animal cells that you can see under the low power lens. Label the parts of the cell that you can see.

4 Now look at your slide using the high power lens.

5 Draw a diagram of one of the cells and label the parts that you can see.

Analyse and conclude

❶ Describe what the animal cell looks like under the microscope.

❷ Would you expect to see a cell wall? Explain your answer.

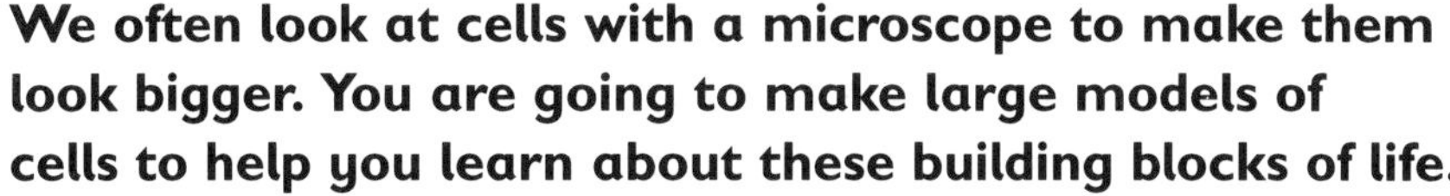

Making a model cell

Activity 6.2C
Core

We often look at cells with a microscope to make them look bigger. You are going to make large models of cells to help you learn about these building blocks of life.

> ⚠ Take care not to spill liquid on the floor. If you do, clear it up straight away.
>
> Wash your hands after using wallpaper paste.

Equipment available

- clear plastic bags (cell membrane)
- green Plasticine (chloroplasts)
- shoe box (cell wall)
- tennis balls (nucleus)
- smaller plastic bag (vacuole)
- liquid or wallpaper paste (cytoplasm)
- water (sap).

Make a model animal cell

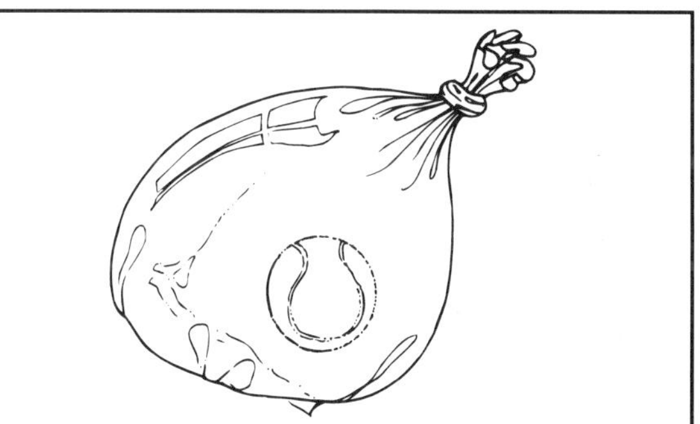

1 Place a tennis ball inside a plastic bag.

2 Put some liquid in the plastic bag and tie a knot at the top to secure it.

Make a model plant cell

3 Place a tennis ball inside a plastic bag.

4 Roll the green Plasticine into lots of marble-sized balls. Flatten them slightly into sausage shapes and put them into the bag.

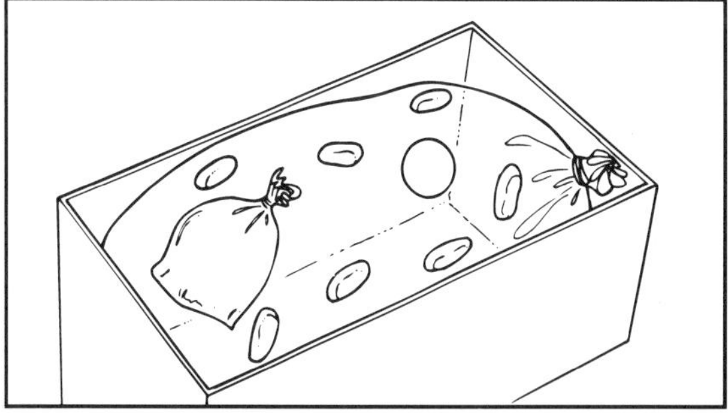

5 Take a smaller plastic bag and put some water in it. Tie a knot at the top and put this bag inside the larger bag.

6 Put some liquid in the large plastic bag and tie a knot at the top to secure it.

7 Put this plastic bag inside the shoe box.

Conclude and evaluate

1 Draw a diagram of each model. Label the cell parts with their names and the material you used to make them.

2 For each item you used in the animal cell model, write down why the material is well suited to represent the cell part.

3 Do the same for the plant cell model.

4 Do you think these are good models? Explain your answer.

Making a model cell

Activity 6.2C
Extension

We often look at cells with a microscope to make them look bigger. You are going to make large models of cells to help you learn about these building blocks of life.

⚠ Take care not to spill liquid on the floor. If you do, clear it up straight away.

Wash your hands after using wallpaper paste.

Equipment available

- clear plastic bags
- green Plasticine
- shoe box
- tennis balls
- water
- liquid or wallpaper paste.

Make a model animal cell

1 Decide what you will use for the cell membrane.

2 Choose a nucleus and place this inside the cell membrane.

3 Decide what you will use as cytoplasm. Add this to your model to finish it off.

Make a model plant cell

4 Start with the cell membrane again.

5 Add a nucleus.

6 Decide what you will use to make chloroplasts. Think about what these should look like.

7 Decide how you will show the sap vacuole. Think about what it should look like.

8 Decide how you will make the cell wall to complete your model.

Conclude and evaluate

1 Draw a diagram of each of your models. Label the cell parts with their names and the material you used to make them.

2 For both models, write down why the material you used was well suited to represent each part.

3 Do you think these are good models? Explain your answer.

4 How are your cell models different from how cells would look under a microscope?

What do plants need for photosynthesis?

Activity 6.3A
Core

In photosynthesis, plants use light energy to turn carbon dioxide and water into sugars. The plant stores sugars as a substance called starch.

You are going to test whether leaves carry out photosynthesis without sunlight, and without carbon dioxide. If there is starch in the leaves, they have been carrying out photosynthesis.

Wear eye protection.

Ethanol is flammable. Do not use a Bunsen burner near it.

Take care with boiling water.

Iodine solution is harmful. It can stain your skin and your clothes.

Do

1 Set up the plant as shown in the diagram.

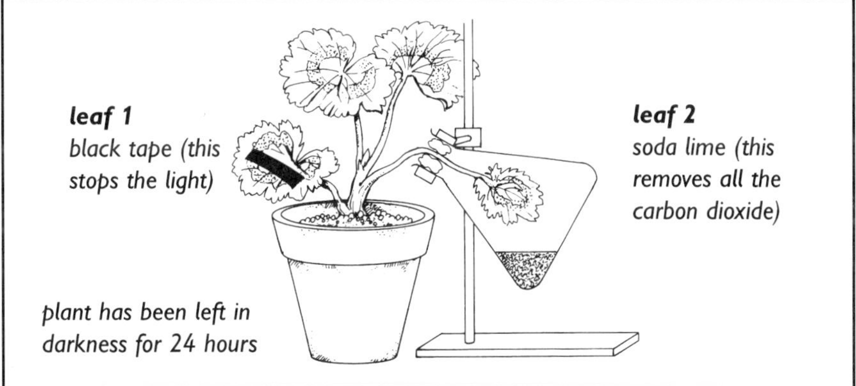

2 Leave the plant in a light place for 24 hours.

3 Take leaves 1 and 2 off the plant. Also take one more leaf (leaf 3) which is untreated. Make sure you remember which leaf is which! You can do this by cutting a different shape out of the side of each leaf and noting which leaf has which shape.

4 Using forceps, place the leaves in 50 cm^3 of boiling water in a beaker. After 2 minutes, turn off the Bunsen burner.

5 Take the leaves out of the water and soak them in warm ethanol in a water bath until they go colourless, as shown.

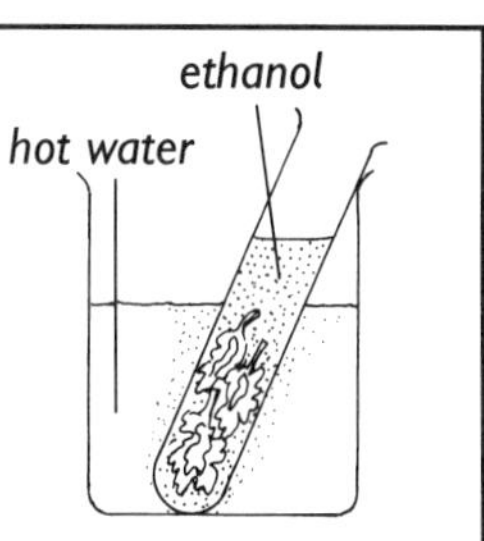

6 Dip the leaves in cool water and dry them carefully with a paper towel.

7 Put the leaves on a white tile and test them with a few drops of iodine. This turns from orange to black if there is starch present.

Record

8 Record the results of the starch test for each leaf.

Analyse and conclude

1 What do the results for leaf 1 tell you about photosynthesis?

2 What do the results for leaf 2 tell you about photosynthesis?

3 What was the purpose of leaf 3 in the experiment?

4 Why do you think the leaves were kept in the dark for 24 hours before the start of the experiment?

What do plants need for photosynthesis?

Activity 6.3A
Help

You are going to test whether leaves carry out photosynthesis without sunlight, and without carbon dioxide. If there is starch in the leaves, they have been carrying out photosynthesis. Iodine turns from orange to black if there is starch present.

Work in groups of three. There are three leaves to test for starch. Test one leaf each.

Wear eye protection.

⚠ Ethanol is flammable. Do not use a Bunsen burner near it.

Take care with boiling water.

Iodine solution is harmful. It can stain your skin and your clothes.

1 Record your results in the table below.

Leaf	Observation (colour change)
Leaf 1 (black tape – no sunlight)	
Leaf 2 (sodium hydroxide solution – no carbon dioxide)	
Leaf 3	

Analyse and conclude

❶ Complete these sentences.
Iodine solution will change from .... to .... if starch is present in the leaf. If starch is present in the leaf, it means the leaf has been carrying out ....

❷ What happened to the iodine on leaf 1?

....

❸ What does this tell you about photosynthesis in leaf 1?

....

❹ What happened to the iodine on leaf 2?

....

❺ What does this tell you about photosynthesis in leaf 2?

....

❻ What happened to the iodine on leaf 3?

....

❼ What does this tell you about photosynthesis in leaf 3?

....

❽ What was the purpose of leaf 3 in the experiment?

....

What gas is made in photosynthesis?

Activity 6.3B
Core

A plant uses carbon dioxide and water to make food by photosynthesis. You are going to find out what else is made during photosynthesis.

You are going to collect a gas from a plant and test it with a glowing splint. If the splint relights, the gas is oxygen.

⚠ Take care with Bunsen burners.

Do

1 Set up the beaker as shown in the diagram.

2 Fill the test tube with water. Put your thumb over the end then turn the test tube upside down. Take care no air gets in the test tube.

3 Carefully lower the test tube into the beaker so the end you are holding is under the water above the funnel.

4 Remove your thumb and lower the test tube over the end of the funnel.

5 Leave it on a window sill for 24 hours.

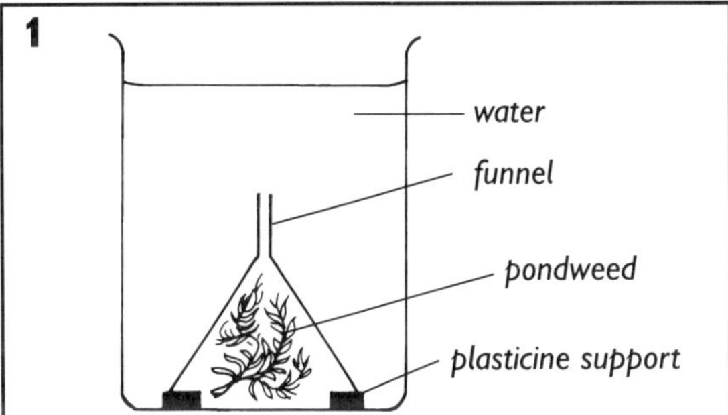

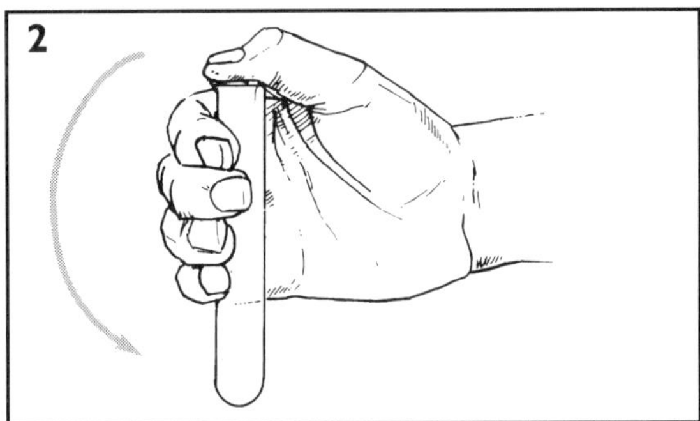

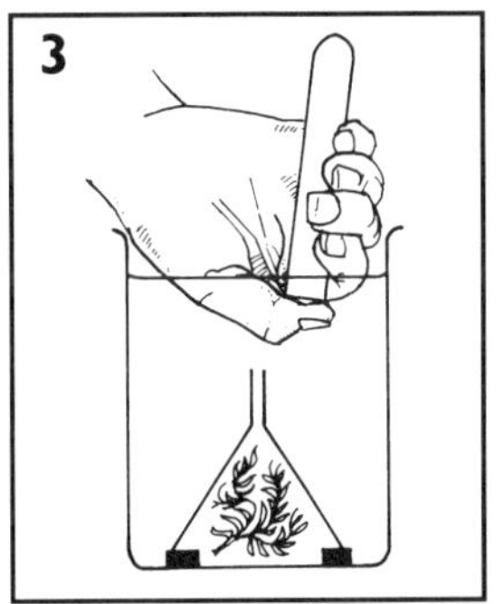

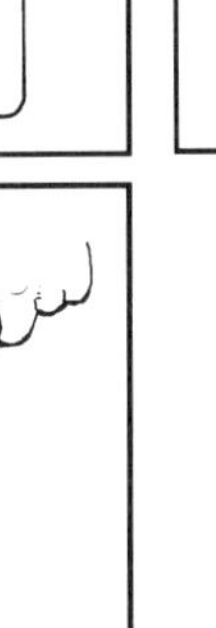

Next lesson:

6 Take a splint and blow it out so that it is glowing.

7 Slide your thumb over the end of the test tube under the water, then remove the test tube carefully. Turn the right way up.

8 Taking care not to let all the collected gas escape, quickly remove your thumb and place the glowing splint inside the test tube.

8

Record

9 Record what happens to the splint.

Analyse and conclude

❶ What gas was produced during this experiment?

❷ Think about how you might be able to make the plant produce the gas faster. Suggest ways you might try.

❸ What else is produced by photosynthesis?

When do plants grow the fastest?

Activity 6.3C
Core

You are going to follow the growth of a plant over three days using datalogging equipment. You are going to use a position sensor to find out when a plant grows the fastest.

⚠ Do not eat the seeds or plants.

Wash your hands afterwards.

Do

1 Set up the apparatus as shown. The cotton must be tight.

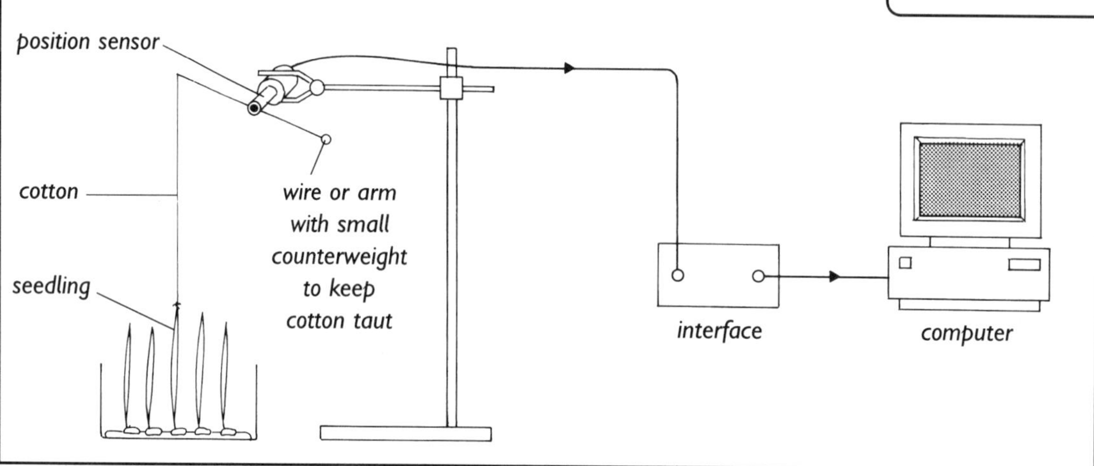

2 Set up the computer to record the growth. Note down the time that you started.

3 Leave the plant by a window for three days. Make sure the plant has enough water.

The computer will show a graph of the growth of the seedling against the time taken to grow.

Record

4 Draw a sketch of the graph shown on the computer (or your teacher may give you a printout).

5 Label your graph with the time when you started the experiment.

Analyse and conclude

❶ When did the plant grow the quickest? Why do you think this is?

❷ When did the plant grow the slowest? Why do you think this is?

Evaluate

❸ Think about how this experiment could be made better. Would each of the following suggestions improve the experiment or not? Explain your answers.

- doing the experiment a few times
- using more plants
- carrying out the experiment for a shorter period of time
- carrying out the experiment for a longer period of time

Looking at leaves

Activity 6.4
Core

The leaf of a plant carries out photosynthesis. Each part of the leaf has a special job to help it carry out photosynthesis. You are going to look at a leaf under a microscope.

⚠ Take care with microscopes and slides.

Your teacher will give you a slide with a very thin slice of leaf on it.

Do

1 Put the slide on the microscope stage.

2 Focus on your slide using the low power lens.

3 Now look at the leaf using the high power lens.

Record

4 Make a careful drawing in pencil to show what the leaf looks like under the microscope.

5 Label the parts of the leaf you can see.

6 If you have time, write a short explanation of what each part does and how it helps the leaf carry out photosynthesis.

6.4

Looking at leaves

Activity 6.4
Core

The leaf of a plant carries out photosynthesis. Each part of the leaf has a special job to help it carry out photosynthesis. You are going to look at a leaf under a microscope.

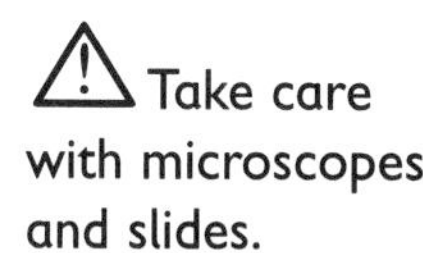

⚠ Take care with microscopes and slides.

Your teacher will give you a slide with a very thin slice of leaf on it.

Do

1 Put the slide on the microscope stage.

2 Focus on your slide using the low power lens.

3 Now look at the leaf using the high power lens.

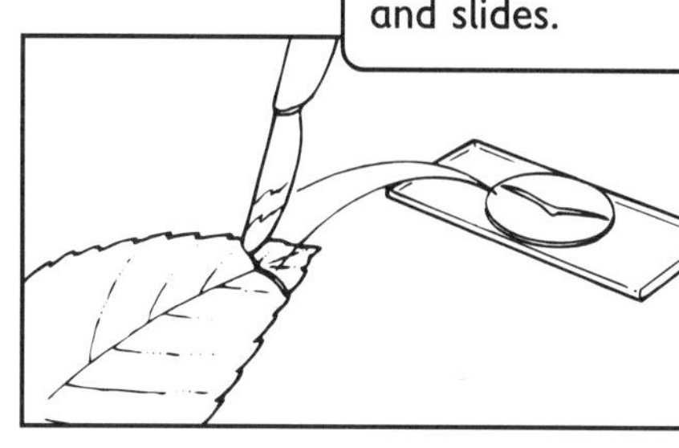

Record

4 Make a careful drawing in pencil to show what the leaf looks like under the microscope.

5 Label the parts of the leaf you can see.

6 If you have time, write a short explanation of what each part does and how it helps the leaf carry out photosynthesis.

Looking at root hairs

Activity 6.5A
Core

The roots of a plant absorb water and minerals for the plant. They do this through tiny root hairs. You are going to look at a root under a microscope.

⚠ Take care with microscopes and slides.

Your teacher will give you a slide with a very thin slice of root on it.

Do

1. Put the slide on the microscope stage.
2. Focus on your slide using the low power lens.
3. Now look at the root hair using the high power lens.

Record

4. Make a careful drawing in pencil to show what the root looks like under the microscope. Make sure you include the structure of the root hair.
5. Label the parts you can see.

Analyse

❶ How does the structure of the root help the plant absorb water and minerals from the soil?

❷ What other job does the root do in the plant?

Looking at root hairs

Activity 6.5A
Core

The roots of a plant absorb water and minerals for the plant. They do this through tiny root hairs. You are going to look at a root under a microscope.

⚠ Take care with microscopes and slides.

Your teacher will give you a slide with a very thin slice of root on it.

Do

1. Put the slide on the microscope stage.
2. Focus on your slide using the low power lens.
3. Now look at the root hair using the high power lens.

Record

4. Make a careful drawing in pencil to show what the root looks like under the microscope. Make sure you include the structure of the root hair.
5. Label the parts you can see.

Analyse

❶ How does the structure of the root help the plant absorb water and minerals from the soil?

❷ What other job does the root do in the plant?

Water transport in celery

Activity 6.5B
Core

Take care with the knife. It is very sharp.

Take care with microscopes and slides.

Do not eat the celery.

Water and minerals are taken up from the soil into the roots of the plant. They are transported around the plant through the veins. You are going to look at these veins using a microscope.

Do

1 Stand some celery stalks in red dye. Leave them overnight.

2 The next day, look at how far the dye has moved up the stalk. Record your observations.

3 Use a knife to cut a thin cross section of dyed celery stalk.

4 Place the section onto the slide. Put a few drops of distilled water on the section. Carefully lower a coverstrip over the slide as shown.

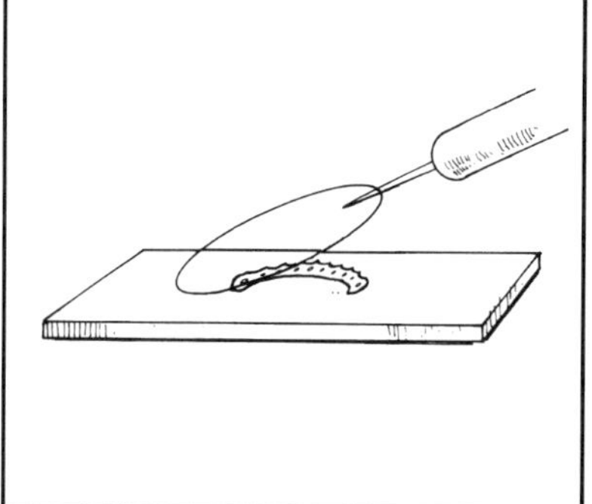

Record

5 Draw a sketch of what you can see.

Analyse and conclude

1 Look back at how far the dye moved up the stem. How far up the plant do you think the veins go?

2 What is the job of the veins in the plant?

3 Describe how the structure of the vein helps it to carry out its job in the plant.

Flower structure

Plants make flowers so that they can reproduce. You are going to make a labelled diagram showing the parts of a flower, and what each part does.

1 Copy the diagram. Use these words to label the parts of the flower.

anther ovary petal stigma style filament

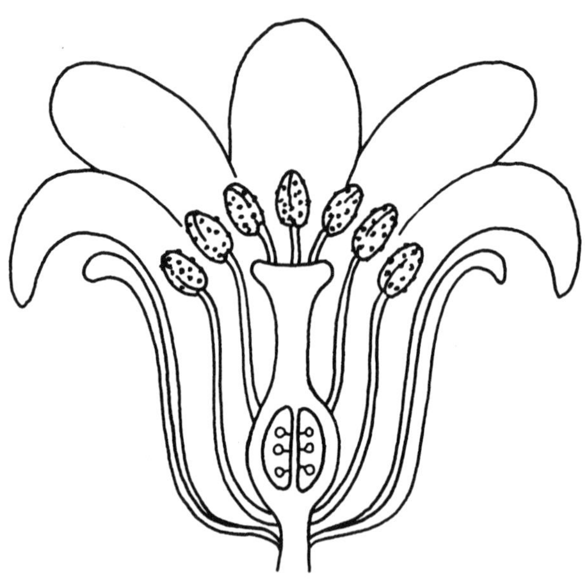

2 Then add the job of each part of the flower to your diagram.

often coloured and scented to attract insects
stalk that holds the anther
joins the stigma to the ovary
pollen lands here during pollination
contains the egg cell
pollen is made here

Analyse and conclude

1. What is the female sex cell called in a flower?
2. What is the male sex cell called?
3. How does the male sex cell get to the female part of the flower? What do we call this process?

Growing pollen tubes

Activity 6.6B
Core

⚠ Take care with microscopes and slides.

Do not eat the plants.

Wash your hands after touching the plants.

After the pollen lands on the stigma, a pollen tube grows down the style. This pollen tube grows into the ovary and then enters the ovule until it reaches the egg cell. The pollen nucleus passes down this tube to join with the egg cell.

You are going to observe the growth of the pollen tube.

Do

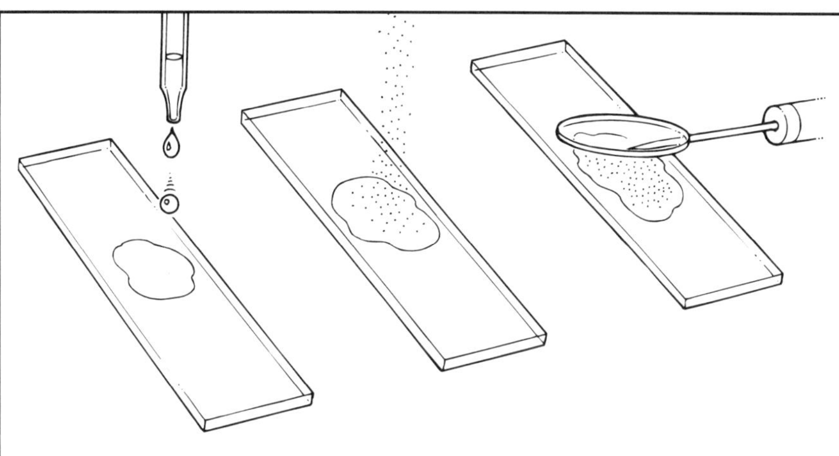

1 Place a few drops of sucrose solution onto a cavity slide.

2 Place some pollen grains in the solution, either by shaking the flower or using a fine art brush.

3 Lower a coverslip over the slide.

4 Leave the pollen grains for about 30 minutes in a warm place (about 25–30 °C).

5 Place the slide onto the microscope stage.

6 Observe the pollen grains every 10 minutes.

Record

7 Record your observations about the growth of the tubes.

8 Draw a flow diagram showing what happens when the pollen tube grows.

Activity 6.6B
Extension

Analyse and conclude

❶ What is the job of the pollen tube?

❷ What is it called when the pollen nucleus joins with the egg cell nucleus?

How pollination happens

Activity 6.6C
Extension

Pollination is the transfer of pollen from the anther to the stigma.

If the pollen is transferred from the anther to the stigma of the same plant, it is called self-pollination. If the pollen is transferred from one plant to a different plant, it is called cross-pollination.

The pollen can be transferred by different methods, such as insects or the wind. You are going to look at different sorts of pollination.

Insect pollination

The insects are attracted to the flowers because they have colourful, scented petals and nectar. The anthers and stigmas are inside the flowers to make sure the insects rub against them. The pollen is sticky so that it will stick to the insects.

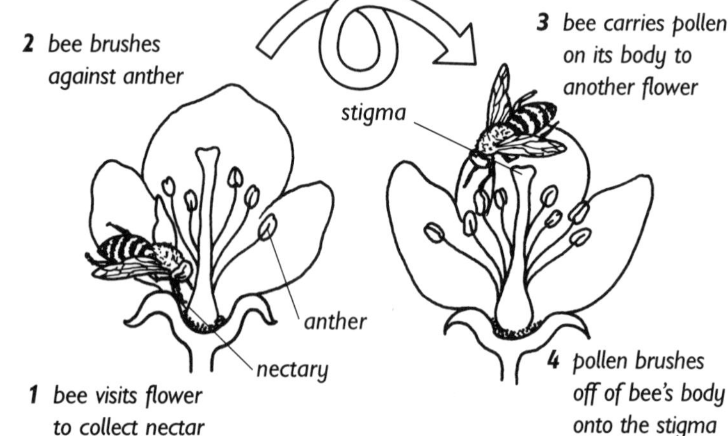

Wind pollination

Wind-pollinated flowers have their anthers outside the flower so the pollen can be spread easily by the wind. They produce lots of pollen and have feathery stigmas to catch the pollen.

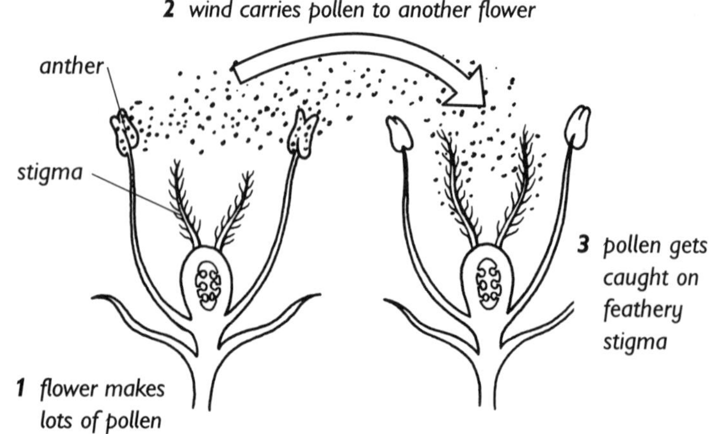

1. What is the difference between self-pollination and cross-pollination?
2. List three things that attract insects to certain flowers.
3. Describe the things that help make sure that the pollen sticks to the insect, and then is transferred to the style of the next flower.
4. Describe the things that help make sure that the pollen grains are transferred from one flower to another in wind-pollinated plants.
5. What process happens after the flower has been pollinated?

7 Metals

Unit map

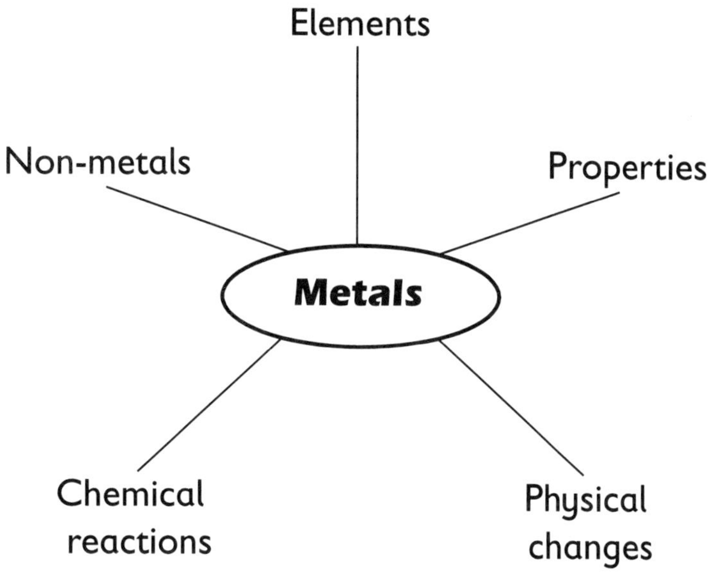

Elements

Non-metals

Properties

Metals

Chemical reactions

Physical changes

7 Metals

Unit map

Use these words to help you copy and complete your unit map.

shiny	atom	boiling
conductor	symbols	burning
magnetic	periodic table	compound
corrosion	group	mixture
melting point	period	oxide
boiling point	classification	chloride
reversible	rusting	sulphide
irreversible	melting	

Making iron and steel

Activity 7.1A
Extension

In this activity you will learn more about iron, where it comes from and how it is made into different types of useful metal.

Iron is not found as iron. It is found as **minerals**. Iron minerals are found in rocks. Rocks that are rich in minerals are called **ores**. Ores are mined from the ground.

Iron minerals have to be changed into iron metal by a chemical reaction. Heating the minerals with charcoal changes the iron minerals into iron metal, but only at very high temperatures. These high temperatures are only possible when bellows are used to blow air into the fire.

When iron is first made, it contains many impurities. One way of removing the impurities is by hammering, or **forging**. This type of iron is called **wrought iron**. It is flexible and rather soft. It can be made harder by **quenching**. This is when the iron is heated, hammered and then plunged into cold water.

forging

Iron is an odd metal. Mixing iron with carbon changes the way it behaves. Iron with 2–4% carbon has a lower melting point than 100% iron. This is called **cast iron** because it can be melted and cast (poured into moulds). Cast iron is brittle and hard.

casting

Iron has been widely used in Europe for over 3000 years. Making iron uses charcoal, both to provide the carbon needed to make the iron, and as a fuel. Charcoal is made by heating wood in pits. Britain used to be covered in forests, but most of the trees were cut down to make charcoal. This continued until the 17th century when coke was used instead. Coke was made from coal rather than trees.

Mixing iron with less than 2% carbon makes **steel**. Steel is an amazing material. It is very strong, not brittle and very hard.

Steel could be used in only very small amounts until 1856, when Henry Bessemer invented a way of making large amounts of cheap steel. He blew oxygen through cast iron. Some of the carbon was burnt, reducing the carbon content to less than 2%.

We use steel to build bridges, buildings, make cars, knives and needles. Many more items are made using a steel tool or machine.

1. Iron is not found as a pure metal. How is it found in the Earth?
2. How are iron minerals converted into iron metal?
3. Explain how wrought iron is made harder.
4. Why is it easier to make a large amount of cast iron than a large amount of wrought iron?
5. Why did making iron lead to a loss of forests?
6. Changing from charcoal to coke solved one environmental problem but caused another. Suggest how mining coal damages the environment.
7. How did Henry Bessemer change cast iron into steel?

A better knife

Activity 7.1B
Core

You are going to write a story about what makes iron knives better than bronze knives.

Mursilis is a young Hittite blacksmith living in Anatolia in 1200 BC. He is trying to sell his new iron knives but the customers are not sure. They want bronze knives. He has to convince them that iron is better.

1. Write a story about how Mursilis tried to sell his friend Hattusilis an iron knife. Use the information in the boxes below to help you.

Iron knives:
- do not break
- have a very sharp edge if you sharpen them
- go blunt if you do not sharpen them
- go rusty unless you oil them.

Bronze knives:
- break easily
- are not very sharp
- do not get blunter, but cannot be sharpened
- do not go rusty.

Hattusilis says, 'I want to buy a knife.'
'Here is an iron knife,' Mursilis replies. 'An iron knife is good because…

Hattusilis shakes his head. 'I want a bronze knife because…

Hattusilis adds, 'Iron knives are not as good because…

'You just have to look after the iron knife properly,' Mursilis argues.
'You have to …

Hattusilis decides…

Mursilis feels…

Properties of metals

Activity 7.2A
Core

You are going to investigate the properties of metals.

1 Make a table like the one below.

Name of metal	Is it shiny?	Is it magnetic?	Does it conduct electricity?	Does it conduct heat energy?

Do

Follow steps **2–5**. Record the results in your table.

2 Polish a piece of each metal. Is it shiny?

3 Test each metal with a magnet. Does it stick to the magnet? If the metal sticks, it is magnetic.

⚠ Wash your hands after handling metals.

4 Make a simple circuit like the one in the diagram.

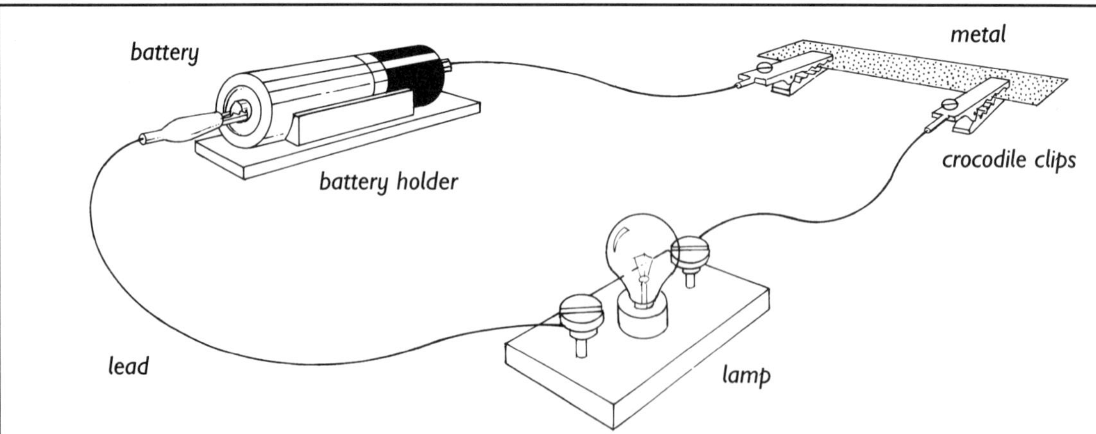

Put each metal in the circuit in turn. Does the lamp light? If the lamp lights, the metal conducts electricity.

5 Watch the experiment your teacher shows you. Did each metal conduct heat energy?

Analysing and concluding

1. Which metals were shiny?
2. Which metals were magnetic?
3. How did you know that these metals were magnetic?
4. Which metals conducted electricity?
5. How did you know that the metals conducted electricity?
6. Which metals conducted heat energy?
7. How did you know that the metal conducted heat energy?
8. Some metals conduct heat energy better than others. Which metal was the best conductor of heat energy?

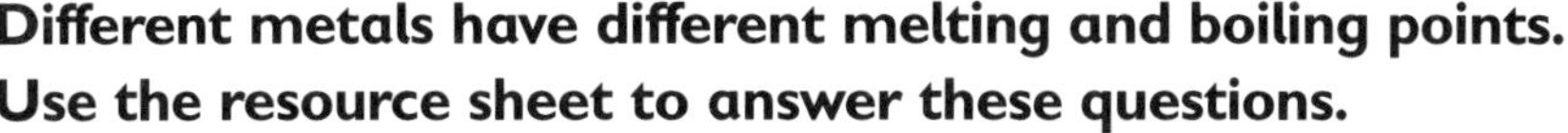

Solid, liquid or gas?

Activity 7.2B
Core

Different metals have different melting and boiling points. Use the resource sheet to answer these questions.

1. Which metals melt and boil between –200 °C and 1600 °C?
2. Which metals melt between –200 °C and 1600 °C, but do not boil between these two temperatures?
3. Which metal has the highest melting point?
4. Which metal has the lowest melting point?
5. Which metal has a melting point of 650 °C?
6. Which metal has a boiling point of 760 °C?
7. Which metals will be solids at 1000 °C?
8. Which three metals would boil if you heated them to 1000 °C?
9. Titanium has a melting point of 1660 °C. What would you see if titanium was on the chart?
10. Scientists are building a space probe to go to Venus. Temperatures on Venus can be as high as 460 °C. The scientists are not using any tin or lead in the space probe. Why not?

Solid, liquid or gas?

Activity 7.2B
Extension

Different metals have different melting and boiling points. Use the resource sheet to answer these questions.

1. Which metal has the highest melting point?
2. Which metal has the lowest melting point?
3. Which metal has a melting point of 650 °C?
4. Which metal has a boiling point of 760 °C?
5. Which metals will be solids at 1000 °C?
6. Which four metals would boil if you heated them to 1000 °C?
7. Titanium has a melting point of 1660 °C. What would you see if titanium was on the chart?
8. Lead has a melting point of 238°C. Why is it difficult to show this accurately on the chart?
9. Identify metals X and Y using information on the resource sheet.
10. Scientists are building a space probe to go to Venus. Temperatures on Venus can be as high as 460 °C. Which of the metals in the chart could be used to build the space probe? Explain why you chose these metals.

Solid, liquid or gas?

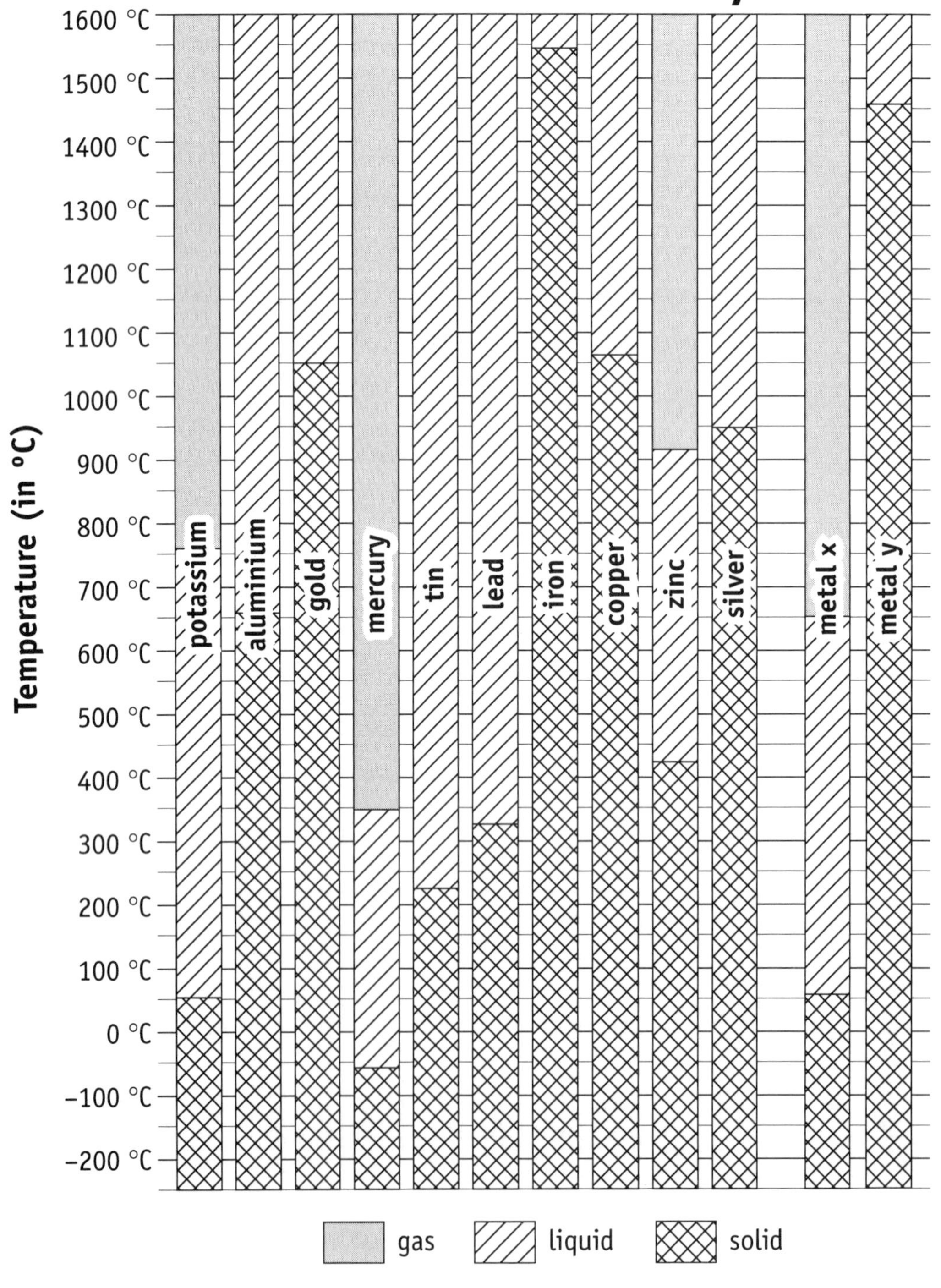

Use this table to help you answer Extension question 9.

Name of metal	Melting point (°C)	Boiling point (°C)
caesium	29	669
chromium	1857	2670
lithium	181	1342
magnesium	649	1107
nickel	1455	2725
titanium	1660	3231

Solid, liquid or gas?

Activity 7.2B
Help

Different metals have different melting and boiling points. Use the chart below to answer these questions.

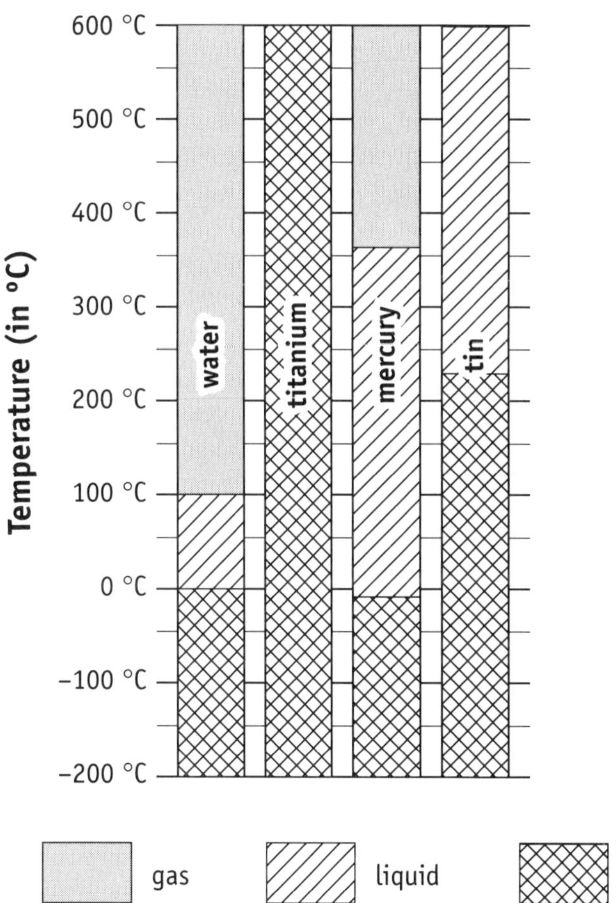

1 Find water on the chart.

❶ Is water a solid, a liquid or a gas at –100 °C?

❷ Is water a solid, a liquid or a gas at 200 °C?

❸ Is water a solid, a liquid or a gas at 400 °C?

2 Find mercury on the chart.

❹ Is mercury a solid, a liquid or a gas at –100 °C? (Put a ruler along –100 °C.)

❺ Is mercury a solid, a liquid or a gas at 200 °C? (Put a ruler along 200 °C.)

❻ Is mercury a solid, a liquid or a gas at 400 °C? (Put a ruler along 400 °C.)

3 Scientists are building a space probe to land on Venus. On Venus the temperature is 460 °C. The space probe is made of metal.

❼ Which metal would you use, titanium, tin or mercury?

❽ Why did you choose this metal and not the others?

Metallic elements

Activity 7.3B
Core

Use the database to answer these questions.

1. How many elements are in the database?
2. How many of the elements are metals?
   (Select the metals using a **filter**.)
3. Which is the metal with the highest melting point?
   (**Sort** the metals according to melting point in *descending* order.)
4. Which is the metal with the lowest melting point?
   (**Sort** the metals according to melting point in *ascending* order.)
5. Which metal is the best conductor of heat energy?
   (**Sort** the metals according to *How well does it conduct heat energy?* in *descending* order.)
6. Which metal is used to line the reactors in nuclear power plants?
   (**Find** 'reactor' in the *Uses* column.)
7. Which metal has the symbol Y?
   (**Find** 'Y' in the *Symbol* column. Click on *Find entire cells only.*)
8. Which metal melts at 29 °C?
   (**Find** '29' in the *Melting point* column.)
9. Which metals are magnetic?
   (Select the *magnetic metals* using a **filter**.)
10. How many of the metals are good conductors of electricity?
    (Select the metals with a rating of 10 using a **filter**. Make sure you are searching through all records of metals.)

Time left?

11. Name three metals that are very good conductors of electricity.
12. Name three metals that are poorer conductors of electricity than tin.

Non-metallic elements

Activity 7.4B
Core

Use the database to answer these questions.

1. How many records are about non-metals?
   (Select out the non-metals.)

2. How many of the non-metals are solids?
   Select out the solids. This is done using the *Appearance at room temperature* column as follows:
   - Look under the filter at the top of the column. Select *custom.*
   - Type ***solid** into the box to the right of *equals.* Click on *OK.* This will select any entry which ends in the word 'solid'.)

3. How many of the non-metals are liquids?

4. How many of the non-metals are gases?

   (Re-select all the non-metals. Select out the gases in the same way as you selected out the solids in question 2.)

   [Another way of selecting all the gases would be to pick out all the non-metals with a boiling point less than 25 °C (room temperature). See question 5.]

5. How many non-metals have a boiling point less than 0 °C?

   (Make sure you have all the non-metals selected.)
   - Look under the filter at the top of the column. Select *custom.*
   - Look at the first box. It probably says *equals.* Look in the drop down menu for this box. Select *is less than.*
   - Go to the next box (to the right). Type in **0**. Click on *OK.*

6. **a** Which non-metal is *used by cells to release energy?*

   b Which non-metal is used in *light sensors?*

   c Which non-metal is used to make *explosives?* Give two other uses of this non-metal element.

   (Use the **Find** function to answer these questions. Make sure you have all non-metals selected at the beginning.)

7. Name two non-metallic elements which are poisons.

   (Use the filter to make your selection. Use *custom, equals* and ***poison***.)

Grouping metals

Activity 7.5
Core

Some metals react when in air. Some metals react with water. You are going to sort different metals into groups.

1 Look at cards below for the metals **gold**, **potassium**, **sodium**, **iron**, **copper** and **lithium**.

1 Use the information on the cards to put the metals into two groups.

2 Explain carefully how you decided on these two groups.

2 Look at cards below for the metals **silver** and **caesium**.

3 Which groups would you put these metals into?

4 Explain your reasons.

Gold – Au
Reaction in air: none
Reaction in water: none

Potassium – K
Reaction in air: burns; fire is very difficult to put out
Reaction in water: bursts into flames

Sodium – Na
Reaction in air: burns; fire is very difficult to put out
Reaction in water: fizzes a lot and pops

Iron – Fe
Reaction in air: no reaction unless water is present
Reaction in water: rusts slowly if oxygen is also present

Copper – Cu
Reaction in air: slowly reacts over many years
Reaction in water: slowly reacts over many years

Lithium – Li
Reaction in air: burns; fire is very difficult to put out
Reaction in water: fizzes a lot

Silver – Ag
Reaction in air: reacts very slowly, going slightly black
Reaction in water: slowly reacts over many years

Caesium – Cs
Reaction in air: burns; fire is very difficult to put out
Reaction in water: explodes

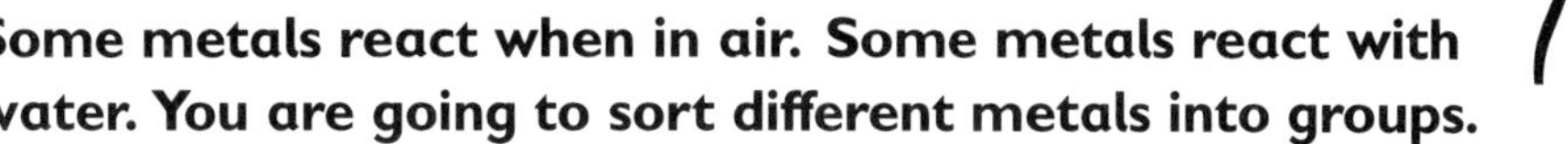

7.5 Grouping metals

Activity 7.5
Help

Some metals react when in air. Some metals react with water. You are going to sort different metals into groups.

1 Look at cards for the metals **gold**, **potassium**, **sodium**, **iron**, **copper** and **lithium**.

Fizzing, popping and bursting into flame show a very fast reaction.

1 Which three metals react quickly in air?

....

....

2 Which two metals react slowly in air?

....

3 Which metal does not react in air? ....

2 Next, you have to sort the metals into two groups.

4 Which metals are in your first group?

....

5 Which metals are in your second group?

....

6 Explain carefully how you decided. ....

....

3 Look at cards for silver and caesium.
Look at your two groups above.

7 Which group would you put silver into? Explain why.

....

8

Which group would you put caesium into? Explain why.

....

Making iron sulphide

You are going to make iron sulphide from iron and sulphur.

You can write a word equation to show the chemical reaction:

iron + sulphur → iron sulphide

Wear eye protection throughout this experiment.

Take care!
Iron filings irritate the eyes.
Wash your hands afterwards.

Equipment available

- test tube containing iron and sulphur
- test tube holder
- Bunsen burner
- heatproof mat

Do

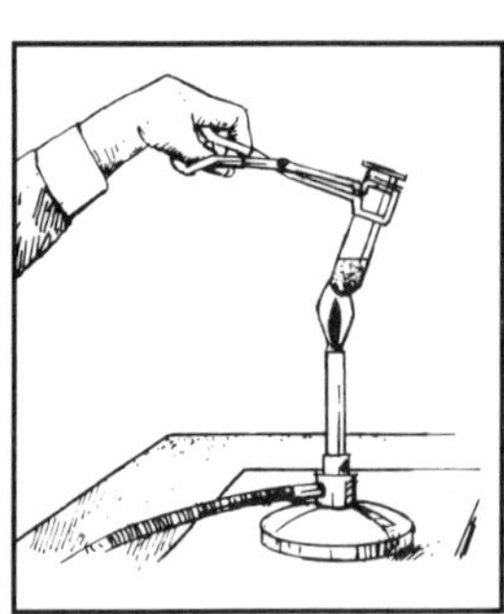

1 Heat the iron and sulphur as shown. Point the open mouth of the tube away from yourself and other pupils. Make sure you hold the bottom of the test tube in the hottest part of the Bunsen flame.

2 Be patient. You will have to heat for a long time.

3 The iron and sulphur will start to glow. The chemical reaction has begun. Heat until it stops glowing.

4 Place the test tube on the heatproof mat. Do not touch it for 10 minutes.

5 While your iron sulphide is cooling, look at the iron, the sulphur and the iron sulphide.

Analyse

1 What does the sulphur look like?

2 What does the iron look like?

3 What does the iron sulphide look like?

4 Which of the substances are magnetic? (Run the magnet along the side of the jar.)

5 Write down one way in which the iron sulphide is different from sulphur.

6 Write down one way in which the iron sulphide is different from iron.

7 What did you see when the chemical reaction was happening?

Do

6 After 10 minutes, try to remove the iron sulphide from the test tube. Turn the test tube upside down and tap it gently against the heatproof mat.

7 If the iron sulphide is stuck, take the test tube to your teacher.

8 Test your iron sulphide with a magnet to see if it is magnetic.

Analyse

8 Is the iron sulphide magnetic?

9 Is a new substance made?

10 Are the properties of the new substance the same as or different from the iron and sulphur? Describe them.

Recording reactions

Activity 7.6B
Core

In this activity you are going to use word equations to show chemical reactions.

Oxides

When a metal reacts with oxygen it makes an **oxide**. Most oxides have simple names, like magnesium oxide and copper oxide.

Non-metals also react with oxygen to make oxides. 'Hydrogen oxide' has a special name. 'Hydrogen oxide' is **water**.

Carbon forms two oxides when it burns. This means we need two different names. When carbon is burned with a lot of oxygen it makes **carbon dioxide**. When carbon burns and there is a lack of oxygen, it makes **carbon monoxide**.

1 Use *Skill sheet 7: Word equations* and the information above to write word equations for the following reactions:

❶ calcium and oxygen

❷ carbon and oxygen when there is a lot of oxygen

❸ carbon and oxygen when there is a limited amount of oxygen

❹ hydrogen and oxygen.

Reactions of metals with other non-metals

Metals also react with non-metals other than oxygen. For example:

- metals react with chlorine to make **chlorides**
- metals react with sulphur to make **sulphides**

2 Write word equations for the following reactions:

❺ sodium and chlorine

❻ calcium and chlorine

❼ potassium and sulphur

Recording reactions

In this activity you are going to use word equations to show chemical reactions.

Oxides

When a metal reacts with oxygen it makes an **oxide**. Most oxides have simple names, like magnesium oxide and copper oxide.

1. Complete this word equation. It shows the reaction between calcium and oxygen.

   calcium + oxygen → ....

Non-metals also react with oxygen to make oxides. 'Hydrogen oxide' has a special name. 'Hydrogen oxide' is **water**.

2. Complete this word equation. It shows the reaction between hydrogen and oxygen.

   hydrogen + oxygen → ....

Carbon forms two oxides when it burns. This means we need two different names. When carbon is burned with a lot of oxygen it makes **carbon dioxide**. When carbon burns and there is a lack of oxygen, it makes **carbon monoxide**.

3. Complete this word equation. It shows the reaction of carbon and oxygen when there is lots of oxygen.

   carbon + oxygen → ....

4. Complete this word equation. It shows the reaction of carbon and oxygen when there is a lack of oxygen.

   carbon + oxygen → ....

Reactions of metals with other non-metals

Metals also react with other non-metals. For example, metals react with chlorine to make **chlorides**.

5. Complete the word equation. It shows the reaction between calcium and chlorine.

   calcium + chlorine → ....

Metals also react with sulphur to make **sulphides**.

6. Complete the word equation. It shows the reaction between potassium and sulphur.

   potassium + sulphur → ....

Recording reactions

Activity 7.6B
Extension

In this activity you are going to use word equations to show chemical reactions.

It takes less time to write a word equation than to write a description. Scientists follow the same rules for writing word equations, so everyone knows what they mean.

Oxides

When a metallic element reacts with oxygen it makes an **oxide**. Most oxides have simple names, like magnesium oxide and copper oxide.

Non-metallic elements also react with oxygen to make oxides. 'Hydrogen oxide' has a special name. 'Hydrogen oxide' is **water**.

Carbon forms two oxides when it burns. This means we need two different names. When carbon is burned with a lot of oxygen it makes **carbon dioxide**. When carbon burns and there is a lack of oxygen, it makes **carbon monoxide**.

Sulphur can form more than one oxide when it burns. One of these oxides is **sulphur dioxide**.

1 Use *Skill sheet 7: Word equations* and the information above to write word equations for the following reactions:

❶ calcium and oxygen

❷ carbon and oxygen when there is a limited amount of oxygen

❸ carbon and oxygen when there is a lot of oxygen

❹ when sulphur dioxide is made

❺ hydrogen and oxygen

❻ strontium and oxygen

Reactions with other non-metallic elements

Metallic elements react with other non-metallic elements. For example:

- chlorine makes **chlorides**
- sulphur makes **sulphides**
- bromine makes **bromides**
- fluorine makes **fluorides**
- iodine makes **iodides**
- nitrogen makes **nitrides**.

2 Write word equations for the following reactions:

❼ magnesium and bromine

❽ calcium and fluorine

❾ sodium and iodine

❿ potassium and sulphur

⓫ magnesium and nitrogen

⓬ calcium and chlorine

Will it rust?

Activity 7.7A
Core

You are going to carry out an investigation about rusting.

FIRST LESSON: Plan and predict

1 Plan an investigation about rusting. Read the information in the speech bubbles to help you.

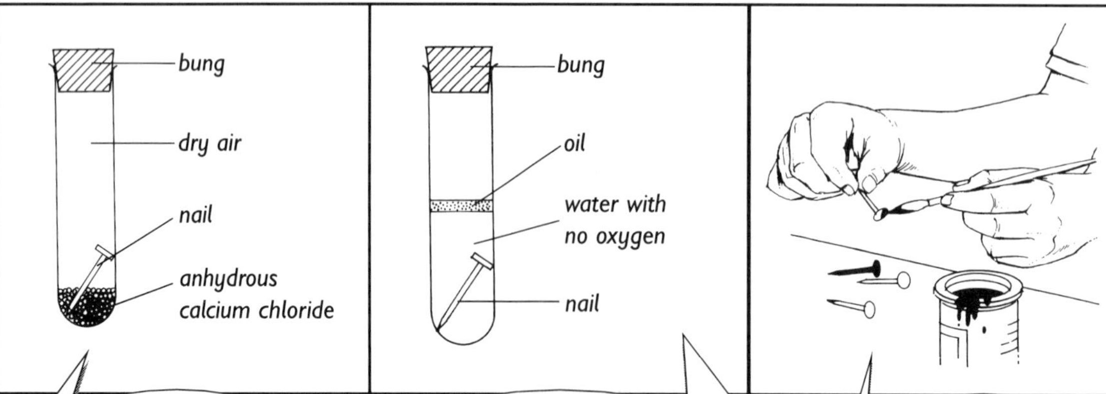

2 Look at your plan.

- Which variable are you changing?
- Which variable are you measuring or observing?
- Is it a fair test?

3 Make a prediction. How will your investigation turn out? Explain your reasons for your prediction.

4 Show your plan to your teacher before you carry it out.

Do

5 Set up your investigation. Make sure that your test tubes are labelled. Put your experiment somewhere safe.

6 Prepare your results table.

SECOND LESSON: Observe and record

7 Look at the nails. Record your results in your table.

Analyse and conclude

8 Think about what your results show. Write a few sentences to describe your results.

9 Look at your prediction. Do your results agree with your prediction?

Evaluate

10 Imagine you were doing your investigation again. How would you improve it?

Will it rust?

Activity 7.7A
Help

You are going to carry out an investigation about rusting.

FIRST LESSON: Plan and predict

1 Pick one question to answer.

- Is oxygen needed for rusting?
- Is water needed for rusting?
- Does painting stop rusting?

Write your question down.

2 Look at these diagrams. Which test tubes do you need to set up?

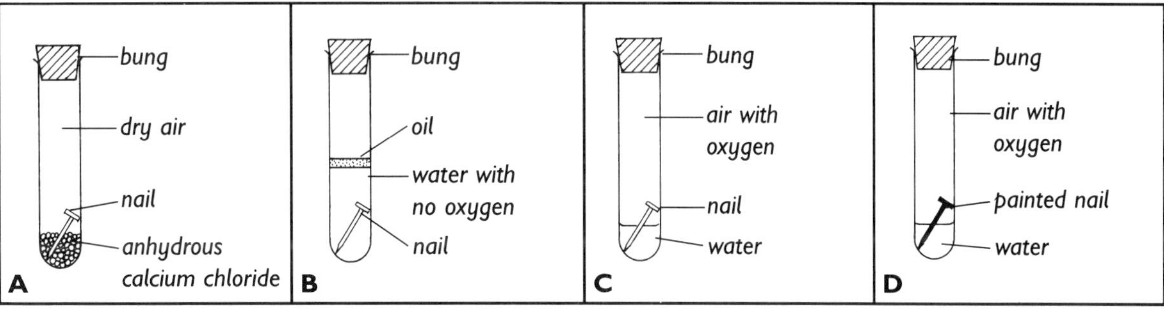

3 Write down your plan. Show it to your teacher.

4 Make a prediction. Which nails will go rusty? Why?

Write your prediction down.

Do

5 Set up your experiments. Remember to label each test tube.

6 Make a table for your results like the one below.

Test tube (A, B, C or D)	Was oxygen present?	Was water present?	Was the nail ? painted	Did the nail go rusty?

SECOND LESSON: Observe and record

7 Look at your nails. Which have gone rusty?

8 Write your results in your table.

Analyse and conclude

9 What answer do your results give to your question?

10 Was your prediction correct?

Evaluate

11 Imagine doing your investigation again. How would you improve it?

Metals
7.7
B

Rusty screws

Activity 7.7B
Core

Kirsten runs a small company that makes screws. The company makes screws of three different materials: iron, stainless steel and solid brass. You are going to sort out which screws are suitable for different customers.

Look at this information about the three types of screws.

Material of screw	Does it rust?	Appearance	Cost
iron	yes	brown when rusty, can stain the surrounding materials	£0.52 per pack
stainless steel	no	silver	£2.80 per pack
brass	no	rich yellow	£5.39 per pack

Kirsten has three different customers. She wants to sell the correct screws to each customer.

Look at the information about each customer.

I am Mr Brown, a builder. I use screws to join pieces of wood inside the houses. The screws will not show.

I am Mr Pink. I make double-glazed windows. I offer a 30 year guarantee. The handles and hinges are screwed together.

I am Miss Green. I make expensive hinges and door handles for antique furniture. Many of my designs are made to look as if they are two or three hundred years old.

Imagine you are Kirsten.

1. Decide which screws would be best for each customer.
2. Make a list of the things you should say to each customer to explain why the screws are the best ones for them.

7.7
B

Rusty screws

Activity 7.7B
Help

Kirsten runs a small company that makes screws. You are going to sort out which screws are suitable for different customers.

Look at the table. It shows two types of screws.

Material of screw	Does it rust?	Appearance	Cost
iron	yes	brown when rusty, can stain the surrounding materials	£0.52 per pack
stainless steel	no	silver	£2.80 per pack

Kirsten is selling screws to Mr Brown and Mr Pink. She needs to explain to them which screws are best for their work.

Read about Mr Brown and Mr Pink.

I am Mr Brown, a builder. I use screws to join pieces of wood inside the houses. The screws will not show.

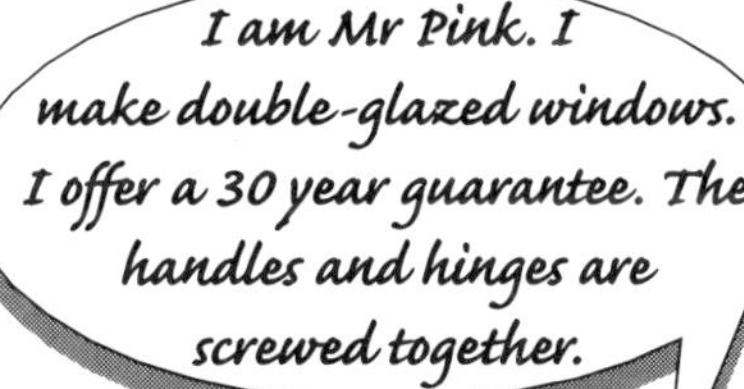
I am Mr Pink. I make double-glazed windows. I offer a 30 year guarantee. The handles and hinges are screwed together.

Imagine you are Kirsten.

1. Should Mr Brown buy iron screws or stainless steel screws?

   ....

2. What will you say to Mr Brown? ....

   ....

3. Should Mr Pink buy iron screws or stainless steel screws?

   ....

4. What should you say to Mr Pink? ....

   ....

Rusty screws

Activity 7.7B
Extension

Kirsten runs a small company that makes screws of four different materials: iron, nickel-plated iron, stainless steel and solid brass. You are going to sort out which screws are suitable for different customers.

Look at this information about the four types of screws.

Material of screw	Does it rust?	Appearance	Cost
iron	yes, it will rust	unattractive when rusted, can stain the surrounding materials	£0.52 per pack
nickel-plated iron	only when nickel coating has worn away	silver, until rusting begins	£1.11 per pack
stainless steel	no	silver	£2.80 per pack
brass	no	rich yellow	£5.39 per pack

Kirsten has four different customers. She wants to sell the correct screws to each customer. Look at the information about each customer.

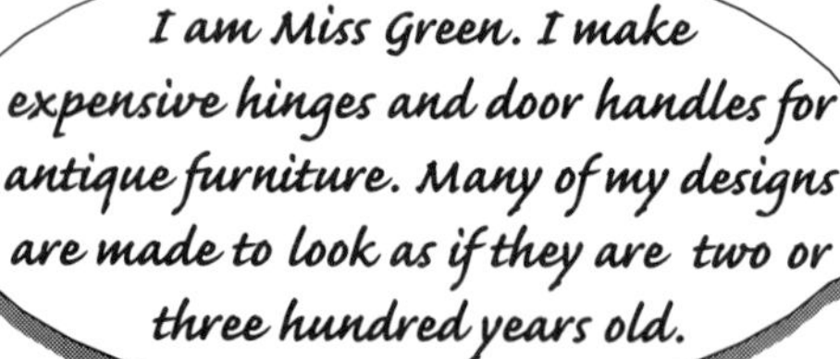

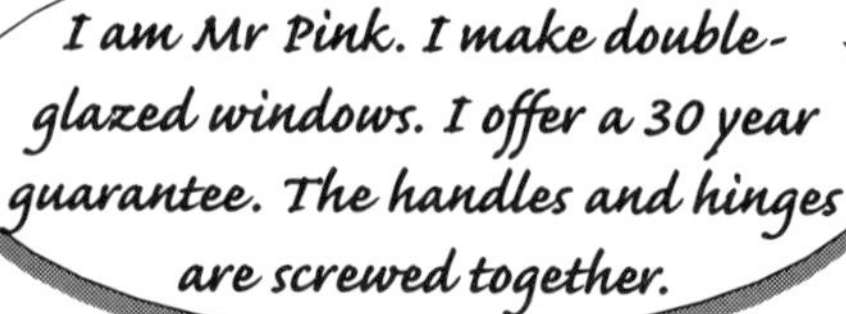

Imagine you are Kirsten.

1. Decide which screws would be best for each customer.
2. Make a list of the things you should say to each customer to explain why the screws are the best ones for them.

Which particles are present?

Activity 7.8A
Core

All materials are made up of atoms. You are going to look for the atoms in different materials.

The diagrams show some of the atoms in four different materials.

copper *carbon* *chlorine* *hydrogen* *sodium* *mercury* *oxygen*

A

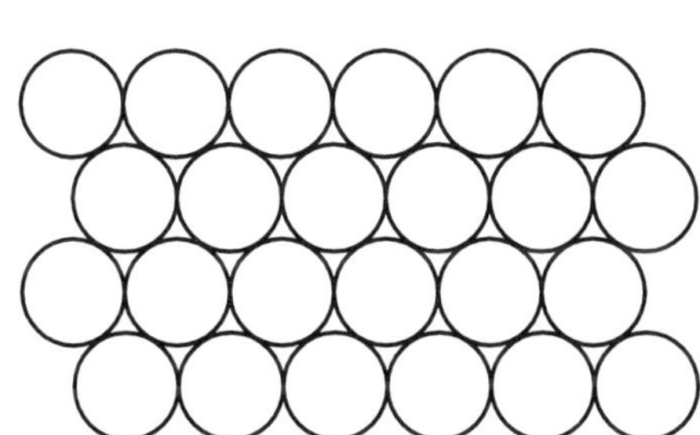

B

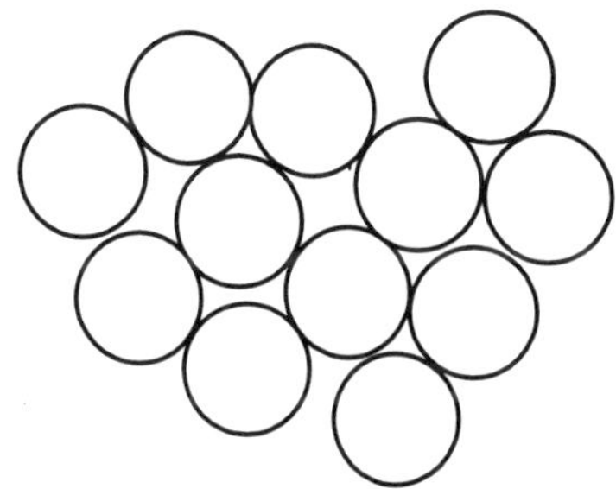

C

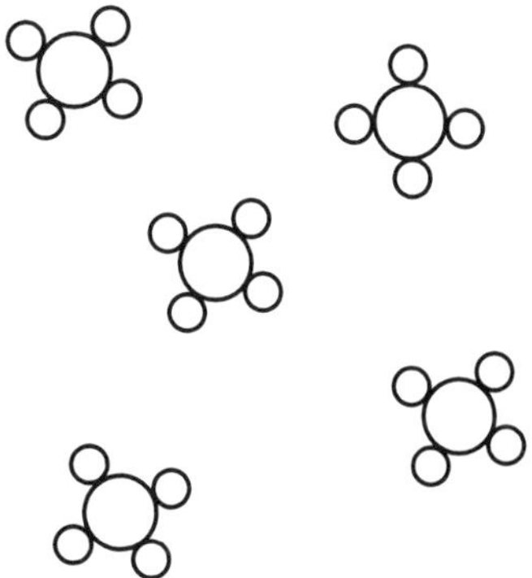

D

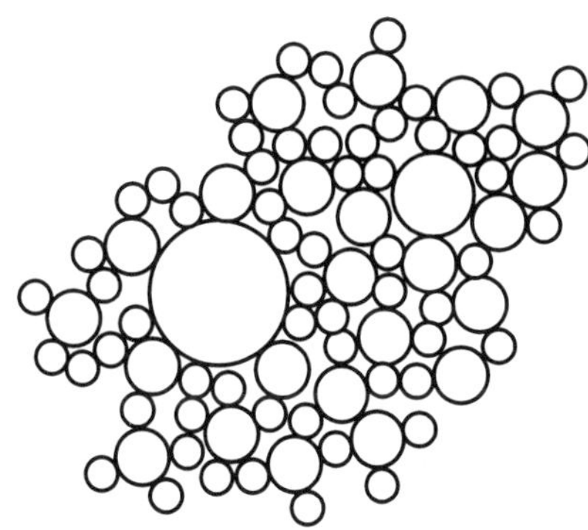

1. Which material is a solid?
2. Which material is a gas?
3. Which two materials are liquids?
4. Which materials are elements?
5. Which material could be copper?
6. Which material could be mercury?
7. Methane is made of carbon and hydrogen atoms joined up. Which material is the pure compound called methane?
8. Which material is a solution of sodium chloride?
9. Which of the four materials is a mixture of different substances?

Formulae

Activity 7.8B
Extension

You are going to work out the formulae of different materials by working out the ratio of atoms in each.

The diagrams show the atoms in five different materials.

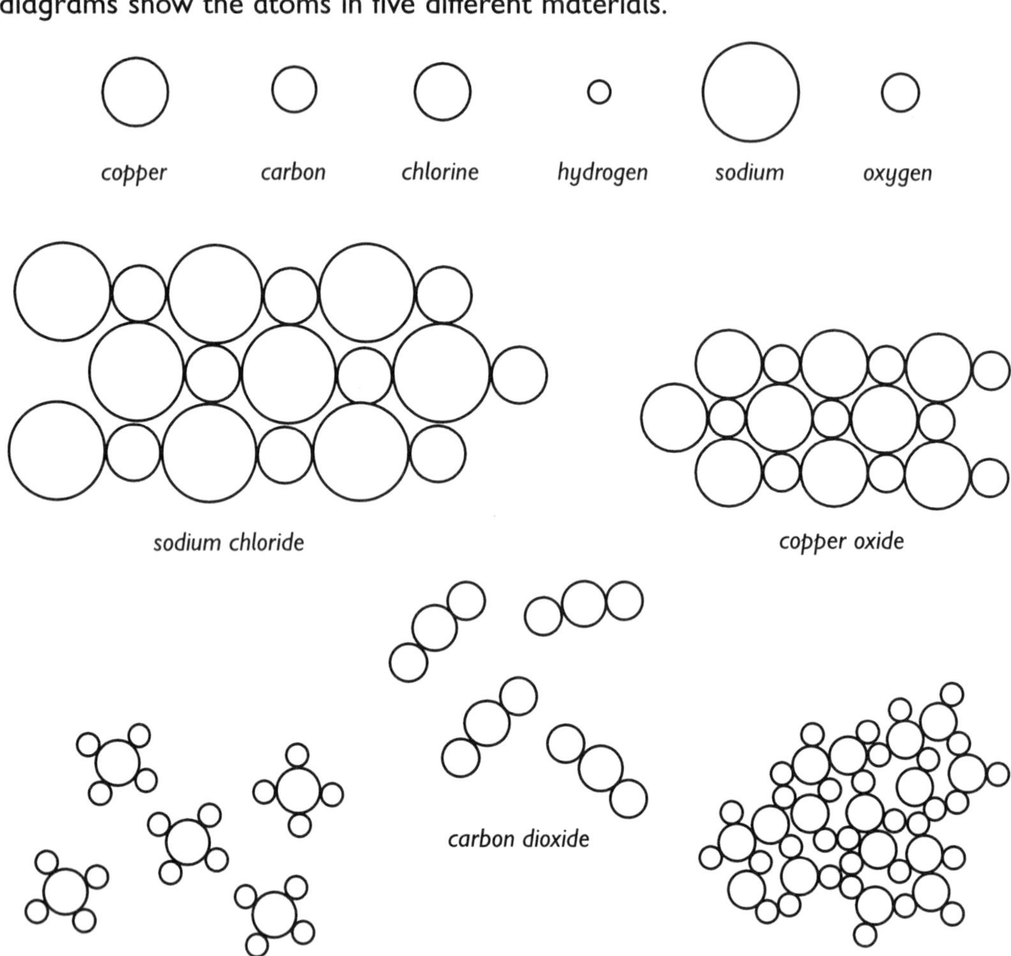

Study the diagram of sodium chloride. There are 9 sodium atoms and 9 chlorine atoms. The ratio of sodium to chlorine is 9:9. This can be simplified to 1:1. We write NaCl, which is a short way of saying there is one sodium atom for every one chlorine atom.
NaCl is the **formula** for sodium chloride.

1. What is the ratio of copper atoms to oxygen atoms in copper oxide?
2. What is the formula for copper oxide?

Not all compounds have a 1:1 ratio. Study the diagram of carbon dioxide. There are 4 carbon atoms and 8 oxygen atoms. The ratio of carbon atoms to oxygen atoms is 4:8, which can be simplified to 1:2. We write the formula for water as CO_2, to show that there are twice as many oxygen atoms as carbon atoms.

3. What is the ratio of hydrogen atoms to oxygen atoms in water?
4. What is the formula for water?
5. What is the ratio of carbon atoms to hydrogen atoms in methane?
6. What is the formula for methane?

8 Forces

Unit map

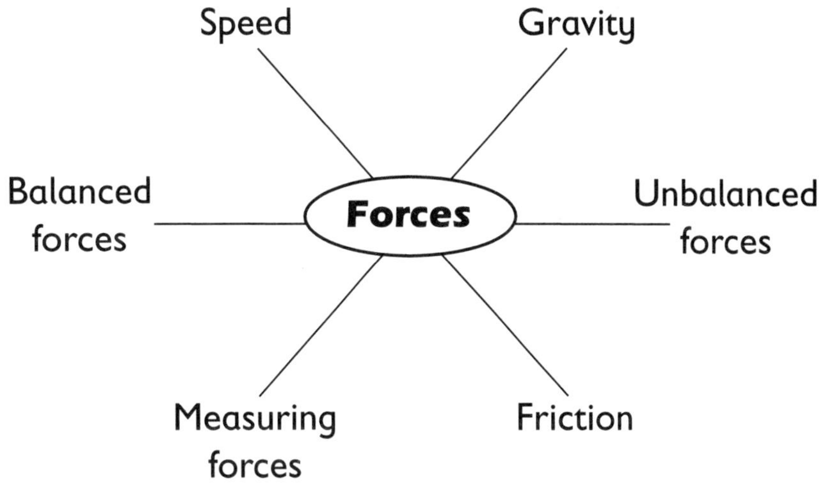

Speed

Gravity

Balanced forces

Forces

Unbalanced forces

Measuring forces

Friction

8 Forces

Unit map

Use these words to help you complete your unit map.

push	rub	distance travelled
pull	force arrows	time taken
weight	move	mass
newton	faster	kilogram
lubricant	slower	surface
air resistance	upthrust	heat energy
streamlined	steady speed	

Measuring forces

Activity 8.1A
Core

There are several different types of equipment for measuring forces. You are going to measure forces using newtonmeters and newton scales. Newton scales are scales that measure a person's weight in newtons.

Practise

1 Write down the reading shown on each newtonmeter here.

A

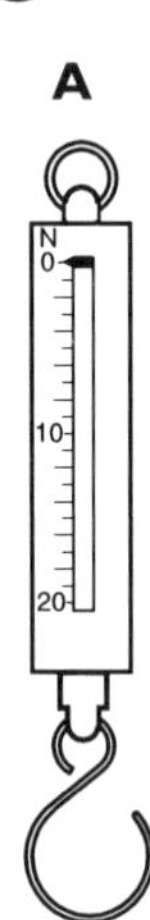

B

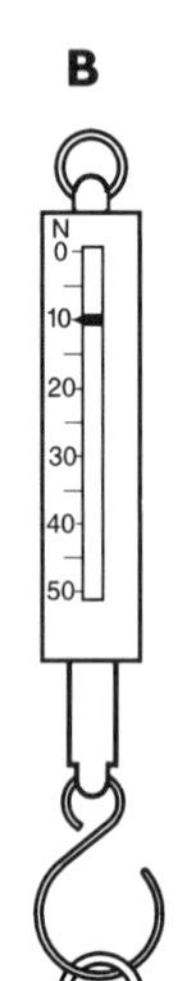

C

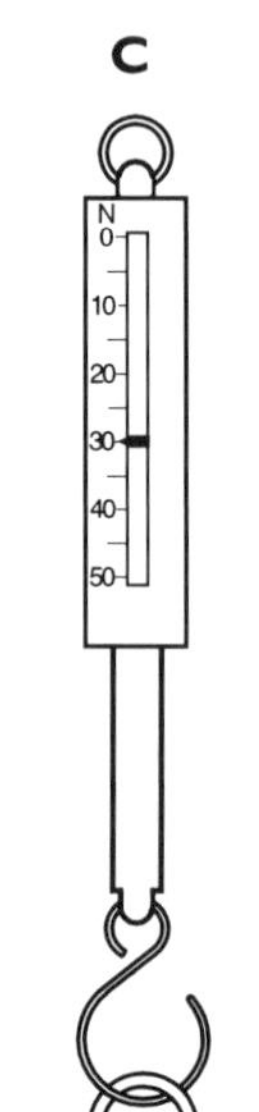

D

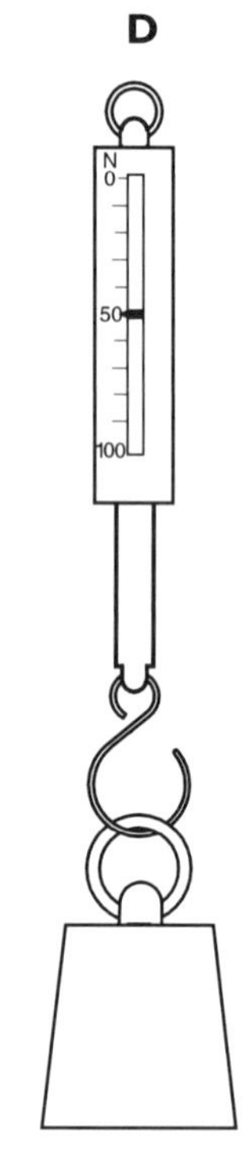

E

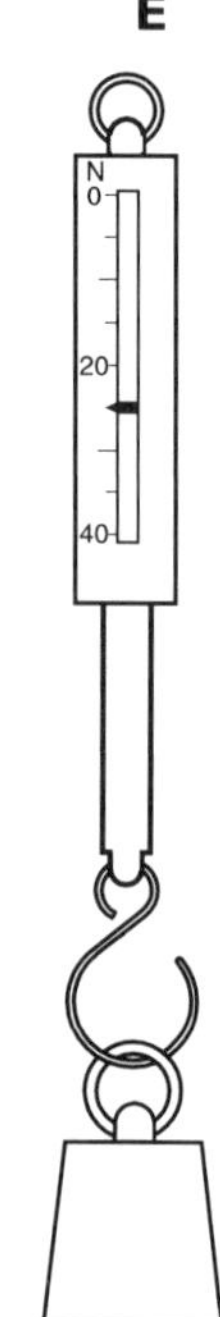

F

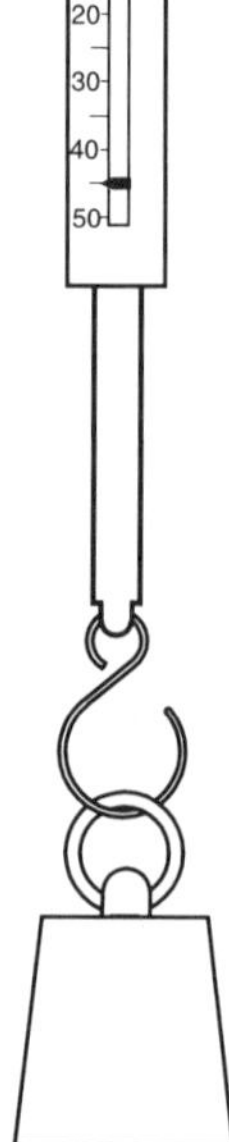

Do

1. Use a newtonmeter to measure these forces:
   - the weight of a textbook
   - the weight of a pencil case
   - the weight of a shoe.

   You can use string to attach each object to the newtonmeter.

   Make a table to record your results.

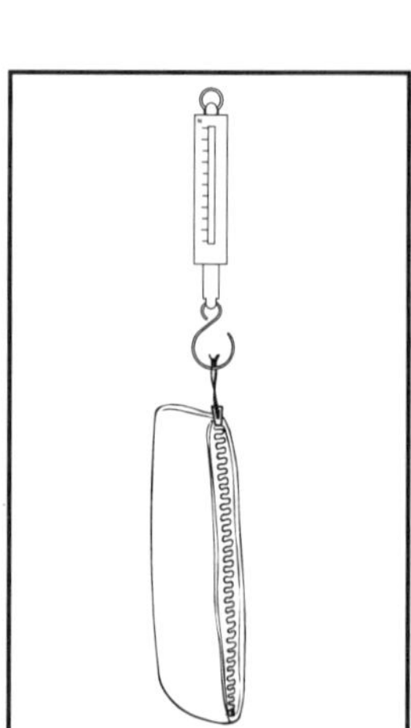

2. Use the newton scales to find the force when you:
   - stand on them
   - press down on them as hard as you can with the palm of one hand.

   Make a table to record your results.

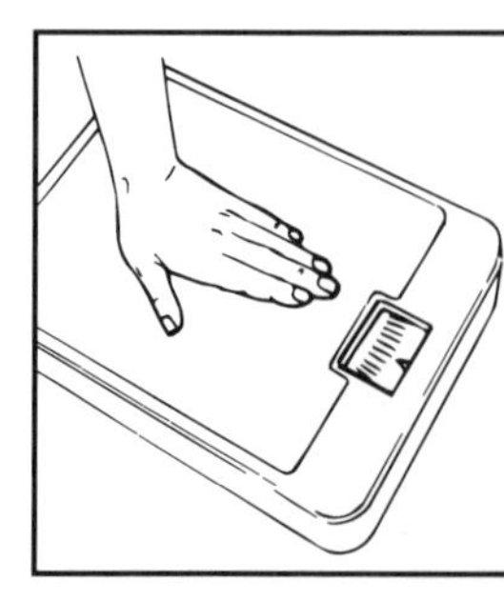

Analyse and conclude

2 Using the newtonmeter, which object weighed the most?

3 Which way of pressing on the newton scales produced the biggest force?

Forces in everyday life

Activity 8.1B
Core

Everything we do in life uses forces. You are going to think about how useful forces are to us in everyday life.

Imagine you have met a visitor from outer space. She is collecting information about life on Earth to take back home with her. She has asked you to help her write a report about how people use forces.

1. Write a report for the visitor to take back. You can use some of the ideas below to help you, or you can use your own ideas.

> Useful forces on Earth
> Forces are all around us.
> We use these forces every day: …
>
> Forces are measured using …
>
> Gravity is a force that …
>
> If I woke up in the morning and there were no forces, life would be different because …

8.1 B

Forces in everyday life

Activity 8.1B
Core

Everything we do in life uses forces. You are going to think about how useful forces are to us in everyday life.

Imagine you have met a visitor from outer space. She is collecting information about life on Earth to take back home with her. She has asked you to help her write a report about how people use forces.

1. Write a report for the visitor to take back. You can use some of the ideas below to help you, or you can use your own ideas.

> Useful forces on Earth
> Forces are all around us.
> We use these forces every day: …
>
> Forces are measured using …
>
> Gravity is a force that …
>
> If I woke up in the morning and there were no forces, life would be different because …

Forces

8.2 Mass and weight

Activity 8.2
Core

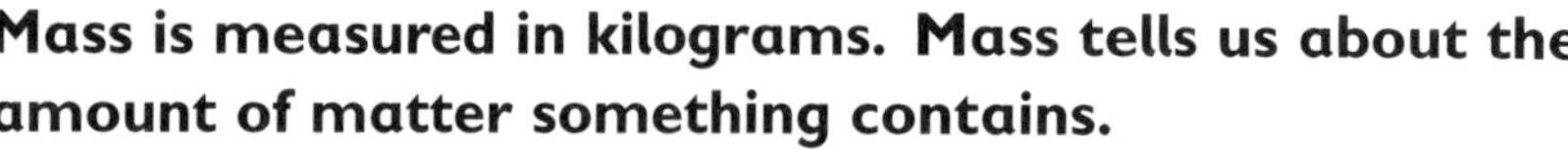

Mass is measured in kilograms. Mass tells us about the amount of matter something contains.

Weight is measured in newtons. Weight tells us about the force of gravity pulling down on something.

You are going to answer some questions about mass and weight.

Apples on Earth

An apple has a mass of about 100 g. On Earth it will weigh about 1 N.

> **Remember**
> On Earth, 1 kg weighs 10 N.
> 1 kg = 1000 g

1. What is the mass of 10 apples?
2. How much do 10 apples weigh?
3. What is the mass of a box of apples that weighs 500 N?

Apples on the Moon

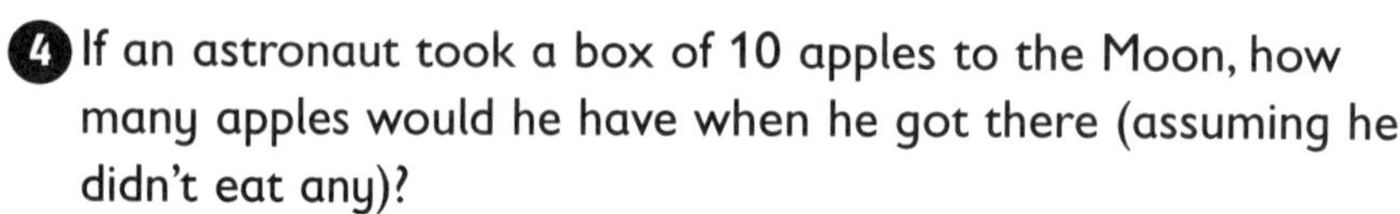

4. If an astronaut took a box of 10 apples to the Moon, how many apples would he have when he got there (assuming he didn't eat any)?

If the number of apples doesn't change, then the mass will stay the same.

5. What will be the mass of the apples on the Moon?
6. How much will the 10 apples weigh on the Moon?
7. If the astronaut eats 5 of the apples, what is the mass of all the apples that are left? Where is the rest of the mass?

> **Remember**
> On the Moon, the pull of gravity is about one-sixth that on Earth.
> To calculate the weight of an object on the Moon you divide its weight on Earth by 6.
> 1 kg weighs about 1.5 N on the Moon.

8. What is the mass of a space buggy that weighs 450 N on the moon?

Sending spacecraft

9. The space shuttle has a mass of about 100 000 kg. How much does it weigh on Earth? How much would it weigh if it landed on the Moon?

NASA would like to send a mission to Mars. The heavier something is, the more fuel it takes to launch it. Fuel is very expensive.

10. NASA would like to launch the Mars probe from the Moon. Why do you think they want to do this? Explain your answer.

Shoe soles

Activity 8.3A
Core

You going to investigate the relationship between the mass of a shoe and the force needed to pull it against friction.

Equipment available

- a set of masses
- a shoe
- a newtonmeter
- string
- a suitable surface to pull the shoe over.

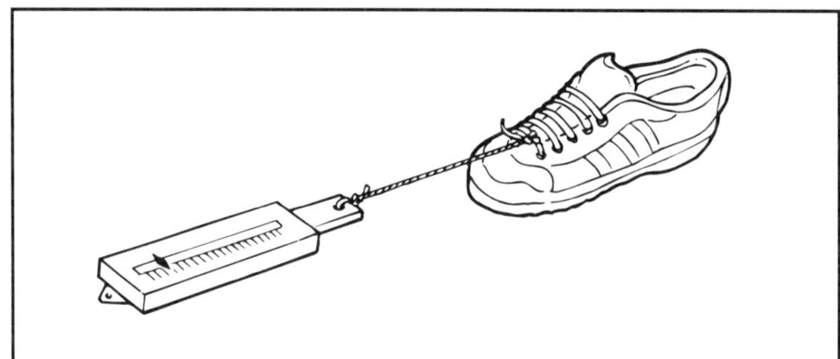

Plan

1 Decide how you are going to make the experiment fair.

2 Decide how many times you will do the experiment.

3 Decide how you are going to record the results.

Do

4 Choose a suitable shoe and a surface for the experiment.

5 Tie the newtonmeter to the shoe.

6 Pull the shoe without any masses inside it, so that it moves at a steady speed across the surface.

7 Record the force shown on the newtonmeter.

8 Repeat steps **4** to **6** six times, putting a 100 g mass in the shoe each time until the mass inside the shoe is 600 g (six masses). Pull the shoe at the same steady speed in each experiment.

Analyse and conclude

9 Draw a line graph of your results. Put mass along the bottom and force up the side.

❶ What happens to the size of force needed to pull the shoe as the mass increases?

❷ Why do you think this happens? Use the word friction in your answer.

Evaluate

❸ How could you improve this experiment?

Activity 8.3A
Extension

❹ Plan an experiment to do one of the following:

- compare how much grip is given by the soles of different running shoes
- find the safest track surface for running on in wet weather
- find the best shoes for a safe landing for a skydiving team.

A world without friction

Activity 8.3B
Core

Friction is very useful in everyday life. You are going to think about what might happen if there was no friction.

1 Write a story about life without friction. You can use some of the ideas below to help you, or you can use your own ideas.

The day there was no friction

Without friction, cars, buses and bicycles …

When you walk, …

It would be very dangerous to be a parachutist because …

Sometimes friction is not useful. Machines …

Heat energy is made when there is friction. This is useful because …

Forces
8.3
B

A world without friction

Activity 8.3B
Core

Friction is very useful in everyday life. You are going to think about what might happen if there was no friction.

1 Write a story about life without friction. You can use some of the ideas below to help you, or you can use your own ideas.

The day there was no friction

Without friction, cars, buses and bicycles …

When you walk, …

It would be very dangerous to be a parachutist because …

Sometimes friction is not useful. Machines …

Heat energy is made when there is friction. This is useful because …

8.4 Unbalanced forces

Activity 8.4
Core

Unbalanced forces make things move faster, move slower or change their shape. Unbalanced forces can also make moving objects change direction. You are going to answer some questions about unbalanced forces.

1. Look at the objects below. For each one, write down whether an unbalanced force is acting. If so, explain where it has come from.

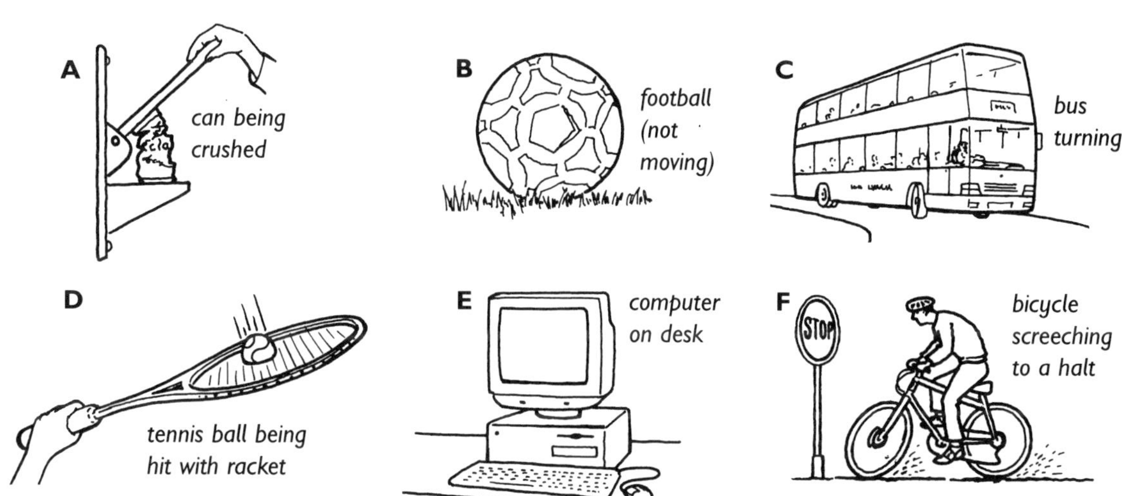

Friction is a force that stops things moving, or slows them down when they are moving. Friction acts in the opposite direction to the movement. If you want to start something moving, or speed it up, you need a force larger than friction.

2. For each of the following, draw a diagram with force arrows to show the force making the movement and the friction force. Remember: the longer the arrow, the larger the force.
   - a car driving along
   - a person opening a drawer
   - you sliding down a rope
   - a shopper pushing a trolley

3. Draw a picture of a game of tennis or rounders. Add arrows to show all the unbalanced forces.

4. Draw a picture of a rocket leaving the Earth. Add arrows to show the main forces on the rocket.

Unbalanced forces

Activity 8.4
Extension

The forces on an object are unbalanced when one of the forces is bigger than the other. We can draw force diagrams with arrows showing the direction of each force. The size of the force is shown by the length of the arrow.

You are going to find out the sizes of the forces in the questions below.

1. Who will win the tug-of-war? What is the size of the unbalanced force?

2. A horse pulls a cart with a force of 400 N. There is a force of friction on the cart's wheels of 300 N.

   Draw a force diagram and say what happens to the cart.

3. A team of circus trainers is pulling an elephant. The trainers pull with a force of 1500 N. The elephant pulls back with a force of 2000 N.

   Draw a force diagram to show the forces on the trainers and elephant. Calculate the size of the unbalanced force. Which way will they all move?

4. A tug boat pulls a ship with a force of 4000 N. The weight of the ship pulls against the tug with a force of 3500 N.

   Draw a force diagram and calculate the size of the unbalanced force. What will happen?

Making bridges

Bridges need to be built to support their own weight and the weight of the load that will cross them. The downward forces must be balanced by the upward forces. There are many different types of bridge, such as the beam bridge, the suspension bridge and the arch bridge.

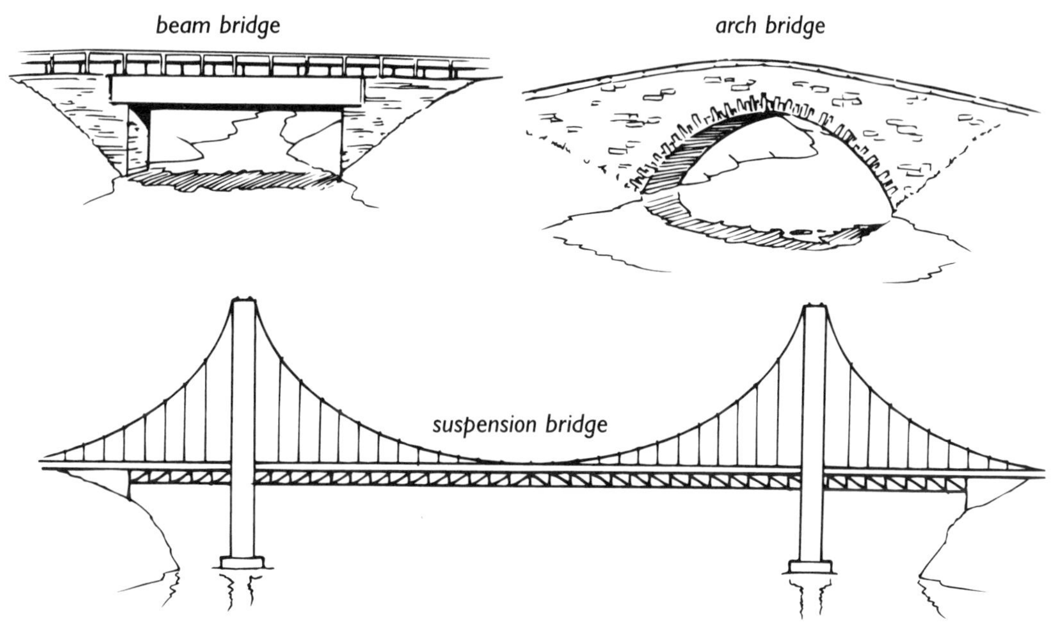

You are going to design, make and test a bridge using straws, paper and sticky tape.

Plan

1 Design a bridge using the materials provided. Draw a diagram of the bridge. Label your diagram.

Do

2 Build your bridge.

3 Test your bridge by loading it with 100 g masses until it breaks.

Analyse and conclude

4 Compare your bridge and its test results with the other bridges in the class.

❶ Which bridge supported the most masses?

❷ Why do you think it was the best?

❸ Draw a diagram of your bridge before it broke. Add arrows to show the forces acting on the bridge.

❹ Which forces must balance if the bridge is not going to collapse?

Evaluate

❺ If you were planning to build a bridge again, how would you change your design? How would you test the bridge?

Stretching

When you hang weights on the end of a spring, the spring stretches. A newtonmeter has a spring inside it. When you hang weights on the newtonmeter, the spring pulls up with a force equal to the force of the weight pulling down. The forces are balanced.

An elastic band stretches too when you hang weights on it. You are going to hang weights on a spring and an elastic band and compare how much they stretch. This is called the extension.

Wear eye protection.

Take care not to knock yourself on the clamp stand when bending down.

Be careful not to drop weights on your feet.

Do

1 Make a table like the one below. You will need six rows.

Weight in N	Position in mm	Extension in mm (position – zero point)

2 Set up the apparatus as shown in the diagram **A**.

3 Record the position of the base of the spring with a holder but no weights, in millimetres. This is your zero point.

4 Put a 1 N weight on the holder as shown in diagram **B**. Record the new position in your table.

5 Add weights one at a time and record the positions for 2 N, 3 N, 4 N, 5 N and 6 N.

6 Fill in the extension column of your table by subtracting the zero point from each measurement.

7 Repeat steps **1** to **6** using an elastic band instead of a spring.

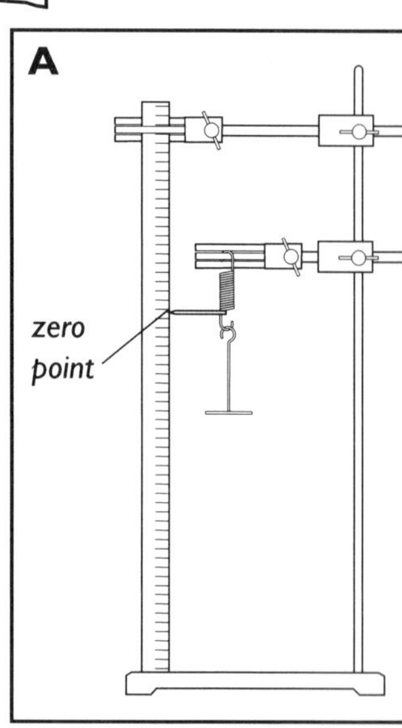

Analyse and conclude

8 Plot a line graph of your results for the spring. Put weight along the bottom and extension up the side. Draw a line of best fit using a ruler.

9 Plot another graph for the elastic band.

1 How is the extension of the rubber band different from the extension of the spring when you hang weights on them?

2 Is there a relationship between the weight on the spring and the amount it extends? Describe the relationship.

3 Is there a relationship between the weight on the elastic band and the amount it extends? Describe the relationship.

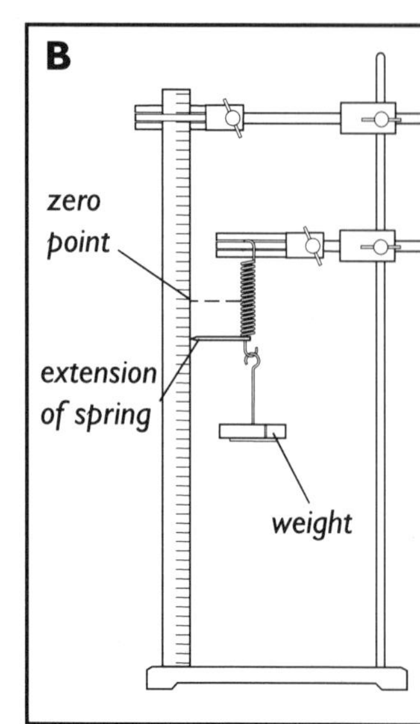

Evaluate

4 How could you make your results more reliable?

5 Plan an experiment to find out if all springs extend in the same way.

Balanced forces

Activity 8.5C
Help

The forces on an object are balanced when the forces are the same size and act in opposite directions.

You are going to think about balanced forces in the questions below.

1. The picture shows a boat about to float away down the river. Draw a force arrow showing where a rope must pull it to stop the boat floating off.

2. Here is a picture of Katrina floating on a lilo. The arrow shows her weight pulling her down. Draw a force arrow to show the balanced force that she needs from the water if she is not going to get wet.

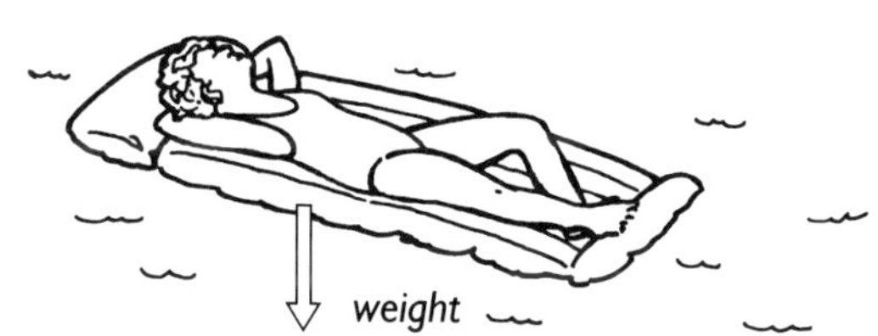

3. This book is not falling. There must be a force on it from the table. Draw an arrow to show the missing force.

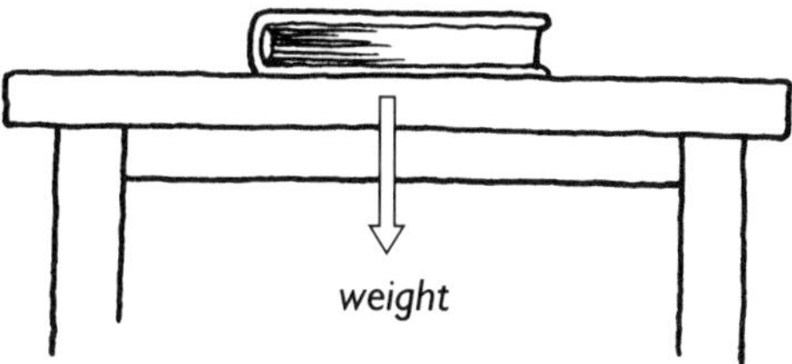

4. This parachutist is falling at a steady speed. Draw an arrow to show the force that is balancing his weight.

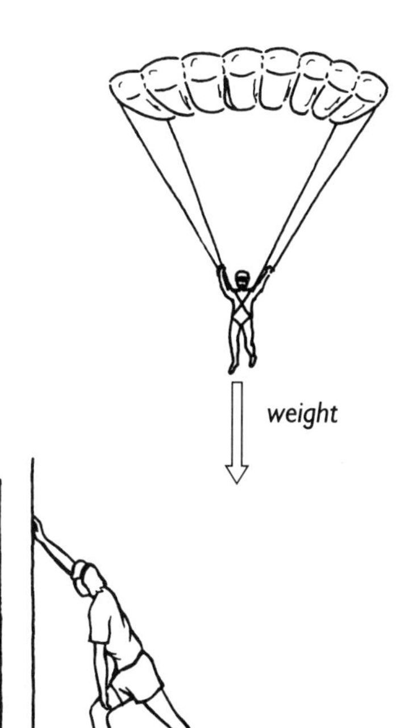

5. This athlete is pushing against a wall to stretch the muscles in her leg. Draw arrows that show her pushing force, and the balanced force from the wall that stops her falling over.

Speeding trolleys

Activity 8.6A
Core

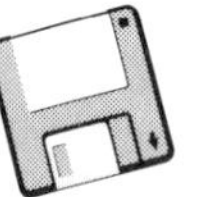

You are going to use light gates and datalogging software to measure the speed of a trolley travelling down a ramp. You are going to change the height of the ramp and see how this affects the speed of the trolley.

⚠ Keep feet and fingers away from speeding trolleys.

Support ramps carefully so they can't fall.

Do

1 Decide how you will record your results.

2 Set up the apparatus as shown in the diagram. You are going to measure the speed of the trolley.

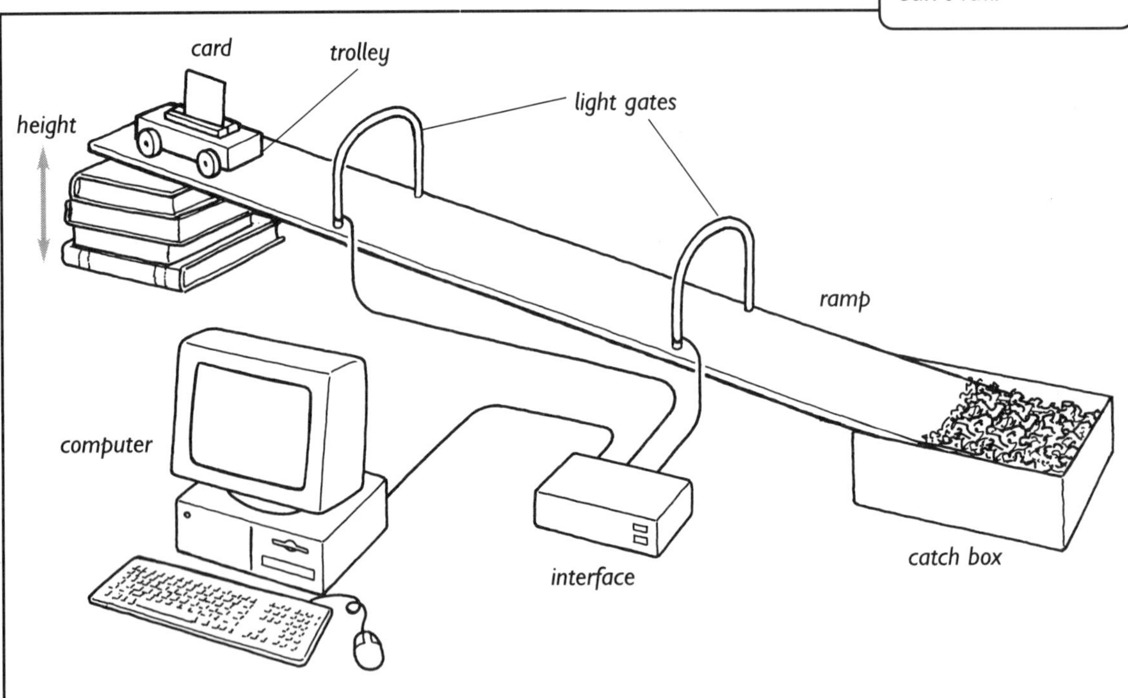

3 Start with the height of the ramp at 10 cm. Hold the trolley at the top of the ramp, let it go and the computer will measure its speed.

4 Repeat the experiment with ramp heights of 20 cm, 30 cm, 40 cm, 50 cm and 60 cm.

Analyse and conclude

❶ Draw a bar chart of your results (or your teacher may give you a printout).

❷ What happens to the speed of the trolley when the height of the slope is increased?

Evaluate

❸ Can you think of any improvements to this experiment?

Speed freak

Activity 8.6B
Core

The speed of an object can be found by using:

$$\text{speed} = \frac{\text{distance travelled}}{\text{time taken}}$$

Use the equation above to calculate the speed in the following questions. Make sure you give units with your answers.

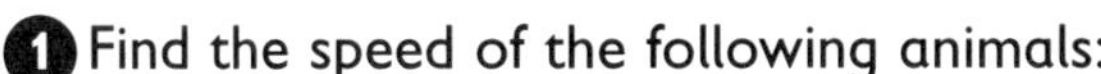

1. Find the speed of the following animals:
   - a cat that runs 20 metres in 2 seconds
   - a dog that walks 40 metres in 8 seconds
   - a kangaroo that jumps 800 metres in 10 seconds.

2. At the school sports day, Mark runs the 100 m in 10 s while James runs the 200 m in 25 s. Who was faster?

3. Find out the speed of each train in the table below. Which one is travelling the fastest?

Train	**Train A**	**Train B**	**Train C**
Journey	From Liverpool to London	From Leeds to London	From Ashford to London
Distance	240 km	200 km	60 km
Time taken	3 hours	2 hours	1.5 hours

4. A plane travels from Vienna to London, a distance of 800 km, in 75 minutes. What is the speed of the plane?

Life story

Unit map

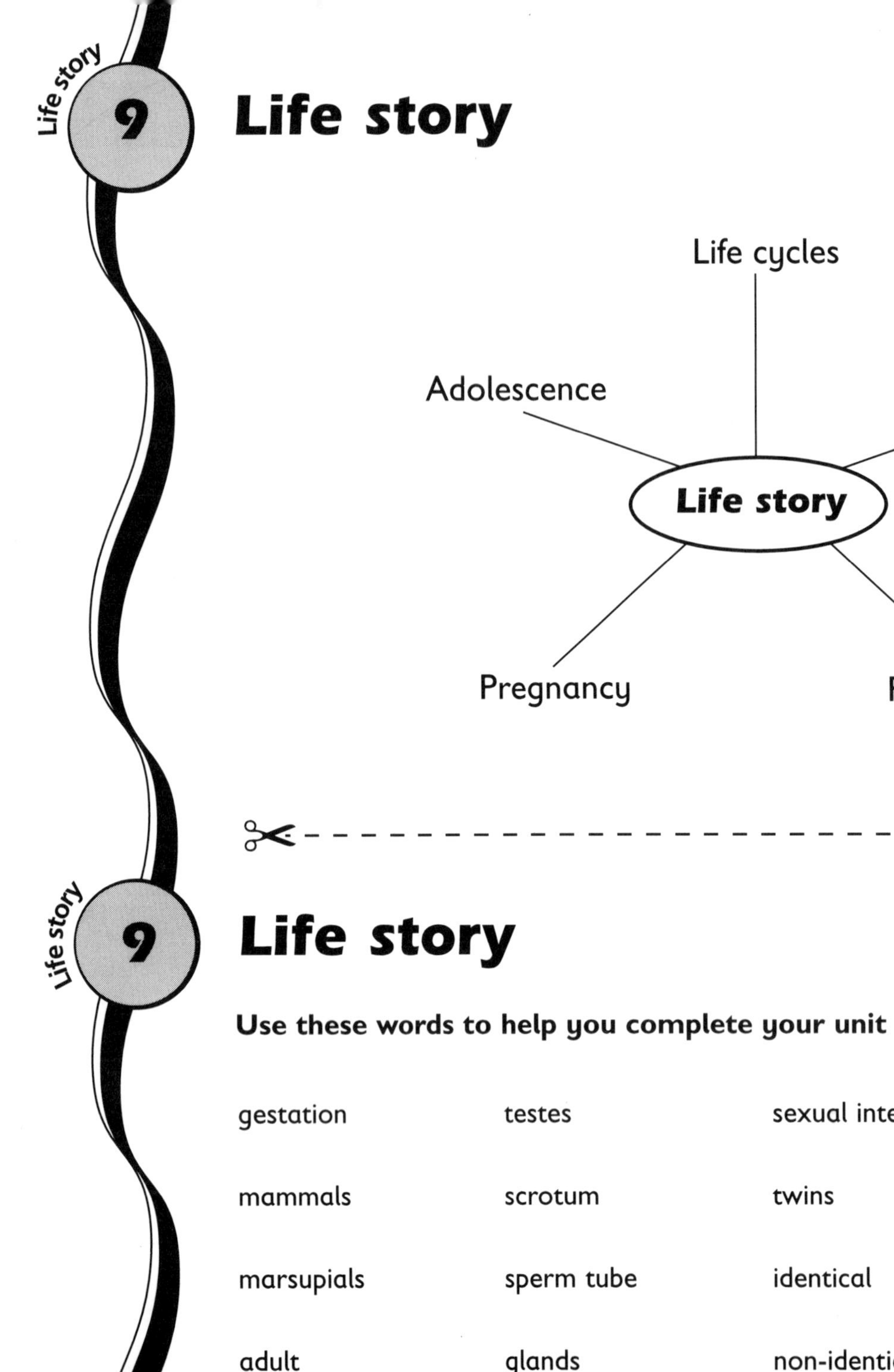

Life story

Unit map

Use these words to help you complete your unit map.

gestation	testes	sexual intercourse	birth
mammals	scrotum	twins	afterbirth
marsupials	sperm tube	identical	puberty
adult	glands	non-identical	hormones
baby	semen	infertility	testosterone
child	penis	implantation	oestrogen
adolescent	ovaries	embryo	menstrual cycle
male	oviducts	fetus	menopause
female	uterus	placenta	growth spurts
sperm	cervix	cord	
eggs	vagina	amnion	

9.1 Life cycles

Activity 9.1
Core

There are four main stages in the human life cycle. Each stage lasts for a different amount of time. You are going to compare the life cycles of a human and a penguin.

The four main stages in the human life cycle are shown below. They are in the wrong order.

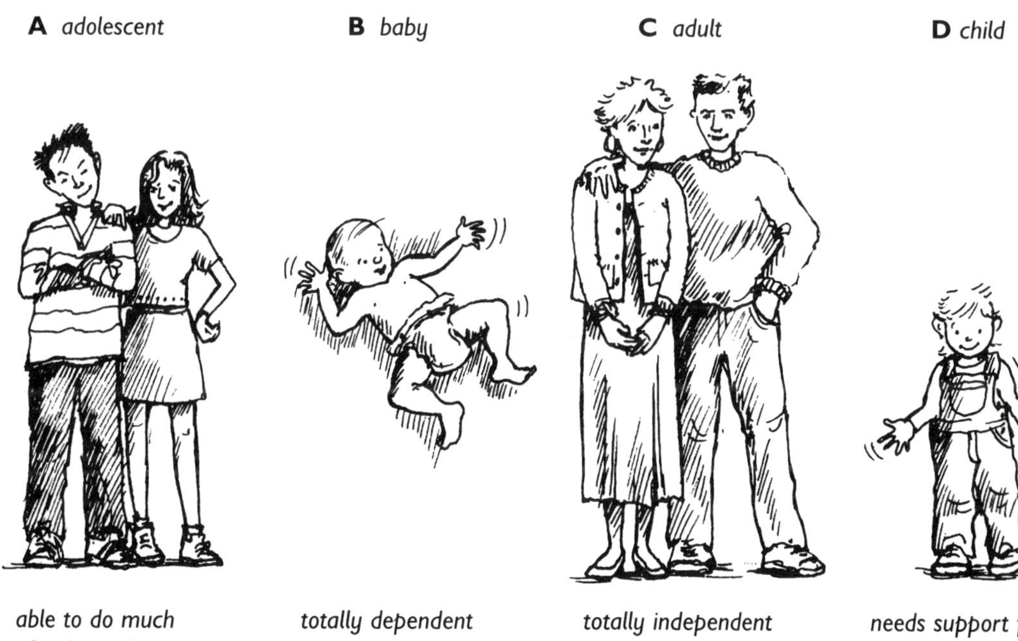

1 Work out the correct order of stages, then draw a life cycle for the human as a flow diagram.

Here is a time line for the life cycle of an Emperor penguin.

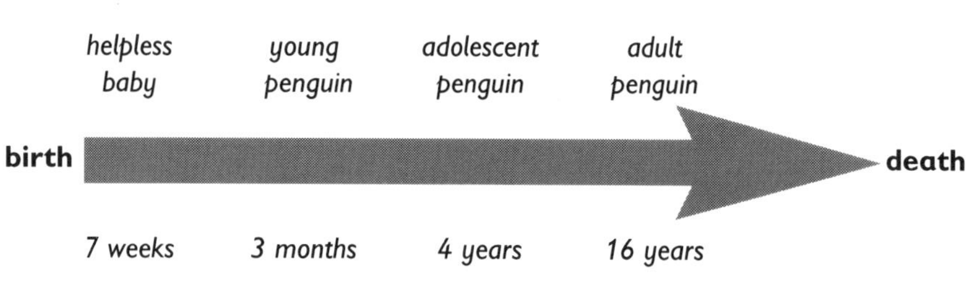

2 Draw a time line to show the four main stages in the human life cycle. Write below each stage the amount of time in years that it lasts.

3 Put an X where you are on the time line.

4 Compare your time line with the one for the penguin.

- What similarities are there? Describe them.
- What differences are there? Describe them.
- How do you think these differences help the human and the penguin?

Male parts

Activity 9.2A
Core

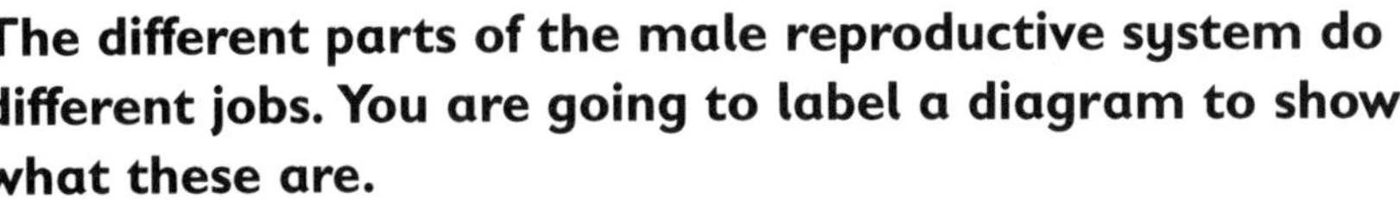

The different parts of the male reproductive system do different jobs. You are going to label a diagram to show what these are.

Copy and label the diagram below.

1. Write the name of each part of the system on the diagram.
2. Under each name, write a few words to describe what job it does.

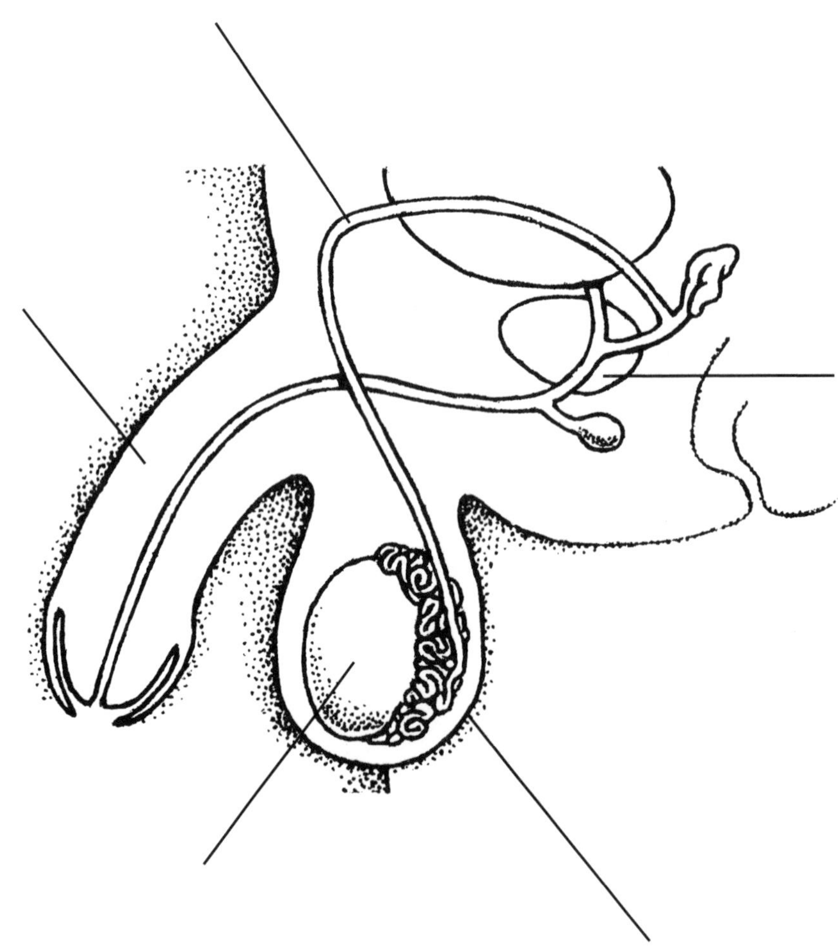

Male parts

The different parts of the male reproductive system do different jobs. You are going to label a diagram to show what these are.

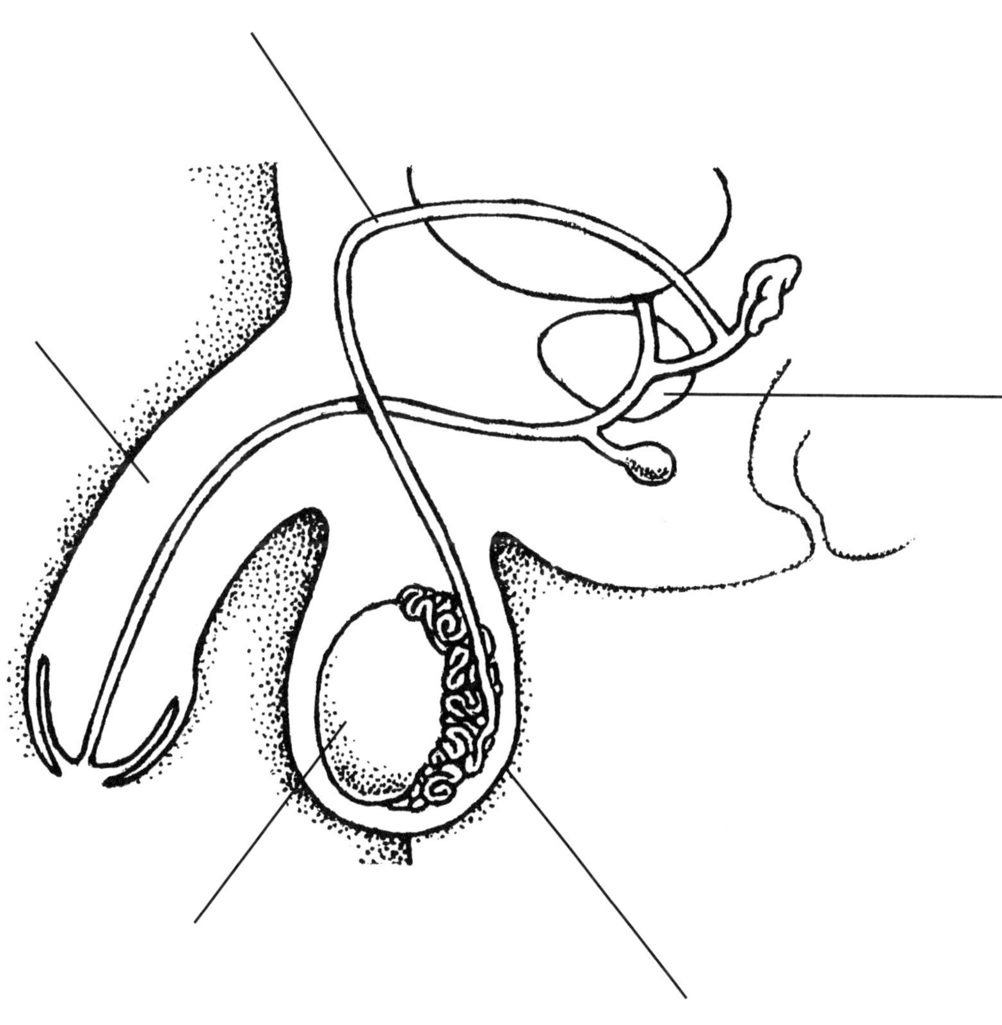

1. Use these words to label each part of the diagram.

   testis scrotum sperm tube penis glands

2. The boxes below describe what each part does. Cut out each box and stick it by the correct label.

carries sperm to the penis	carries sperm out of the body	where the sperm are made

add fluids to sperm to make semen	a bag of skin which holds the testes

Female parts

Core

You are going to label a diagram of the female reproductive system to show the different parts and what they do.

Copy and label the diagram below.

1. Write the name of each part of the system on the diagram.
2. Under each name, write a few words to describe what job it does.

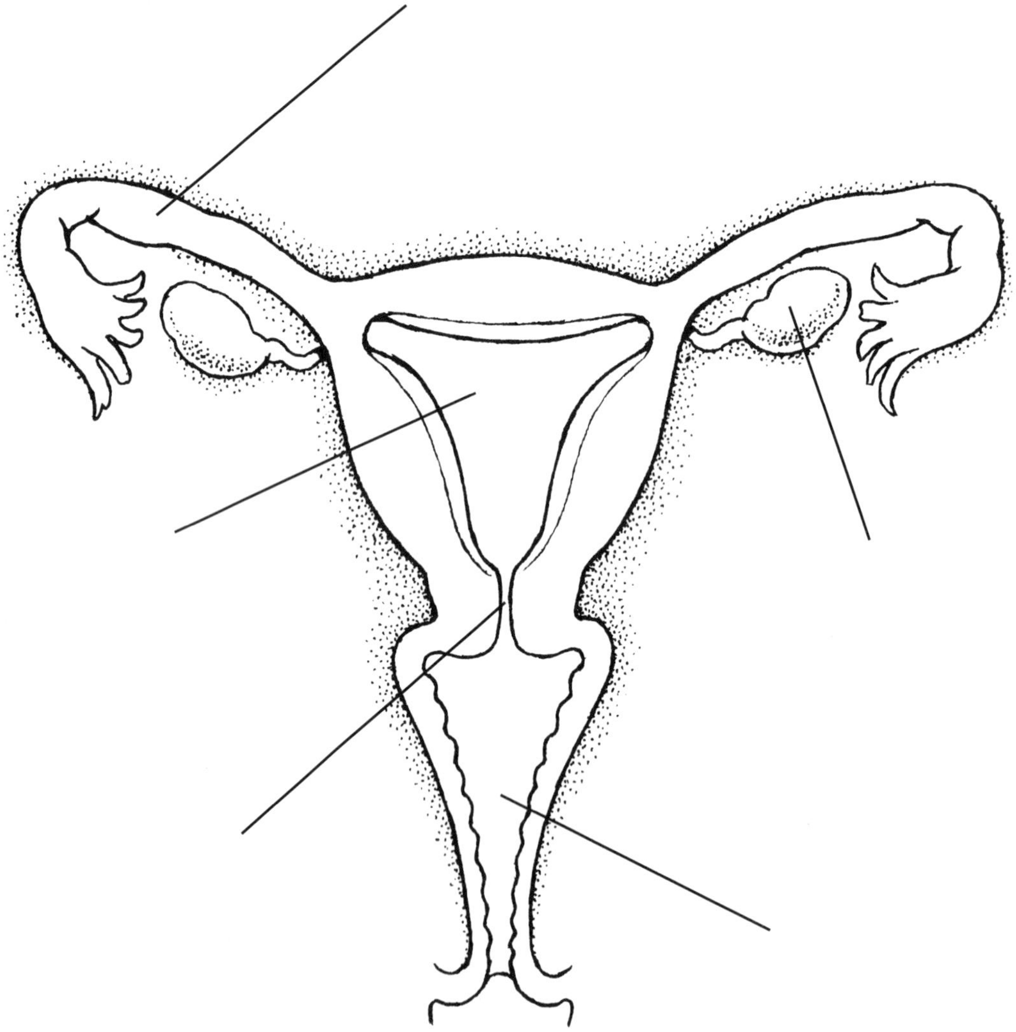

Female parts

You are going to label a diagram of the female reproductive system to show the different parts and what they do.

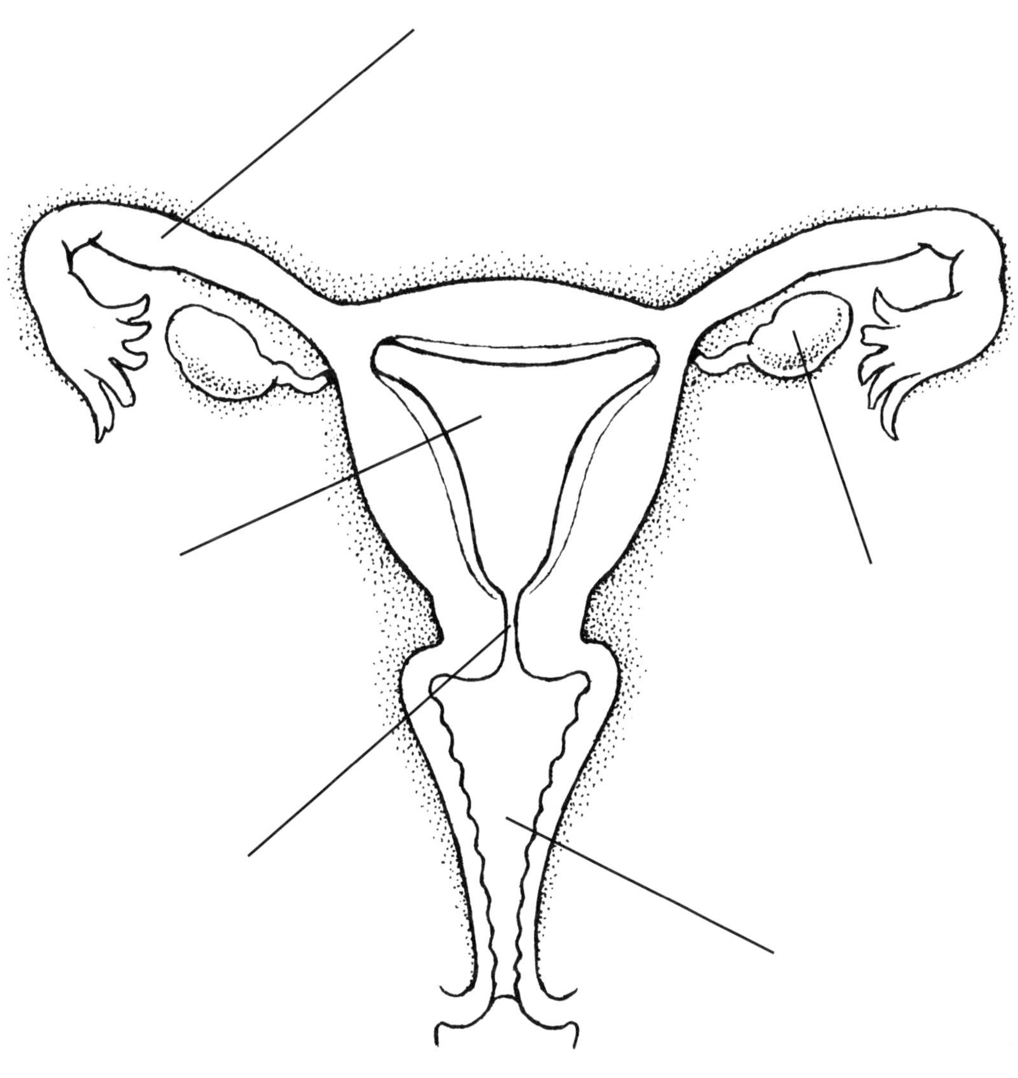

1. Use these words to label each part of the diagram.

uterus cervix oviduct ovary vagina

2. The boxes below describe what each part does. Cut out each box and stick it below the correct label.

the opening of the uterus	receives the sperm	where the eggs are made
carries the egg to the uterus	where the baby grows	

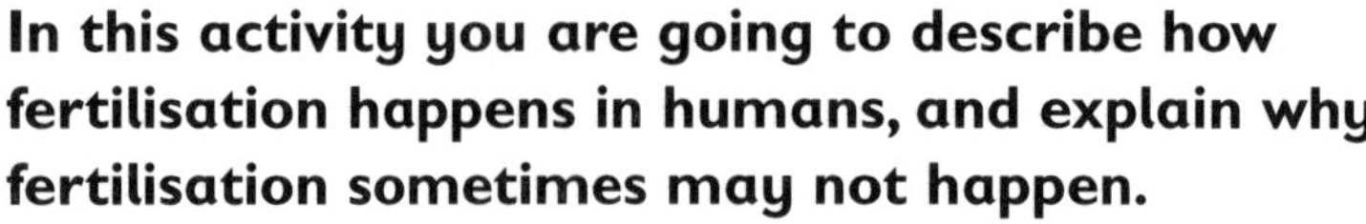

Fertilisation

In this activity you are going to describe how fertilisation happens in humans, and explain why fertilisation sometimes may not happen.

The statements below describe how fertilisation happens in humans. They have been mixed up.

1 Write out the statements in the correct order.

a The sperm start to swim from the vagina into the uterus. The sperm swim through the uterus and then into both oviducts.

b The nucleus of the sperm joins with the nucleus of the egg. This is called fertilisation. The fertilised egg will become a baby.

c When a man and a woman have sexual intercourse, the man's penis enters the woman's vagina.

d If there is an egg in the oviduct the sperm will surround it. The first sperm to reach the egg burrows into it.

e Sperm are released from the penis into the vagina.

Sometimes a couple find they are unable to have a baby. There may be something wrong with the male or the female reproductive system so fertilisation doesn't happen. This is called **infertility**.

Possible problems are:

- the man is not producing much sperm
- the woman's oviducts are blocked
- the woman is not making an egg every month.

2 Explain for each of these problems why fertilisation may not happen.

Sperm meets egg

In some animals the sperm meets the egg inside the female's body. In others, this takes place outside the body. You are going to compare animals with these different types of fertilisation.

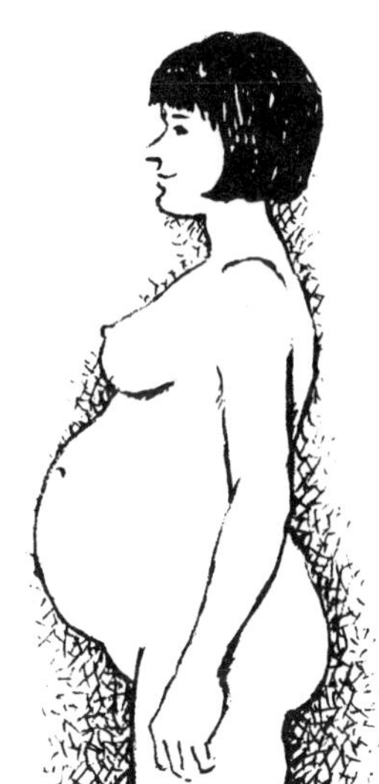

In humans, fertilisation takes place inside the woman's body. This is called **internal fertilisation**. The advantage of this is that there is a good chance of a sperm meeting the egg and a baby developing. The human looks after its offspring as it develops.

In some animals, such as frogs and fish, fertilisation takes place outside their bodies. This is called **external fertilisation**. The female frog produces many eggs so that there is a chance that some of these eggs will be fertilised. The frog does not look after its offspring. They develop independently.

This table shows the average number of eggs released at one time.

Animal	Type of fertilisation	Number of eggs
human	internal	1
cat	internal	4
frog	external	250
dog	internal	6
trout	external	5000
eagle	internal	2

1. Compare the number of eggs for each animal. Describe the relationship between the type of fertilisation and the number of eggs.
2. Why do you think a human needs only one egg at a time?
3. Why do you think a trout needs thousands of eggs?
4. Which of these animals look after their babies once they are born/hatched? Why might this affect the number of eggs they have?

Turtles have internal fertilisation, but lay over 100 eggs at a time. They bury their eggs in a beach and then leave them. When the babies hatch they have to make their own way to the water.

5. Why do you think the turtle lays so many eggs?

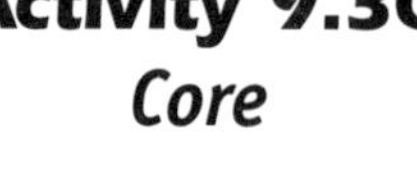

The sperm's story

To make a baby, a sperm must meet an egg to fertilise it. You are going to write a story about how this happens.

❶ Imagine you are a sperm. Write a story or make a strip cartoon about your journey to the egg to fertilise it. Use the ideas below to help you.

The Journey of a Sperm

Hello, my name is ... and I am a ...
I started my journey inside the ...
where it was ...
which is an ideal temperature for making ...
Then I swam up the ...
After that I ...
Once inside the vagina I ...
Finally I made it to the egg. I had to ...

Life story
9.3
C

The sperm's story

To make a baby, a sperm must meet an egg to fertilise it. You are going to write a story about how this happens.

❶ Imagine you are a sperm. Write a story or make a strip cartoon about your journey to the egg to fertilise it. Use the ideas below to help you.

The Journey of a Sperm

Hello, my name is ... and I am a ...
I started my journey inside the ...
where it was ...
which is an ideal temperature for making ...
Then I swam up the ...
After that I ...
Once inside the vagina I ...
Finally I made it to the egg. I had to ...

The fetus

Activity 9.4
Core

The human fetus takes about 9 months to develop fully. This is the time a woman is pregnant. You are going to label a diagram of a woman nearing the end of her pregnancy.

1 Label the diagram below.

- Write the name of each part.
- Write a few words to describe what each part does.

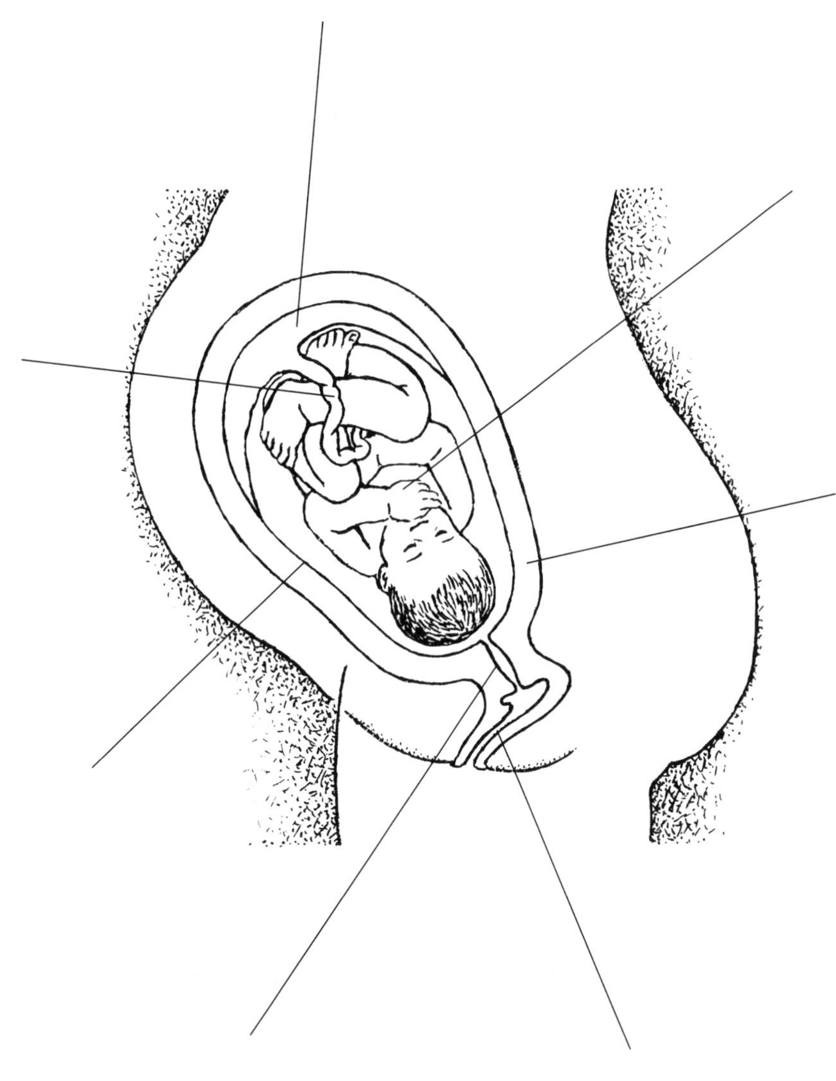

The fetus

Activity 9.4
Help

The human fetus takes about 9 months to develop fully. This is the time a woman is pregnant. You are going to label a diagram of a woman nearing the end of her pregnancy.

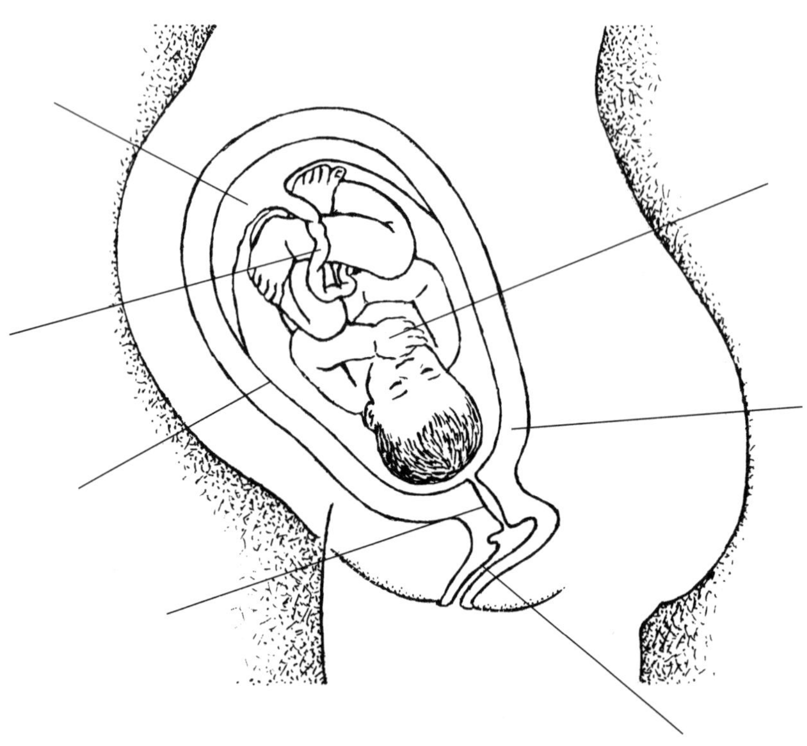

1 Use these words to label each part of the diagram.

fetus placenta cord amnion uterus cervix vagina

2 Use the same words to complete this table.

Name of part	Job of part
	protects the baby from bumps
	joins the placenta to the baby
	supplies the baby with food and oxygen
	place that feeds and shelters the baby
	the developing baby
	the baby is pushed out here
	ring of muscle at entrance of uterus which widens to let the baby out

9.4 The fetus

Activity 9.4
Extension

The human fetus takes about 9 months to develop fully. During this time, the mother's body is like a life support machine for the baby. You are going to describe the parts of the mother's body that perform this job.

1. Imagine you are a growing fetus. Write a description of the parts of the life support machine and how they work to help you live and grow.

   Use the diagram below to remind you of the parts that you need to describe.

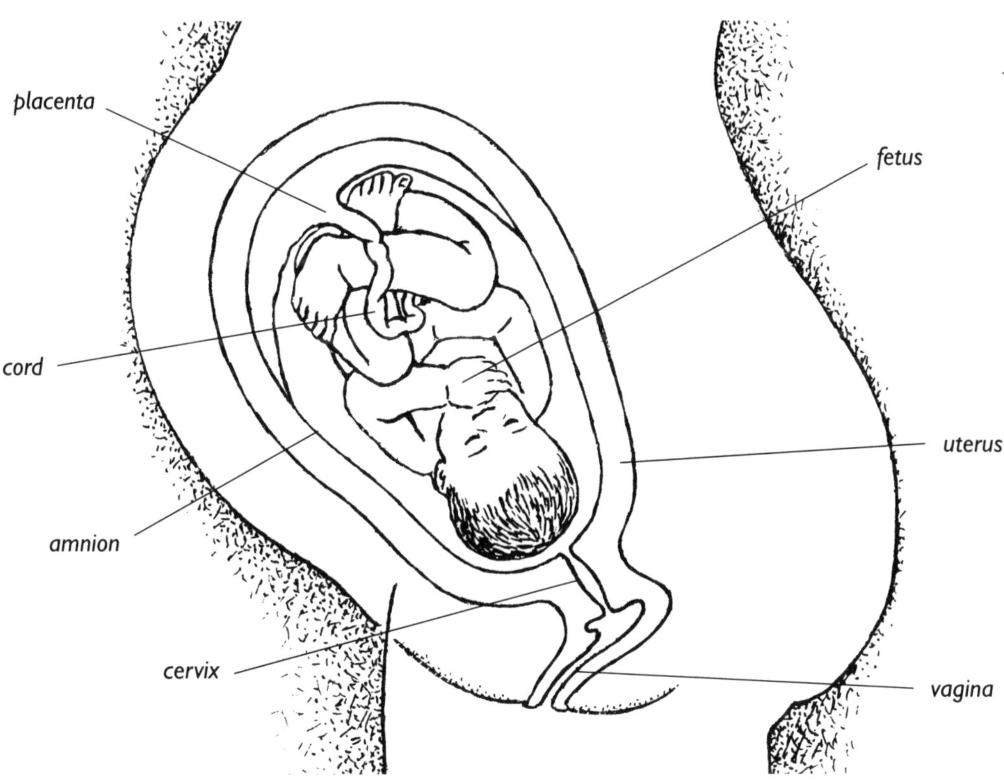

When babies are born before 39 works they may need special care. Babies that are born too early are called **premature**. They are put into an incubator machine that provides some of the same support as the mother's body.

2. List the things you think an incubator can provide in place of the mother. List the things it cannot provide.

Growth spurts

Activity 9.5
Core

Teenagers grow faster for a couple of years than they grew since being toddlers. This fast growth is called a growth spurt.

The graph below shows the average height of girls and boys today. You are going to analyse the information about girls and boys by answering the questions about the graph.

A graph can tell you how fast or slow something is happening. A steep line shows faster growth. A less steep line shows slower growth.

1. Between what ages are girls taller than boys?
2. At age 12 girls are taller than boys. At what age will boys be taller than girls again?
3. At age 6, how much taller are boys than girls?
4. At age 18, how much taller are boys than girls?
5. How much do girls grow between ages 16 and 18?
6. How much do boys grow between ages 16 and 18?
7. Who grows the most between ages 16 and 18?
8. At age $10\frac{1}{2}$ are girls or boys growing faster?
9. At age $13\frac{1}{2}$ are girls or boys growing faster?
10. At what age between 0 and 18 do girls and boys grow fastest?
11. The estimated average height data for a man aged 18 years in the 19th century is 165 cm. Why do you think this differs from the recently collected data above?

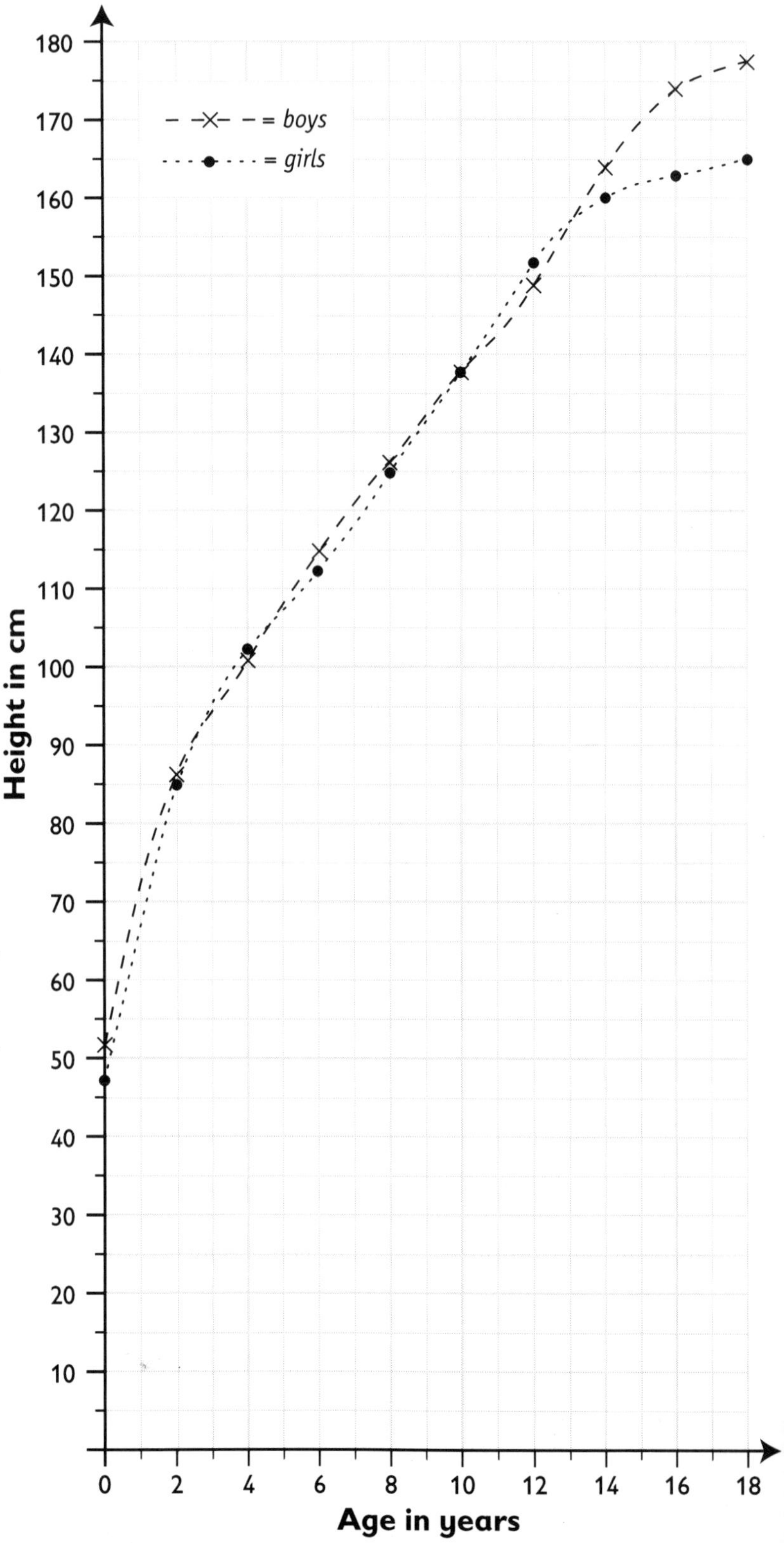

Safety in the lab

Skill sheet
1

Class 7Z is very noisy and careless. They never listen to what the teacher says. Here is a picture of them in the lab.

Make a table like the one below.

Hazard	Why it is dangerous?	What should be done instead?

1. Identify the different safety hazards there are in this lab. There are at least 17 of them to find. Write them in the left-hand column of your table.
2. Explain why each action is a hazard in the middle column.
3. Explain what they should do to make it safe in the right-hand column.

Lighting a Bunsen burner

Skill sheet
2

The diagram below shows the main parts of a Bunsen burner.

The Bunsen burner is attached to a gas supply by rubber tubing.

The gas is lit using a match or a splint.

Wear eye protection.

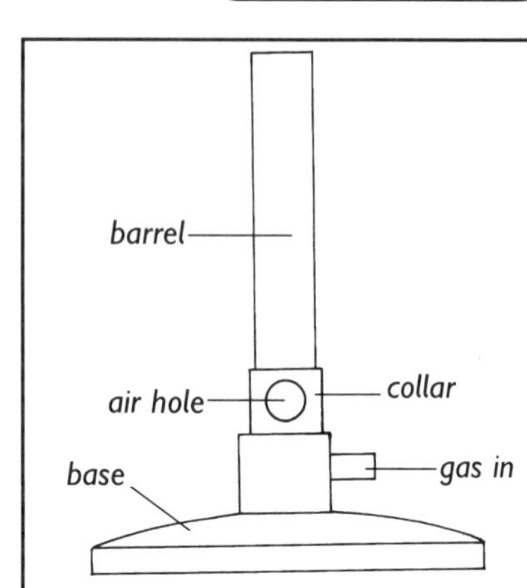

1 Place the Bunsen burner onto a heatproof mat.
2 Attach the rubber tubing firmly onto a gas tap.
3 Close the air hole completely.
4 Put on your eye protection.
5 Light a splint.
6 Turn on the gas tap.
   - Quickly light the gas with the splint.
   - Once a flame appears from the Bunsen burner, move your hand away quickly.
7 Turn the collar to get the correct flame for the experiment.
8 Always leave the air hole closed when you walk away from the Bunsen burner.

Lighting a Bunsen burner

Skill sheet
2

The diagram below shows the main parts of a Bunsen burner.

The Bunsen burner is attached to a gas supply by rubber tubing.

The gas is lit using a match or a splint.

Wear eye protection.

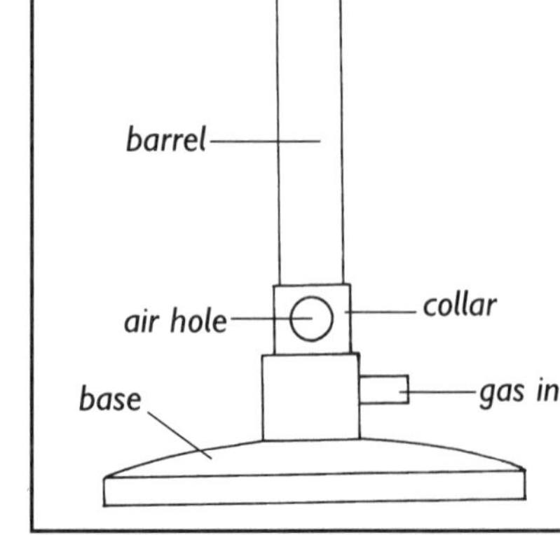

1 Place the Bunsen burner onto a heatproof mat.
2 Attach the rubber tubing firmly onto a gas tap.
3 Close the air hole completely.
4 Put on your eye protection.
5 Light a splint.
6 Turn on the gas tap.
   - Quickly light the gas with the splint.
   - Once a flame appears from the Bunsen burner, move your hand away quickly.
7 Turn the collar to get the correct flame for the experiment.
8 Always leave the air hole closed when you walk away from the Bunsen burner.

Heating substances

Skill sheet 3

Different flames are needed to heat different types of substances. The diagram below shows which flame should be used for heating solid substances and liquids with a Bunsen burner.

The diagram also shows the flame which must be left on when the Bunsen is not being used. This flame is called the safety flame. It looks yellow.

If the flame is too big, adjust the gas at the gas tap.

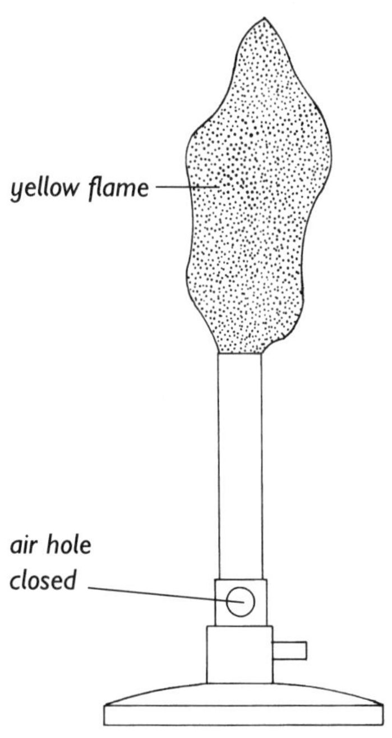

This is known as a safety flame and must not be used for heating substances.

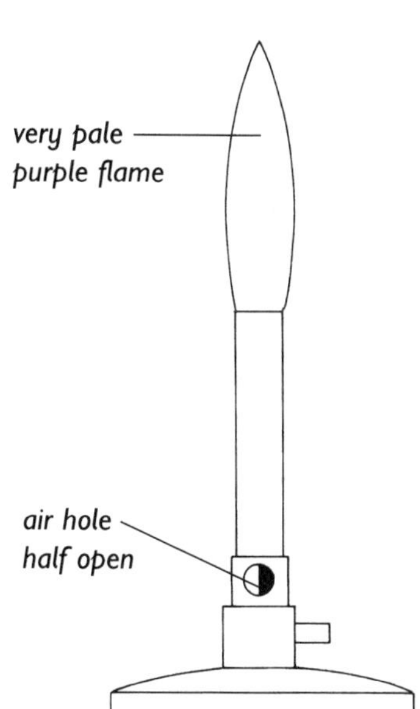

This flame can be used for heating most substances and it is always used for heating liquids.

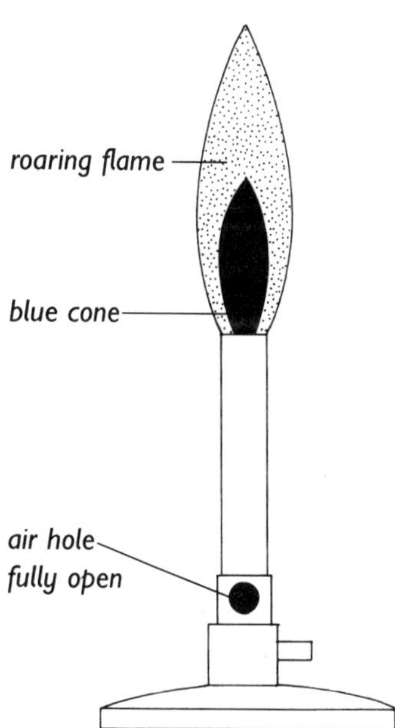

This is the hottest flame and is used to heat solids. The hottest part of the flame is just above the blue cone.

Heating solids

When you are heating solids in test tubes:

- hold the test tube with a test tube holder near the top of the tube
- heat at an angle as shown in the diagram
- do not point the tube towards anybody
- heat the tube for a short amount of time and check to see if anything is happening
- keep heating a little longer each time and keep on checking.

Heating liquids

When you are heating liquids in boiling tubes:

- fill the boiling tube no more than a third full
- use a boiling tube holder or clamp the tube
- heat at an angle as shown in the diagram
- do not point the tube towards anybody
- watch the liquid carefully and if it starts to boil remove the tube from the flame.

Energy transfer diagrams

Stored energy is shown using a box.

Energy stored in a stretched elastic band *as* ***strain energy***	*Energy stored in* the battery *as* ***chemical energy***	*Energy stored in* the sky diver *as* ***gravitational energy***

The words in the box tell you:

- where the energy is being stored
- what type of energy is being stored.

Energy being transferred is written on an arrow.

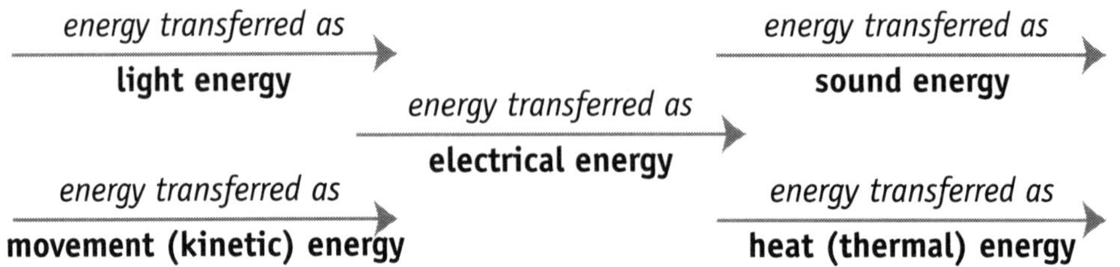

The arrow tells you:

- where the energy is coming from and where it is going.

The words tell you:

- what type of energy is being transferred.

Devices that transfer energy but do not store it are shown between arrows. Sometimes the energy is changed from one type to another in a device.

Energy transfer diagrams can branch. They can show more than one energy transfer.

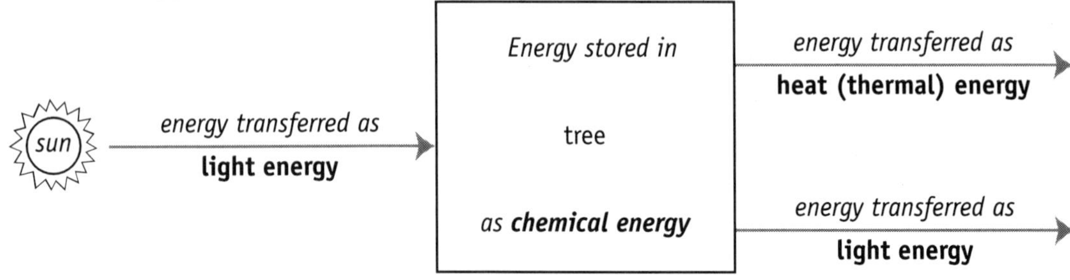

This energy transfer diagram shows:

- energy being transferred into a tree during photosynthesis
- the tree storing the energy
- the energy being released during burning.

5 Drawing charts and graphs

Choosing the right type of chart or graph

Ask yourself, 'What is the input variable?'

If it is a number that can have any value...
like 1.2, 4.8, 7.9, 16.8
... then you want a **line graph**.

*Variables like this are **continuous variables**.*

If it is has values ...
like red, green, blue
or tall, medium, short
or January, March, April
...then you want a **bar chart**.

*Variables like this are **discontinuous variables**.*

Which way round?

That is easy! The **input variable** (the thing you change) goes along the bottom and the **outcome variable** (the thing you measure) goes up the side.

Remember

- give the graph a title
- label the axes
- if there are units, put them on the axes
- make sure each point is in exactly the right place

Bar charts look like this:

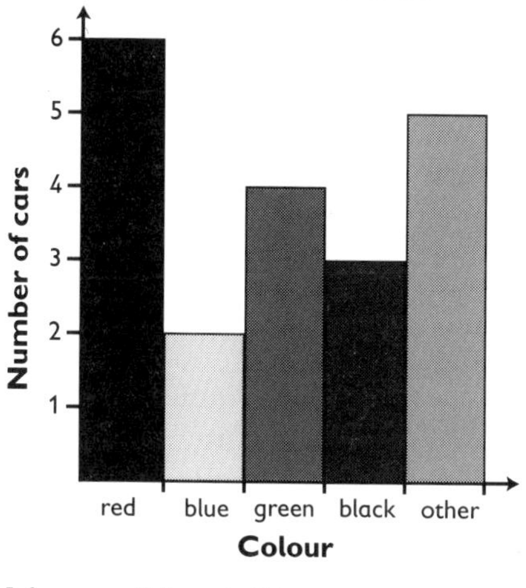

Line graphs look like this:

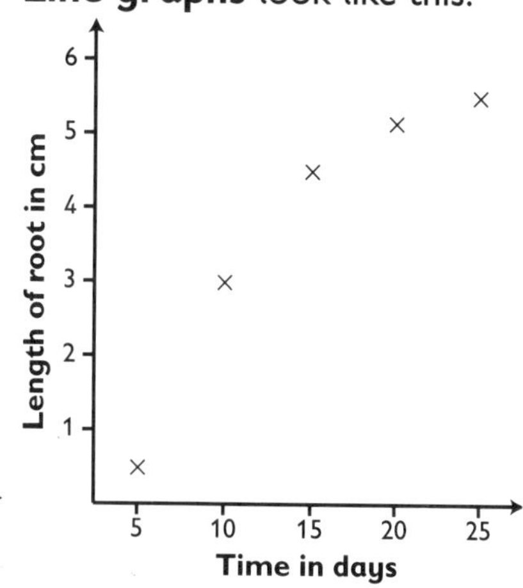

Lines of best fit

When you are drawing a line graph **do not join the crosses**. Instead, **look for the pattern**. The line of best fit should show the pattern. The pattern can be a straight line or a curve.

The pattern looks like a straight line:

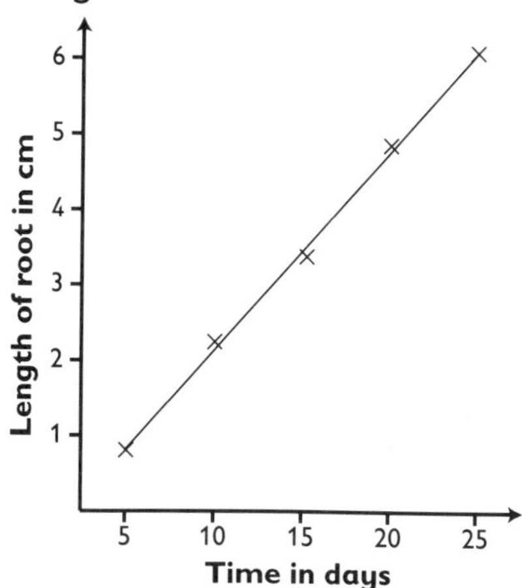

The pattern looks like a curve:

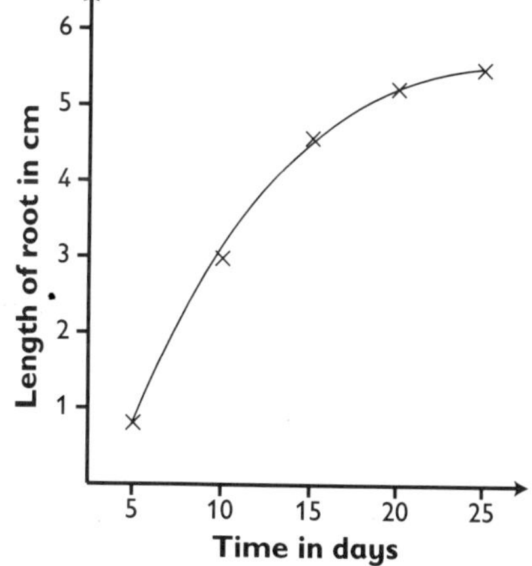

Interpreting graphs

Bar charts

Using the bar chart you can tell that:

- there are 6 red cars, 2 blue cars, 4 green cars, 3 black cars and 5 cars of other colours
- that there are 20 cars altogether (by adding up all the bars).

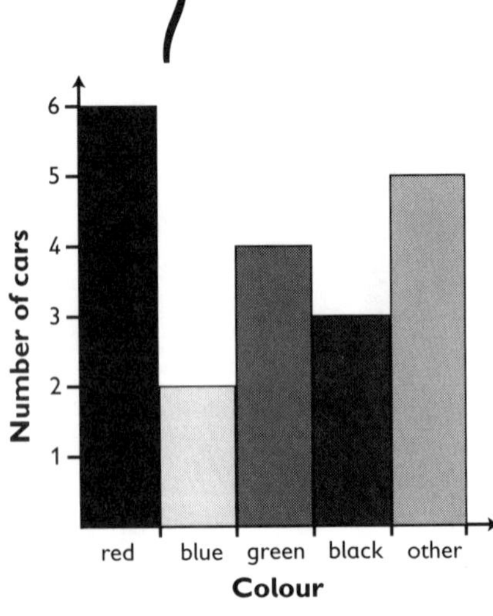

Line graphs

If there is a pattern to the line graph, then there is a relationship between the input variable and the outcome variable.

Using graph **A** you can tell that:

- as the time increases, the distance increases
- the straight line slopes upwards
- the slope of the line stays the same
- when the time increases by 5 s, the distance always increases by about 10 m.

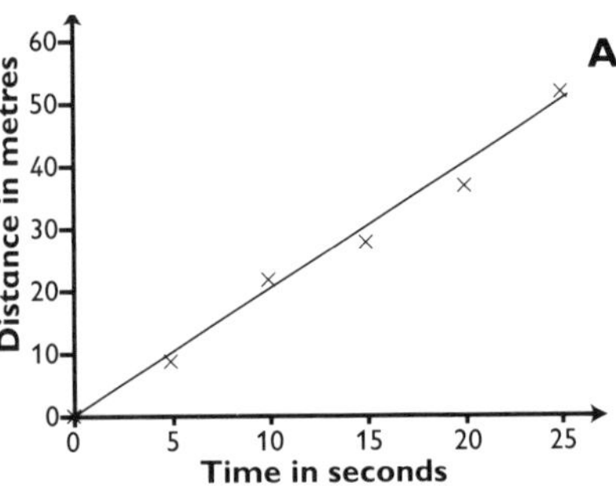

Using graph **B** you can tell that:

- as the time increases, the distance increases
- the curve slopes upwards
- the slope increases as the time increases
- at the beginning, when the time increases by 5 s the distance increases by about 2.5 m
- at the end, when the time increases by 5 s the distance increases by about 20 m.

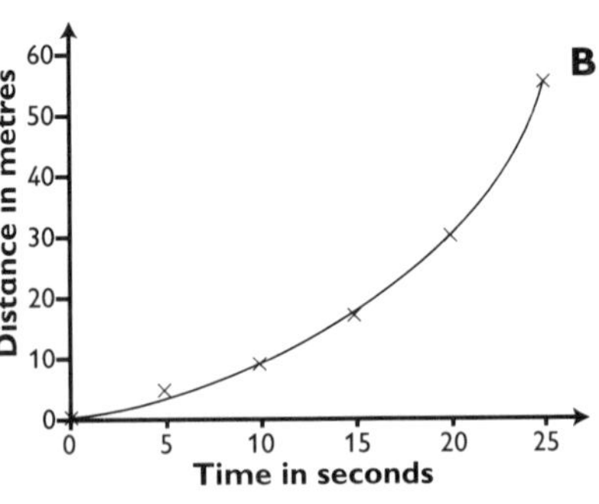

Using graph **C** you can tell that:

- as the time increases, the speed decreases
- the straight line slopes downwards
- the slope of the line stays the same
- when time increases by 5 seconds, the speed always decreases by about 10 m/s.

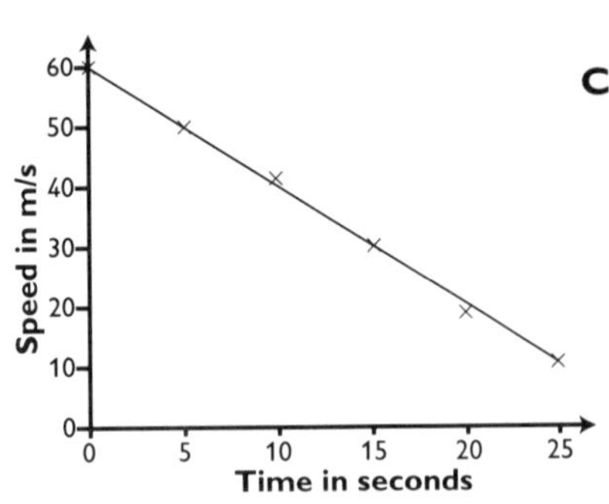

Using graph **D** you can tell that:

- as the volume increases, the pressure decreases
- the curve slopes downwards
- the slope decreases as the volume increases
- at the beginning, when the volume increases by $5\,m^3$ the pressure decreases by about 20 Pa
- at the end, when the volume increases by $5\,m^3$ the pressure decreases by 2 Pa.

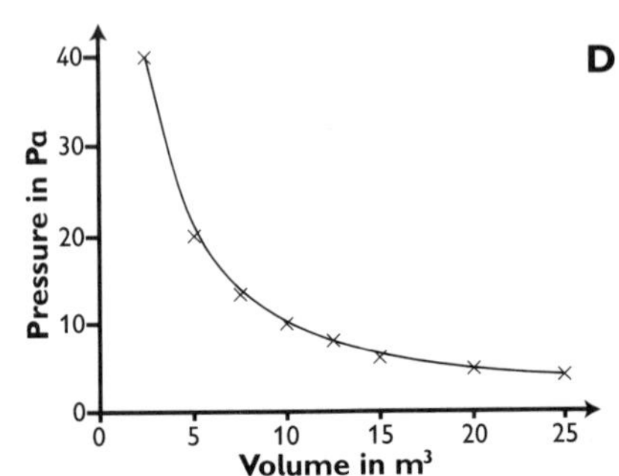

7 Word equations

Word equations are used to show chemical reactions.

You start with... You end up with...

methane + oxygen → carbon dioxide + water

The substances you start with are put on the left.

A plus sign is put between the substances.

These substances are called **reactants**.

The arrow shows the chemical reaction happening.

The substances you end up with are put on the right.

Again, a plus sign is put between the substances.

These substances are called **products**.

Some common reactions

- Burning magnesium:
  magnesium + oxygen → magnesium oxide
- Photosynthesis:
  carbon dioxide + water → glucose + oxygen
- Respiration:
  glucose + oxygen → carbon dioxide + water
- Neutralising acid:
  hydrochloric acid + sodium hydroxide → sodium chloride + water
- Displacing copper:
  copper sulphate + zinc → zinc sulphate + copper

Using a microscope

Microscopes are very delicate pieces of equipment. They are easy to break and expensive to mend! You must be very careful when using one. Make sure you carry it around properly and never touch the glass of the lenses.

⚠ Take care!
Be very careful with microscopes.
Do not reflect sunlight up through the microscope.

Looking at your slides

1 Turn the lenses so that the shortest lens (one with the lowest number) is pointing down at the stage.

light goes into your eye

eyepiece lens

4 Before you look down the microscope, move the lens nearest the slide down until it is just above the slide.

objective lenses of different strengths (make things look bigger)

focusing knobs

2 Place your slide on the stage. Hold it in place with the metal clips.

5 Look down the eyepiece and slowly turn the focusing knob so that the lens moves **away** from the slide.

3 Arrange the lamp/mirror so that light shines up through the hole in the stage.

6 Carefully focus until you get a clear picture.

mirror or light source (depends on type of microscope)

stage

clip to hold slide in place on the stage

Looking closer

7 To look at cells in more detail you need to use a higher magnification. Turn the lenses until the middle lens is pointing down at the stage.

8 Turn the fine focusing knob to get a clear picture.

Writing frame:
Plan an investigation

Skill sheet
9

Title ...

The aim of this activity is to ...

I am trying to find out ...

What I think will happen is ...

I think this will happen because ...

I am going to need ...

For safety reasons, I will ...

I will set up my equipment like this ...
(attach any diagrams)

Fair testing is important, so the things I will keep the same are ...

During the activity, I will look for ...

I will count ...

I will measure ...

The number of measurements I will take is ...

I will repeat my experiment to...

Writing frame: Report an investigation

Title …

Method

The aim of this activity was to …

Firstly, I …

Then, I …

My reason for doing this was …

Finally, I …

Results

(attach your tables and graphs)

Analyse and conclude

I have found out …

What I thought would happen was …

If I compare my results with my prediction, I can see that …

My graph shows that …

This is because …

Evaluate

I found it easy to …

Although, it was hard to …

My results …

A more accurate way of doing this experiment would be …

If I had more time, I would …

Writing frame: Explanation

Skill sheet
11

Title …

The process/device I am going to explain is designed to …

At the first stage, the …

Next the …

This is followed by …

Finally …

Writing frame: Event

Title …

It was …

The weather was …

We began …

Next, we …

Interestingly, …

Later in the day …

Finally …

I thought the day was …

Writing frame: Debate

Title …

We think that …

The arguments for are …

Our research shows that …

On the other hand …

The information supporting this can be found …

We have seen that …

The evidence clearly points to the conclusion that …

Writing frame: Discussion

Title …

The issue is …

The points for are …

The points against are …

We have heard that …

The view of most people is that …

Writing frame: Research

Skill sheet
15

The topic I am researching is …

Questions I need to answer are …	Answers	Extra details	Source

Writing frame: Timeline

Date:
Person/event:

Date:
Person/event:

Date:
Person/event:

Date:
Person/event:

Date:
Person/event:

Date:
Person/event:

What does energy mean to you?

KS2 precursor concepts	*Science PoS*
Although not covered at KS2, pupils will know from everyday experience that energy has something to do with running about, with food and with fuels.	–

Activity	*Description*	*Differentiation*
	Energy circus – A circus of four activities. **A: Energy from food** – A selection of foods for pupils to divide into 'high energy' and 'low energy' foods. **B: Energy in fuel** – Heating water in a boiling tube for 1 minute with a candle. **C: Energy to run** – One student runs on the spot while another saunters on the spot for 1 minute. **D: Energy to lift** – One student lifts as many sandbags as possible from floor to bench, while another lifts one sandbag every 5 seconds for the same time.	Core

Setting the scene

This spread introduces 'energy' as a word in everyday use. The **unit map** can be used to help brainstorm key words and ideas about the unit topics.

Answers to book questions

Red book

a e.g. chocolate, Lucozade, milk, meat, butter, oil
b e.g. carrots, celery, apple, cucumber, grapefruit
c e.g. coal, oil, natural gas, petrol, wood
d hot, sweaty, tired
e running the marathon
f e.g. bricklaying, scaffolding, building, working in a laundry, nursing, postal delivery, furniture removals
g lifting ten bricks
h e.g. hotplate, fire, kettle, boiling water
i use a thermometer
j e.g. candle, Bunsen burner, torch, fire, firework
k e.g. turn off lights when not in the room
l shout, sing, beat drums, turn rattles

1 a burning match (A), star (C)
b whistle (B), kettle (E)
c burning match (A), kettle (E)
d runner (F), pole-vaulter (G), bricklayer (H)
e kettle (E)
f chocolate bar (D), sweet (I)
g pole-vaulter (G), bricklayer (H)

2 –

Green book

a e.g. chocolate, Lucozade, milk, meat, butter, oil
b e.g. coal, oil, natural gas, petrol, wood
c hot, sweaty, tired
d e.g. bricklaying, scaffolding, building, working in a laundry, nursing, postal delivery, furniture removals
e e.g. people, bath, water, cup of tea, radiator
f e.g. candle, Bunsen burner, torch, fire, firework
g e.g. stereo, TV, computer, hairdryer, microwave
h shout, sing, beat drums, turn rattles

1 burning match (A), star (C)
2 whistle (B), kettle (E)
3 burning match (A), kettle (E)
4 runner (F), pole-vaulter (G), bricklayer (H)
5 kettle (E)
6 chocolate bar (D), sweet (I)
7 pole-vaulter (G), bricklayer (H)

Activity 1.1
Extension

Energy circus

Purpose

To get pupils thinking about energy, through a series of simple activities.

Running the activities

Divide the class into eight groups. Have two stations for each activity. Rotate every 5 minutes. This is only an elicitation activity; it should not take more than 20–25 minutes. The activities relate to the first four sections of the book spread. Alternatively, elect a group to do each activity and then report back to the class.

Expected outcomes

Pupils develop an appreciation that energy is involved in many processes.

Pitfalls

Make sure pupils muddle the different foods before the next group arrives. **(1.1A)**

Safety notes

Warn pupils that no food should be consumed in a laboratory. **(1.1A)**
Remind pupils doing **1.1B** to wear eye protection and beware of the hot apparatus, particularly as the apparatus may be hot when they arrive at that station.
Asthmatics may have to take care when taking strenuous exercise. **(1.1C, 1.1D)**

What is energy?

Key ideas	*Science PoS*
Things that move have energy. We call this kinetic/movement energy. Energy given out as light is called light energy. Energy given out as sound is called sound energy. Energy that warms is called thermal/heat energy.	1.2c, 4.5e

Activity	*Description*	*Differentiation*
	A: Energy out! – A display of objects about the room. Pupils decide if the objects are giving out light energy, sound energy or heat energy, or whether they are moving.	Core
	B: Energy everywhere! – Linked to questions **c** and **d** (red book) or e and f (green book). Alternative or additional.	Core

Answers to book questions

Red book

a i light energy – e.g. candle, electric light bulbs, Sun, stars, fire, TVs

ii sound energy – e.g. humans, musical instruments, bells, whistles, radios, TVs

iii thermal energy – e.g. fire, Sun, radiators, cookers, irons

b –

c –

1 a sound energy – e.g. people, TV, radio

b light energy – e.g. lights

c kinetic energy – e.g. people, video recorder

d thermal energy – e.g. people, TV, video recorder, radiator

2 a e.g. people, animals

b e.g. fire, Sun

c e.g. people, animals, thrown objects such as spears and stones

d e.g. fire, people, animals

3 no machines or electric devices in Stone Age village

Green book

a the skater is moving

b we see light and are warmed by it

c we hear a sound

d it warms the clothes, we can feel the heat from it

e –

f –

1 a the TV gives out light energy, sound energy and heat energy

b a kettle gives out heat energy and sound energy

c the hands of the clock move and it may tick (make a sound)

2 it moves
it makes a sound
it lights up the room and warms us

3 a e.g. people, animals

b e.g. fire, Sun

c e.g. people, animals, thrown objects such as spears and stones

d e.g. fire, people, animals

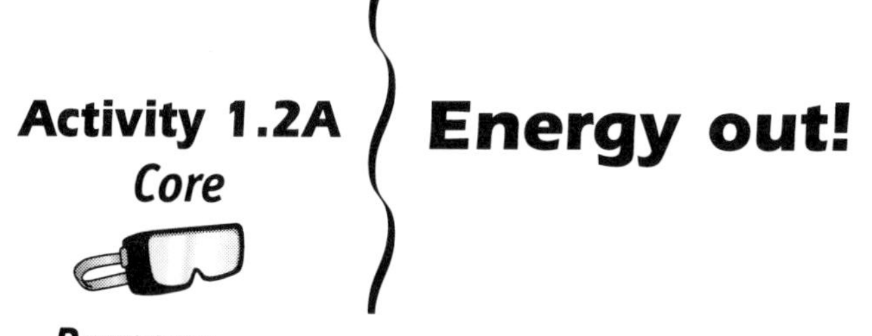

Activity 1.2A Core — Energy out!

Purpose

For pupils to appreciate through observation that energy is given out whenever something happens.

Running the activity

Objects should be spread about the room, each with an appropriate instruction card. For example:

- a ball to drop
- a spinning top to spin
- matches to strike (one at a time!)
- lights in the room
- a lit Bunsen burner
- a kettle to boil some water
- a bell to strike
- musical instruments, such as a guitar to pluck a string
- a toy to wind up
- a battery torch to switch on and off
- a lit candle
- the Sun out of the window
- a hot water bottle to feel
- a whistle to blow (and disinfect afterwards)
- a tray of marbles to tip and roll

Pupils make a table as shown on the activity sheet.

Expected outcomes

Pupils develop an appreciation that energy is given off by a large range of devices.

Safety notes

Anything blown into should be disinfected after use.
Beware of hot objects like Bunsen burners and matches.

Activity 1.2B Core — Energy everywhere!

Purpose

For pupils to identify movement, light, sound and heat energy.

Running the activity

Pupils look at a picture and list different types of energy.
Less able pupils may find it helpful to colour code the different types of energy directly onto their sheets. They can put in a key in the space below the questions.

Answers

1. Stars and Moon (if night), Sun (if day), light bulbs. Some pupils may mention other items they have seen at fairs, e.g. flames, burning cigarettes and chemiluminescent plastic jewellery.
2. People, loud speakers, carriages rushing through the air, squeaky machinery, surfaces rubbing together.
3. Sun (if day), light bulbs, people, machinery, surfaces rubbing together.
4. People, carriages on all rides, spinning carousel, the train in the ghost ride, big wheel, children coming down the helter skelter, carriages on roller coaster.

Energy on the move

Key ideas	Science PoS
Energy can be moved from place to place. We say that the energy is transferred. Energy transfers can be shown using energy transfer diagrams. Energy carried by electricity is called electrical energy.	4.5e

Activity	Description	Differentiation
	A: Energy in, energy out – Identifying energy being transferred out of electrical devices.	Core
	B: Move it! – Drawing energy transfer diagrams.	Core, Help, Extension

Other relevant material

Skill sheet 4: Energy transfer diagrams

ICT opportunities

CD-ROMs: Biography of James Prescott Joule in *Eyewitness Science Encyclopedia 2.0* (DK Multimedia) and in *Encarta 95* (Microsoft).

Answers to book questions

Red book

a **i** camera film, eyes
ii microphone, ears
iii thermometer, skin

b iron – thermal energy
radio – sound energy
drill – kinetic energy and sound energy
cooker – thermal energy

c —(electrical energy)→ *cooker* —(thermal energy)→

d —(electrical energy)→ *TV* —(sound energy)→ / —(light energy)→ / —(thermal energy)→

1 —(electrical energy)→ *hairdryer* —(sound energy)→ / —(kinetic energy)→ / —(thermal energy)→

2 —(electrical energy)→ *washing machine* —(sound energy)→ / —(kinetic energy)→ / —(thermal energy)→

3 —(kinetic energy)→ *dynamo* —(electrical energy)→ *lamp* —(light energy)→

Green book

a light energy – camera film, eyes
sound energy – microphone, ears
heat energy – thermometer, skin

b see red book answer **b** (less able pupils will use 'heat' and 'movement' energy)

c see red book answer **c** (less able pupils will use 'heat' energy)

1 Energy is carried into the hairdryer by *electricity*. We call this *electrical* energy. The hairdryer gives out air, which has *movement* energy and *heat* energy. The hairdryer also gives out *sound* energy.

2 see red book answer **1** (less able pupils will use 'heat' energy and 'movement' energy)

3 see red book answer **d** (less able pupils will use 'heat' energy)

Activity 1.3A Core

Energy in, energy out

Purpose

To prepare pupils to write energy transfers by observing them.

Running the activity

Spread mains electrical devices about the room. For example:

- a desk lamp
- an iron/soldering iron
- a radio or cassette player
- a fan
- a room heater
- curling tongs/hair styling brush

Pupils observe energy transfers and fill in a table as given on the activity sheet.

Expected outcomes

Pupils complete the table and prepare to begin writing energy transfers.

Pitfalls

Do not use a food processor, tumble dryer, television or electric kettle as these are used in the next activity.

Safety notes

All hot objects require a warning notice: **WARNING – HOT**
Do not use any electrical device which could trap fingers or cut.

Energy 1.3 B

Move it!

Activity 1.3B
Core, Help, Extension

Purpose

To introduce written energy transfers, applying what pupils learned in **1.3A** to some different domestic appliances.

Running the activity

Pupils complete some given energy transfer diagrams. In addition, they could also draw their own energy transfer diagrams for some of the other devices recorded in the previous activity.

Core and Extension: Pupils copy and complete diagrams.

Help: Pupils write on the sheets to complete the diagrams.

Other relevant material

Skill sheet 4: Energy transfer diagrams

Expected outcomes

Pupils feel confident about trying to draw their own energy transfer diagrams.

Pitfalls

Copying and completing the energy transfer diagrams could be laborious. If you do not want to re-use the sheets for another class, you may find it easier for all pupils to write the answers directly onto their sheets.

Answers

Core: Missing words are as follows:

1 a movement
b electrical, movement, heat, sound
c electrical, TV
d electrical, energy transferred as heat energy, as sound energy, as movement energy

Help: Missing words are as follows:

1 a electrical
b movement
c electrical, movement, heat, sound

Extension: Missing words are as follows:

1 a kinetic, sound, thermal
b electrical, kinetic, thermal, sound
c electrical, TV
d electrical, energy transferred as thermal energy, as sound energy, as kinetic energy

Stored energy

Key ideas	*Science PoS*
Energy stored because a material is being pulled or pushed is called strain energy. Energy stored in fuels, food or batteries is called chemical energy. Energy stored in something because it is lifted up is called gravitational energy	1.2 cmp, 4.5e

Activity	*Description*	*Differentiation*
	A: Stored energy – Deciding how energy is stored in different objects.	Core
	B: Cotton reel racers – Finding out how much energy can be stored in an elastic band.	Core, Help

Other relevant material

Skill sheet 4: Energy transfer diagrams

Answers to book questions

Red book

a e.g. rubber band, spring, ball, bow, catapult

b e.g. food, petrol, oil, coal, wood

c The skier is lifted up by the ski lift.

d A, strain energy

e C

f The energy is in the girl as kinetic energy.

g

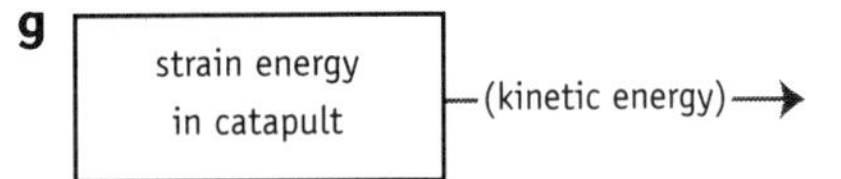

h When the catapult is pulled back as far as it will go.

1 a strain energy

b gravitational energy

c chemical energy

d gravitational energy

e chemical energy

f strain energy

2

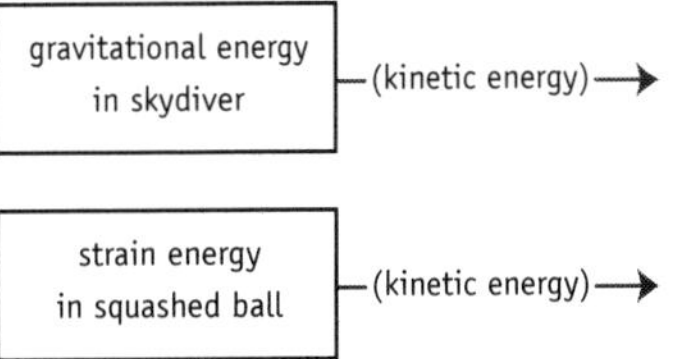

gravitational energy in skydiver → (kinetic energy)

strain energy in squashed ball → (kinetic energy)

Green book

a e.g. rubber band, spring, ball, bow, catapult

b The skier is lifted up by the ski lift.

c A

d strain energy

e C

f gravitational energy

g B

1 a gravitational energy

b chemical energy

c strain energy

2 skydiver – movement energy

firework – light energy, heat energy, sound energy, movement energy

squashed ball – movement energy

3 See red book answer **2** (less able pupils will use 'heat' and 'movement' energy)

Stored energy

Activity 1.4A
Core

Activity notes

Purpose

To consider how and where energy is stored, through a series of demonstrations.

Running the activity

A series of mini-demonstrations are placed around the room and pairs of pupils tour them, guided by their activity sheets.
Alternatively, the teacher could demonstrate from the front of the class, whereupon larger demonstrations may be desirable.

Expected outcomes

Pupils complete a table, as shown on the activity sheet.

Safety notes

Pupils should wear eye protection for demonstrations with stretched elastic bands (cotton reel racer).

Energy 1.4 B

Cotton reel racers

Activity 1.4B
Core, Help

Purpose

To allow pupils to develop their ideas about stored energy in a enjoyable context.

Running the activity

Pupils work in small groups to develop and test a cotton reel racer, as shown on their activity sheets. Then as a class they race their cotton reel racers in a Derby, where the distance covered and movement time are measured and recorded.

Core: Pupils are given some guidance at each stage.

Help: Pupils are told what to do, and record their results on the sheet.

Expected outcomes

Pupils record the characteristics of their cotton reel racer and its 'race results'. They then suggest improvements.

Pitfalls

It is essential to check that a working cotton reel racer can be built out of the components being supplied. A working model would help struggling groups, who may find it difficult to interpret the diagram.

Safety notes

Pupils should wear eye protection as the rubber bands may be over-wound.

Answers

Answers will depend on the pupils' experiments.

Fuel for life

Key ideas	*Science PoS*
Energy is stored in food as chemical energy.	1.2gik, 4.5ae

Activity	*Description*	*Differentiation*
	A: Energy in food – Burning foods to heat water with the energy released.	Core
	B: How much energy? – Using a combined database and spreadsheet to calculate the energy in a meal.	Core

Answers to book questions

Red book

a 350 kJ
b 600 kJ
c 1 hour
d 5 hours
e –
1 a butter
b walking up a slope
c 1500 kJ
d 2.5 hours
2 –

Green book

a 350 kJ
b 1 hour
c 1975 kJ
d 5 hours
e –
1 a butter
b walking up a slope
c 1500 kJ
2 to get advice about how to lose weight but stay healthy

Energy in food

Activity 1.5A
Core

Purpose

To show that foods contain a store of energy.

Running the activity

This could be done as a demonstration, if time is short. Alternatively, one group could do the pea and the other the raisin, and they could swap results. Some pupils could do **1.5A** while others did **1.5B**.

Other relevant material

Skill sheet 2: Lighting a Bunsen burner
Skill sheet 4: Energy transfer diagrams

Expected outcomes

One raisin has more energy than one pea, if the raisin and pea are average sized.

Pitfalls

Check that the temperature rise is reasonable for one pea and one raisin of the size given. If not, it may be necessary to alter the volume of water accordingly.

Safety notes

Pupils should wear eye protection while burning the pea/raisin and heating water. Make sure the peas are 'pre-drilled' to avoid pupils stabbing themselves with a needle.

Answers

1 –

2 The pea should have given out more heat energy.

3 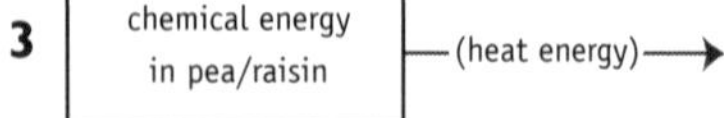

How much energy?

Activity 1.5B
Core

Purpose

To show pupils that standard tables of nutritional information can be used to calculate the energy content of meals, that databases are good ways of extracting a small amount of required information from a large, complex source, and that spreadsheets are ways of doing complex, multi-stage calculations.

Running the activity

This PC-based activity uses a Microsoft® *Excel* spreadsheet with an inbuilt database available on the CD-ROM that accompanies this pack.

ICT opportunities

ICT Pos 1c Using a database

Expected outcomes

Pupils complete the spreadsheet and calculate the energy content of the meal.

Answers

1 5220 kJ

Sound energy

Key ideas	*Science PoS*
Sound is made by vibrations. The eardrum vibrates when sound enters the ear. Sound needs a material to travel though. It cannot travel through a vacuum.	1.2gk, 4.3gi

KS2 precursor concepts	*Science PoS*
That vibrations make sounds and require a medium.	KS2 4.3eg

Activity	*Description*	*Differentiation*
	A: Bell in a vacuum demonstration – A teacher demonstration to show that sound does not travel through a vacuum.	Core (no pupil sheets)
	B: Investigating sound – Finding out if sound travels through different materials.	Core

Answers to book questions

Red book

a it vibrates

b sound energy to kinetic energy

c kinetic energy to electrical energy

d along the nerve

e e.g. Sound can travel through a variety of media, including gases, liquids and solids. However, sound cannot travel through a vacuum.

1 the shuttle

2 through the air

3 The eardrum vibrated.

4 The floor was vibrating, because the sound travelled through the floor.

5 There is no air on the Moon.

6 The vibrations could travel through the ground and floor.

Green book

a it vibrates

b along the nerve

c no

1 the skin of the drum

2 through the air

3 it vibrates

4 No, sound cannot travel through a vacuum.

Activity notes

Bell in a vacuum demonstration

Activity 1.6A
Core (no pupil sheets)

Purpose

To demonstrate to pupils that sound does not travel in a vacuum.

Running the activity

This is intended as a teacher demonstration. There are no activity sheets.
Practise using the vacuum pump in advance. Pump out as much air as possible. If the vacuum is good the sound will fade to almost nothing. Then allow air to re-enter, and the volume of sound will increase.

Expected outcomes

Pupils realise that air is needed in the bell jar for sound to travel.

Pitfalls

Make sure the bell is suspended in the jar, not sitting on a surface (otherwise sound will be transferred from the jar by the vibrations).

Safety notes

Use only a glass bell jar designed to be evacuated. Check the bell jar before use for any chips, cracks or nicks – discard if any are found.
A safety screen is needed between the class and the demonstration.
All present require eye protection.

Energy **1.6 B**

Investigating sound

Activity 1.6B
Core

Purpose

To underscore that sound needs a material or substance through which to travel.

Running the activity

Pupils work in groups, reaching their answers by discussion.

Answers

1 air

2 water

3 wood

4 no

5 a vacuum

6 Sound needs a material/substance to travel through. We know this because sound can travel through air, water and wood but not through a vacuum (no material/substance).

More energy, more sound?

Key ideas	*Science PoS*
Loud sounds can damage your hearing. (Loud sounds transfer a lot of energy.) The larger the amplitude of a vibration, the louder the sound. The larger the frequency of a vibration, the higher the pitch of the sound. Some people can hear higher pitch sounds than others.	4.3ghjk

KS2 Precursor concepts	*Science PoS*
The loudness and pitch of a sound can change.	KS2 4.3f

Activity	*Description*	*Differentiation*
	CRO demonstrations – Teacher demonstrations using a CRO to show the effects of changing first the amplitude and then the frequency of a vibration.	Core (no pupil sheets)

Answers to book questions

Red book

a Sounds above 90–100 dB can damage the nerve in the ears of the people who work in clubs because they are exposed to loud sounds for long periods of time. People visiting clubs are exposed to the loud sounds for only short periods of time.

b i ii

c over 15 kHz but below 20 kHz

d 20 Hz–6 kHz would probably be enough for speech

1 Vibrations with large amplitudes produce loud sounds.
Vibrations with high frequencies produce high-pitched sounds.

2 a Someone working in a noisy factory may lose their hearing because of damage to the nerve in their ears.

b –

Green book

a Sounds above 90–100 dB can damage the nerve in the ears of the people who work in clubs because they are exposed to loud sounds for long periods of time.

b young people

c dogs and bats

1 The *amplitude* of a vibration tells us how big the vibration is. Big vibrations make loud sounds. The *frequency* of a vibration tells us how fast a vibration is. Fast vibrations make sound with a high *pitch*.

2 loud thunderclap – 110 dB
busy street – 70 dB
chatting – 60 dB
whispering – 30 dB

CRO demonstrations

Activity 1.7
Core (no pupil sheets)

Purpose

The first part is to show pupils that louder sounds are caused by larger vibrations, with a larger amplitude.
The second part is to show pupils that higher pitched sounds are caused by more frequent vibrations, with a higher frequency. It also demonstrates the audible range in humans.

Running the activity

These are intended as teacher demonstrations. There are no activity sheets. First turn the volume of the signal up and down, to show that the amplitude of the vibrations alters. Then increase and decrease the pitch to show that the frequency is altered.
To demonstrate the audible range in humans, turn the frequency of the signal generator up and down and point out the change in frequency. Get pupils to all raise their hands and ask them to lower their hands when they no longer hear the sound. Get as many adults as possible to join in. Turn up the frequency of sound until inaudible.

Expected outcomes

Loud sounds have large amplitudes. Quiet sounds have small amplitudes. High-pitched sounds have high frequencies. Low-pitched sounds have small frequencies.
The audible range for humans is about 20 Hz to 20 kHz.

Pitfalls

Practise with the CRO and signal generator in advance.

Safety notes

Keep the volume of sound low.

Energy trails

Key ideas	*Science PoS*
Energy is conserved. It is impossible to create or destroy energy. Most energy can be tracked back to the Sun. When energy is transferred, only some of it can be used.	4.5bg

Activity	*Description*	*Differentiation*
	A: Energy trails – Group work making energy trails.	Core
	B: 'Wasted' energy – Learning that not all the energy ends up where we want it.	Core

Other relevant material

Skill sheet 4: Energy transfer diagrams

Answers to book questions

Red book

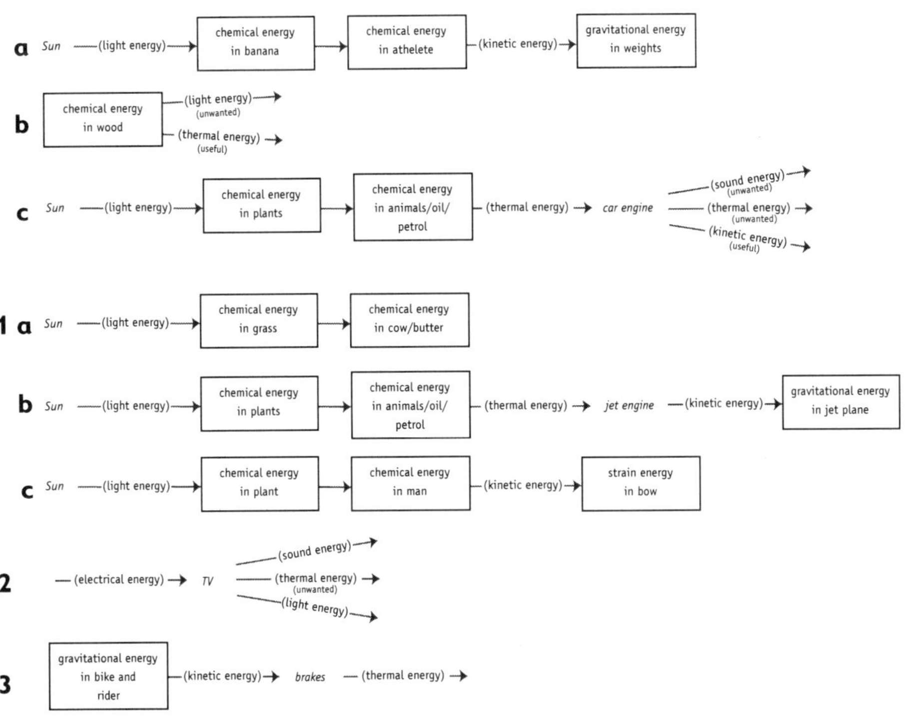

Green book

a the Sun

b the Sun

c missing words from left to right: light, chemical, movement, gravitational

1 Refer to answer for red book question **1**. Pupils may use 'movement energy' instead of 'kinetic energy'.

2 a Refer to answer for red book question **2**. Pupils may use 'heat energy' instead of 'thermal energy'.

b heat energy

Energy trails

Activity 1
Core, Resource

Activity notes

Purpose

To get pupils to realise that almost all energy on Earth derives from the Sun.

Running the activity

Pupils work in groups to make some energy trails based on what they have learned in this unit. There is a resource sheet to accompany this activity.

Other relevant material

Skill sheet 4: Energy transfer diagrams

Expected outcomes

A3 posters to display.

Energy 1.8 B

'Wasted' energy

Activity 1.8B
Core

Purpose

For pupils to realise that not all the energy ends up where we want it when energy is transferred.

Running the activity

Pupils answer the questions on the sheet.

Other relevant material

Skill sheet 4: Energy transfer diagrams

Answers

1 electrical energy
2 movement/kinetic energy, heat/thermal energy, sound energy
3 —(electrical energy)→ *hairdryer* — (heat energy)→ / (movement energy)→ / (sound energy)→
4 drying wet hair
5 heat energy, movement energy
6 sound energy
7 chemical energy (in petrol/diesel)
8 movement/kinetic energy, heat/thermal energy, sound energy
9 —(heat energy)→ *car engine* — (heat energy)→ / (movement energy)→ / (sound energy)→
10 move
11 movement/kinetic energy
12 heat/thermal energy, sound energy

The best fuel?

Developing thinking skills

A class discussion led by the teacher can be used to introduce the context of the spread. Pupils can then work in small groups, ideally in pairs. The questions in the text are intended to prompt either whole class discussion or small group discussion, as appropriate. The teacher will have the opportunity to intervene and challenge individual pupils. It is advisable not to tell the pupils the answers, but to ask them another question which takes them forward in their thinking. This will help them to develop higher thinking skills. Many of the questions are very open and do not have a simple answer. It is useful to allow some time for pupils to feedback ideas to the class after the group work.

Think about: fair tests and variables

This activity allows pupils to refine their ideas about a fair tests. They are given a flawed experimental design to criticise and then asked for a better version. The context is not simple, which should provide opportunities for discussion. The language is that of CASE: the independent variable is referred to as the input variable and the dependent variable is referred to as the outcome variable. The word relationship is used in the Higher text (red book): this refers to how the input variable (the independent variable) affects the outcome variable (the dependent variable). There is an opportunity to plot a line graph. Lines of best fit are introduced at this early stage, to try to avoid a habit of 'joining the dots'.

Key ideas	*Science PoS*
The things that change during an investigation are called variables. In a fair test, you keep most of the variables the same. You change one variable. This is called the input variable. You measure one variable to get your results. This is called the outcome variable.	1.2d

KS2 Precursor concepts	*Science PoS*
Fair tests	KS2 1.2d

Activity	*Description*	*Differentiation*
	The best fuel? – A teacher demonstration of the experiment described in the pupils' book (heating water with lighter fuel).	Core (no pupils sheets)

Other relevant material

Skill sheet 5: Drawing charts and graphs; Skill sheet 6: Interpreting graphs

Answers to book questions

Red book

a to make it a fair test, and so results could be compared across the class
b to make it a fair test, and so that results could be compared across the class
c 61°C
d no, they used a different mass of fuel
e no, would have used 2g of fuel to make it a fair test
f mass of fuel
g temperature of water at the end
h amount of water, temperature of water at start
i –
j yes, as the mass of fuel increases, the temperature rise increases

Green book

a to make it a fair test, and so results could be compared across the class
b to make it a fair test, and so that results could be compared across the class
c 61°C
d no, they used 5g not 2g
e yes
f no, they could not compare the fuels as the mass is different
g no, would have used 2g of fuel
h mass of fuel
i temperature rise
j amount of water and temperature at start

The best fuel?

Activity 1.9
Core (no pupil sheets)

Purpose

To familiarise pupils with the experiment discussed in the text, so that they can concentrate on the task.

Running the activity

This is intended as a teacher demonstration. There are no activity sheets.
Set up the apparatus as shown in the textbook.

Pitfalls

Mineral wool will be needed for the lighter fuel, to act as a wick.

Safety notes

All present require eye protection.

The birthday party

Setting the scene

This spread introduces solids, liquids and gases and some of their properties. The **unit map** can be used to help brainstorm key words and ideas about the unit topics.

KS2 precursor concepts	*Science PoS*
Pupils should know the difference between solids, liquids and gases.	KS2 3.1e

Activity	*Description*	*Differentiation*
	The birthday party – Finding solids, liquids and gases in a picture (based on the book spread 2.1) and describing some changes of state taking place.	Core

Answers to book questions

Red book

a it will solidify/freeze
b it was turning from liquid to solid (freezing)
c helium is lighter than air
d they are lighter (less dense) than the lemonade and so float
e it was melting
f it started to melt

1 –

2 a any five solids
b water, any bench solutions
c air, natural gas (methane)

3 –

Green book

a it melted
b it will become solid
c it was turning from liquid to solid (freezing)
d it melts/becomes liquid
e the gas in it was lighter than air
f they are lighter (less dense) than the lemonade so they float
g it was melting
h so that it would melt a little and soften

1 from top to bottom: solid, liquid, solid, gas, liquid

2 When you heat a solid it can turn into a *liquid*. This is called *melting*. If you boil a liquid, it will turn into a *gas*. Freezing happens when a *liquid* turns into a *solid*.

3 –

The birthday party

Activity 2.1
Core

Purpose

To reinforce the book spread.

Running the activity

After reading the book spread, this activity can be used so pupils identify all the different examples of solids, liquids and gases in the picture and list them. Less able pupils could colour in the solids, liquids and gases in three different colours.

Answers

1,2,3 refer to picture

4 it is melting/becoming liquid

5 it will freeze/become solid

6 it is melting/becoming liquid

7 it is evaporating/becoming a gas/steam

Solids, liquids and gases

Key ideas	*Science PoS*
Solids are hard and have a fixed shape and fixed volume. Liquids have a fixed volume. They are runny and can be poured. Gases do not have a fixed shape or a fixed volume. They take the shape of their container. They can be squashed easily.	3.1b

KS2 precursor concepts	*Science PoS*
Compare solids, liquids and gases based on their properties.	KS2 3.1e

Activity	*Description*	*Differentiation*
	Classifying materials – Sorting different materials into solids, liquids and gases by their properties.	Core

ICT opportunities

CD-ROM: *States of Matter* (New Media, PO Box 4441, Henley-on-Thames, RG9 3YR).

Answers to book questions

Red book

1 Everything in the world is made of *matter.* Solids, liquids and gases are the three kinds of *matter.*

2

Property	Solid	Liquid	Gas
Easy to pour	✗	✔	✔
Easy to squash	✗	✗	✔
Fixed shape	✔	✗	✗
Fixed volume	✔	✔	✗

3 Air can be squashed so will absorb more shocks

4 hard, fixed shape, can't be squashed/fixed volume

Green book

a any five solids

b two of: hard, fixed shape, can't be squashed/fixed volume

c not hard, runny/can flow/can be poured, can change shape, can't be squashed/fixed volume

d can be squashed/can change volume, can change shape, can flow, not hard

1 Everything in the world is made of *matter.* Solids, liquids and gases are the three kinds of *matter.*

2

Property	Solid	Liquid	Gas
Easy to pour	✗	✔	✔
Easy to squash	✗	✗	✔
Fixed shape	✔	✗	✗
Fixed volume	✔	✔	✗

3 hard, fixed shape, can't be squashed/fixed volume

Classifying materials

Activity 2.2
Core

Activity notes

Purpose

To classify materials and explain reasons for choices.

Running the activity

Pupils decide whether given materials are solid, liquid or gas and make a table to show this. Pupils then list properties of solids, liquids and gases.

Answers

1

Solid	Liquid	Gas
gold	mercury	air
glass	lemonade	oxygen
iron	oil	carbon dioxide
brick	water	
plastic		

2 solids – hard, fixed shape, fixed volume

3 liquids – fixed volume, runny/can be poured, do not have a fixed shape

4 gases – do not have a fixed shape or fixed volume, take on the shape of their container, can be squashed easily

Particle power

Key ideas	*Science PoS*
Everything is made of particles. In a solid, the particles are very close and in a neat pattern. In a liquid, the particles are slightly further apart and have a less regular pattern. In a gas, the particles are far apart and have no pattern at all. Solids and liquids are more dense than gases.	1.2cglm, 3.1ab

Activity	*Description*	*Differentiation*
	A tight squeeze – Investigating whether solids, liquids and gases can be squashed.	Core, Help

Other relevant material

Particles can be modelled using coins or counters on an overhead projector – this makes them visible to the whole class.

ICT opportunities

CD-ROM: *States of Matter* (New Media, PO Box 4441, Henley-on-Thames, RG9 3YR)

Answers to book questions

Red book

a particles very close together
b particles can move a little
c particles always moving

1 Solids have a fixed shape because their particles are *joined strongly*.
Gases fill all of their container because their particles are *always moving*.
Liquids are hard to squash because their particles are *close together*.

2 The particles spread out – much farther apart.

3 The particles are much closer together in a solid – more particles in a given volume.

4 The water – it is denser so is much smaller and easy to carry.

Green book

a very close together, neat pattern
b higgledy-piggledy, close together
c very far apart, all over the place (random)
d particles constantly moving

1 Solids have a fixed shape because their particles are *joined strongly*.
Gases fill all of their container because their particles are *always moving*.
Liquids are easy to pour because their particles can *move a little*.

2 The particles are very close together and don't move much.

3 a neither – both the same
b water
c water

A tight squeeze

Purpose

To introduce pupils to predicting and explaining results through a simple practical activity.

Running the activity

Pupils investigate how easy it is to squash a solid, liquid and gas.

Core: Pupils make a prediction then are given the experimental method. They have to devise a way of recording their results (a table), analyse their results and explain them in terms of particles.

Help: The teacher can either show pupils what to do or give them the full instructions on the Core sheet. This Help sheet is for pupils to record their predictions, results and conclusions.

Pitfalls

Test the sand before the water, otherwise any water left in the syringe will make the sand damp.

Expected outcomes

Pupils discover that air can be squashed but sand and water cannot.

Safety notes

Pupils need to keep their fingers firmly over the ends of the syringes to prevent water from squirting. Wet floors can be slippery.

Answers

Core: **1** The air should be squashed the most.

2 Because the particles in a gas have space to move together.

3 Depends on prediction.

4 The gas will be squashed the most.

5 The particles in a gas have space to move together. In the solid and liquid the particles are close together and cannot be squashed closer.

Help: **1** I think that *air* can be squashed the most. I think this because *the particles in a gas have space to move together.*

2 Depends on prediction.

3 I found out that the *air* could be squashed the most. This happens because the particles in a *gas* are *close together* and so can be *squashed closer.*

Moving particles

Key ideas	*Science PoS*
Particles move faster when they are heated. They slow down when they are cooled. A solid melts because the particles move away from each other. A liquid evaporates because the particles move around on their own. These changes are called changes of state.	3.1b, 3.2c

KS2 precursor concepts	*Science PoS*
The idea of changes of state and that they can be reversed.	KS2 3.2d

Activity	*Description*	*Differentiation*
	A: Moving particles – Using peas in a box to model particles in changes of state.	Core
	B: Role play – particles – Understanding changes of state in terms of the movement of particles.	Core

ICT opportunities

CD-ROM: *States of Matter* (New Media, PO Box 4441, Henley-on-Thames, RG9 3YR).

Answers to book questions

Red book

a melting
b the snowman shrinks and leaves a puddle
c they would evaporate

1 When you heat particles, they move *faster*. When you cool particles, they move *slower*.

2 solid – jiggle about, don't move far
liquid – move a bit more, can move around each other
gas – move at random in all directions

3 –

Green book

a jiggle about, don't move far
b move a little, can move around each other
c move at random in all directions

1 When you heat particles, they move *faster*.
When you cool particles, they move *slower*.

2 –

Moving particles

Purpose

To model particles and changes of state, and pull out the elements of the model.

Running the activity

Pupils make a model of a solid using peas to represent particles. This is then shaken to represent heating the solid until it turns into a liquid, then into steam.
If using a totally clear box, this activity could be demonstrated to the whole class by placing the box on an overhead projector.

Safety notes

Be careful not to let peas fall on the floor, otherwise people may slip.

Answers

1 solid ice – step 4, liquid water – step 5, water vapour (steam) – step 6

2 shaking the peas more and more

3

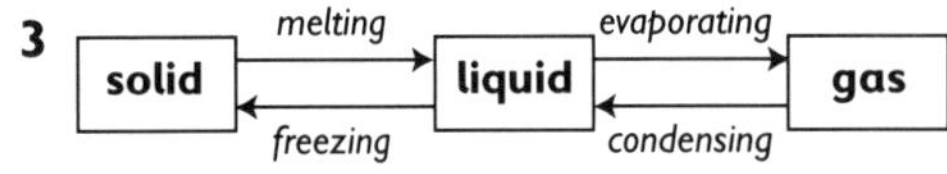

Changing state
2.4
B

Role play – particles

Activity 2.4B
Extension

Purpose

To learn about particles in a fun context through modelling (kinesthetic learning).

Running the activity

Pupils act out the roles of particles in solids, liquids and gases. This should be carried out in a large space if possible. It could be done with a whole class if a large enough space is available. Alternatively a small group could be used to demonstrate it to the rest of the class.

Safety notes

Take care that the pupils do not get too carried away when they are a gas, running about too quickly and bumping into each other too energetically!

Answers

1 moving only very slightly, very close together

2 moving quickly all over the place, spaced out

3 as a liquid – moved faster, spread out slightly

4 as a gas

5

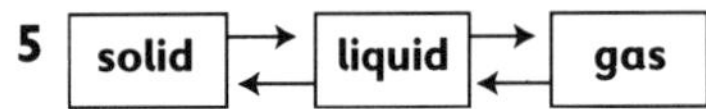

Dissolving

Key ideas	*Science PoS*
A solute is a substance that dissolves in a liquid called a solvent. The particles in the solute break apart and mix with the particles in the solvent. The mixture of solute dissolved in solvent is called a solution. Different solutes dissolve in different solvents.	2.1a–p, 3.1b, 3.2b

KS2 precursor concepts	*Science PoS*
Some solids dissolve in water to give solutions. This process is reversible.	KS2 3.2d, 3.3b

Activity	*Description*	*Differentiation*
	Investigating dissolving – Guiding pupils through an investigation into the dissolving of sugar.	Core, Help, Extension

Answers to book questions

Red book

1. If you stir salt into water, it will *dissolve*. The salt is called the *solute* and the water is called the *solvent*. The mixture of salt and water is called a *solution*.
2. use hot water, stir it, use granulated sugar/ crush the sugar lump
3. The particles will be moving around more and so can be mixed up more easily.

Green book

a sugar
b water

1. If you stir salt into water, it will *dissolve*. The salt is called the *solute* and the water is called the *solvent*. The mixtures of salt and water is called a *solution*.
2. use hot water, stir it, use granulated sugar/or crush the sugar lump

Investigating dissolving

Activity 2.5
Core, Help, Extension

Activity notes

Purpose

To introduce pupils to doing a complete Sc1 investigation with guidance.

Running the activity

This is an investigation into the variables which affect the rate that sugar dissolves.

Core: Pupils have to find out which dissolves fastest – lump, granulated or caster sugar. They have to think about the variables that will affect the rate of dissolving, then plan and carry out an experiment to test their prediction. The sheet gives some guidance through each stage of the investigation.

Help: For less able pupils, photocopy the top half of the Core sheet showing the introduction and equipment available but use the Help sheet for more guided predictions, plans, etc. Pupils can write their answers and record their results on this sheet.

Extension: Pupils have to think about all the variables that affect the rate of sugar dissolving, then chose one variable to investigate. They plan their own investigations with some guidance.

You will need to check all pupils' plans before they carry out their investigations.

Tip: Weigh a sugar lump first, then get pupils to use the same weight of granulated and caster sugar.

Expected outcomes

Pupils should discover that caster sugar dissolves the fastest, and that the rate of dissolving increases with temperature. Extension pupils may also find that stirring increases the rate of dissolving.

Pitfalls

Pupils may have trouble determining the exact end point when all the sugar has dissolved. This may lead to errors in their results.

They may have some difficulty in understanding the theory behind why a sugar lump dissolves slower than a powder.

Safety notes

Hot water can scald – remind pupils to take care.

Pupils should also be reminded not to eat or taste the sugar.

Answers

Core:
1 I think caster sugar will dissolve fastest and lump sugar will dissolve slowest.
2 In lump sugar the grains are packed together so it takes time for them to separate and mix with the water particles. In caster sugar the grains are smaller and loosely packed so they can mix more easily with the water particles.
3 temperature, stirring
4 depends on pupil's hypothesis
5 depends on pupil's hypothesis

Help:
1 caster sugar
2 In caster sugar the grains are smaller and loosely packed so they can mix more easily with the water particles.
3,4 depend on results
5 I found out that the caster sugar dissolved the fastest. I think this happened because the grains are smaller and loosely packed so they can mix more easily with the water particles.

Extension: answers depend on variable chosen and results

Separating mixtures

Key ideas	*Science PoS*
Distillation can be used to separate a pure liquid from a solution. Chromatography is a way of separating a mixture of dyes.	3.1gh

KS2 precursor concepts	*Science PoS*
Basic ways of separating different types of mixtures.	KS2 3.3acde

Activity	*Description*	*Differentiation*
	A: Distillation – A teacher demonstration of the distillation of salt water, then completing a flow diagram.	Help
	B: Looking at mixtures – Interpreting a pie chart of the composition of air.	Core

Answers to book questions

Red book

a boil – break away and move upwards

b condense – become a liquid

c dye D

d two dyes

e Green is the most soluble, then mauve, and blue is the least soluble.

1 To separate salt and water, we can use a method called *distillation*. The water is boiled and turns into a gas. The water *vapour* reaches the condenser where it cools down and *condenses*. This pure water is called *distilled* water.

2 Chromatography experiment to separate colours.

3 Tap water produces limescale which can clog it up, distilled water doesn't.

Green book

a boil – break away and moves upwards

b condense – become a liquid

c dye D

d dye B

e dye A

1 To separate salt and water, we can use a method called *distillation*. The water is boiled and turns into a gas. The water *vapour* reaches the condenser where it cools down and *condenses*. This pure water is called *distilled* water.

2 Try separating the colours using chromatography.

Distillation

Activity notes

Purpose

A teacher demonstration to help pupils concentrate on observing.

Running the activity

This is a demonstration of distillation. Pupils should write down their observations and the results.

Help: Pupils can fill in this sheet either during or after the process has been demonstrated.

Expected outcomes

Pupils should observe the distillation process and understand the different stages and changes of state that occur.

Safety notes

All present should wear eye protection.

Use anti-bumping granules or a couple of bits of pot in the flask. Ensure the whole apparatus is stable. Do not let the flask boil dry.

Answers

1 Here the *salty water* is heated until it *boils*.

2 The water turns into a *gas* and *moves up* the tube. It is called water *vapour*.

3 The gas is cooled down until it turns into a *liquid*. This process is called *condensation*.

4 The liquid drips out of the tube into a test tube. It is called *distilled* water.

Changing state **2.6 B**

Looking at mixtures

Activity 2.6B
Core

Purpose

To interpret data.

Running the activity

Pupils analyse the pie chart and answer questions based on it.

Answers

1 nitrogen

2 21%

3 1%

4 any three of carbon dioxide, hydrogen and any noble gases

Crime and colours

Developing thinking skills

A class discussion led by the teacher can be used to introduce the context of the spread. Pupils can then work in small groups, ideally in pairs. The questions in the text are intended to prompt either whole class discussion or small group discussion, as appropriate. The teacher will have the opportunity to intervene and challenge individual pupils. It is advisable not to tell the pupils the answers, but to ask them another question which takes them forward in their thinking. This will help them to develop higher thinking skills. Many of the questions are very open and do not have a simple answer. It is useful to allow some time for pupils to feedback ideas to the class after the group work.

Think about: analysing results

This unit will be based on the concepts of chromatography introduced in the last spread (bridging). Pupils will be asked to consider different chromatograms. The first chromatogram is very simple and can be used to allow concrete preparation. Pupils then have to use their knowledge of chromatography to analyse the chromatograms of the kidnapping suspects. They should argue why there is not enough evidence to prove who is the kidnapper (cognitive conflict). Pupils should be encouraged to explain fully their thinking behind each of the questions in the text (metacognition).

Key ideas	*Science PoS*
Analyse experimental data and draw conclusions. Consider whether this data is sufficient to draw conclusions. Analyse chromatograms.	1.2klno, 3.1h

ICT opportunities

Use the Internet to find out about forensic science.

Answers to book questions

Red book

a three
b green, they moved the furthest
c Mr Brown's, because the position of the dyes in the kidnapper's sample of ink matches the dyes in Mr Brown's sample of ink
d someone else could have used his pen, more than one of these pens, many pens may use the same ink

1 solar yellow, sunny yellow
2 sunburst yellow
3 mellow yellow
4 no – they do not contain sunburst yellow
5 yes – they contain sunburst yellow
6 food labels which show what additives (E numbers) are in them

Green book

a three
b green
c Mr Brown's, because the position of the dyes in the kidnapper's sample of ink matches the dyes in Mr Brown's sample of ink
d someone else could have used his pen, more than one of these pens, many pens may use the same ink

1 two
2 solar yellow, sunny yellow
3 one
4 sunburst yellow
5 mellow yellow
6 no – they do not contain sunburst yellow
7 yes – they contain sunburst yellow

Lookalikes

Setting the scene

This spread is designed to activate prior knowledge of the life processes. The **unit map** can be used to brainstorm key words and ideas about the unit topics.

KS2 precursor concepts	*Science PoS*
Pupils should know that there are life processes, including nutrition, movement, growth and reproduction, common to plants and animals including humans.	KS2 2.1ab

Activity	*Description*	*Differentiation*
	Survival – Pupils take on the role of explorers planning a trip to the North Pole. Each pupil selects and prioritises items to take with them.	Core

ICT opportunities

Is there life on other planets? The SETI Institute (Search for Extraterrestrial Intelligence) is conducting a survey of the galaxy using the world's largest radio telescopes.

Website: http://www.set-inst.edu/Welcome.html

Answers to book questions

Red book

1 a move, sense

b respire, grow, reproduce, feed, excrete

c get energy from fuel cells, do without food/water, do without a toilet

2 The humans may not survive 110 years, so you need some robots.
Robots do not have the power to think, so you need some humans.
Air and food for humans may run out, so you need some robots.

3 Deprive Zac of oxygen – he will survive. Deprive Zac of food – he will survive. Monitor Zac's behaviour – he will not excrete or eliminate waste.

4 Test the slime to see if it takes in oxygen/see if it survives without oxygen. Monitor whether it photosynthesises/eats food, reproduces or gets rid of waste. Measure to see if it grows.

Green book

a move, breathe, sense, grow, reproduce, feed, get rid of waste

b move, sense

1 a move

b move

c grow

2 Test the slime to see if it takes in oxygen/see if it survives without oxygen. Monitor whether it photosynthesises/eats food, reproduces or gets rid of waste. Measure to see if it grows.

Activity 3.1
Core

Survival

Purpose

To encourage group discussion, making choices and giving reasons for those choices.

Running the activity

Pupils take on the role of explorers preparing for an ice walk across the North Pole. They have to select five items each to pack into their rucksacks. Pupils should work in groups of 4–6, preferably of mixed ability. They will need a large piece of paper to record their decisions on. Give a time limit for the activity (approximately 10 minutes). Suggest that each group chooses a person to write and a person who will give a brief report (no more than 2 minutes) back to the class.

Expected outcomes

Pupils should realise that their selection and prioritising of items to take on the trip relate to the life processes, and that by sharing and co-operating with each other they can take more.

Pitfalls

Arguments may become rather heated!

Sorting out living things

Key ideas	*Science PoS*
We can sort living things into groups with similar features. This is called classification. Vertebrates are animals with a backbone. Invertebrates are animals without a backbone.	1.2fgjk 2.4b

KS2 precursor concepts	*Science PoS*
Pupils should know: • how to make and use keys (Red book pupils only); • how locally occurring animals and plants can be identified and assigned to groups • that the variety of plants and animals makes it important to identify them and assign them to groups. For the activity, pupils should know: • about the different plants and animals found in different habitats • how to use food charts to show feeding relationships in a habitat.	KS2 2.4abc, 2.5bd

Activity	*Description*	*Differentiation*
	**Pond survey** – Pupils visit a pond and make observations. They collect samples of pond water for microscopic analysis back in the laboratory, then classify the organisms into the major taxonomic groups.	Core, Help

Answers to book questions

Red book

a Find out if it carries out all of the life processes.

b He might have compared the size of the elephant's tooth with teeth of elephants at that time. If the measurements were the same, the extinct elephant would have been the same size. If the extinct elephant's tooth was 2x bigger then it would have been 2x bigger than the elephants at that time.

c vertebrates – seal, cod arctic tern; invertebrates – starfish, octopus, crab

1 Put all of the organisms with similar features in one group.

2 Plants are green and make their own food.

3 Fungi feed on rotting material.

4 robin, toad, rat, snake, bat, squirrel

5 –

Green book

a Find out if it carries out all of the life processes.

b Put organisms that have similar features into one group.

c seal, cod, arctic tern

1 We can sort living things into *groups*. All of the *organisms* in a group have *similar* features. Each group can be sorted into *smaller* groups.

2 vertebrates – human, horse, polar bear, cod; invertebrates – octopus, spider, starfish

Activity 3.2
Core, Help, Resource (1,2)

Pond survey

Purpose

To observe a wide range of living things, sort and classify them into the major taxonomic groups and begin to appreciate that there is a pyramid of numbers.

Running the activity

Core: Pupils visit a pond and observe the living things they can see. They bring back samples of the pond water to make observations in the laboratory. They then classify the organisms they have observed into the major taxonomic groups.

There are two resource sheets with pictures of plants and animals (invertebrates and vertebrates) they are likely to find.

Help: Pupils carry out the Core activity but use their Help sheets to record their observations.

Other relevant material

Skill sheet 8: Using a microscope

Expected outcomes

Hopefully the results will reveal more invertebrates than vertebrates, so pupils can begin to appreciate that there is a pyramid of numbers.

Pitfalls

If you do not have a school pond, advance planning is necessary.

Safety notes

Refer to school and LEA policy and ensure parental consent, adequate supervision, etc. if the pond is away from the school site.

Remind pupils not to pick plants and to take care of living specimens which will be returned to the pond after the activity.

Disposable plastic gloves should be worn if plants are sampled by hand. Broken skin should be covered by waterproof plasters. Hands need to be washed afterwards.

Remind pupils to take care with microscopes. Never use a microscope where the Sun's rays might reflect off the mirror into it.

Answers

Core: **1** Vertebrates feed on invertebrates / many of the invertebrates are herbivores / many of the vertebrates are carnivores / one vertebrate needs lots of invertebrates to feed on.

Help: **1** The group which had the most living this in it was *invertebrates*. There are more *invertebrates* than *vertebrates* in the pond because *vertebrates* feed on *invertebrates*.

More animal groups

Key ideas	Science PoS
Vertebrates are classified into five groups. The groups are mammals, birds, reptiles, amphibians and fish. Each group has different features.	1.2k 2.4b

KS2 precursor concepts	Science PoS
(See Book notes 3.2)	

Activity	Description	Differentiation
	A: All backbone! – Pupils use the CD-ROM *Dangerous Creatures* to find information about vertebrates.	Core, Extension
	B: Vertebrates game – Pupils play a board game to gain familiarity with the characteristics of the vertebrate groups.	Core

Answers to book questions

Red book

1 mammals – we feed our young on milk from mammary glands, babies develop inside bodies and we have a hairy skin

2 eggs with a hard shell, feathers, wings

3 dry and scaly

4 They go back to water to lay their eggs. Yes, because amphibian's eggs are jelly-like and would dry out on land.

5 through gills

6 Birds and reptiles lays eggs on land, so need shells for protection. Human eggs develop inside the mother's body so no shell is needed.

7 Amphibian lays jelly-like eggs / lays eggs in water / has smooth, moist skin / lives partly on land.

Reptile lays eggs with a leathery shell / lays eggs on land / has dry, scaly skin / lives mainly on land.

Green book

a mammals

b feathers and wings

c dry and scaly

d to lay eggs

e through gills

1 Missing from each column:
Vertebrates – birds, fish
Features – eggs with a leathery shell, dry and scaly skin; eggs like jelly, smooth and moist skin

2 on land

3 mammals

Activity 3.3A
Core, Extension

All backbone!

Purpose

To develop ICT research skills. The activity may be used to support pupils in their independent research. For some, it may lead on to extension work. Alternatively the multimedia approach could support less able pupils in their learning.

Running the activity

Pupils find information about vertebrates from the Microsoft® CD-ROM *Dangerous Creatures*. This is a comprehensive multimedia package.

Core: The computer may be available in the laboratory to be accessed by pupils during the lesson. Some schools may wish to put the activity into the school library or open learning centre as an enrichment or homework exercise.

Extension: If pupils have time left after completing the Core sheet, they can continue their searches with this extra sheet.

ICT opportunities

ICT PoS 2a: Reaching conclusions by exploring information from a CD-ROM.

Expected outcomes

Pupils have an understanding of a wider variety of vertebrates and which groups they belong to.

Answers

Core:

1 Wolves communicate with all kinds of visual signals as well as with a variety of sounds.

2 Although vultures prefer food that is already dead, many will also dine on rodents and baby birds.

3 By keeping its head still and wiggling its worm-like tail, an Australian death adder tricks its prey into coming close enough to bite. The snake's powerful venom paralyses its victim in seconds.

4 to warn other animals that they are dangerous to eat

Extension: Answers will vary for **5, 8, 11, 14, 17**. To answer the following questions, pupils will need to recall information from the book spread.

6 furry/hairy skin

7 on milk that they make in mammary glands

9 wings and/or legs

10 feathers / wings / eggs with a hard shell / most can fly

12 on land

13 to keep warm

15 living on both land and water

16 like jelly

18 using gills

19 scales

Vertebrates game

Activity 3.3B
Core,
Resource (3)

Purpose

To gain familiarity with the characteristics of the vertebrate groups. This activity may also be used for revision or as informal assessment to check on how well pupils have understood the key ideas of the book spread.

Running the activity

The groups should ideally be mixed ability. There is scope for pupils to use and develop interpersonal and linguistic skills through discussion and kinesthetic skills through mime and acting.

Photocopy the resource sheets to make the game. You may wish to enlarge these and print them on coloured card. Laminated copies will be reusable.

There is scope for differentiation by changing the questions on the cards.

Expected outcomes

Pupils have an understanding of a wider variety of vertebrates and which groups they belong to.

Pitfalls

Pupils may become rather noisy as they enjoy making their friends pay their forfeits. If preferred, the 'Can you?' tasks can be replaced with quieter activities.

Make no bones about it

Key ideas	*Science PoS*
Invertebrates are divided into seven groups. The groups are jellyfish, starfish, flatworms, roundworms, segmented worms, molluscs and arthropods. The arthropod group is split into crustaceans, centipedes and millipedes, spiders and insects.	1.2k, 2.4b

KS2 precursor concepts	*Science PoS*
(See book notes 3.2)	

Activity	*Description*	*Differentiation*
	Suits of armour – Pupils use the CD-ROM *Dangerous Creatures* to find information about invertebrates.	Core

Answers to book questions

Red book

1 a type of body
  b segmented worms
2 a an invertebrate with jointed legs
  b a centipede has legs
3 Jelly fish, starfish, flatworms, roundworms, segmented worms. He could not see all the differences between organisms that we can see today.
4 –

Green book

a type of body
b segmented worms
c an invertebrate with jointed legs
d a centipede has legs
1 flatworm, starfish, crustacean
2 an insect has 6 legs and a 3-part body; a spider has 8 legs and a 2-part body

Suits of armour

Activity 3.4
Core

Purpose

To develop ICT research skills. The activity may be used to support pupils in their independent research. The multimedia approach could support less able pupils in their learning.

Running the activity

Pupils find information about arthropods from the Microsoft® CD-ROM *Dangerous Creatures*.

The computer may be available in the laboratory to be accessed by pupils during the lesson. Some schools may wish to put the activity into the school library or open learning centre as an enrichment or homework exercise.

ICT opportunities

ICT PoS 2a: Reaching conclusions by exploring information from a CD-ROM

Expected outcomes

Pupils have an understanding of a wider variety of arthropods and how they are classified.

Answers

1 a shell

2 it has 6 jointed legs (and a hard exoskeleton)

3 it has 8 legs and 2 parts to its body (to answer the question pupils will have to recall information from the book spread)

4 A millipede has 2 pairs of legs on each segment. A centipede has 1 pair of legs on each segment. Millipedes eat plants. Centipedes have venomous claws.

Differences count

Key ideas	*Science PoS*
We call the differences between living things variations. If there are enough differences between organisms, they are different species. Some of the variations between the members of a species are inherited from their parents, some are caused by their surroundings. (Red book only) Discontinuous variation means having either one feature or another. In continuous variation, there are lots of inbetweens.	1.2gjk 2.4a

Activity	*Description*	*Differentiation*
	Spot the species! – Pupils compare live specimens or drawings of a frog and a toad and list their similarities and differences. They should realise that there are sufficient differences for them to belong to different species.	Core, Help

Answers to book questions

Red book

a –

b –

c sport/training/hair styles/tattoos/diet/sun-tanning

1 e.g. reindeer have antlers, long hair, different body shape to wolves

2 The polar bear and seal belong to different species. The polar bear and brown bear are varieties of the same species.

3 Some of the differences have been inherited from our parents and some have been caused by our surroundings and lifestyle. Parents with different features, surroundings and lifestyles mean lots of differences between us.

4 e.g. height, weight, fitness, knowledge, hairstyle, etc.

5 a discontinuous

b discontinuous

Green book

a –

b –

c sport/training/hair styles/tattoos/diet/sun-tanning

1 There are *differences* between members of the same *species*. These differences are called *variations*. Some of these differences are inherited from the *parents*. Differences in the *surroundings* or upbringing also cause variation.

2 The polar bear and seal belong to different species. The polar bear and brown bear are varieties of the same species.

Spot the species!

Purpose

Pupils observe and list similarities and differences between a frog and a toad.

Running the activity

Drawings are provided on the sheets, but colour photographs or live specimens could be used if available.

Core: Pupils are prompted to design their own table for recording their observations.

Help: Pupils write down their observations in the table provided.

Expected outcomes

Pupils should realise that there are sufficient differences for toads and frogs to belong to different species.

Safety notes

Live specimens (if used) should be handled with care.

Hands should be washed with soap and hot water before and after handling.

Answers

Core: **1** no

Help: **1** different

Born to survive

Key ideas	Science PoS
Many animals are adapted to survive in their habitat. Some animals are adapted to survive in the cold. They have fur or fat to insulate them from the cold. Some animals are camouflaged to hide from other animals. Some animals change their behaviour to help them cope with changes in temperature.	1.2a–p, 2.5bc

KS2 precursor concepts	Science PoS
Pupils should know how animals are suited to their environment and about feeding relationships in a habitat. For the Higher spread (red book), they should understand the terms predator and prey.	KS2 2.5bc

Activity	Description	Differentiation
	A: Bear necessities – Pupils use the CD-ROM *Dangerous Creatures* to find information about how the polar bear is adapted to survive in the Arctic.	Core
	B: A winter coat – A datalogging practical in which pupils use temperature sensors to investigate whether a layer of cotton wool helps to keep water in a flask hot. This relates to animals in winter growing a thicker layer of fur.	Core, Help, Extension

Answers to book questions

Red book

a might be eaten by a killer whale / might sink

b Camouflage is important to the baby seal because it has a white coat at first and then a short, sleek, dark coat which gives better protection against the dark sea. The killer whale is a *predator* of the baby seal. It eats baby seals, so they are its *prey*. The seal's mother instinctively knows when her baby seal is ready to swim – it will have a dark coat and be strong enough. This is called *parenting*.

c to shelter from the heat of the sun

1 It has a thick coat made of hollow hair which provides good insulation.

2 Its white coat camouflages it against the snow, so that other animals including humans cannot see it easily.

3 Arctic foxes, hares, caribou and cattle have long hair or thick fur to keep them warm. The Arctic fox and hare grow longer fur for the winter. Seals and whales have a thick layer of insulating fat.

4 Baby seals cannot swim so live on land. Their white coat camouflages them against the snow. As they grow into adults they learn to swim. Their black coat camouflages them against the sea.

5 Gerbils burrow into the sand to avoid the midday heat.
Camels face the sun at midday exposing the minimum of their body surface.
Lizards sunbathe to warm up or shelter to stay cool.

6 –

Green book

a thick coat (for insulation), white coat (for camouflage against the snow)

b features that help a living thing blend in with its surroundings

c to shelter from the midday sun

d to stay cool/avoid the heat of the sun

1 Polar bears and seals are *adapted* to survive in the cold. Polar bears have a *thick/white* coat. Seals have *fat* called blubber. Both of these help to keep them *warm* in winter

Bear necessities

Purpose

To develop IT research skills.

Running the activity

Pupils find information about polar bears from the Microsoft® CD-ROM *Dangerous Creatures*.

The computer may be available in the laboratory to be accessed by pupils during the lesson. Some schools may wish to put the activity into the school library or open learning centre as an enrichment or homework exercise.

ICT opportunities

ICT PoS 2a: Reaching conclusions by exploring information from a CD-ROM

Expected outcomes

Pupils should be able to describe how the polar bear is adapted to survive in the cold Arctic climate.

Answers

1 a seals, walruses, musk, oxen, reindeer, foxes, fish and crabs
b by biting and crushing it with powerful jaws

2 Garbage is not good for bears. The polar bear's normal diet is 100% meat.

3 It waits for dinner to appear in a seal's air hole. When a seal comes up to take a breath, the bear lunges to grab its dinner and often dives into the water in pursuit of its prey.

4 They need extra insulation. They develop a thick layer of fat under their skin or grow a dense coat of hollow hair.

5 They stay in a den dug out of the ground until they are three months old.

6 It has a thick white coat for camouflage and warmth in the winter. This is replaced by a thinner summer coat that may be grey, red or tan.

Activity 3.6B Core, Help, Extension

A winter coat

Purpose

To practise datalogging as part of a full Sc1 investigation.

Running the activity

This activity tests whether a layer of cotton wool helps to keep the water in a flask hot. This relates to animals in winter growing a thicker layer of fur. The activity should be carried out in small groups.

Core: Pupils are given equipment but have to decide how to set it up. The sheet leads them through a full investigation.

Help: The teacher carries out the experiment as a demonstration. Pupils draw a graph and analyse the results.

Extension: Pupils are told what they need to investigate, and given some suggestions for things to think about. They then have to devise an experiment and write up their results as a report.

ICT opportunities

ICT PoS 2b: Datalogging

Expected outcomes

Pupils should realise from the model that a thicker layer of fur keeps the heat in.

Pitfalls

Make sure the water is at the same temperature in both flasks to within 2–3°C at the start, otherwise analysis of results is difficult.

Safety notes

Remind pupils of the dangers of hot water. In cases of scalding, cool the skin at once with plenty of running water, and keep it in the cold water for 10 minutes.

Pupils should wear eye protection.

The teacher or technician should dispense the hot water from the kettles.

Answers

Core: **1** The flask with cotton wool/insulation will cool down slower than the flask without cotton wool/insulation.

2, 3, 4, 5 depend on results of experiment

6 e.g. start temperature of water, setting up apparatus, volume of water, length of recording time, repeating the experiment

Help: **1** I think that the flask with insulation will cool down slower than the flask without insulation.

2, 3, 4 depend on results of experiment.

The right size?

Developing thinking skills

A class discussion led by the teacher can be used to introduce the context of the spread. Pupils can then work in small groups, ideally in pairs. The questions in the text are intended to prompt either whole class discussion or small group discussion, as appropriate. The teacher will have the opportunity to intervene and challenge individual pupils. It is advisable not to tell the pupils the answers, but to ask them another question which takes them forward in their thinking. This will help them to develop higher thinking skills. Many of the questions are very open and do not have a simple answer. It is useful to allow some time for pupils to feedback ideas to the class after the group work.

Think about: displaying data and comparing two samples

Pupils are introduced to the idea of human height as a variable that shows a continuous spread, and the need to sample a wide range of data in order to make comparisons and draw conclusions. The context is drawn from a comparison of the heights of Inuit children with children from the USA.

The concrete preparation leads pupils through the need to take a large enough sample in order to see the whole range, and comparing the extremes to show up the maximum difference.

They discuss the graphical display of the data and try to resolve whether the Inuit stature is an inherited feature, a consequence of environment or a combination of both.

Some cognitive conflict will arise as they begin to challenge grandfather's statement and question whether the data presented is sufficient to form the basis for a conclusion. Teachers will have the opportunity to challenge pupils, asking them to explain their thinking.

Key ideas	*Science PoS*
Variation in height within our species has both environmental and inherited causes. Height is a variable that shows a continuous spread. A large sample is needed to show the range. Graphs can be used to make comparisons and decide whether the data is sufficient to draw conclusions.	1.2gimo 2.4a

Activity	*Description*	*Differentiation*
	Class heights – Pupils measure their heights and enter them into a spreadsheet. They use the spreadsheet to sort, display and analyse the data. They are asked evaluate the usefulness of a spreadsheet.	Core, Help

Other relevant material

Reference for the book spread can be found on the Internet: Canadian Journal of Rural Medicine Website: http://www.cma.ca/cjrm/vol%2D3/issue%2D1/0012.htm

Skill sheet 6: Interpreting graphs

continued

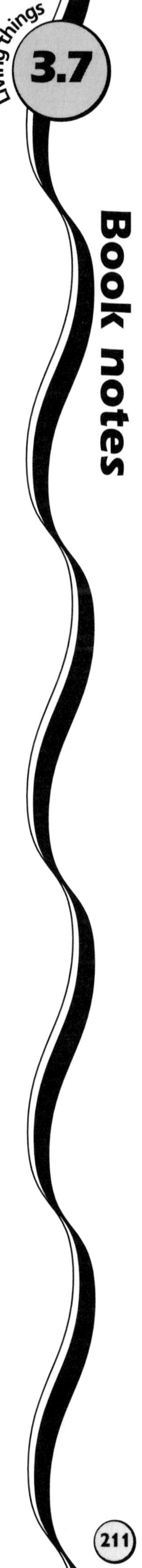

Answers to book questions

Red book

a to see the complete range

b chose some tall, medium and small

1 to see any differences

2 no / very little

3 the Inuits grew at a slower rate / were smaller

4 boys are usually taller than girls

5 weights, diet, disease statistics, seasonal variations – because these all affect growth

6 Some will say 'yes' because the data shows a difference in height early in the children's lives, before the environment has had a chance to affect them.

Others will say 'no' because there is no significant difference at birth or in the first 6 months, and there is a difference as soon as they are subjected to environmental influences.

Some might pick up that the Inuits are heavy, although they are short which does not support the theory that they are small because of a poor diet.

It is important that pupils can explain their answers (metacognition).

7 Some will say 'yes' because the trend will continue, the difference is inherited. Others will say 'no' because 25 years is a long time and there will be changes in the environment which might cause variation. Again, it is important for pupils to explain there thinking.

Green book

a it is passed on through families / it is the best shape for keeping warm / any answer relating to environmental factors, e.g. diet, cold weather, illness, stress of surviving in the cold

b to see the complete range

c choose some tall, medium and small

1 There is a *small* difference in the heights of the Inuits and American girls when they are 12 months old. As they get older, the gap *widens*. The Inuit girls grew *slower* than the girls in the USA.

2 weights, diet, disease statistics, seasonal variations – because these all affect growth

Class heights

Activity 3.7
Core, Help

Purpose

To collect, display and analyse data using spreadsheet software.

Running the activity

Pupils should work in small groups measuring each other's heights. They should visit the computer when they are ready and enter their results into the spreadsheet (Microsoft® *Excel*). The analysis may be done in a plenary part of the lesson. The class data may be made available on a network. There is scope for combining data from other classes.

Core: This sheet gives instructions for the activity.

Help: This sheet gives more guidance on how to use the spreadsheet.

The *Excel* spread sheet is available on the CD-ROM which accompanies this pack. Alternatively, if you decide to set up your own spreadsheet you will need the following columns:

	A	B	C	D	E	F
1	CLASS HEIGHTS					
2						
3		table 1			table 2	
4		Name	Height cm		Range cm	Number of people in the range
5					121 to 130	
6					131 to 140	
7					141 to 150	
8					151 to 160	
9					161 to 170	
10					171 to 180	
11						

ICT opportunities

ICT PoS 1c: Analysing data gathered, 4a: Reflect critically on their use of ICT.

Expected outcomes

Pupils should be able to apply some of the ideas from the 'Think about' spread 3.7 in the book.

Pitfalls

Small classes may not give a large enough range to show a normal distribution, but class results can be combined. You may need to alter the 'Range cm' categories.

Safety notes

Warn pupils to hold/carry metre rules in a safe position.

Answers

These depend on the data collected.

The burning question

Setting the scene

This spread is designed to activate prior knowledge of burning. Pupils are used to reading text in narrative form at Key Stage 2 and some of them find the transition to reading science texts difficult. The story in this spread is designed to bridge that gap, boosting pupils' confidence and gaining their interest.
The **unit map** can be used to brainstorm key words and ideas about the unit topics.

KS2 precursor concepts	*Science PoS*
Pupils should know that burning materials results in the formation of new materials and that the change is not usually reversible.	KS2 3.2g

Activity	*Description*	*Differentiation*
	The burning question – Pupils brainstorm and give presentations demonstrating what they already know about burning. There is scope to use the following skills: intrapersonal (individual, reflective work); interpersonal (discussion); linguistic; artistic; musical and kinesthetic (mime); and numerical (ordering).	Core

Answers to book questions

Red book

1 a e.g. paper, cardboard, fabrics
b e.g. stone, some metals, concrete
2 because the wood was wet
3 a heat, light, sound
b light, heat
c light, sound, heat
4 an irreversible change
5 Answers will vary.
6 Either answer is correct depending on level of understanding.
7 Answer should describe a method of collecting gases, e.g. funnel and tubing.
8 It prevents oxygen getting to the fire.

Green book

a yes (might give examples)
b ash
1 a When a material burns, we see a *flame*.
b Burning is a change that is not *reversible*.
c For a material to burn, you need to give it *heat/air*.

The burning question

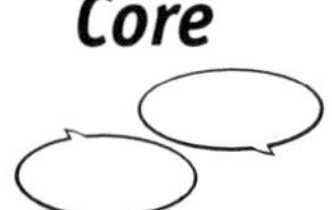

Purpose

To brainstorm in groups and give presentations demonstrating what pupils already know about burning.

Running the activity

Pupils first brainstorm individually using the unit map and make their own version of the map. This could be collected in and used as a guide to assessing each pupil's level of understanding at the start of the topic, and to inform future planning.

Then the class works in groups of three or four to share their ideas and draw a large map. They choose one of their words and prepare a presentation to the class to explain it. Large pieces of paper should be provided for the combined map and the presentation. It is useful to ask each pupil to write in a different colour so that you can assess their individual written contributions.

Pupils have different preferred learning styles, and there is scope within the activity for them to use the following skills: intrapersonal (individual, reflective work); interpersonal (discussion); linguistic; artistic; musical and kinesthetic (mime); and numerical (ordering).

During the presentations, the teacher might build up a concept map of what the pupils already know on the board or OHP and use this to summarise the lesson.

Other relevant material

Unit map

Expected outcomes

Pupils activate their prior knowledge of burning, and present this in a variety of ways.

How does it happen?

Key ideas	*Science PoS*
The part of the air needed for burning is called oxygen. Oxygen is also needed for life. Flammable materials burn more easily than others. Fires need fuel, oxygen and heat to burn.	1.2fgk 3.2h

KS2 precursor concepts	*Science PoS*
(See Book notes 4.1)	–

Activity	*Description*	*Differentiation*
	Putting fires out – Pupils compare how quickly sand, water and foam put out a fire.	Core, Help

Answers to book questions

Red book

a The more air available, the longer the candle burns.

b 21%

1 oxygen

2 so that they can breathe in a burning building, as fire uses up oxygen

3 Something that is flammable burns easily.

flammable

4 to stop them burning as easily/prevent them from melting and sticking to the skin/because they give off poisonous gases when they burn

5 fuel, oxygen and heat.

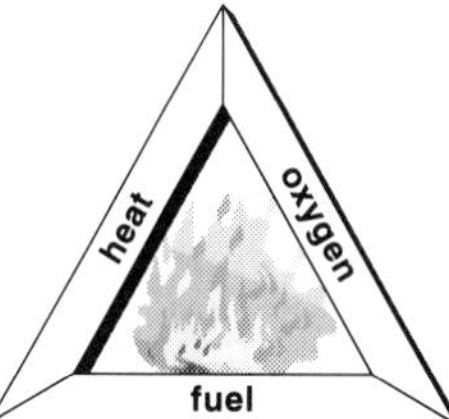

6 heat

Green book

a the one under the biggest jar

b oxygen

c –

d e.g. cigarette ends, putting furniture too close to a gas fire, a spark from an open fire

1 Materials that burn easily are called *flammable*. The gas in the air used in burning is called *oxygen*. To put a fire out, you must take away the fuel, the *heat/oxygen* or the *oxygen/heat*.

2

flammable

3

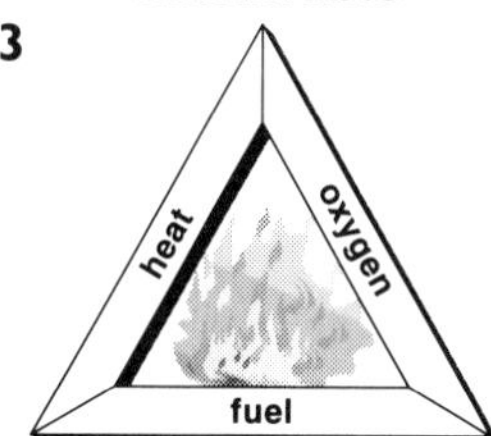

4 heat

Putting fires out

Activity 4.2
Core, Help

Activity notes

Purpose

To evaluate the effectiveness of different methods of putting out fires.

Running the activity

Pupils set up mini fires and use sand, water and foam to put them out. They time how long each fire takes to go out.

Core: The method is given for the experiment, and there are structured questions for analysis and evaluation.

Help: This gives a framework for recording, analysing and evaluating. Diagrams only are provided for the method, so the pupils will need help to carry out the experiment, or it could be carried out as a demonstration.

Expected outcomes

Pupils should compare how quickly each method puts the fire out, and also compare their ease of use. They should realise how each method breaks the fire triangle.

Pitfalls

The activity can be messy. Pupils should dry the bench and use a fresh heatproof mat or tin lid, if sufficient are available, for each of the three fires. A collection of clean, used small food cans (e.g. catfood tins) are ideal for setting the fires in.

Safety notes

Wear eye protection.

Ensure pupils keep their fires small and remind them about the risks of using acids.

The foam may be acid and its use should be carefully controlled.

Answers

Core:

1 sand or water

2 depends on results

3 water or foam

4 water

5 They remove part of the fire triangle: sand prevents oxygen reaching the fuel, water removes heat, foam prevents oxygen reaching the fuel.

Help:

1 The easiest way to put out the fire was *sand* or *water*.
The fire was put out fastest by (*depends on results*).
The most mess to clear up was left by *sand*.

2 The best method to use on a large fire would be *water*.

3
- using sand, *oxygen or fuel*
- using water, *heat*
- using foam, *oxygen or fuel*

Burning changes

Key ideas	*Science PoS*
Substances join with oxygen to make oxides. This is a chemical change. Some metals burn in air to make oxides. (The red book introduces word equations.)	1.2fgjk, 3.1ef, 3.3a

KS2 precursor concepts	*Science PoS*
Pupils should know that reversible changes result in the formation of new materials that may be useful.	KS2 3.2f

Activity	*Description*	*Differentiation*
	Burning metals – Pupils burn magnesium, iron and copper and see that they produce new substances – oxides, and release energy.	Core (with Extension questions), Help

Other relevant material

Skill sheet 7: Word equations (for red book)

Answers to book questions

Red book

1 There is black ash, soot and perhaps pieces of metal and brick which have turned black.

2 Oxides, formed when a substance burns and joins with oxygen in the air.

3 It produces a new substance/you cannot get back the substance you started with.

4 They give out flashes, sparks and colours when they make oxides.

5 a gives out a white flash and makes a white powder (magnesium oxide)

b gives out sparks and makes iron oxide

c makes a black powder (copper oxide)

6 a iron + oxygen → iron oxide

b copper + oxygen → copper oxide

Green book

a There is black ash, soot and pieces of metal and brick which have turned black.

b copper oxide

1 They give out flashes, sparks and colours when they make oxides.

2 a gives out a white flash and makes a white powder (magnesium oxide)

b gives out sparks and makes iron oxide

c makes a black powder (copper oxide)

Burning metals

Activity 4.3
Core (Extension), Help,

Purpose

To observe magnesium, iron and copper as they are heated, analyse what is happening and select the best metal for making a distress flare.

Running the activity

Pupils work in small groups, or alternatively, the teacher might choose to demonstrate this experiment. The three metals are heated in a Bunsen burner flame and the pupils record their observations.

Core: Instructions are given for the experiment. Pupils draw up their own table to record the observations, and questions prompt them to draw conclusions.

Extension: There are optional Extension questions at the foot of the Core sheet, which can be cut off if not required. The questions ask pupils to write word equations.

Help: A table is provided for recording, and structured questions lead to conclusions. The method is not described on this sheet, so pupils will need help to carry out the experiment following the Core sheet, or the sheet could be used to accompany a teacher demonstration.

Other relevant material

Skill sheet 2: Lighting a Bunsen burner
Skill sheet 7: Word equations (for Extension)

Expected outcomes

Pupils see that when magnesium, iron and copper burn, they produce new substances (oxides) and release energy.

Safety notes

Wear eye protection.

Only small pieces of the metals should be provided.

Warn pupils to take care heating the metals. Copper compounds are harmful.

Burning magnesium should be viewed through blue glass or pupils told to look away when they have seen how bright it is.

Answers

Core:
1 magnesium oxide, iron oxide, copper oxide
2 light energy/heat energy
3 magnesium, because it gives out the most light energy

Extension:
4 magnesium + *oxygen* → magnesium oxide
iron + oxygen → *iron oxide*
copper + *oxygen* → copper oxide
5 calcium + oxygen → calcium oxide

Help:
1 magnesium oxide, iron oxide, copper oxide
2 light energy/heat energy
3 magnesium
4 magnesium

Useful burning

Key ideas	*Science PoS*
Fuels store energy. Energy is released when fuels burn. There are many different fuels. The body uses food as fuel. We measure energy in joules, J.	1.2fgijk 3.2h 4.5ae

Activity	*Description*	*Differentiation*
	A: How much energy? – This is a teacher demonstration using a temperature sensor to illustrate how energy can be transferred by burning a fuel.	Core (Help)
	B: A good fuel? – Pupils burn different fuels and evaluate them against a set of criteria.	Core, Help

Answers to book questions

Red book

a petrol, cereal, milk, bacon, sausage, baked beans, eggs, toast, sandwich, gas, chocolate

1 –

2 e.g. it has a store of energy, it gives out heat energy when it burns.

3 you use heat energy, light energy is wasted

4 coal

5 e.g. to keep warm, to move around, for electrical activity in the brain

Green book

a petrol, cereal, milk, bacon, sausage, baked beans, eggs, toast, sandwich, gas, chocolate

b **i** petrol **ii** candle wax

c candle wax, charcoal, gas, petrol e.g. wood, coal, foods

d It is being transferred from the charcoal to the food, making the food hot.

1 A fuel *stores* energy. We call this *chemical* energy. When a fuel *burns*, the stored energy is released as *heat* energy and *light* energy.

2 a William

b Jenny

c William

How much energy?

Activity 4.4A
Core (Help)

Purpose

To analyse and conclude from observations. Pupils also make a plan for a similar experiment using fair testing.

Running the activity

Pupils see how heat energy can be transferred to water by burning a fuel. A temperature sensor and datalogging software are used to monitor the energy transfer. This activity should be carried out as a teacher demonstration because of the potential hazards involved in burning a fuel close to electrical equipment.

Core/Help: The Core sheet gives a format for recording and analysing for pupils to copy and complete. If preferred, it could be used as a write-on Help sheet.

Other relevant material

Skill sheet 6: Interpreting graphs

ICT opportunities

ICT PoS 2b: Datalogging

Expected outcomes

A measurable temperature rise should be observed. This should help pupils appreciate that energy is transferred from the burning fuel to the water.

Safety notes

Wear eye protection.

Methylated spirits is highly flammable – use only the stated amount.

Ensure that the electrical wiring is kept well away from the flame.

Answers

1 –

2 –

3 As the fuel burned, the temperature of the water *rose* or *got higher* or *went up*. As the fuel burned, *energy* was transferred from the fuel to the water.

4 Answers should refer to using equal volumes/masses of fuel and water.

Activity 4.4B
Core, Help

A good fuel?

Purpose

To make observations and evaluate fuels against a set of criteria, and consider whether the experiment is a fair test.

Running the activity

Pupils work in small groups. They burn samples of different fuels and make observations. They are prompted to score the fuels according to four given criteria, and to rank the fuels.

Core: Pupils plan their own results table. Instructions are given to carry out the experiment with four fuels, and questions lead them to evaluate the experiment and plan further experiments.

Help: A table is provided for recording, for three fuels. The questions provide a more structured format for the evaluation of the fuels. The method is not described on this sheet, so pupils will need help to carry out the experiment as set out in the Core sheet, or use the Help sheet to accompany a teacher demonstration.

Other relevant material

Skill sheet 2: Lighting a Bunsen burner

Expected outcomes

Pupils gain an awareness of factors other than energy content that affect the quality of a fuel.

Pitfalls

Some fuels such as coal are difficult to light, and may need to be demonstrated by the teacher. The liquid fuels should be tested by the teacher if pupils cannot be trusted to use only two drops.

Safety notes

Wear eye protection. Only two drops of liquid fuels should be used, and small amounts of solid fuels. Warn pupils to take care heating the fuels and to wash their hands after the experiment.

Answers

Core: **1** –

2 No, the amounts of fuels were not measured.

3 –

4 e.g. cost, pollution, ease of storage

Help: **1** –

2 An ideal fuel is *easy* to light. It burns for the *longest* time. It gives off the *least smoke*. It leaves the *least* ash.

What's special about fuels?

Key ideas	*Science PoS*
The fuels we burn contain carbon, and so does food.	1.2fgk
When carbon burns, it joins with oxygen in the air to make carbon dioxide.	3.1e
Carbon dioxide is a gas which turns limewater milky.	3.2h

KS2 precursor concepts	*Science PoS*
Pupils should know that burning materials results in the formation of new materials and that this change is not usually reversible.	KS2 3.2g

Activity	*Description*	*Differentiation*
	What happens when a fuel burns? – Pupils collect the gas from a burning candle and bubble it through limewater to show that carbon dioxide gas is released when the wax burns.	Core, Help

Answers to book questions

Red book

a cleaner/more convenient/more efficient/cheaper

1 It contains carbon and stores energy.

2 It came from dead trees. The trees were squashed under the ground and gradually changed to coal.

3 Carbon. They produce carbon dioxide when they burn.

4 Trap the gas with a funnel and pass it through limewater. The limewater turns milky.

5 Carbon dioxide is 'heavier than' air so it sinks and covers the fuel, stopping oxygen getting to it. Tip – point directly over the flame to cover the fuel with carbon dioxide gas.

Green book

a ash

b It came from dead trees. The trees were squashed under the ground and gradually changed to coal.

1 Most fuels contain *carbon*. When carbon burns, it *joins* with oxygen to make an *oxide* of carbon. This is a *gas* called *carbon dioxide*.

2 Trap the gas with a funnel and pass it through limewater. The limewater turns milky.

Activity 4.5
Core, Help

What happens when a fuel burns?

Purpose

To illustrate that carbon dioxide is produced during burning. The gas from a burning candle is bubbled through limewater.

Running the activity

Pupils may carry out the experiment in small groups, or the teacher might choose to demonstrate.

Core: Pupils are given a method for the experiment, and questions prompt them to draw conclusions.

Help: The method is not given, and the teacher may prefer to use this sheet to accompany a demonstration. The questions are more structured to help pupils draw conclusions.

Expected outcomes

The gas from the burning candle turns the limewater milky, showing that carbon dioxide gas is released when the wax burns.

Safety notes

Wear eye protection. Warn pupils to take care with the burning candle, and not to touch the hot wax.

Answers

Core:

1. The gas turned the limewater milky.
2. A burning candle gives off carbon dioxide.
3. carbon dioxide
4. smoke or water

Help:

1. The gas from the burning candle turned the limewater *milky*. This shows that the burning candle produces *carbon dioxide*.
2. smoke or water

It's all about reactions

Key ideas	Science PoS
When a fuel burns, a chemical reaction called combustion takes place.	1.1ac
A word equation shows what happens in a chemical reaction.	3.1f, 3.2gh
(Red book only) Equations must balance.	
Hydrocarbons are fuels that contain carbon and hydrogen.	

KS2 precursor concepts	Science PoS
(See Book notes 4.5)	

Activity	Description	Differentiation
	The day we discovered oxygen – Using a report of one of Lavoisier's experiments, the pupils put themselves in the place of a scientist of that time and write their diary for the day. The activity may be used to develop literacy skills and to place science in a historical context.	Core, Help

Other relevant material

Skill sheet 7: Word equations

Answers to book questions

Red book

1 New substances are formed/you cannot get back the substances you started with.

2 combustion

3 to give the particles energy to start reacting

4 A chemical reaction called combustion takes place. Each carbon particle joins with two oxygen particles to form a carbon dioxide particle. Hydrogen joins with oxygen to produce water.

5 hydrogen + oxygen → water

Green book

a combustion

b carbon dioxide

1 When coal burns, oxygen *particles* in the air *join* with particles of carbon in the coal. They make *bigger* particles of a new substance called *carbon dioxide*.

2 carbon + oxygen → *carbon dioxide*

Activity 4.6
Core, Help, Resource

The day we discovered oxygen

Activity notes

Purpose

To develop literacy skills and to place science in a historical context.

Running the activity

Using a report of one of Lavoisier's experiments, the pupils put themselves in the place of a scientist of that time and write their diary for the day.

Pupils could discuss the activity in pairs, write their diaries individually than then redraft each other's work in pairs.

Core: The pupils are given a framework to help them write their diary entries, using the Resource sheet for information.

Help: The diary framework on the write-on sheet includes more detail.

Other relevant material

Resource sheet 4.6

Expected outcomes

Pupils practise narrative writing, and start to develop an awareness of the history of scientific discovery.

Getting hotter

Developing thinking skills

A class discussion led by the teacher can be used to introduce the context of the spread. Pupils can then work in small groups, ideally in pairs. The questions in the text are intended to prompt either whole class discussion or small group discussion, as appropriate. The teacher will have the opportunity to intervene and challenge individual pupils. It is advisable not to tell the pupils the answers, but to ask them another question which takes them forward in their thinking. This will help them to develop higher thinking skills. Many of the questions are very open and do not have a simple answer. It is useful to allow some time for pupils to feedback ideas to the class after the group work.

Think about: relationships between variables

Pupils are introduced to the idea of a relationship between two variables using a model to investigate the greenhouse effect. The terms input variable, outcome variable and relationship are reinforced. The red book spread develops the concept of the straight-line graph as a picture of the relationship between two proportional variables. The green book spread allows for the development of literacy skills by practising terminology, e.g. hot, hotter, hottest.

Key ideas	*Science PoS*
We use the word relationship to describe how the outcome variable changes when we change the input variable.	1.2cgijklmp
(Red book only) A straight-line graph shows that there is a relationship between the variables.	3.2i
Scientists use a model to represent a real situation that is difficult to test.	

Activity	*Description*	*Differentiation*
	Grow your own greenhouse effect – A temperature sensor is used to compare the temperatures inside and outside a glass jar, which represents a greenhouse. This is a datalogging activity which starts with a prediction and leads pupils through the stages of a full investigation.	Core, Help

Other relevant material

Skill sheet 6: Interpreting graphs

ICT opportunities

ICT PoS 1b: Obtaining information well matched to purpose.

Research information about global warming is available at http://www.globalwarming.org/

continued

Getting hotter ⋙ continued

Answers to book questions

Red book

a input variable – carbon dioxide level, outcome variable – temperature

b 22 °C

1 29 °C

2 yes, reasoning based on relationship derived from the model or no, the model is flawed/changes in carbon dioxide levels are difficult to measure

3 It will increase, appropriate reasoning *or* it will not increase, we might burn fewer fossil fuels.

4 e.g. set up a long-term experiment, try to get data about the Earth since this is only a model, test other input variables such as levels of other gases in the air.

5 a Ice-caps will melt, causing sea levels to rise, resulting in flooding.

b The weather will get warmer, with more extremes.

c Food supplies will suffer because crops will fail as a result of floods and weather changes.

Green book

a carbon dioxide in the air

b because the carbon dioxide in the air has the same effect as the glass in a greenhouse

c As the carbon dioxide increases, the Earth gets *warmer*.

d The Earth would get cooler.

e carbon dioxide level

f temperature

1 a Both the carbon dioxide level and the temperature in the biodome have *increased* over the 5 days.

b As the carbon dioxide level *increased*, the temperature became *higher*.

2 –

Activity notes

Grow your own greenhouse effect

Activity 4.7
Core, Help

Purpose

To carry out a datalogging activity which starts with a prediction and leads pupils through the stages of a full investigation. A temperature sensor is used to compare the temperatures inside and outside a glass jar, which represents a greenhouse.

Running the activity

The activity is intended as a teacher demonstration. The equipment should be set up to record while pupils are working on the book spread.

Core: Pupils are asked to make a prediction and plan a results table. They go on to obtain, analyse and evaluate the results.

Help: The sheet gives a more structured format for analysis and conclusion only.

Other relevant material

Skill sheet 6: Interpreting graphs

ICT opportunities

ICT PoS 2b: Datalogging

Expected outcomes

The temperature difference obtained will depend on the ambient conditions. On a hot sunny day, a significant temperature difference can be obtained after half an hour, but you may wish to set the experiment up to record over a day and discuss how and why both graphs follow the same pattern.

Pitfalls

A sunny day is essential.

Answers

Core: **1** The air inside the jar was hotter, because the glass helped to keep the heat energy inside.

2 Refer to prediction.

3 No, difficult to keep the room temperature constant, or sensors may have received different amounts of light.

4 e.g. leave it for longer, do the experiment outside (central heating fluctuations may have affected the results), repeat it for reliability, cover the jar with a glass lid

Help: **1** At the end of the experiment, the temperature inside the jar was *higher* than at the start of the experiment.
The glass stops some of the heat energy *escaping* from the greenhouse. The plants stay *warm*.

At the touch of a switch

Setting the scene

This spread asks pupils to think about the importance of electricity in their lives. They then trace the development of the domestic electric light bulb. The lesson could be started by reading this spread by candlelight.

The text draws on Key Stage 2 work on circuits. The **unit map** can be used to brainstorm key words and ideas about the unit topics.

KS2 precursor concepts	*Science PoS*
Pupils should know:	KS2 1.1a
• about the part that science has played in the development of many of the things that they use	1.1ac
• that a complete circuit, including a battery or power supply, is needed to make electrical devices work.	4.1a

Activity	*Description*	*Differentiation*
	Developing the light bulb – Pupils read the biographies of Davy, Swan and Edison and answer the questions on the sheet.	Extension

Other relevant material

Skill sheet 4: Energy transfers

The following teacher demonstrations can be carried out to illustrate the development of the electric filament lamp:

- increase the current in a wire until it glows, then breaks
- show pupils a carbon filament lamp and compare this with a modern clear light bulb.

ICT opportunities

Biographies of Humphry Davy in the CD-ROM *Eyewitness Encyclopedia of Science 2.0* (Dorling Kindersley), *The Way Things Work* (Dorling Kindersley) and *Encarta* (Microsoft®).

Biographies of Edison in the CD-ROM *The Way Things Work* and *Encarta*.

Biography of Swan in the CD-ROM *The Way Things Work*.

Answers to book questions

Red book

a –

b –

c It goes out, because the circuit has been broken so it is no longer being heated.

d The platinum burned when it became hot.

e The filaments burned.

f so that the filament would not burn

g The tungsten filaments lasted longer.

h A coiled filament is longer, so there is more glow.

Green book

a –

b –

c the electricity

d It glows.

e The filament burned and broke.

f It lasted longer.

g It was longer so it made a bigger glow

▷▷▷ continued

At the touch of a switch ▷▷▷ continued

Answers to book questions

Red book

1 It is cleaner (no smoke), easier to turn on and off, brighter, needs less maintenance.

2 It would be better if they did not give out so much heat energy (wasted energy), if they were made of an unbreakable material and if the filament did not break after it was used for a long time.

3 1801 – Davy tried out a platinum filament lamp
1850 – Swan started to make filament lamps
1875 – (Sprengel and Crookes) invented the pump to take the air out of the bulbs
1878 – Swan invented a successful filament lamp (with a carbon filament)
1879 – Edison invented a successful filament lamp (also with a carbon filament)
1911 – tungsten filaments introduced
1913 – coiled filament introduced

4 –

Green book

1 It is cleaner (no smoke), easier to turn on and off, brighter, needs less maintenance.

2 a It gives out bright light and it is cheap.

b It would be better if it did not give out so much heat energy (wasted energy), if it was made of an unbreakable material and if the filament did not break after it was used for a long time.

3 –

Activity 5.1 *Extension* Developing the light bulb

Purpose

To extend understanding of the historical development of the light bulb, for more able pupils.

Running the activity

Pupils work individually or in pairs to read the biographies of the scientists and answer the questions on the sheet.

ICT opportunities

Biographies of Humphry Davy in the CD-ROM *Eyewitness Encyclopedia of Science 2.0* (Dorling Kindersley), *The Way Things Work* (Dorling Kindersley) and *Encarta* (Microsoft®).

Biographies of Edison in the CD-ROM *The Way Things Work* and *Encarta*.

Biography of Swan in the CD-ROM *The Way Things Work*.

Expected outcomes

Pupils gain an insight into how scientific discoveries can stem from the work of several scientists working at different times, and appreciate the commercial value of inventions.

Answers

1 carbon, because you can heat it to a higher temperature before it melts

2 Platinum is much more expensive than carbon.

3 **a** carbon dioxide **b** platinum oxide

4 If the number of light bulbs in the pupil's home is *n*, the sum is £$(n \times 5000000 \times 2)/(4 \times 240)$. If *n* is 10, the patent was worth about £104000 per year in Britain.

5 –

Circuit training

Key ideas	*Science PoS*
We get energy from electricity to make things work. You need a complete circuit for energy to be transferred.	4.1c

KS2 precursor concepts	*Science PoS*
Pupils should know that a complete circuit, including a battery or power supply, is needed to make electrical devices work.	KS2 4.1a

Activity	*Description*	*Differentiation*
	A: Find the fault – Pupils visit circuits set up around the room that do not work, and decide what is wrong with them, to check their understanding that a complete circuit is needed for a transfer of energy.	Core (no pupil sheets)
	B: Switch on! – Pupils solve the puzzles of circuit diagrams with multiple switches.	Core, Extension

Note

The word 'battery' is used in this unit although, in reality, we are using 'cells'. The symbol for a cell is used, yet referred to as a battery. This is to avoid confusion with cells in Life Processes and Living Things, and to access the pupils' experiences.

Other relevant material

Skill sheet 4: Energy transfer diagrams

ICT opportunities

A useful piece of software for making circuits is available on the CD-ROM *Crocodile Clips 3* (Crocodile Clips Ltd). *Crocodile Clips 3 Elementary* can be downloaded from: www.crocodile-clips.com/education/.

Answers to book questions

Red book

a chemical energy in battery → (electrical energy) → lamp → (light energy) →, (thermal energy) →

b B, F

c A, D, E

d C

1

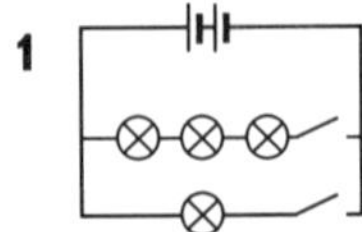

2 a 4

b 3

c Lamps lit column: 1, 2, 3, 4; 2; 1, 2, 4; 1, 2, 3; 2.

3 No battery – open up and check; flat battery – test with battery checker on packet or try in another device; batteries wrong way around – open up and check; lamp blown – look/replace with new lamp; wiring in torch damaged – try with new batteries and new lamp.

Green book

a see **a** red book

b B

1 see **1** red book

2 a 3

b 3

c Lamps lit column: 1, 2, 3; None; 2; 2; 2.

Activity 5.2A
Core (no pupil sheets)

Find the fault

Activity notes

Purpose

To check pupils' understanding that a complete circuit is needed for a transfer of energy. Pupils visit circuits that do not work and decide what is wrong with them.

Running the activity

This is a short activity. It is suggested that the class be divided into pairs, and the pairs grouped (four pairs in a group). The pairs visit each of four circuits and write down what is wrong with each one. At their last circuit, they put the circuit right and prepare to report back to the class.

Four sets of the following experiments are needed for this activity:

- Circuit 1: a series circuit with 1 lamp and 1 battery, but the filament of the lamp is broken
- Circuit 2: a series circuit with 1 lamp and 1 battery, but the leads are both attached to the same side of the lamp
- Circuit 3: a series circuit with 1 lamp and 2 batteries, but one of the batteries is the wrong way round
- Circuit 4: a complicated circuit with, say, 5 lamps and 2 batteries, but one of the leads is not connected. The circuit should be set up so that the leads look muddled.
- 4 spare bulbs ready to replace the faulty one in each circuit 1

Expected outcomes

Circuit 1: the filament lamp has no filament.
Circuit 2: both connections to the lamp are on the same side of the holder.
Circuit 3: the two batteries are different ways around.
Circuit 4: in the spaghetti of wires, one is not connected.

Pitfalls

Make sure that circuits 2, 3 and 4 are not 'mended' by pairs 1, 2 or 3.

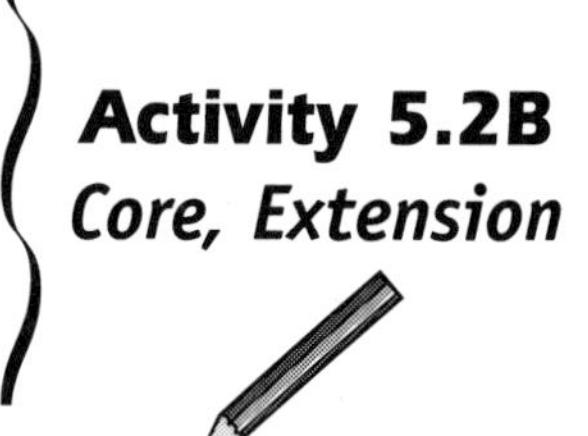

Switch on!

Activity 5.2B
Core, Extension

Purpose

To give pupils experience of problem solving in the context of circuits.

Running the activity

Pupils work individually or in pairs to work out what happens in the circuits on the sheet when the switches are open and closed.

Core: The circuits are straightforward parallel circuits. A table is provided for pupils to copy and complete in order to answer question 5. If preferred, the sheet could be used as a write-on disposable sheet, with the pupils instructed to write in the table on the sheet.

Extension: The circuits are more complex. A table is provided for each circuit for pupils to copy and complete.

Expected outcomes

Pupils solve the problems on the sheet and realise that a complete circuit is needed for a lamp to light.

Answers

Core:

1 A, C

2 A, B, C

3 none

4 D, E, F

5

Switches closed	Lamps lit
1	G
2	H
3	I
1, 2	G, H
1, 3	G, I
2, 3	H, I
1, 2, 3	G, H, I

Extension: **1 Circuit 1**

Switches closed	Lamps lit
1	none
2	A
3	none
4	none
1, 2	A
1, 3	B
1, 4	none
2, 3	A
2, 4	A
3, 4	C
1, 2, 3	A, B
1, 3, 4	B, C
2, 3, 4	A, C
1, 2, 3, 4	A, B, C

Circuit 2

Switches closed	Lamps lit
1	A
2	none
3	B
4	B, E
5	D, E
1, 2	A
1, 3	A, B
1, 4	A, B, E
1, 5	A, D, E
2, 3	B, C
2, 4	B, C, E
2, 5	D, E
3, 5	B, D, E
4, 5	B, D, E
1, 2, 3	A, B, C
1, 4, 5	A, B, D, E
2, 4, 5	B, C, D, E

Current affairs

Key ideas	*Science PoS*
Current is measured in amps, A, using an ammeter. The current is the same on both sides of a lamp. Increasing the number of batteries makes the lamps brighter and increases the current. (Red book only) Increasing the number of lamps decreases the current.	1.1b, 2cgijkl 4.1ab

KS2 precursor concepts	*Science PoS*
Pupils should know: • how changing the number or type of components in a circuit can make bulbs brighter or dimmer • how to represent series circuits by drawings and conventional symbols • how to construct series circuits on the basis of drawings and conventional symbols.	KS2 4.1bc

Activity	*Description*	*Differentiation*
	A: Demonstration: the current either side of a lamp – Teacher demonstration that the current is the same on either side of the lamp in a series circuit.	Core (no pupil sheets)
	B: Investigating current – Pupils see how varying the number of batteries affects the current (Core), and how varying the number of lamps affects the current (Extension).	Core, Extension

Other relevant material

Skill sheet 5: Drawing charts and graphs
Skill sheet 6: Interpreting graphs

Answers to book questions

Red book

a in the circuit
b amps
c the same
d Laura
e Dan
f Laura
g Dan's
h The current gets bigger.

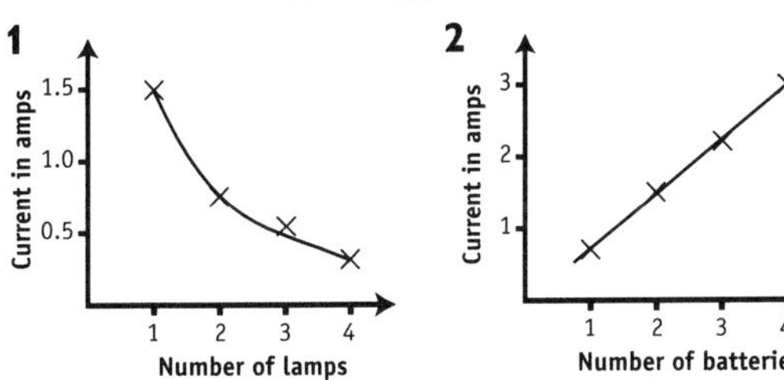

Green book

a in the circuit
b amps
c –
d Dan
e Lucy
f The more batteries there are, the greater the current.

1 There is a current in the *circuit*. We measure current by using an *ammeter*. Current is measured in *amps*. The current is the *same* before and after the lamp.

2 a the one in circuit **D**
b This circuit has the biggest current.
c There would be too much current for the lamp and it would 'blow'.

Demonstration: the current either side of a lamp

Activity 5.3A
Core (no pupil sheets)

Purpose

To demonstrate that the current is the same on either side of the lamp in a series circuit.

Running the activity

This is a teacher demonstration. The circuit should be set up with an ammeter on each side of the lamp.

Expected outcomes

The current shown on both ammeters should be the same.

Pitfalls

It is important that pupils are not distracted by the inaccuracy of the ammeters. Digital ammeters can show readings that vary by ± 0.02 A, and therefore the second decimal place is likely to differ between the ammeters. This distracts pupils, who do not realise that such a difference is within the limits of accuracy of the measuring device. One possible solution is to use digital ammeters that measure only to 0.1 A, or to use analogue meters, which pupils will not read to a hundredth of an amp. The large, old-fashioned display ammeters are ideal.

Activity 5.3B *Core, Extension*

Investigating current

Activity notes

Purpose

To see how varying the number of batteries affects the current (Core), and how varying the number of lamps affects the current (Extension).

Running the activity

Pupils work in pairs or small groups.

Core: Pupils make a prediction about what effect changing the number of batteries will have on the current. They build a circuit from a realistic diagram, and are given a table format for recording their results. They draw a line graph and analyse their results.

Extension: This activity has a similar format to the Core one, except that pupils are looking at the effect of the number of lamps on the current. Circuit diagrams are provided from which to build their circuits, rather than realistic diagrams. Pupils are asked to use their graph to predict the outcome of a further experiment.

More able pupils could do both experiments, or could go straight to the Extension activity and pick up on the Core experiment when groups report back at the end of the lesson.

Other relevant material

Skill sheet 5: Drawing charts and graphs
Skill sheet 6: Interpreting graphs

Expected outcomes

Core: The current should be proportional to the number of batteries in the circuit.

Extension: The current is inversely proportional to the number of lamps. The graph will be a curve with a negative gradient.

Pitfalls

Core: Ensure that pupils do not use too many batteries, or they will 'blow' the lamp. For five 1.5 V batteries, the lamp used needs to be >7.5 V, probably 12 V. The lamp will not glow when one battery is used, but the current will show on the ammeter. If the Core and Extension activities are being run together, pupils will have to be warned which lamp to use.

Extension: The sheet assumes a voltage of 3 V (two 1.5 V batteries). A lamp should be chosen that glows brightly with 3 V. Adding more lamps will make each dimmer, but the ammeter will measure the current. Make sure that the lamps for Core and Extension, which are likely to be different, are kept separately.

Answers

Core:

1 The current should increase.

2 Acceptable reasons include: more electricity flowing around the circuit *or* more batteries will make more electricity.

3 The current should have increased as more batteries were added. The graph should be a straight line. The current doubled as the number of batteries was doubled.

4 Depends on answer to **1**.

Extension:

1 There should be less current with more lamps.

2 Acceptable answers include: the electricity has to flow through more lamps so it slows down *or* the electricity finds it more difficult to flow.

3 The current should have decreased when they added more lamps. The graph should be curved with a negative, decreasing gradient.

4 Depends on answer to **1**.

5 Pupils should try to extrapolate their graph (not easy as it is a curve). They then should read off the current for 6 lamps.

Energy from electricity

Key ideas	*Science PoS*
Voltage is measured across parts of a circuit.	4.1ac
Voltage is measured in volts, V, using a voltmeter.	1.1b
There is a voltage across any part of the circuit where energy is entering or exiting.	1.2cgijkl

KS2 precursor concepts	*Science PoS*
Voltage is not studied at KS2 but pupils have probably made circuits with different numbers of batteries.	–

Activity	*Description*	*Differentiation*
	A: Demonstration: the voltage across different parts of a circuit – Teacher demonstration to show that there is a voltage across those parts of a circuit where energy is put in (the batteries) or leaves (in this case, a lamp).	Core (no pupil sheets)
	B: Investigating voltage: batteries – Pupils find out how the voltage changes when the number of batteries in a circuit is increased: more batteries means more energy being sent out, which means more voltage.	Core, Extension

Answers to book questions

Red book

a i 2.35 V
  ii 2.35 V
  iii 0 V

b at the battery

c at the lamp

d No energy is entering or exiting the circuit at the wires.

e the one across the batteries in circuit **B**; more batteries, more energy entering, so more voltage

f the one in circuit **B**

g 6.0 V

h 3.0 V; because there is no energy leaving at the wires, so it all leaves at the lamp

1 **B**

2 A 3, B 4, C 6, D 2 (each battery is 1.5 V)

Green book

a i yes
  ii yes
  iii no

b at the battery

c at the lamp

d No energy is going into or out of the circuit at the wires.

e **B**; there are more batteries

f circuit **B**

g **B**

h 4 V

1

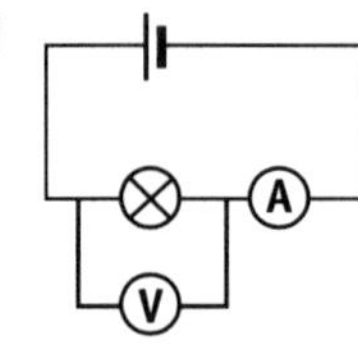

2 B

Activity 5.4A
Core (no pupil sheets)

Demonstration: the voltage across different parts of a circuit

Purpose

To show that there is a voltage across those parts of a circuit where energy is put in (the batteries) or leaves (in this case, a lamp).

Running the activity

The activity is a teacher demonstration. Voltmeters are connected into a simple series circuit across the battery, the lamp, and the leads.

Expected outcomes

The voltage across the battery and the lamp should be the same. There should be no voltage across the leads, as an insignificant amount of energy is lost from the circuit in the leads.

Pitfalls

Use the largest voltmeters available. Use four voltmeters so that pupils can see them simultaneously.

Investigating voltage: batteries

Activity 5.4B
Core, Extension

Purpose

To show pupils how the voltage changes when the number of batteries in a circuit is increased: more batteries means more energy being sent out, which means more voltage.

Running the activity

Pupils work in pairs or small groups.

Core: Pupils make a prediction about how the voltage will change as they add more batteries to a circuit. They build a circuit from a realistic diagram, and are given a table format for recording their results. They draw a line graph and analyse their results.

Extension: This activity has a similar format to the Core one. Circuit diagrams are provided from which to build their circuits, rather than realistic diagrams. Pupils are asked to use their graph to predict the outcome of a further experiment.

Pitfalls

Ensure that pupils do not use too many batteries, or they will 'blow' the lamp. For five 1.5 V batteries, the lamp used needs to be >7.5 V, probably 12 V. The lamp will not glow when one battery is used, but the voltage will register on the voltmeter.

Answers

Core:

1 The voltage will increase with the number of batteries.

2 If there are more batteries more energy is being put into the circuit, so there will be more voltage.

3 It increased (presumably).

4 Depends on pupil's response to **1**.

Extension:

1 The voltage will increase with the number of batteries.

2 If there are more batteries more energy is being put into the circuit, so there will be more voltage.

3 It increased (presumably).

4 Depends on pupil's response to **1**.

5 Pupils should extrapolate the graph to six batteries, and read off the voltage.

Models of electricity

Developing thinking skills

A class discussion led by the teacher can be used to introduce the context of the spread. Pupils can then work in small groups, ideally in pairs. The questions in the text are intended to prompt either whole class discussion or small group discussion, as appropriate. The teacher will have the opportunity to intervene and challenge individual pupils. It is advisable not to tell the pupils the answers, but to ask them another question which takes them forward in their thinking. This will help them to develop higher thinking skills. Many of the questions are very open and do not have a simple answer. It is useful to allow some time for pupils to feedback ideas to the class after the group work.

Think about: models

At Key Stage 3, pupils are meeting concepts for which there is no simple explanation based on what they can see. If they are to go beyond making observations and learning facts, they need to start having a mental picture of what is happening. This mental picture, or model, will be simple and limited but it will be elaborated as they progress into and through Key Stage 4. This spread shows how the ideas developed in earlier lessons are used to make a model. The idea of testing the model is not introduced at this stage.

Key ideas	*Science PoS*
We can use models to think about electricity.	1.1c

KS2 precursor concepts	*Science PoS*
Pupils should know that science is about thinking creatively to explain things and think about causes.	KS2 1.1a

Activity	*Description*	*Differentiation*
	Demonstration: 'class and matches' model – class demonstration to give pupils experience of using models.	Core (no pupil sheets)

Answers to book questions

Red book

- **a** **i** the track
  - **ii** the mine
  - **iii** the power station
  - **iv** the coal
- **b** increase
- **c** The energy goes in at the mine, and out at the power station, so these are where the voltage would be, but it is not very obvious.
- **d** –
- **e** Check diagrams: the matches are the energy (green); the moving pupils are the current (yellow); Mrs Fuller is the battery; Miss Huxley is the lamp; the chalked circle is the circuit (pink).
- **f** –
- **g** e.g. you could have someone counting the numbers of pupils that went by at a certain time.
- **h** e.g. you could have someone counting the matches being given out or the matches being collected.

Green book

- **a** **i** the track
  - **ii** the mine
  - **iii** the power station
  - **iv** the coal
- **b** increase
- **c** The energy goes in at the mine, and out at the power station, so these are where the voltage would be, but it is not very obvious.
- **d** **i** the matches
  - **ii** the chalked circle
  - **iii** the moving pupils
  - **iv** Mrs Fuller; Miss Huxley
- **e** Check diagrams: the match is the energy (green); the moving pupils are the current (yellow); Mrs Fuller is the battery; Miss Huxley is the lamp; the chalked circle is the circuit (pink).

▷▷▷ continued

Models of electricity

>>> continued

Answers to book questions

Red book

1 –

2 Bicycle: the chain is the circuit, the 'energy in' is the movement of the pedals and the 'energy out' is the movement energy of the back wheel. It is difficult to say what the current is.

Roller coaster: the track is the circuit, the moving trucks are the current, the 'energy in' is when the trucks are lifted up but the 'energy out' is less clear – it could be the movement energy of the trucks. The energy carried is difficult (the remaining gravitational potential energy).

Green book

1 a Jackie shows someone giving out the matches (this is the battery) and someone collecting the matches (this is the lamp). She has some walking pupils carrying matches (this is could be current), but there is no complete circuit and there is no current on the far side of the lamp.

b Lester shows the complete circuit and he has the current all around the circuit (the walking pupils). He has half the pupils carrying matches (energy) and half not, but he does not explain where they get the energy from (there is no battery) nor where they give it up (no lamp).

Activity 5.5
Core (no pupil sheets)

Demonstration: 'class and matches' model

Purpose

To give pupils experience of using models.

Running the activity

A 'circuit' is marked on the floor with chalk or tape. The circle must be big enough for all members of the class to walk around at once (the pupils should be quite close together).

One teacher, or a trusted pupil, stands at one side of the circle. He or she is the battery and he or she will put energy into the circuit by giving out matches. Another teacher stands opposite, again on the 'circuit'. He or she is the lamp, and he or she will take energy out of the circuit by taking in the matches and striking them.

The pupils stand on the circle. They walk slowly around the circle and collect a match from the 'battery' as they go by, and deliver the match to the 'lamp'. The pupils themselves actually represent the charge carriers, but as charge carriers have not been introduced, the moving pupils are considered to represent the current. Pupils can be asked to speed up a little to represent an increase in current, or slow down to represent a decrease in current.

Pitfalls

Use the largest type of household matches, so they are easily seen.

Safety notes

If only one teacher is available, he or she should be the 'lamp' (who strikes the matches).

More circuits

Key ideas	*Science PoS*
You can connect lamps in series and in parallel. Parallel circuits have more than one loop. Lamps in parallel are brighter than the same lamps in series, using the same battery. In a series circuit: • the current is the same at all points • the voltage is shared between the lamps. In a parallel circuit: • the current is shared between the loops • the voltage is the same across the battery and each lamp.	4.1a

KS2 precursor concepts	*Science PoS*
Series circuits	KS2 4.1c

Activity	*Description*	*Differentiation*
	A: Series and parallel circuits: current – Pupils set up their own series and parallel circuits and measure the current at three points.	Core, Extension
	B: Series and parallel circuits: voltage – Pupils set up their own series and parallel circuits and measure the voltage across each lamp and across the 'battery'.	Core

ICT opportunities

An explanation of series and parallel circuits is read out in the CD-ROM *Eyewitness Encyclopedia of Science 2.0* (Dorling Kindersley) under 'Physics', 'Electric circuits'.

A useful piece of software for making circuits is available on the CD-ROM *Crocodile Clips 3* (Crocodile Clips Ltd). *Crocodile Clips 3 Elementary* can be downloaded from: www.crocodile-clip.com/education/.

Answers to book questions

Red book

a X 0.1 A, **Y** 0.1 A
b P 0.4A, **Q** 0.2A, **R** 0.2 A
c 1.75 V (7 V shared four ways)
d 7.0 V

Green book

a series
b parallel
c those in the parallel circuit
d X 0.1 A, **Y** 0.1 A
e P 0.4A, **Q** 0.2A, **R** 0.2 A
f parallel
g series

continued

More circuits ⊳⊳⊳ continued

Answers to book questions

Red book

1

	Series circuits	Parallel circuits
Lamp brightness	Dimmer	Brighter
Number of loops	One	More than one
Voltage	Shared	Same
Current	Same	Shared

2

3a, b Coal truck model: series circuit – same as before but there are two identical power stations; half the coal is unloaded at one and half at the other. This works quite well as it explains why the current is the same all the way round but why the voltage is shared across the lamps.

Parallel circuit – same as before but there are two identical power stations and the track branches, with one loop going to one power station and one to the other; half the trucks go one way and half the other. Each truck dumps all its coal (energy) at the power station. A problem is that with half the trucks, you might expect half the total energy. With half the trucks going one way and half the other, the divided current is explained.

Green book

1

Series circuits	Parallel circuits
The lamps are dimmer.	The lamps are brighter.
The voltage across the battery is shared between the lamps.	The voltage is the same across the battery and each lamp.
The current is the same at all points in the circuit.	The current is shared between the loops of the circuit.

2

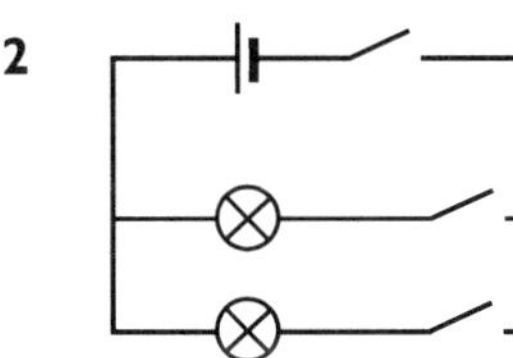

Series and parallel circuits: current

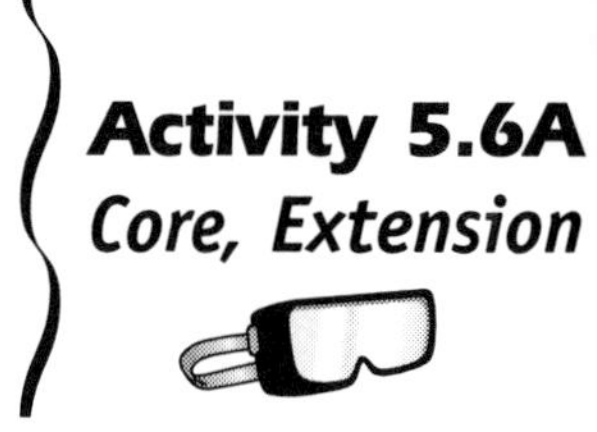

Purpose

To show pupils how to wire series and parallel circuits, and to measure current at different points in them.

Running the activity

Pupils work in pairs or small groups. Some groups could do this activity while others do Activity 5.6B, with all groups reporting back at the end.

Core: The circuit diagrams are given in the table. The table can be photocopied for less able pupils, who will find it difficult to draw so many circuit diagrams.

Extension: Pupils build their circuits from circuit diagrams. They need to construct their own table for recording their results. A final question hints at the mathematical relationship between the currents in different loops of a parallel circuit.

Expected outcomes

The current should be the same at all points in a series circuit.

The current varies at different points in a parallel circuit, dividing at branches.

Answers

Core:

1 Pupils will discuss their own experimental results. They should find that the current is the same in all parts of the circuit.

2 Pupils will discuss their own experimental results. They will notice that the current is not the same in all three positions. Some may notice that the current in position 1 is greater than at positions 2 and 3. Some able students may notice that the currents measured at 2 and 3 add up to the current measured at position 1.

Extension:

1 Pupils should find that the current is the same at all three positions. They should quote their results in their conclusion to support this.

2 Pupils should find that the current is not the same in all three positions. They should quote their results to support this.

3 If you add the currents measured at positions 2 and 3, it equals the current at position 1.

Activity 5.6B
Core

Series and parallel circuits: voltage

Purpose

To show pupils how to wire series and parallel circuits, and to measure voltage across different points in series and parallel circuits.

Running the activity

Pupils work in pairs or small groups. Some groups could do this activity while others do Activity 5.6A, with all groups reporting back at the end.

Expected outcomes

The voltage is different across the components in a series circuit, and adds to the voltage across the battery.

The voltage should be the same across the different components in a parallel circuit.

Answers

1 It is different across different places around the series circuit.

2 It is the same across different places around the parallel circuit.

Magnets

Key ideas	*Science PoS*
A coil of wire connected to a battery makes a magnet. Magnets make magnetic fields. Magnetic fields have magnetic field lines. Like magnetic poles repel. Unlike poles attract. Iron, nickel and cobalt are magnetic metals.	4.1de

KS2 precursor concepts	*Science PoS*
Pupils should know that there are forces of attraction and repulsion between magnets, and forces of attraction between magnets and magnetic materials.	KS2 4.2a

Activity	*Description*	*Differentiation*
	A: What do magnets do? – Pupils can carry out simple experiments with magnets, if they seem unfamiliar with magnets.	Core (Help)
	B: Demonstration: the magnetic field around a bar magnet and a coil – To familiarise pupils with magnetic fields and magnetic field lines. These are visualised using iron filings, and the direction of the field lines is found using a compass. The shape of the magnetic field around a bar magnet and a coil is shown to pupils.	Core (no pupil sheets)
	C: Demonstration: how a coil behaves like a magnet – To show pupils that a coil with a current through it behaves like a bar magnet.	Core (no pupil sheets)

Answers to book questions

Red book

a X
b The compasses would all point to north.
c Check diagrams – two north poles adjacent, or two south poles adjacent.
d The coils are acting as magnets, and opposite poles are together.
e They would no longer pull together they would no longer act as magnets.
f iron, nickel, cobalt

1 a magnetic field
b magnetic field lines
c magnetic materials
d repelling
e attracting

2 Like a bar magnet: has a north and a south pole, attracts magnetic materials, makes a magnetic field with magnetic field lines. Unlike a bar magnet: needs a current to make it work and stops working when you switch the current off.

Green book

a The compasses would all point to north.
b Check diagrams – opposite poles adjacent.
c They would no longer pull together.
d iron, nickel, cobalt
e any two metals except iron, nickel or cobalt (e.g. copper, aluminium, gold, silver)

1 a magnetic field
b magnetic field lines
c magnetic materials
d repelling
e attracting

2 has a north and a south pole, attracts magnetic materials, makes a magnetic field with magnetic field lines

Activity 5.7A
Core (Help)

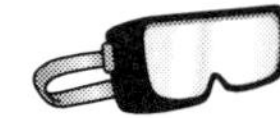

What do magnets do?

Purpose

To provide familiarity with simple bar magnets, for those pupils who need it.

Running the activity

Pupils work in pairs. They test different metals with a bar magnet, see the effect of a magnetic field on a compass, and experiment with pushing magnets together. They look at some statements about magnets and write out the correct ones.

If preferred, the Core sheet could be used as a write-on disposable Help sheet, with answer lines drawn on beside questions 1–4. For question 5, they could tick or colour the correct statements, or cut them out and stick them in their books.

Instead of making detailed notes, pupils could feed back their observations at the beginning of the demonstrations (Activities 5.7B and 5.7C).

Expected outcomes

Pupils find out that iron and nickel are magnetic, but copper and aluminium are not. The compass needle shows the magnetic field. Same poles repel, opposite poles attract.

Pitfalls

Give pupils a time limit for this activity.

Answers

1 iron, nickel

2 The compass needle points towards one end of the magnet and away from the other end.

3 They repel/attract.

4 They attract/repel.

5 Iron sticks to a magnet.
Nickel sticks to a magnet.
Iron and nickel are magnetic materials.
Compasses point towards one end (pole) of the magnet.
Compasses point away from the other end (pole) of the magnet.
Same poles repel.
Unlike poles attract.

Demonstration: the magnetic field around a bar magnet and a coil

Activity 5.7B
Core (no pupil sheets)

Purpose

To familiarise pupils with magnetic fields and magnetic field lines. These are visualised using iron filings, and the direction of the field lines is found using a compass. The shape of the magnetic field around a bar magnet and a coil is shown to pupils.

Running the activity

This teacher demonstration is best done on an overhead projector.

The pattern of the field using iron filings

Put the bar magnet under an overhead transparency and prop up the corners of the transparency so that it is flat. Sprinkle the iron filings thinly onto the overhead transparency and tap gently until they form lines. Focus the overhead projector on the magnetic field lines.

For the coil, best results are obtained using a commercial apparatus produced for the purpose, which has a solenoid in a Perspex platform. Again, it can be used on the overhead projector. Put an overhead transparency under the apparatus to catch the iron filings. Connect the coil to a power supply following the manufacturer's recommendation. Sprinkle the filings on the Perspex platform and tap gently.

The direction of the field using plotting compasses

If see-through compasses are used, this can also be done on the overhead projector. The compasses along the bar magnet will not be projected due to the shadow of the magnet and their direction should be confirmed by a pupil. Compasses should be placed inside as well as around the coil. The electricity should be turned off when the direction of the magnetic field has been seen.

Expected outcomes

The fields around the bar magnet and the coil are similar.

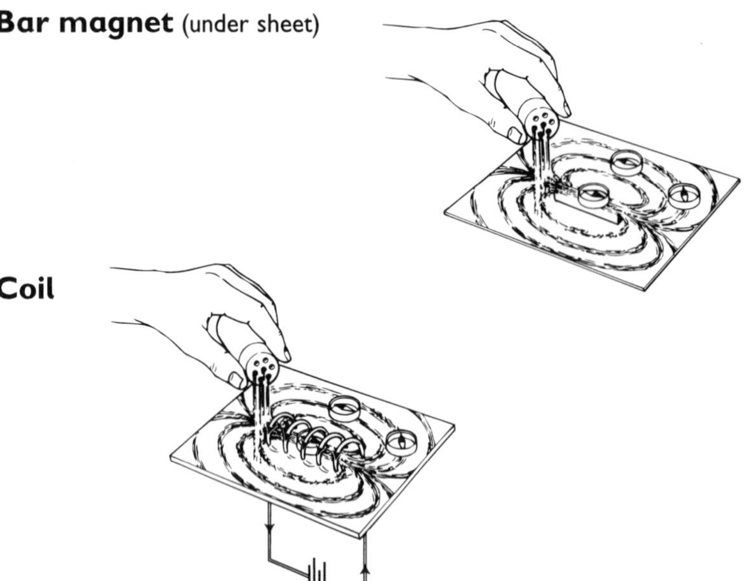

When the electricity is turned off, the compasses point to north.

Safety notes

Wear eye protection. Iron filings are dangerous if they get into the eyes. They may also irritate the skin, especially if skin problems are present. Wash hands after use.

Activity 5.7C
Core (no pupil sheets)

Demonstration: how a coil behaves like a magnet

Purpose

To show pupils that a coil with a current through it behaves like a bar magnet.

Running the activity

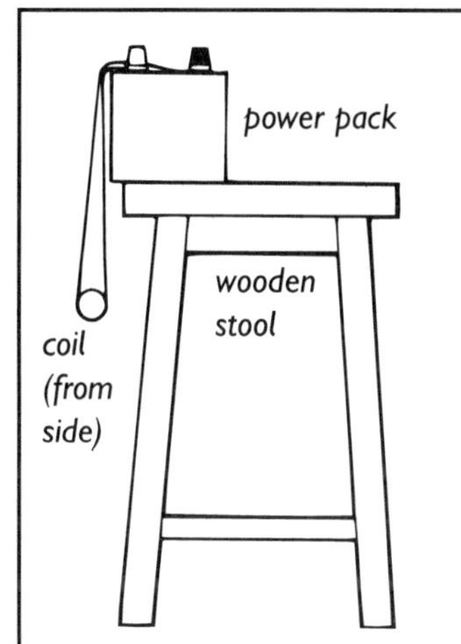

This activity is a teacher demonstration.

First run through what happens when two bar magnets are brought together. They either repel (like poles) or attract (unlike poles). Demonstrate this with large magnets or small but powerful magnets on the overhead projector.

Set up a lightweight coil with a current through it, hanging by the wires from a battery or power pack (see diagram). Bring up one pole of a powerful magnet and the coil will be repelled. Bring up the other pole of the powerful magnet and the coil will be attracted. Do the same for the other side of the coil and show that the two ends of the coil are two different poles. Turn off the electricity and show that the effect is lost.

Expected outcomes

Like poles of the magnet repel; unlike poles attract. One end of the coil behaves like a north pole and the other like a south pole. The effect is lost when the electricity is turned off.

Pitfalls

The coil has to be very light, so 30–32 SWG wire is suitable. Plastic-coated wire is too rigid. Enamel-coated wire is ideal. If only bare wire is available, then the coil must be elongated to prevent short circuits. A 1 cm diameter, 50 turn coil of 30 SWG copper wire with 1 V across it needs a strong permanent magnet to push it. 50 turns is the maximum number with bare wire, as otherwise the coil is too long and will become very floppy. More than 50 turns is possible with enamel-coated wire as the coil can be more compact. However, care must be taken not to make the coil too heavy, or the movement will be too slight to see from a distance.

Safety notes

Increased voltage across the coil gives a more obvious movement, but care must be taken not to allow the coil to overheat.

Electromagnets

Key ideas	*Science PoS*
An electromagnet is a coil of wire with an electric current running through it and a core inside.	1.1b
Electromagnets are made with an iron core so that they can be switched off.	1.2cefgijklnop
Increasing the current in the coil makes an electromagnet stronger.	4.1f
Increasing the number of turns in the coil of an electromagnet also makes it stronger.	

Activity	*Description*	*Differentiation*
	Electromagnets – Pupils carry out a class investigation to establish the three main facts about electromagnets: they need a core of magnetic material, and the magnetic field strength increases with increased number of turns in the coil, and with increased current.	Core, Help, Extension

Other relevant material

Skill sheet 5: Drawing charts and graphs

Skill sheet 6: Interpreting graphs

ICT opportunities

There is a video clip of an electromagnet being used in the CD-ROM *Eyewitness Encyclopedia of Science 2.0* (Dorling Kindersley) under 'Physics', 'Electromagnets'.

Answers to book questions

Red book

a iron and nickel

b Copper and aluminium are not magnetic materials.

c The steel stays magnetic after the current is switched off.

d

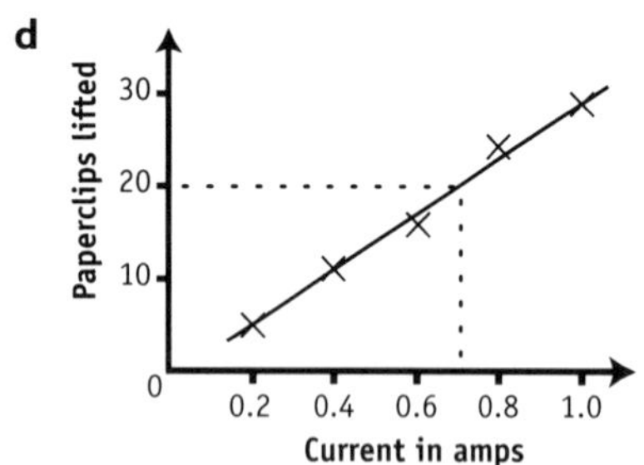

The more current you use, the more paperclips are lifted.

e 20/21 paperclips (see graph)

Green book

a iron and nickel

b iron

c The more current you use, the more paperclips you lift.

d between 9 and 16, approx. 13

e They will not be able to pick up the aluminium cars

1 more current, more turns

2 so that it stops holding the cars when the current is switched off, otherwise you would not be able to get the car off the magnet

3

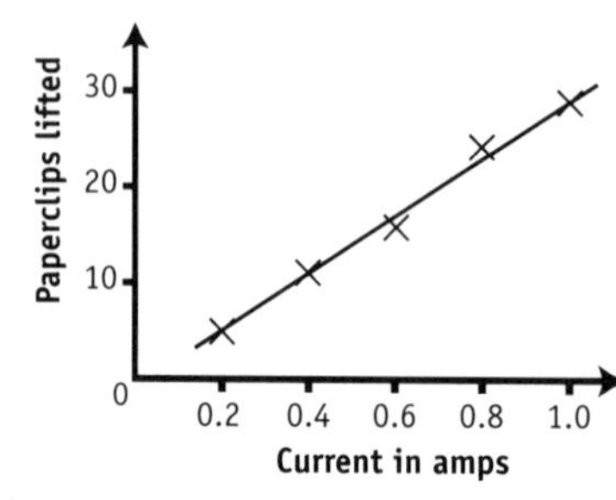

continued

Electromagnets ⊳⊳⊳ continued

Answers to book questions

Red book

f

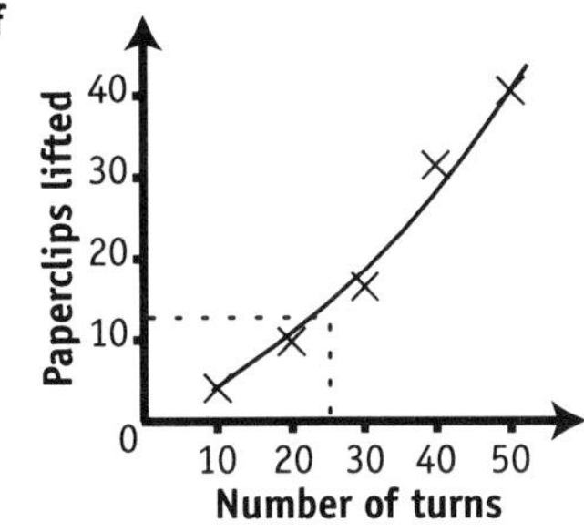

The more turns in the coil, the more paperclips are lifted.

g 13 paperclips (see graph)

h The electromagnet will not pick up the aluminium cars.

1 so that it stops holding the cars when the current is switched off, otherwise you would not be able to get the car off the magnet

2 The electromagnets with iron or nickel cores picked up the paperclips. The electromagnets with copper or aluminium cores did not. This is because iron and nickel are magnetic materials, while aluminium and copper are not. I could test my conclusion by making an electromagnet with a cobalt core. Cobalt is a magnetic material and the electromagnet should pick up the paperclips. If I made an electromagnet with a gold core it will not pick up the paperclips. This is because gold is not a magnetic material.

Electromagnets

Activity 5.8
Core, Help, Extension

Purpose

To establish the three main facts about electromagnets: they need a core of magnetic material, and the magnetic field strength increases with increased number of turns in the coil, and with increased current. To discuss the design of experiments.

This activity is a complete Sc1 investigation, where different groups in the class are assigned different input variables but all measure the same outcome variable.

Running the activity

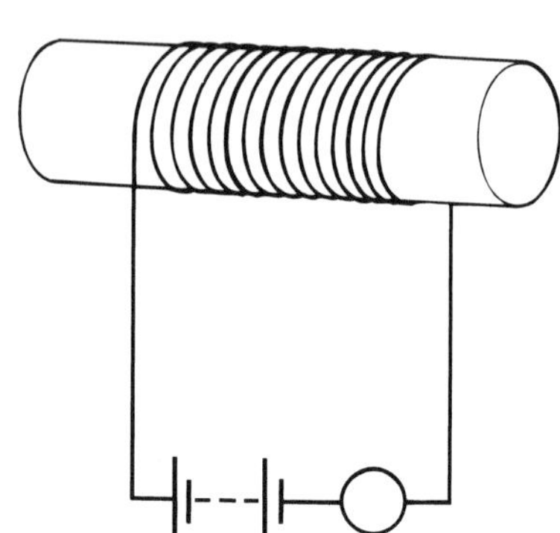

This class investigation should be started by drawing the diagram for the experiment on the board (see right), and giving a demonstration of a simple electromagnet picking up paperclips. Follow with a class discussion as to what could change the strength of an electromagnet. List the variables the pupils suggest. The teacher can then pick out the three variables that are going to be investigated, and establish that the variable being measured is number of paperclips being lifted. Safety precautions should be established (maximum current/voltage).

The discussion should then be developed to introduce the idea of a class investigation. Pupils must understand that, if different groups are going to compare their results, then the 'variables you are keeping the same' must be kept the same across different groups. The teacher should write up the values for the 'variables to be kept the same'. Suggested values are:

- If you are keeping the core the same, it should be **iron**.
- If you are keeping the current the same, it should be **0.5 A**.
- If you are keeping the number of turns the same, it should be **20 turns**.

Pupils should be arranged in ability pairs/groups.

The activity sheets have been written assuming that 'changing the material of the core' is the Help activity for less able pupils. 'Changing the number of turns' and 'changing the current' are addressed by variable-independent sheets at Core and Extension level. If the pupils were in mixed ability groups, the Core sheets could be used and the less able pupils given an additional writing frame for 'Planning and predicting'.

The sheets guide pupils through the investigation and ask them to prepare feedback to the class as a whole. This feedback from different groups should establish the relationship between the three variables and the strength of the electromagnet.

Core: Pupils plan their investigation and make a prediction. They draw a graph and analyse their results. Skill sheets 9 and 10 (writing frames) may be helpful for some pupils.

Help: This covers the investigation into the material of the core. The sheet provides a framework for planning and predicting, and a table for recording.

Extension: This is similar to the Core sheet, but the questions are less directed.

Other relevant material

Skill sheets 5: Drawing charts and graphs
Skill sheets 6: Interpreting graphs

▷▷▷ continued

Activity 5.8
Core, Help, Extension

Stronger electromagnets

continued

Activity notes

Expected outcomes

A 0.5 A current through a 1 m 25 SWG copper wire should give a voltage of 4.5 V.

Success is determined by picking up paperclips.

Changing the core

Iron, steel and (if available) nickel will make electromagnets. Aluminium and copper will not.

Changing the number of turns

Increasing the number of turns will increase the strength of the electromagnet.

Changing the current

0.1 A, 0.2 A. 0.3 A. 0.4 A and 0.5 A currents are realistic. Increasing the current will increase the strength of the electromagnet.

Pitfalls

Too high a current will cause the plastic insulation on the wire to melt. It is best to use power packs with the maximum voltage set to 5 V, or batteries.

Safety notes

Coils can become hot. Electromagnets should be kept on a heatproof mat. Warn pupils not to go higher than the maximum voltage that has been set by the teacher.

The history of microscopes

Book notes

Setting the scene

The unit opens with a historical context charting the development of the microscope and the discoveries it led to. The **unit map** can be used to brainstorm key words and ideas about the unit topics.

KS2 precursor concepts	*Science PoS*
This topic is not covered at KS2, but it makes pupils aware of the part science has played in the development of many of the things they use.	1.1c

Activity	*Description*	*Differentiation*
	A: The parts of a microscope – Pupils learn the parts of a microscope by labelling a diagram.	Core (with Extension question)
	B: A letter from Robert Hooke – This activity is a writing frame to support question **3** in the book. Pupils put themselves in the place of Robert Hooke and write a letter explaining the significance of his new microscope.	Core (Help)

ICT opportunities

Use Microsoft® *Encarta* to research microscopes, Antoni van Leeuwenhoek, Robert Hooke.

Answers to book questions

Red book

a ×40
b ×400

1 a holds the slide
b focuses the image
c controls the amount of light
d sends light up through slide

2 –

3 –

4 –

Green book

a because they could study living things in more detail
b eyepiece, objective
c ×40

1 stage – holds the slide
lens – focuses the image
condenser – controls the amount of light
mirror – sends light up through slide

2 –

3 –

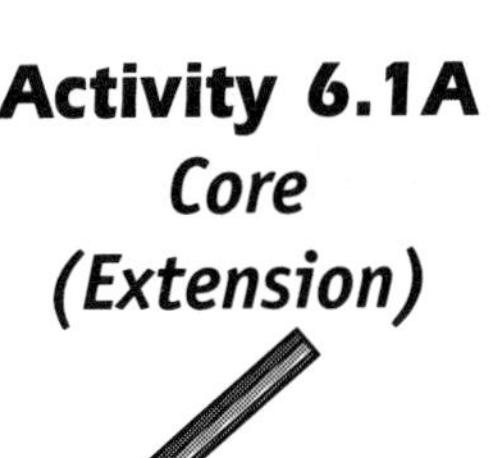

Activity 6.1A
Core
(Extension)

The parts of a microscope

Purpose

To reinforce learning of the parts and function of a microscope by labelling a diagram.

Running the activity

Core: This is a simple labelling activity. The pupils work either individually or in groups. Note that this Core activity uses the worksheet as a write-on disposable sheet.

Extension: There is an optional Extension question at the foot of the Core sheet, which can be cut off if not required. This asks pupils to write their own labels to explain the function of each microscope part.

Other relevant material

Skill sheet 8: Using a microscope

Expected outcomes

Pupils label the diagram to learn the parts of the microscope.

Answers

Core: **1 A** coarse focus
B fine focus
C mirror
D eyepiece
E tube
F objective lens
G stage

Extension: **2 A** to get the slide roughly in focus before using the fine focus
B to focus clearly on the slide
C to send light up through the slide
D second lens that focuses the image/magnifies the image more
E to carry the light from the objective lens to the eyepiece lens
F first lens that magnifies what's on the slide
G to hold the slide

A letter from Robert Hooke

Activity 6.1B
Core (Help)

Purpose

To develop literacy skills and place science in a historical context. Pupils put themselves in the place of Robert Hooke and write a letter explaining the significance of his new microscope.

Running the activity

This activity is a writing frame to support question **3** in the book. Pupils use the introduction on the sheet and what they have read in the book to write their letter. They could discuss the activity in pairs, write their own letters and then compare them.

The instructions on the Core sheet ask pupils to use the ideas provided in the letter framework to write their own letter, but the sheet could be used as a write-on disposable Help sheet instead if preferred.

Expected outcomes

Pupils practise writing letters, and start to develop an awareness of the history of science.

Building blocks

Key ideas	*Science PoS*
All living things are made of cells.	1.1c, 1.2gi
There are two types of cell: animal cells and plant cells.	2.1b
Both types of cell have a cell membrane, cytoplasm and a nucleus.	
Plant cells also have a regular shape, a cell wall, chloroplasts and a vacuole.	

Activity	*Description*	*Differentiation*
	A: Looking at plant cells – Pupils prepare and observe slides of onion cells, using a microscope.	Core
	B: Looking at animal cells – Pupils look at pre-prepared animal cell slides, using a microscope.	Core
	C: Making a model cell – Pupils make models of plant and animal cells.	Core, Extension

Other relevant material

A range of textbooks, Microsoft® *Encarta* or the Internet (see below) could be used to find pictures of cells.

ICT opportunities

Pupils could produce a Microsoft® *Powerpoint* presentation to explain differences between a plant cell and an animal cell.

Website: http//www.cellsalive.com

Question 3 in the Red book provides opportunity for using ICT to produce the poster.

Answers to book questions

Red book

a controls what goes in and out of the cell
b The plant cells have a regular shape, the animal cells do not; the plant cells have a cell wall, the animal cells do not; the plant cells have a sap vacuole, the animal cells do not.

1 a cell membrane, nucleus, cytoplasm, stored food
b Plant cells have a cell wall, chloroplasts, sap vacuole.

2 a nucleus
b cell wall
c sap vacuole
d chloroplasts
e cell membrane
f cytoplasm

3 –

Green book

a controls what goes in and out of the cell
b cytoplasm
c controls everything that happens in the cell
d cellulose
e chlorophyll

1 a A, P
b P
c A, P
d A, P
e P
f P

2 a nucleus
b cell wall
c cell membrane
d cytoplasm

Looking at plant cells

Activity 6.2A
Core

Purpose

To practise using a microscope and reinforce knowledge of cells. Pupils prepare and observe slides of onion cells.

Running the activity

Pupils work in pairs. The activity sheet gives a method for carrying out the practical, along with analysis questions at the end. A microscope could be linked to a video camera (e.g. Flexicam) to display slides to the whole class.

Other relevant material

Skill sheet 8: Using a microscope

Expected outcomes

Pupils produce a labelled drawing of plant cells as seen under the microscope.

Pitfalls

Some pupils may need help with peeling a thin layer of onion skin.

Pupils should take care to avoid introducing air bubbles under the coverslip.

Safety notes

Iodine is harmful. Warn pupils to take care if they are cutting the onion. If in doubt, the pieces of onion could be cut ready for them. Pupils should take care with microscopes and slides.

Answers

1 Pupils should be able to see the cell wall, cytoplasm and maybe the vacuole.

2 because cells are clear

3 as a stain, to make more parts of the cell show up

4 because onions grow underground – they don't photosynthesise

Activity 6.2B
Core

Looking at animal cells

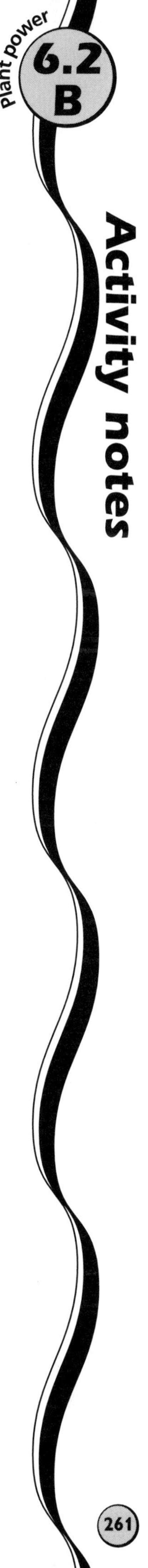

Purpose

To practise using a microscope and reinforce knowledge of cells. Pupils look at pre-prepared animal cell slides.

Running the activity

Pupils work in pairs. The activity sheet gives a method for carrying out the practical, along with analysis questions. A microscope could be linked to a video camera (e.g. Flexicam) to display slides to the whole class.

Other relevant material

Skill sheet 8: Using a microscope

Expected outcomes

Pupils produce a labelled drawing of animal cells as seen under the microscope.

Safety notes

Pupils should take care with microscopes and slides.
Do not ask pupils to carry out the activity using their own cells, because of the risk of infection.

Answers

1 Pupils should be able to see individual, irregular-shaped cells with membranes and sometimes a nucleus, otherwise not many features visible.

2 No, because animals cells do not have cell walls.

Making a model cell

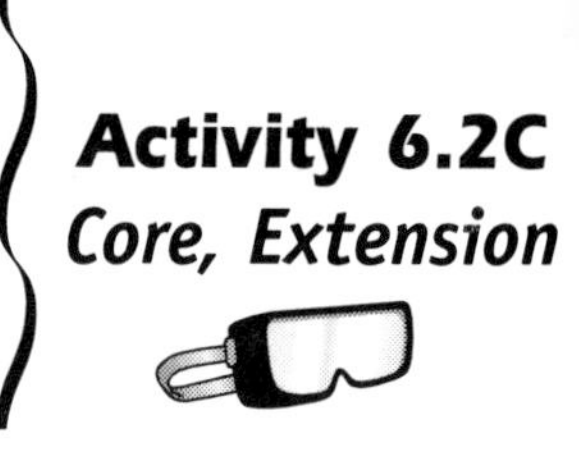

Purpose

To introduce the idea of a model, and to realise what each part of the model represents. Pupils make models of plant and animal cells.

Running the activity

Pupils work in groups. Each group can choose to produce an animal cell, a plant cell or both cell types. You may decide to direct groups to make certain models. Their finished models can be displayed in the classroom.

Core: Pupils are told what each part of the model represents in the cell. They follow the instructions to build the model, and then draw a labelled diagram and answer questions to reinforce their understanding and evaluate the models.

Extension: Pupils are given the apparatus and have to select the best material to represent each part of the cell.

Other relevant material

A range of textbooks, Microsoft® *Encarta* or the Internet could be used to find pictures of cells.

Expected outcomes

Each group should produce large models of cells which can be used for display purposes. This should enable pupils to view the cell as a three-dimensional object rather than just a two-dimensional drawing.

Pitfalls

The activity can be messy. Have plenty of paper towels ready in case of wallpaper paste being spilled.

Some pupils may have difficulty in visualising the cell as a three-dimensional object and may need help in building their models.

Safety notes

Warn pupils to clear up any liquid spilled on the floor to avoid accidents.

Wallpaper paste contains fungicide – wash hands thoroughly after use.

Answers

Core:

1 Check pupils' diagrams.

2 plastic bag (cell membrane) – clear and thin; tennis ball (nucleus) – has membrane and relative size is correct; liquid/paste (cytoplasm) – is jelly-like substance

3 as answer **2**, also: green plasticine (chloroplasts) – right colour for chlorophyll; shoebox (cell wall) – rigid, thicker than cell membrane; smaller plastic bag (vacuole) – thin membrane; water (sap) – is a watery substance

4 Yes, because they show cells in 3D and give an idea of size and what different parts of the cells look like. They make it easier to visualise what plant and animal cells look like.

Extension:

1 Check pupils' diagrams.

2 plastic bag (cell membrane) – clear and thin; tennis ball (nucleus) – has membrane and relative size is correct; liquid/paste (cytoplasm) – is jelly-like substance; green plasticine (chloroplasts) – right colour for chlorophyll; shoebox (cell wall) – rigid, thicker than cell membrane; smaller plastic bag (vacuole) – thin membrane; water (sap) – is a watery substance

3 Yes, because they show cells in 3D and give an idea of size and what different parts of the cells look like. They make it easier to visualise what plant and animal cells look like.

4 e.g. bigger, three-dimensional, you can touch them

Photosynthesis

Key ideas	*Science PoS*
Plants make food by a process called photosynthesis.	1.2gikp
In photosynthesis, plants use light energy, carbon dioxide and water to make sugars and oxygen.	2.3ab

KS2 precursor concepts	*Science PoS*
Pupils should know that plant growth is affected by the availability of light and water, and by temperature.	KS2 2.3a

Activity	*Description*	*Differentiation*
	A: What do plants need for photosynthesis? – Pupils test leaves for starch in order to find out whether a plant needs light and carbon dioxide for photosynthesis.	Core, Help
	B: What gas is made in photosynthesis? – Pupils observe that plants make a gas during photosynthesis, and test the gas to find out whether it is oxygen.	Core
	C: When do plants grow the fastest? – Pupils carry out a datalogging activity to compare the growth of seedlings during daylight and at night. A position sensor is used to monitor the growth.	Core

Answers to book questions

Red book

a They make it themselves in their leaves.
b light, carbon dioxide and water
c because they contain chlorophyll
d oxygen

1 Photosynthesis uses *carbon dioxide* and *water* to make sugars.
The green pigment in plants is called *chlorophyll*.
The gas made in photosynthesis is *oxygen*.

2 a It would go down/decrease/stop, because the plant needs light for photosynthesis.
b It would go down/decrease/stop, because the plant needs carbon dioxide for photosynthesis.

3 for respiration/energy

4 as starch

Green book

a They make it themselves in their leaves.
b light, carbon dioxide and water
c because they contain chlorophyll
d oxygen

1 Photosynthesis uses *water* and *carbon dioxide* to make sugars.
The green substance in plants is called *chlorophyll*.
The gas made in photosynthesis is *oxygen*.

2 a It would go down/decrease/stop, because the plant needs light for photosynthesis.
b It would go down/decrease/stop, because the plant needs carbon dioxide for photosynthesis.

3 carbon dioxide + *water* → sugar + *oxygen*

What do plants need for photosynthesis?

Purpose

To test leaves for starch in order to find out whether a plant needs light and carbon dioxide for photosynthesis.

Running the activity

Pupils work in small groups, or the activity could be carried out as a teacher demonstration. Plants must first be left in the dark for 24 hours to destarch them. After the destarched plants have been set up as shown on the Core sheet, they must be left in a light place for a further 24 hours. The pupils then test the leaves for starch, which should take about 30 minutes. Pupils test three leaves at the same time, cutting a shape in the side of each to identify which are leaves 1, 2 and 3. Alternatively, pupils could test one leaf at a time to ensure they don't get them mixed up. A preheated water bath will be needed for heating the ethanol (see Safety notes below).

Core: The method is given for the activity, and pupils come up with their own format for recording results. Questions ask them to draw conclusions about what the plant needs for photosynthesis. Question 4 could be used as an optional extension question.

Help: This sheet provides a table for pupils to record their results, and more structured questions lead them to their conclusions. Instructions for the experiment are not given on this sheet, so pupils will need help with the activity, or the sheet could be used to accompany a teacher demonstration.

ICT opportunities

Simulation software could be used to change the variables, to see their effect on photosynthesis.

Other relevant material

Skill sheet 2: Lighting a Bunsen burner

Expected outcomes

Iodine will change from orange to black when starch is present in the leaf. The presence of starch indicates that the plant has been photosynthesising. Areas of leaves covered with black tape will not turn iodine black, indicating that the leaf needs light for photosynthesis. Leaves kept in the presence of sodium hydroxide will not turn iodine black, indicating that carbon dioxide is needed for photosynthesis. Leaves that have been kept in the light with carbon dioxide will turn iodine black, indicating that starch has been produced by photosynthesis.

Pitfalls

The plants must be thoroughly destarched before use otherwise false results will be obtained. Old leaves should be avoided. Put soda lime in the conical flasks before the start of this activity.

Safety notes

Ethanol is flammable. Use a hot plate for the waterbath to heat the ethanol. Do not use a naked flame to heat it.

Warn pupils to take care with boiling water. If they scald themselves, cool the skin with plenty of cold running water.

Answers

Core: **1** Light is needed for photosynthesis.

2 Carbon dioxide is needed for photosynthesis.

3 control

4 to destarch the leaves (so that the plant uses up any starch already produced in the leaves)

▷▷▷ continued

Activity 6.3A
Core, Help

What do plants need for photosynthesis? ⊳⊳⊳ continued

Help: **1** Iodine solution will change from *orange* to *black* if starch is present in the leaf. If starch is present in the leaf, it means the leaf has been carrying out *photosynthesis*.

2 no colour change

3 Light is needed for photosynthesis.

4 no colour change

5 Carbon dioxide is needed for photosynthesis.

6 colour changed to black

7 Starch is present, so the leaf has been photosynthesing.

8 control

Activity 6.3B
Core

What gas is made in photosynthesis?

Purpose

To observe that plants make a gas during photosynthesis, and test the gas to find out whether it is oxygen.

Running the activity

The pupils work in groups, or the activity can be run as a teacher demonstration to save time. Pupils are instructed to set up the experiment and leave it for 24 hours on a window sill. The gas that has collected the next day is tested with a glowing splint, or the gas can be produced more quickly by shining a lamp on the plant.

Questions lead pupils to draw conclusions and analyse the experiment.

Expected outcomes

The glowing splint will be relit, showing that the gas that is produced by the photosynthesising plant is oxygen.

Answers

1 oxygen

2 e.g. shine a bright light on the plant throughout the 24-hour period, grow the plant in an enriched atmosphere of carbon dioxide

3 food/sugars/glucose

When do plants grow the fastest?

Activity 6.3C
Core

Purpose

To carry out a datalogging activity to compare the growth of seedlings during daylight and at night. A position sensor is used to monitor the growth.

Running the activity

This activity will probably be run as a teacher demonstration unless there are enough position sensors available for each group of pupils. The growing seedlings are set up and left by a window for three days. The results are more convincing if the experiment can be left longer.

Pupils are asked questions leading them to a conclusion, and also to evaluate the experiment.

Pitfalls

Do not forget to water the seedlings. The position sensor connections are often very delicate and easily disturbed by pupils, perhaps from other classes.

Other relevant material

Skill sheet 6 : Interpreting graphs

ICT opportunities

ICT Pos 2b: Datalogging

Expected outcomes

The position sensor will indicate a general increase in size. There will be a marked increase in the growth of plants during the day, that may be less obvious with younger plants.

Safety notes

Warn pupils not to eat the plants.

Answers

1 during the day, as there is more photosynthesis then

2 during the night, as there is no photosynthesis then

3
- Doing the experiment a few times would make the results more reliable, in case a mistake was made.
- Using more plants would make the results more reliable, in case there was something wrong with the plants.
- Carrying out the experiment for a shorter period of time would not improve the experiment.
- Carrying out the experiment for a longer period of time would make the results more obvious to see.

Leaf structure

Key ideas	*Science PoS*
The plant makes its food by photosynthesis in the leaves.	1.2gi
Leaves have a large surface to trap as much sunlight as possible.	2.3ab
Leaves have stomata so gases can move in and oxygen can move out.	

KS2 precursor concepts	*Science PoS*
Pupils should know that plants need light, water and air to produce new material for growth, and understand the importance of the leaf in this process.	KS2 2.3b

Activity	*Description*	*Differentiation*
	Looking at leaves – Pupils look at pre-prepared leaf slides, using a microscope.	Core

Answers to book questions

Red book

a They are flat, broad, green and thin.
b **i** from the air, through the air holes
ii from the soil, through the roots

1 waxy layer – stops water being lost
palisade cell – photosynthesis happens here
stomata – allow gases into and out of the leaf
vein – transports substances to the leaf

2 a to carry out as much photosynthesis as they can
b so that they get the light
c large surface area to catch as much light as possible

3 Humans (and all other organisms) need oxygen for respiration.

Green book

a They are flat, broad, green and thin.
b carbon dioxide, light and water
c air holes, air spaces, veins, chloroplasts
d so that they get the light
e chloroplasts

1 All plants need *carbon dioxide*, *water* and light energy to make their food. Inside the palisade cells are parts called *chloroplasts*. These contain a green substance called *chlorophyll*.

2 waxy layer – stops the leaf losing water
palisade cell – photosynthesis happens here
stomata – let gases into and out of the leaf
vein – carries substances to the leaf

3 a carbon dioxide
b oxygen

4 through the stomata

Looking at leaves

Purpose

To practise using a microscope and reinforce knowledge of the structure and function of the leaf. Pupils look at pre-prepared leaf slides.

Running the activity

Pupils work in pairs. The activity sheet gives a method for carrying out the practical, and directs pupils to record a labelled diagram of the slide. Question 6 could be used as an optional extension question. A microscope could be linked to a video camera (e.g. Flexicam) to display slides to the whole class.

Other relevant material

Skill sheet 8: Using a microscope

Expected outcomes

Pupils produce a labelled drawing of a section through the leaf as seen under the microscope.

Safety notes

Pupils should take care with microscopes and slides.

The root of the problem

Key ideas	*Science PoS*
The roots of a plant hold it firm/anchor it in the ground, and absorb water and minerals.	1.2gi
Root hairs are tiny parts with a large surface to absorb water.	2.3d
Water is transported around the plant through the veins.	

KS2 precursor concepts	*Science PoS*
Pupils should know that the root anchors the plant, and that water and minerals are taken in through the root and transported through the stem to other parts of the plant.	KS2 2.3c

Activity	*Description*	*Differentiation*
	A: Looking at root hairs – Pupils look at pre-prepared slides of roots showing root hairs, using a microscope.	Core
	B: Water transport in celery – Pupils observe coloured water travelling up the veins in a celery stalk, and observe a dyed vein using a microscope.	Core

Other relevant material

Skill sheet 8: Using a microscope

Answers to book questions

Red book

a discussion question: to find water, which may be deep in the soil, and to anchor the plant firmly in the soil

1 e.g. to carry out photosynthesis, for transporting substances within the plant, to keep the cells firm, to keep the plant upright, without it they would wilt and die

2 taking in water and nutrients and anchoring the plant in the soil

3 They have a large surface area.

4 –

Green book

a discussion question: to find water, which may be deep in the soil, and to anchor the plant firmly in the soil

b taking in water and minerals, and holding the plant firm in the soil

c very thin hair-like structures

d to transport water, minerals and dissolved food/sugars

1 The roots take *water* into the plant. Roots are also important because they *hold* plants *firm* in the soil. The ends of the roots have very tiny structures called *root hairs*. Water passes up the plant through the *veins*.

2 e.g. to carry out photosynthesis, for transporting substances within the plant, to keep the cells firm, to keep the plant upright, without it they would wilt and die

3 –

Looking at root hairs

Activity 6.5A
Core

Purpose

To practise using a microscope and reinforce knowledge of the structure and function of the root. Pupils look at pre-prepared slides of roots showing root hairs.

Running the activity

Pupils work in pairs. The activity sheet gives a method for carrying out the practical, and directs pupils to record a labelled diagram of the slide. A microscope could be linked to a video camera (e.g. Flexicam) to display slides to the whole class.

Other relevant material

Skill sheet 8: Using a microscope

Expected outcomes

Pupils produce a labelled drawing of a root as seen under the microscope.

Safety notes

Pupils should take care with microscopes and slides.

Answers

1 The root hairs provide a large area for absorption.

2 holds it firm in the soil

Activity 6.5B
Core

Water transport in celery

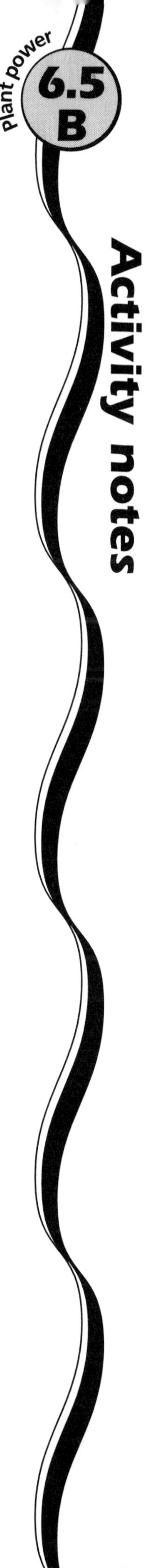

Purpose

To observe coloured water travelling up the veins in a plant, and to reinforce knowledge of the structure and function of veins in plants.

Running the activity

Pupils work in groups. They are instructed to leave celery stalks in dyed water overnight and observe them the next day. To carry out the activity in the same day, the celery stalks need to be left for at least a few hours before they are used. Alternatively, a cool hair dryer blowing over the leaves will speed up the movement of dye up the stalk.

Pupils then make a slide of a thin cross-section and observe it under a microscope. Structured questions lead them to analyse the structure and function of the veins.

As a demonstration in parallel with this activity, a white carnation can be left in dyed water overnight to show pupils that the dye travels up the veins and colours the flower.

Other relevant material

Skill sheet 8: Using a microscope

Expected outcomes

The celery stalk will become stained in the veins that carry water (xylem). With a very thin cross-section of the stalk, the structure of the stained veins should become clearly visible under a light microscope.

Pitfalls

Make sure pupils cut very thin cross-sections. Some pupils may need help with this.

Safety notes

Pupils must use knives carefully, and take care with microscopes and slides. Remind pupils not to eat the celery.

Answers

1 all the way up to the leaves

2 to transport water up the plant

3 e.g. it is a long thin tube

Plant reproduction

Book notes

Key ideas	*Science PoS*
Flowers contain the sex parts of the plant. The male sex cells are the pollen grains. The female sex cells are the egg cells. Pollination is the transfer of the pollen grains from the anther to the stigma. Fertilisation happens when the nucleus of the pollen grain joins with the nucleus of an egg cell.	1.2gi 2.1d

KS2 precursor concepts	*Science PoS*
Pupils should know about the life cycle of flowering plants, including pollination, fertilisation, seed dispersal and germination.	KS2 2.3d

Activity	*Description*	*Differentiation*
	A: Flower structure – Pupils label a diagram of a flower.	Core (with Extension questions)
	B: Growing pollen tubes – Pupils use a microscope to observe the growth of a pollen tube.	Core (with Extension questions)
	C: How pollination happens – Pupils read an account and answer questions about pollination methods.	Extension

Answers to book questions

Red book

a to reproduce

b The pollen sticks to the bee's body when it visits a flower. The bee visits another flower and the pollen rubs off its body onto the stigmas.

1 stigma – receives the pollen grains
carpel – female part of a flower
anther – makes the pollen grains
stamen – male part of a flower

2 –

Green book

a to reproduce

b male parts of a flower

c stigma, style and ovary

d male – pollen grains, female – egg cells

e the joining of the pollen nucleus and the egg cell nucleus

1 stigma – receives the pollen grains
carpel – female part of a flower
anther – makes the pollen grains
stamen – male part of a flower

2 The pollen sticks to the bee's body when it visits a flower. The bee visits another flower and the pollen rubs off its body onto the stigmas.

3 In pollination, pollen grains transfer from the *anther* to the *stigma*. Fertilisation happens when the nucleus of the *pollen grain* joins with the nucleus of the *egg cell*. The fertilised cell forms an *embryo plant* which is a tiny new plant inside the seed.

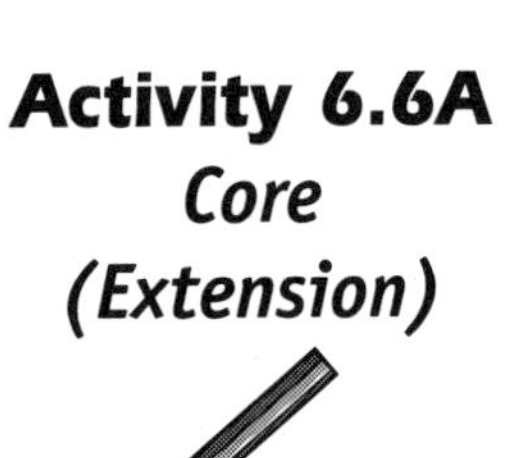

Activity 6.6A Core (Extension)

Flower structure

Purpose

To reinforce learning of the structure and function of the parts of a flower.

Running the activity

Core: This is a simple labelling activity. Pupils are instructed to copy the diagram and add the correct labels for the flower parts. They add the function of each part to their diagram. If preferred, the sheet could be used as a disposable write-on Help sheet.

Extension: There are optional Extension questions at the foot of the Core sheet, which can be cut off if not required. These ask more detailed questions about the process of plant reproduction.

Expected outcomes

Pupils label the diagram to learn the parts of the flower.

Answers

Core:

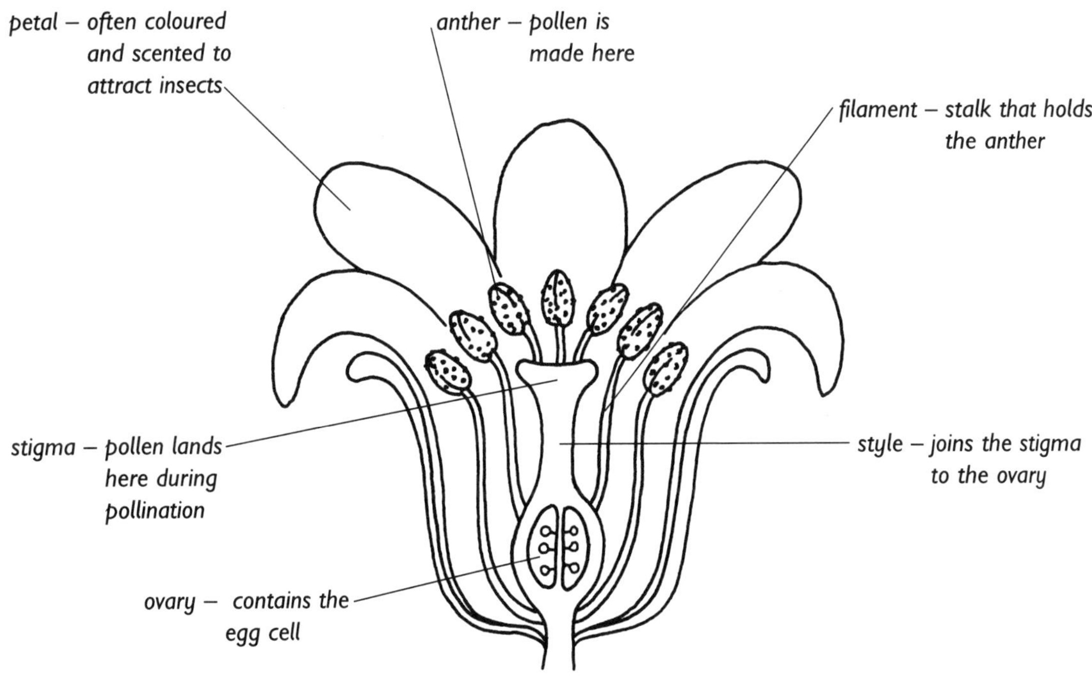

Extension: **1** egg cell

2 pollen grain

3 carried by insects or the wind, pollination

Growing pollen tubes

Activity 6.6B
Core
(Extension)

Purpose

To use a microscope to observe the growth of a pollen tube, and reinforce understanding of plant reproduction.

Running the activity

Pupils work in pairs.

Core: Pupils prepare a slide of pollen grains in sucrose solution. These must be left in a warm place for 30 minutes before being observed under the microscope. The pollen grains could be incubated ready before the lesson if time is short. Pupils observe and record the growth of the pollen tube during the lesson.

Extension: There are optional Extension questions at the foot of the Core sheet, which can be cut off if not required. These ask more detailed questions about the process of fertilisation.

Other relevant material

Skill sheet 8: Using a microscope

Expected outcomes

The pupils will observe the growth of the pollen tube over 10-minute periods using a microscope, and draw a flow diagram to record their observations.

Safety notes

Pupils should take care with microscopes and slides. Remind them not to eat any plant material and to wash their hands afterwards.

Plant pollens may cause allergic reactions in asthmatics and those who suffer from hayfever.

Answers

Extension:

1 It carries the nucleus of the pollen grain from the stigma down to the egg cell in the ovule.

2 fertilisation

3 An embryo plant forms, surrounded by a seed and a fruit.

Activity 6.6C *Extension* — How pollination happens

Purpose

To develop knowledge and aid comprehension of methods of pollination.

Running the activity

Extension: This sheet provides pupils with extra details on pollination. The pupils read the sheet and answer the questions that follow.

Expected outcomes

Pupils develop their knowledge of pollination.

Answers

1 In self-pollination, pollen is transferred from the anther to the stigma of the same flower. In cross-pollination, pollen is transferred from one flower to the stigma of another flower.

2 colour, scent, nectar

3 The anthers are inside the flower so the insect rubs against them to get to the nectar. The stigma is inside the flower so pollen rubs off the insect onto the stigma. The pollen is sticky.

4 The anthers are outside the flower so the pollen can easily blow away. Lots of pollen is produced. The stigmas are outside the flower. They are feathery to help catch the pollen.

5 fertilisation

Scaling up and down

Developing thinking skills

A class discussion led by the teacher can be used to introduce the context of the spread. Pupils can then work in small groups, ideally in pairs. The questions in the text are intended to prompt either whole class discussion or small group discussion, as appropriate. The teacher will have the opportunity to intervene and challenge individual pupils. It is advisable not to tell the pupils the answers, but to ask them another question which takes them forward in their thinking. This will help them to develop higher thinking skills. Many of the questions are very open and do not have a simple answer. It is useful to allow some time for pupils to feedback ideas to the class after the group work.

Think about: scale

The teacher could begin by giving examples of using scale – e.g. maps, diagrams, instructions for self-assembly furniture. Link this with the concept of the cell drawings the pupils have made in previous activities. The activity in the book then leads them through several examples of using scale. We have only used a scale factor as a way of showing how much bigger or smaller something is. The concept of using ratios such as 50:1 or 1:50 will be covered later.

Key ideas	*Science PoS*
Thinking about the concept of scale diagrams: scaling up and scaling down	–

ICT opportunities

A spreadsheet such as Microsoft® *Excel* can be used to calculate the scale factor, real height, etc.

Answers to book questions

Red book

a discussion question
b Mrs Beetroot 160 cm, Nick 120 cm, Aileen 80 cm
c divide by the scale factor
d Mrs Beetroot 8 cm, Nick 6 cm, Aileen 4 cm
e Science book 30 ÷ 3, 10; house 800 ÷ 40, 20; TV 60 ÷ 12; 5

1 10
2 length of car 30; length of pencil 20; width of garden 30
3 –

Green book

a discussion question
b Mrs Beetroot 160 cm, Nick 120 cm, Aileen 80 cm
c divide by the scale factor
d Mrs Beetroot 8 cm, Nick 6 cm, Aileen 4 cm

1 length of car 300; height of car 5; length of pencil 20; height of bicycle 4
2 –

Metals through the ages

Setting the scene

Pupils consider the properties of materials (a KS2 topic) in a new context, the history of metallurgy. The idea that useful materials are produced from raw materials by chemical reactions (an important KS3 concept) is introduced. The spread emphasises an important aspect Sc1, the importance of science and technology in the development of products used in everyday life.

The **unit map** can be used to help brainstorm key words and ideas about the unit topics.

KS2 precursor concepts	*Science PoS*
Different materials have different properties.	KS2 3.1a
The terms strong, hard, flexible (H) and brittle (H).	1.1c

Activity	*Description*	*Differentiation*
	A: Making iron and steel – A comprehension activity for the fluent reader. An alternative or extension of the comprehension activity in the book.	Extension
	B: A better knife – A writing frame to support the story-writing question in the book. Pupils consider properties of iron and bronze.	Core

Optional demonstration

The book spread may be supported with a display of different metals. Any objects will do if samples are not available. Include a modern kitchen knife made of steel and point out that this would have been a 'king's ransom' three thousand years ago, worth more than a knife made of gold!
The display could include samples or items made of:

- copper
- bronze
- wrought iron
- cast iron
- steel (a modern kitchen knife)

ICT opportunities

Biographies of Sir Henry Bessemer are available on the CD-ROMs *Encarta* (Microsoft®) and *The Way Things Work* (Dorling Kindersley). *Encarta* has an image of an engraving showing Bessemer Steel Production. It also contains entries about the different types of iron, and iron and steel manufacture, but these are too complex for Year 7 pupils.

Answers to book questions

Red book

a gold, silver, copper and bronze
b the Hittites
c the Chinese
d Henry Bessemer
e makes it harder but less flexible

Green book

a gold, silver, copper and bronze
b the Hittites
c the Chinese
d Henry Bessemer
e gold
f makes it harder but less flexible

continued

Metals through the ages ⊳⊳⊳ continued

Answers to book questions

Red book

f Large amounts of carbon (about 3%) make the iron harder and more brittle. An intermediate amount (0.5–2.0%) makes steel which is harder and more flexible. Almost no carbon (less than 0.1%) makes wrought iron, which is flexible
and soft.

g First make cast iron (heat iron minerals with charcoal/coke) and then burn off some of the carbon.

1 finding gold, making copper, making bronze, making wrought iron, making small amounts of steel, making cast iron, making large amounts of steel

2 –

3 Reading down each column:

Steel	Copper	Bronze	Wrought iron	Cast iron
rock	rock	rock	rock	rock
yes	yes	no	yes	no
yes	no	yes	no	yes

Green book

g steel

h first make cast iron (heat iron minerals with charcoal/coke) and then burn off some of the carbon

1 When you bend steel it *does not* break. Bronze and cast iron *do* break when bent. Steel is *harder* than wrought iron or copper. Steel knives keep a *sharper* edge than wrought iron or copper knives. Steel knives *do not* break easily.

2 –

Activity 7.1A *Extension*

Making iron and steel

Purpose

A more challenging and extending treatment of the history of metallurgy, which goes well beyond what is given in the book.

Running the activity

This comprehension exercise would be suitable for an able student with good reading skills.

Answers

1 Iron is found as iron minerals in rocks called iron ores.

2 The iron mineral is reacted with carbon (as charcoal or coke).

3 By quenching (heating, hammering and plunging into cold water).

4 Making cast iron does not require hammering, so it is easier to do on a large scale.

5 Charcoal was used to change the iron minerals into iron. Charcoal is made from wood and most of the forests were cut down to make charcoal.

6 Mining involves digging coal from the ground. If it is an open cast mine large areas of landscape are dug up, destroying many habitats for animals and plants. Even if the pits are underground, there are still the waste (slag heaps) and the machinery. Also, roads or railways will have to be built to and from the mines.

7 He blew oxygen through cast iron. This burned off most of the carbon, so that there was less than 2% and the cast iron became steel.

Activity 7.1B *Core (Help)*

A better knife

Purpose

A writing frame to support question 2 (L) and question 3 (H) in the book.

Running the activity

Pupils could write their own story or use the writing frame as a prompt. For less able pupils it could be used as a write-on Help sheet.

What is a metal?

Key ideas	*Science PoS*
Metals are shiny. Metals are good conductors of electricity and heat (thermal) energy. A few metals, including iron, are magnetic. Most metals are solids at room temperature.	1.2e 3.1ad

KS2 precursor concepts	*Science PoS*
That magnetic behaviour, electrical conductivity and thermal conductivity can vary from material to material.	KS2 3.1abc

Activity	*Description*	*Differentiation*
	A: Properties of metals – A short experiment testing samples of different metals, followed by a demonstration of thermal conductivity (with the same metals if possible).	Core
	B: Solid, liquid or gas? – Pupils use a chart like that in the book to answer more questions about melting and boiling points.	Core, Help, Extension

Answers to book questions

Red book

a the steel cans stick to a magnet, the aluminium cans do not

b mercury

c potassium

d iron

e potassium, mercury and zinc

f The mercury in a thermometer has to be liquid, i.e. between these temperatures.

1 aluminium, brass (copper and zinc), bronze (copper and tin), chromium, copper, gold, iron, lead, mercury, nickel, potassium, silver, steel (iron and carbon), tin, zinc

2 –

Green book

a the steel cans stick to a magnet, the aluminium cans do not

b mercury

c potassium

d potassium

e iron

1 copper

2 any one of: stainless steel, cast iron, aluminium, copper

3 iron, nickel, cobalt

4 any two metals not iron, nickel or cobalt

5 aluminium, brass (copper and zinc), bronze (copper and tin), chromium, copper, gold, iron, lead, mercury, nickel, potassium, silver, steel (iron and carbon), tin, zinc

Activity 7.2A Core

Properties of metals

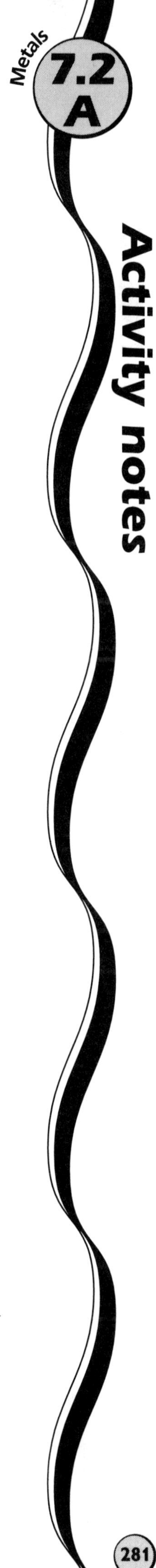

Purpose

To emphasise the properties of metals with a concrete activity.

Running the activity

Pupils carry out simple experiments to investigate the appearance and magnetic properties of a range of metals, and whether or not they conduct electricity.

Experiments on the thermal conductivity of metals involve using large and/or expensive pieces of apparatus, so it is assumed that this experiment will be a demonstration. This may be shown using the classic demonstration, with rods of metal leading from a box filled with hot water to a drawing pin held with wax, or the commercially available samples of metal with in-built temperature-sensitive strips.

Every effort should be made to use the same metals for each experiment, but this is unlikely to be entirely successful as nickel should be included as another example of a magnetic metal, yet is unlikely to be included in a commercial apparatus for comparing thermal conductivity.

Expected outcomes

Pupils record their results in a table of properties then answer questions based on their results.

Pitfalls

Samples of metals should be cleaned with a commercial cleaner, e.g. Brasso.

Get the pupils to test their circuit first to show that battery and lamp are functioning.

Make sure that the joints between the rods and the box of water are water-tight.

Safety notes

Most safety problems are avoided if the thermal conductivity experiment is a demonstration.

Pupils should wash their hands after handling metals.

Check for sharp edges to metal samples.

Answers

1 All the metals are shiny when polished.

2 Iron, nickel and cobalt are the only magnetic metals.

3 They stuck to the magnet.

4 All the metals should conduct electricity in this experiment.

5 They lit the lamp.

6 All the metals conduct heat energy.

7 Probably copper, depending on the selection of metals chosen.

Solid, liquid or gas?

Activity 7.2B
Core, Help, Extension

Purpose

To improve pupils' understanding of melting points and boiling points (PoS 3.1a).

Running the activities

Core: This version is for those who have accepted the concept that different materials have different melting and boiling points but need reinforcement.

Extension: This version is for pupils who have mastered the concept that changes in state occur at different temperatures and would benefit from further reinforcement and challenge. Metals X and Y are for extension pupils only.

Help: This version is for pupils who have yet to cope with the concept of changes in state occurring at different temperatures for different materials.

Note that *Core* and *Extension* questions are given on the first sheet, and both use the chart on the Resource sheet. You will need to blank off metals X and Y and the table when photocopying the Resource sheet for Core pupils. *Help* has a sheet with its own, simpler chart.

Answers

Core:

1. potassium, mercury and zinc
2. aluminium, gold, tin, lead, iron, copper and silver
3. iron
4. mercury
5. aluminium
6. potassium
7. gold, iron and copper
8. potassium, mercury and zinc
9. it would be the colour for solid from top to bottom
10. tin and lead would both melt

Extension:

1. iron
2. mercury
3. aluminium
4. potassium
5. metal Y, gold, iron and copper
6. metal X, potassium, mercury and zinc
7. it would be the colour for solid from top to bottom
8. Each division is 10°C, so looks like 240°C.
9. Metal X is caesium, metal Y is nickel
10. Only those with a melting point above 460°C, i.e. metal Y (nickel), aluminium, gold, iron, copper and silver.

Help:

1. a solid
2. a gas
3. a gas
4. a solid
5. a liquid
6. a gas
7. titanium
8. mercury is a gas at 400°C and tin is a liquid

Metals as elements

Key ideas	*Science PoS*
We call the simplest type of particle an atom. An element is a substance with only one type of atom. Many metals are elements. Each element has a symbol. We arrange the elements in the periodic table. The periodic table has groups (columns) and periods (rows).	1.2k 3.1cd

KS2 precursor concepts	*Science PoS*
That magnetic behaviour, electrical conductivity and thermal conductivity can vary from material to material.	KS2 3.1abc

Activity	*Description*	*Differentiation*
	A: Display of metallic elements – Pupils learn about the appearance of various metallic elements, including the hazardous ones they need to know about.	Core (no pupil sheets)
	B: Metallic elements – Pupils use a database of elements to answer questions about metals.	Core

ICT opportunities

Most CD-ROM encyclopedias have an interactive periodic table. However, the majority are far too complicated for Year 7 pupils. One of the best is in the *Eyewitness Encyclopedia of Science 2.0* (Dorling Kindersley), but this still includes complicated terms.

The version of the periodic table shown in the book is based on that given at: www.webelements.com

Answers to book questions

Red book

a A and C

b 26 symbols – not enough

c caesium – Cs, calcium – Ca, chromium – Cr, copper – Cu, cadmium – Cd, cerium – Ce, curium – Cm, californium – Cf, cobalt – Co

d left

1 Brass is not an element because it contains copper atoms and tin atoms. Copper is an element because it contains only copper atoms.

2 Sarah. F is not a metal because it is at the far right of the periodic table.

3 No. Joe is only considering English names for the elements.

Green book

a A and C

b Fe

c **i** 26

ii 26

iii 118

iv no

d calcium – Ca, cobalt – Co, copper – Cu

e left

1 one type of atom.

2 Brass is not an element because it contains copper atoms and tin atoms. Copper is an element because it contains only copper atoms.

3 Sarah. F is not a metal because it is at the far right of the periodic table.

Display of metallic elements

Activity 7.3A
Core (no pupil sheets)

Purpose

For pupils to learn about the appearance of metallic elements, including the ones they will read about but not usually encounter because they are hazardous.

Running the activity

Pupils are shown samples of lithium, sodium, potassium and mercury. They are not allowed to handle these samples.

The other samples (magnesium, aluminium, calcium, iron, nickel, copper and zinc) may be passed around the class in sealed bottles for pupils to examine.

This activity could be run in conjunction with 7.3B, by dividing the class into two groups and swapping over.

Expected outcomes

Pupils learn about the appearance of elements and the hazards involved with handling them.

Pitfalls

Teachers must ensure that pupils do not open the sample bottles.

Safety notes

All elements should have the appropriate hazard warning symbols (see Hazcards).

The samples of potassium, lithium and sodium should be under oil, the containers sealed and each placed within another, unbreakable, container which is also sealed.

The sample of mercury should be very carefully sealed and the container placed within a second container which is also sealed.

Activity 7.3B *Core* Metallic elements

Purpose

To establish that there are a large number of elements and that information is known about each of them. To use a database to handle a large amount of information.

Other relevant material

The database for this activity is on the CD-ROM that accompanies this pack.

ICT opportunities

ICT PoS 1c Using a database

Most CD-ROM encyclopedias have an interactive periodic table. However, the majority are far too complicated for Year 7 pupils. One of the best is in the *Eyewitness Encyclopedia of Science 2.0* (Dorling Kindersley), but this still includes complicated terms.

Running the activity

The database is meant for pupils at all stages in KS3. It contains information not needed at this stage, nor for this activity. The teacher may wish to 'hide' the columns *Appearance, Position in periodic table* and *Density* to make what appears on the screen less intimidating.

If the number of computers is limited, this activity could be run in conjunction with 7.3A by dividing the class into two groups and swapping over.

Expected outcomes

Pupils learn about the properties of metals. They realise that metallic elements vary in their properties, despite sharing many basic characteristics. Pupils gain experience of handling large amounts of information using a database.

Answers

1 79

2 53

3 tungsten

4 mercury

5 silver

6 zirconium

7 yttrium

8 caesium

9 chromium, iron and nickel

10 21

11 Three of: lithium, beryllium, sodium, magnesium, aluminium, potassium, calcium, cobalt, nickel, copper, zinc, molybdenum, ruthenium, rhodium, silver, cadmium, indium, tungsten, osmium, iridium, gold

12 Three of: manganese, bismuth, radium, plutonium

Non-metals

Key ideas	*Science PoS*
Some elements are non-metals.	1.2k
Most non-metals are not shiny.	3.1d
Most non-metals do not conduct electricity.	
Most non-metals do not conduct heat (thermal) energy.	
Some non-metals are solids, some are liquids and some are gases at room temperature.	

Activity	*Description*	*Differentiation*
	A: Display of non-metallic elements – Pupils learn about the appearance of various non-metallic elements, including the hazardous ones they need to know about.	Core (no pupil sheets)
	B: Non-metallic elements – Pupils use a database of elements to answer questions about non-metals.	Core

ICT opportunities

Most CD-ROM encyclopedias have an interactive periodic table. However, the majority are far too complicated for Year 7 pupils. One of the best is in the *Eyewitness Encyclopedia of Science 2.0* (Dorling Kindersley), but this still includes complicated terms.

Answers to book questions

Red book

a No. They are not shiny, they do not conduct electricity, they do not conduct heat energy, they are not solids at room temperature.

b right

c i No – it is not shiny, does not conduct electrical, does not conduct thermal energy, is not solid at room temperature.

ii No – it is not shiny, does not conduct electrical, does not conduct thermal energy.

iii Diamond is not a metal. It is not shiny, does not conduct heat energy nor electricity. Graphite does conduct heat energy and electricity but is not shiny. Carbon is on the right of the periodic table. It is, on balance, not a metal.

d right

e to kill bacteria in water treatment plants

1 a bromine

b chlorine

c sulphur

d oxygen

2 They are mostly not shiny, they do not conduct electricity, they do not conduct heat energy.

3 a Diamond. It does not conduct electricity and heat energy.

b Graphite. It does conduct electricity and heat energy.

Green book

a i no

ii no

iii no

b no

c no

d right

e no

f not shiny, does not conduct electricity, does not conduct heat energy, is not a solid at room temperature

g right

h no

i not shiny, does not conduct heat energy, does not conduct electricity

1 a bromine

b chlorine

c sulphur

d oxygen

2 they are not shiny, they do not conduct electricity, they do not conduct heat energy

3 a non-metal

b it is not shiny, it does not conduct electricity, it does not conduct heat energy, it is a gas at room temperature.

Activity 7.4A
Core (no pupil sheets)

Display of non-metallic elements

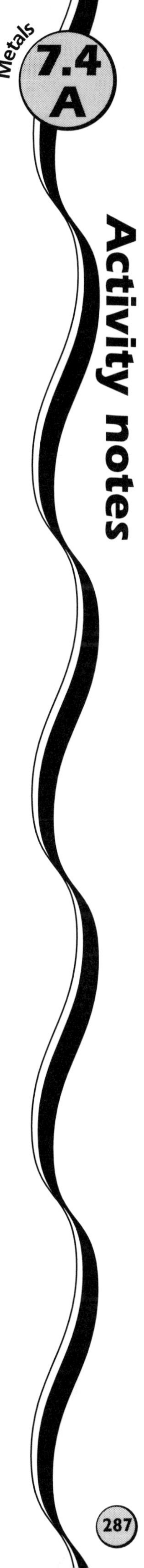

Purpose

For pupils to learn about the appearance of non-metallic elements, including the ones they will read about but not usually encounter because they are hazardous.

Running the activity

Pupils are shown samples of chlorine and bromine. They are not allowed to handle these samples.

The other samples (hydrogen, helium, carbon, nitrogen, oxygen, sulphur and iodine) may be passed around the class in sealed bottles for pupils to examine.

This activity could be run in conjunction with 7.4B, by dividing the class into two groups and swapping over.

Expected outcomes

Pupils learn about the appearance of elements and the hazards involved with handling them.

Pitfalls

Teachers must ensure that pupils do not open the sample bottles.

Safety notes

All elements should have the appropriate hazard warning symbols (see Hazcards). The samples of chlorine gas and bromine should be in sealed containers and each placed within another sealed container. An unopened vial of bromine can be used, but this should be placed inside another container and packed so that it is visible from one side but will not rattle around.

Non-metallic elements

Activity 7.4B
Core

Purpose

To establish that there are a large number of elements and that information is known about each of them. To use a database to handle a large amount of information.

Other relevant material

The database for this activity is on the CD-ROM that accompanies this pack.

ICT opportunities

ICT PoS 1c Using a database

Most CD-ROM encyclopedias have an interactive periodic table. However, the majority are far too complicated for Year 7 pupils. One of the best is in the *Eyewitness Encyclopedia of Science 2.0* (Dorling Kindersley), but this still includes complicated terms.

Running the activity

The database is meant for pupils at all stages in KS3. It contains information not needed at this stage, nor for this activity. The teacher may wish to 'hide' the columns *Position in periodic table*, *Is it a magnetic material?* and *Density* to make what appears on the screen less intimidating.

If the number of computers is limited, this activity could be run in conjunction with 7.4A by dividing the class into two groups and swapping over.

Expected outcomes

Pupils learn about the properties of metals. They realise that metallic elements vary in their properties, despite sharing many basic characteristics. Pupils gain experience of handling large amounts of information using a database.

Answers

1 21

2 9

3 1

4 11

5 11

6 **a** oxygen
  b selenium
  c nitrogen (fertilisers, proteins)

7 chlorine, arsenic

Getting it right

Developing thinking skills

A class discussion led by the teacher can be used to introduce the context of the spread. Pupils can then work in small groups, ideally in pairs. The questions in the text are intended to prompt either whole class discussion or small group discussion, as appropriate. The teacher will have the opportunity to intervene and challenge individual pupils. It is advisable not to tell the pupils the answers, but to ask them another question which takes them forward in their thinking. This will help them to develop higher thinking skills. Many of the questions are very open and do not have a simple answer. It is useful to allow some time for pupils to feedback ideas to the class after the group work.

Think about: classification

Grouping elements gives pupils a opportunity to classify objects in a non-biological context. It also gives them a grounding for studying the periodic table in KS4. A crucial part of the activity is having to follow the 'thinking' of the imaginary pupils as they struggle with cognitive conflict. The pupils also have to explain how they solved the problem which was presented to them. Activity 7.5A gives pupils an opportunity to classify elements, using an unfamiliar context. They again have to explain how they came to their decisions (opportunity for metacognition).

Key ideas	*Science PoS*
Classification of elements	3.1d

Activity	*Description*	*Differentiation*
	Grouping metals – Classification exercise based on chemical rather than physical properties.	Core, Help

Answers to book questions

Red book

a **i** copper, iron, nickel, selenium, carbon, sulphur

ii mercury, bromine, chlorine

iii No – does not give the two groups given at the top of the page. Not all solids are metals and one metal (mercury) is not a solid.

b **i** iron, nickel

ii copper, mercury, selenium, carbon, sulphur, bromine, chlorine

iii No – does not give the groups at the top of the page. Not all metals are magnetic.

c **i** copper, mercury, iron, nickel, carbon

ii selenium, sulphur, bromine, chlorine

iii No – does not give the groups at the top of the page. Graphite (carbon) conducts electricity but is not a metal.

d **i** copper, mercury, iron, nickel, selenium

ii carbon, sulphur, bromine, chlorine

iii No – does not give the groups at the top of the page. Selenium is shiny but is not a metal.

e Tony's has only one wrong (selenium). Yasmin's only has one wrong (carbon).

f Which elements are shiny *and* conduct electricity?

1 They all have some properties of metals. Boron conducts heat energy, silicon is shiny and conducts heat energy, phosphorus conducts electricity. However, they are all non-metals. None of them pass the test 'Be shiny *and* conduct electricity'.

Green book

a **i** copper, aluminium, iron, nickel, sulphur

ii mercury, hydrogen, bromine, chlorine

iii No – does not give the groups at the top of the page.

b **i** iron, nickel

ii copper, aluminium, mercury, hydrogen, sulphur, bromine, chlorine

iii Not all metals are magnetic.

c **i** copper, mercury, iron, nickel, aluminium

ii hydrogen, sulphur, bromine, chlorine

iii Yes, Yasmin's idea gives the groups at the top of the page.

d **i** Lillian's idea would have carbon as a metal.

ii Joe's idea would have carbon as a non-metal.

iii Yasmin's idea would have carbon as a metal.

e Is it shiny? This would put all the elements given in the correct group.

1 Diamond is a non-metal because it has none of the properties of metals. Graphite has some of the properties of the metals – it conducts heat and electricity, but it is not shiny or magnetic. So carbon is more like a non-metal than a metal.

Grouping metals

Activity 7.5
Core, Help

Activity notes

Purpose

Another opportunity for pupils to develop classification skills and to explain their reasoning (opportunity for metacognition).

Running the activity

This could be done in groups or by individuals.

Core: Pupils answer the questions on the sheet. The cards do not need to be cut out.

Help: Cut out the information cards from the Core sheet to use with the questions on the Help sheet.

Answers

Some pupils may group metals differently to the pattern suggested here.

Core: **1** One group: potassium, lithium, sodium. Other group: copper, iron, gold.

2 One group is those elements that react quickly with water, the other is elements that react slowly or not at all.

3 Silver would go with copper, iron and gold. Caesium would go with potassium, lithium and sodium.

4 Silver reacts slowly with water. Caesium reacts quickly with water.

Help: **1** potassium, sodium and lithium

2 iron, copper

3 gold

4 potassium, sodium, lithium

5 iron, copper and gold

6 The first group all react quickly with water/make fires which are difficult to put out. Others react slowly or not at all.

7 Silver goes with gold, copper and iron because it reacts slowly.

8 Caesium goes with potassium, sodium and lithium because it reacts quickly.

Heating metals

Key ideas	*Science PoS*
No new substances are made during physical changes. New substances are made in a chemical reaction.	1.2g
An oxide is made when a metal reacts with oxygen. A chloride is made when a metal reacts with chlorine. A sulphide is made when a metal reacts with sulphur.	3.1ef, 3.3a

KS2 precursor concepts	*Science PoS*
Some changes are reversible and others are not. Non-reversible changes result in the formation of new materials.	KS2 3.2dfg

Activity	*Description*	*Differentiation*
	A: Making iron sulphide – Pupils react iron and sulphur, and consider the properties before and after heating.	Core
	B: Recording reactions – Pupils practise writing word equations.	Core, Help, Extension

Other relevant material

Optional demonstration of burning magnesium (see Technician's Notes).
Skill sheet 7: Word equations

Answers to book questions

Red book

a mercury
b gallium
c sodium
d cadmium
e it would form a pool of silver liquid
f Melting magnesium is a physical change, while burning magnesium is a chemical reaction.
g lithium + oxygen → lithium oxide
h lithium + chlorine → lithium chloride
i zinc + sulphur → zinc sulphide
1 a potassium + chlorine → potassium chloride
b aluminium + oxygen → aluminium oxide
c calcium + sulphur → calcium sulphide
2 melting ice, boiling water, dissolving sugar
3 bubbles (gas being made), or colour change (new substance being made)
4 magnesium fluoride

Green book

a mercury
b gallium
c cadmium
d a pool of silvery liquid
e a bright flame and the shiny metal changes into a white powder
f Melting is a physical change, burning is a chemical reaction.
g lithium + oxygen → *lithium oxide*
1 melting ice, boiling water, dissolving sugar
2 a magnesium + *oxygen* → magnesium oxide
b aluminium + oxygen → *aluminium oxide*
c sodium + *chlorine* → sodium chloride
d potassium + chlorine → *potassium chloride*
3 potassium + oxygen → potassium oxide

Making iron sulphide

Purpose

Pupils carry out a chemical reaction and consider that a new substance has been made by comparing the product (iron sulphide) with the starting materials (sulphur and iron filings).

Running the activity

A well-ventilated room is required for this experiment. Sets of one sealed jar of sulphur, one sealed jar iron filings, one sealed jar iron(II) sulphide and one magnet should be placed about the room for student groups to share.

Each group of pupils heats the iron/sulphur until it starts and then stops glowing. They then place the test tube on the heatproof mat to cool. Once cool, they try to tap the iron(II) sulphide out of the test tube. If this fails, they should take the test tube to the teacher, who will break the test tube and pick out the iron(II) sulphide.

Expected outcomes

The mixture in the test tube will start to glow, indicating that a chemical reaction is happening. The glow will stop when the reaction is complete. If the mixture was well mixed and there was a slight excess of sulphur, the lump of iron(II) sulphide made should not stick to a magnet.

Pitfalls

The mixture of iron and sulphur must be carefully prepared. Only a small amount of the mixture should be placed in each combustion tube.

The iron(II) sulphide often becomes stuck in the bottom of the test tube. The teacher should ensure that the test tube is wrapped in newspaper before breaking it with a mallet.

Safety notes

Iron filings are a hazard. They cause irritation and are very dangerous if they get into the eyes. Placing the mixture into the test tubes reduces the risk.

The room must be well ventilated for the iron and sulphur reaction.

Pupils should wear goggles, both for observing the demonstration and for carrying out the experiment.

The test tubes become extremely hot. They should be left for 10 minutes to cool. If necessary, the teacher should remove the iron(II) sulphide from the test tube by breaking the test tube. This creates a hazard and the broken glass should be disposed of carefully.

Answers

1 yellow powder

2 dark (grey) powder

3 dark (grey) powder solid

4 iron

5 colour

6 iron sulphide is not attracted to the magnet

7 it glowed

8 no

9 yes

10 The iron sulphide is a solid. This is the same as the sulphur and the iron. It is a different colour (dark grey) to both the sulphur and the iron. It is not magnetic, as the iron is.

Activity 7.6B
Core, Help, Extension

Recording reactions

Purpose

To give pupils practice at writing word equations.

Other relevant material

Skill sheet 7: Word equations

Running the activity

Core: This concentrates on oxides, with chlorides and sulphides briefly mentioned.

Help: Pupils only complete word equations rather than writing them from scratch. It also concentrates on oxides, with chlorides and sulphides only briefly mentioned.

Extension: This is more demanding with more reading required. It also introduces iodides, fluorides and nitrides but only as examples following the same patterns as oxides, chlorides and sulphides.

Answers

Core:

1 calcium + oxygen → calcium oxide
2 carbon + oxygen → carbon dioxide
3 carbon + oxygen → carbon monoxide
4 hydrogen + oxygen → water
5 sodium + chlorine → sodium chloride
6 calcium + chlorine → calcium chloride
7 potassium + sulphur → potassium sulphide

Extension:

1 calcium + oxygen → calcium oxide
2 carbon + oxygen → carbon monoxide
3 carbon + oxygen → carbon dioxide
4 sulphur + oxygen → sulphur dioxide
5 hydrogen + oxygen → water
6 strontium + oxygen → strontium oxide
7 magnesium + bromine → magnesium bromide
8 calcium + fluorine → calcium fluoride
9 sodium + iodine → sodium iodide
10 potassium + sulphur → potassium sulphide
11 magnesium + nitrogen → magnesium nitride
12 calcium + chlorine → calcium chloride

Help:

1 calcium oxide
2 water
3 carbon dioxide
4 carbon monoxide
5 calcium chloride
6 potassium sulphide

Rusting

Key ideas	*Science PoS*
Iron rusts when oxygen and water get to it.	1.2acdgiklp
Rusting turns iron into iron oxide.	3.2h
Rusting is one type of corrosion. Corrosion destroys metals.	

KS2 precursor concepts	*Science PoS*
Fair tests	KS2 1.2d

Activity	*Description*	*Differentiation*
	A: Will it rust? – An investigation into the conditions required for rusting to occur.	Core, Help
	B: Rusty screws – Pupils apply their knowledge of rusting in a context.	Core, Help, Extension

Answers to book questions

Red book

a it turns to iron oxide/becomes brown and crumbly
b A, D
c A, B, C, D
d A, D, E
e A, D
f iron, oxygen and water
g to check iron did not go rusty on its own
h The oil stops the water getting to the iron.
i The paint stops the water and the oxygen from getting to the iron.
j Chromium in the steel forms a layer of chromium oxide on the surface which stops oxygen and water getting to the iron.
k An iron bucket would rust. A tin bucket would not rust but would be expensive. A tin-coated iron bucket would be cheaper and the tin would stop the iron rusting by keeping away oxygen and water.

1 Chemical reaction – a new substance is made and it is non-reversible.

2 A will not rust – no iron.
B will rust – it contains oxygen and water and they can get to the iron.
C will not rust – no water.
D will not rust – water and oxygen cannot get to iron because of a layer of chromium oxide.

3 Make them of stainless steel or aluminium.
Paint iron/steel cars with many layers of paint.
Plate iron/steel cars with another metal.

Green book

a iron oxide
b A
c A, B
d A, C
e A
f iron, oxygen and water
g The paint stops the oxygen and water reaching the iron.
h The tin stops the oxygen and water reaching the iron.
i The chromium reacts with the oxygen and makes a layer of chromium oxide. This stops the oxygen and water reaching the iron.

1 irreversible

2 chemical reaction – a new substance is made, the change is irreversible

3 A will not rust – no iron.
B will rust – it contains oxygen and water and they can get to the iron.
C will not rust – no water.
D will not rust – water and oxygen cannot get to iron because of a layer of chromium oxide.

4 paint it

Activity 7.7A Will it rust?

Core, Help

Metals 7.7 A

Activity notes

Purpose

To reinforce that water and oxygen are both needed for rusting. To give pupils experience of planning and carrying out a simple investigation.

Running the activity

This activity takes place over two lessons. Planning and carrying out the experiment takes place in the first lesson. Observing, recording and analysing the results takes place in a later lesson (3–7 days), when the nails have had time to rust.

Core: Pupils are expected to plan their own investigation, so the number of test tubes per group may vary. The actual experiment is limited, with only plus/minus values for the variables, so the planning exercise is left rather open. Check the pupils' plans before they carry out their experiments.

Help: This version is much more structured, guiding pupils at each stage. Check the pupils' plans before they carry out their experiments.

Expected outcomes

The iron nail exposed to air and water will rust in 3–7 days. Nails from which oxygen and/or water have been successfully excluded will not rust.

Pitfalls

Purchased iron nails often have grease on the surface to prevent rusting.

Failure to deoxygenate the water often causes this experiment to give anomalous results.

Safety notes

Calcium chloride is classified as an irritant. The paint used is likely to contain a hazardous solvent.

Activity 7.7B Rusty screws

Core, Help, Extension

Metals 7.7 B

Purpose

For pupils to apply their knowledge of rusting in a context.

Running the activity

The context is company that makes screws for different purposes.

Core: Pupils compare iron, stainless steel and brass screws.

Help: Pupils compare just iron and stainless steel screws. This is a write-on sheet.

Extension: Pupils compare iron, nickel-plated iron, stainless steel and brass screws.

continued

Rusty screws ⊳⊳⊳ continued

Activity 7.7B
Core, Help, Extension

Answers

Core:

Customer	Question 1	Question 2
Mr Brown	iron screws	• indoor use (will not be exposed to water) • do not show (appearance not important) • cost is only relevant factor, so should buy cheapest
Miss Green	brass screws	• product is expensive, so cost is less of a factor • many old door handles and hinges are made of brass, so brass screws would fit in • appearance is very important
Mr Pink	stainless steel screws	• the windows will get wet from time to time, particularly if left open, so the nails could rust: a rust proof screw is needed • double glazing is an expensive product, people will complain if it is discoloured with rusty streaks • Mr Pink is offering a 30-year guarantee, so it is worth him investing in stainless steel screws • brass screws would look out of place

Help:

1 iron screws

2 Your screws will not get rusty, as you only use them indoors and they will not get wet.

3 stainless steel screws

4 The screws in the windows might get wet. Rusty screws look bad and may turn the window frames brown. The customers are paying a lot. You are offering a 30-year guarantee. You need to spend the extra money.

Extension:

Customer	Question 1	Question 2
Mr Brown	iron screws	• indoor use (will not be exposed to water) • do not show (appearance not important) • cost is only relevant factor, so should buy cheapest
Miss Green	brass screws	• product is expensive, so cost is less of a factor • many old door handles and hinges are made of brass, so brass screws would fit in • appearance is very important
Mr Black	nickel-plated iron	• outdoor use, so nails will be exposed to oxygen and water, therefore iron nails cannot be used as they would rust • cost is important to Mr Black, so he would not buy the more expensive stainless steel screws • he does not need the brass screws as appearance is not very important
Mr Pink	stainless steel screws	• the windows will get wet from time to time, particularly if left open, so the nails could rust: a rust proof screw is needed • double glazing is an expensive product, people will complain if it is discoloured with rusty streaks • Mr Pink is offering a 30-year guarantee, so it is worth him investing in stainless steel screws rather than nickel plated screws which may rust as the years go by: the extra money is worth it • brass screws would look out of place.

Compounds

Key ideas	*Science PoS*
A compound is a substance with more than one type of atom joined together. A pure substance contains only one element or compound. (Red book) A molecule is a group of atoms joined together.	3.1efg, 3.2g

Activity	*Description*	*Differentiation*
	A: Which particles are present? – Pupils distinguish between elements, compounds and mixtures using diagrams showing particles.	Core
	B: Formulae – More able pupils work out the formulae of different compounds using the ratio of atoms.	Extension

Other relevant material

Skill sheet 7: Word equations

Answers to book questions

Red book

a magnesium and oxygen

b 2

c 1:1

d 11

e 1 carbon : 2 oxygen

1 5

2 5

3 3

4 nitrogen, oxygen, helium

5 2

6 water, carbon dioxide

7 An element is a substance with only one type of atom. A compound is a substance with more than one type of atom joined up.

Green book

a magnesium and oxygen

b sodium and chlorine

c hydrogen and oxygen

d carbon and oxygen

1 a Element contain *one type of atom.*

b Compounds contain *more than one type* of atom joined together.

2 a drawings of nitrogen molecule, oxygen molecule, helium atom, carbon dioxide molecule, water molecule

b 3

c nitrogen, oxygen, helium

d 2

e carbon dioxide, water

Book notes

Activity notes

Which particles are present?

Activity 7.8A
Core

Purpose

To reinforce the concepts of elements, compounds and mixtures and revisit solids, liquids and gases so that links are made between topics.

Running the activity

Pupils answer questions based on diagrams of particles in different materials.

Answers

1 A
2 C
3 B and D
4 A and B
5 A
6 B
7 C
8 D
9 D

Metals 7.8 B

Formulae

Activity 7.8B
Extension

Purpose

To introduce formulae to the most able pupils.

Running the activity

Pupils work out the ratios of atoms present in different materials, and from these work out their formulae.

Answers

1 9:9 = 1:1
2 CuO
3 52:26 = 2:1
4 H_2O
5 5:20 = 1:4
6 CH_4

Sports day

Setting the scene

The unit opens with a look at forces in the context of a school sports day. The spread quickly covers work on forces from Key Stage 2 as a foundation for the rest of the unit.

The **unit map** can be used to brainstorm key words and ideas about the unit topics.

KS2 precursor ideas	*Science PoS*
Pupils should know: • that objects are pulled downwards because of the gravitational attraction between them and the Earth • that forces act in particular directions and can be measured.	KS2 4.2bce 1.2gi

Activity	*Description*	*Differentiation*
	A: Measuring forces – Pupils practise reading newtonmeter scales, and use newtonmeters and newton scales to measure forces.	Core
	B: Forces in everyday life – Pupils write a report for an alien about how forces are useful in everyday life on Earth. The activity supports question 2 on the book spreads.	Core

Answers to book questions

Red book

- **a** newtonmeter/newton scale/force measurer/spring balance
- **b** newtons
- **c** push (throw)
- **d** push/air resistance
- **e** distance travelled and time taken
- **f** He is pushed by the pole, his shoes and the pole make friction with the ground.
- **g** gravity
- **h** it would be deeper
- **i** towards the centre of the Earth
- **j** because gravity pulls her downwards

1 Forces can change the shape of an object, or make it move faster, or make it move slower (or change its direction).

2 e.g. for movement, to open cans, to cut up food, to open doors, etc.

3 weight

Green book

- **a** newtons
- **b** push (throw)
- **c** push/air resistance
- **d** push
- **e** towards the centre of the Earth
- **f** because gravity pulls her downwards

1 A force can change the *shape* of an object. A force can make something move *faster* or *slower*.

2 e.g. for movement, to open cans, to cut up food, to open doors, etc.

3 weight/gravity

Measuring forces

Activity notes

Purpose

To practise reading newtonmeter scales, and to use newtonmeters and newton scales to measure forces.

Running the activity

Pupils work individually at first to answer question 1, which asks them to read the newtonmeter scales pictured on the sheet. This helps ensure they will read the newtonmeters correctly for the practical that follows. They continue in pairs to measure forces using the newtonmeter and newton scales, recording their results in a table that they draw for themselves. The practicals are quite short and the teacher may add other objects for the pupils to weigh.

Expected outcomes

Pupils gain experience in reading newtonmeter scales, and in using newtonmeters and newton scales correctly. They begin to appreciate the relationship between mass and weight, and compare forces of different sizes.

Answers

1 A 0N B 10N C 30N D 50N E 25N F 45N

2 –

3 standing

Forces 8.1 B

Forces in everyday life

Activity 8.1B
Core

Purpose

To develop literacy skills and relate science to everyday life. Pupils write a report for an alien about how forces are useful in everyday life on Earth.

Running the activity

The activity accompanies question 2 in the textbooks. Pupils work individually or in pairs to write their report. They can use the ideas provided on the sheet to write their own report.

ICT opportunities

Activity 8.1B can be carried out on a computer using a word-processing package such as Microsoft® *Word*.

Expected outcomes

Pupils practise writing for an audience that does not share their day-to-day experiences. They gain an awareness of the role of forces in everyday life.

Forces and gravity

Key ideas	*Science PoS*
Gravity is the force that pulls everything towards the centre of the Earth. Weight is the force of gravity on an object. Weight is a force, measured in newtons, N. Mass is a measure of how much matter an object is made of. Mass is measured in kilograms, kg.	4.2b

KS2 precursor concepts	*Science PoS*
Pupils should know that objects are pulled downwards because of the gravitational attraction between them and the Earth.	KS2 4.2b

Activity	*Description*	*Differentiation*
	Mass and weight – Pupils reinforce learning of the relationship between mass and weight, by carrying out calculations to convert between the two.	Core

ICT opportunities

The CD-ROM *Eyewitness Encyclopedia of Science 2.0* (Dorling Kindersley) provides a good background resource.

Answers to book questions

Red book

a on the Earth
b 100 N
c 80 N
d 1000 N

1 a Weight is the force of gravity on an object.
b Mass is a measure of how much matter an object is made of.
c Gravity is the force that pulls everything towards the centre of the Earth.

2 a 700 N
b 550 N
c 880 N

3 a 60 N
b 10 N
c 150 N

4 a The bigger the mass, the greater the gravitational force.
b The greater the distance between two objects, the smaller is the gravitational force between them.

Green book

a towards the centre of the Earth
b 100 N
c on the Earth
d 100 N
e 550 N

1 Weight is the force of *gravity* on an object. We measure weight in *newtons*.

Mass is a measure of how much *matter* an object is made of. Mass is measured in *kilograms*.

Your mass is the same on Earth and on the Moon but your *weight* is different.

2 a 700 N
b 550 N
c 880 N

3 Gravity is the force that pulls everything towards the centre of the Earth.

Mass and weight

Activity 8.2
Core

Purpose

To reinforce learning of the relationship between mass and weight, and to carry out calculations to convert between the two.

Running the activity

Pupils work individually or in pairs to answer the questions on the sheet.

Expected outcomes

Pupils gain confidence in calculating mass and weight.

Answers

1 1000 g or 1 kg

2 10 N

3 50 kg

4 10

5 1000 g or 1 kg

6 0.15 N

7 500 g or 0.5 kg, in the astronaut

8 300 kg

9 1 000 000 N on Earth, 150 000 N on the Moon

10 The probe will weigh less on the Moon. It requires less fuel to launch. It will be less expensive to launch/it can go further with the same amount of fuel.

Friction

Key ideas	Science PoS
Friction is a force that is exerted/acts when things rub against each other.	4.2d
Air resistance is a form of friction.	1.2gikp
We can reduce or increase friction.	

KS2 precursor concepts	Science PoS
Pupils should know that friction, including air resistance, slows moving objects and may prevent others from moving.	KS2 4.2c

Activity	Description	Differentiation
	A: Shoe soles – Pupils carry out an investigation to find the relationship between the mass of a shoe and the force needed to pull it against friction.	Core (with Extension question)
	B: A world without friction – Pupils write about their imagined experiences if there was no friction, to develop literary skills and relate science to everyday life. The activity supports question 2 on the book spreads.	Core

Answers to book questions

Red book

a rough surfaces

b smooth/shiny surfaces

c e.g. brakes against wheels, tyres against the road, hands against ropes when rock climbing, pegs for hanging out washing

d Sophie's

1 a e.g. use lubricants, make machinery parts smooth, use rollers, separate surfaces with air

b streamlining

2 –

3 –

Green book

a rough surfaces

b smooth/shiny surfaces

c e.g. brakes against wheels, tyres against the road, hands against ropes when rock climbing, pegs for hanging out washing

d oil it

e e.g. sharks, submarines, aeroplanes

1 Friction is made when two surfaces *rub together*.

Where there is friction, *heat* energy is given out.

Friction can be reduced by using *lubricants* such as oil and *grease*.

When air causes friction, it is called *air resistance*.

2 –

3 –

Shoe soles

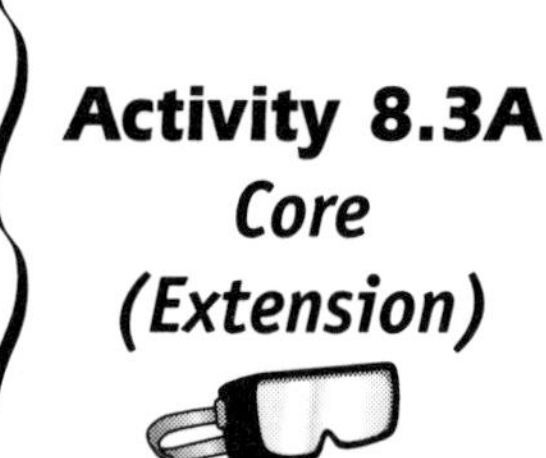

Purpose

To investigate the relationship between the mass of a shoe and the force needed to pull it against friction.

Running the activity

Core: Pupils work in groups towards a full investigation. They write their plans before they start, then carry out the experiment and draw a graph of their results. They analyse their results and evaluate the experiment.

To make the experiment a fair test, the surface, shoe and masses should be the same in each experiment.

Pupils should carry out each reading at least twice to obtain average results. The experiment will not take long to complete so this will not be too time-consuming. Pupils should record their results in a table which has columns for 'Force needed in newtons' and 'Mass in grams'.

Extension: There is an optional Extension question at the foot of the Core sheet, which can be cut off if not required. It asks pupils to suggest a modification to relate the experiment to a real-life problem.

Other relevant material

Skill sheet 5: Drawing charts and graphs

ICT opportunities

The results from Activity 8.3A can be graphed using a spreadsheet such as Microsoft® *Excel*.

Expected outcomes

Pupils carry out an investigation, and see that the heavier the shoe, the greater the friction.

Pitfalls

Care should be taken to make accurate readings when looking at newtonmeters side-on. It is difficult to read the newtonmeter at the same time as pulling it along – one pupil should pull while the other takes the reading.

Answers

Core:

1 As the mass in the shoe increases, so does the force needed to pull the shoe.

2 A greater mass causes more friction between the sole of the shoe and the surface.

3 e.g. repeat the experiment more times, use a more accurate newtonmeter or a pressure sensor

Extension: **4** –

Activity 8.3B
Core

A world without friction

Purpose

To develop literacy skills and relate science to everyday life. Pupils write about their imagined experiences if there was no friction.

Running the activity

The activity accompanies question 2 in the textbooks. Pupils work individually or in pairs to write their story. Pupils can use the ideas provided on the sheet to write their own story.

Expected outcomes

Pupils practise their writing skills and gain an awareness of the role of friction in everyday life.

Book notes

Unbalanced forces

Key ideas	*Science PoS*
Unbalanced forces can act on an object that is not moving. The object starts to move in the direction of the bigger force. Unbalanced forces can act on a moving object. If the bigger force is in the same direction as the movement, then the object moves faster. If the bigger force is in the opposite direction to the movement, then the object moves slower.	4.2c

KS2 precursor concepts	*Science PoS*
Pupils should know how to measure forces and identify the direction in which they act.	KS2 4.2e

Activity	*Description*	*Differentiation*
	Unbalanced forces – Pupils practise drawing force diagrams, to reinforce learning of the effects of unbalanced forces on an object.	Core, Extension

ICT opportunities

Pupils can produce Microsoft® *Excel* spreadsheets to calculate resultant forces.

Answers to book questions

Red book

a **A**

b **C**

c **B**

d The force acting against its movement (e.g. friction) is greater than Dipal's push.

e 950 N

1 a The object starts to move.

b The object moves faster.

c The object moves slower.

2 6 N

Green book

a **A**

b **C**

c **B**

d The force acting against its movement (e.g. friction) is greater than Dipal's push.

e **D** will move to the left, **E** will move upwards.

1 When there are unbalanced forces acting on an object, the object starts to *move*. It moves in the direction of the *bigger* force and it gets faster.

When the bigger force is in the same direction as the movement, the object moves *faster*.

When the bigger force is in the opposite direction to the movement, the object moves *slower*.

2 Check lengths of arrows.

Activity 8.4 Core, Extension — Unbalanced forces

Purpose

To reinforce learning of the effects of unbalanced forces on an object, and to practise drawing force diagrams.

Running the activity

Pupils work individually or in pairs to answer the questions on the sheet.

Core: Pupils should use the force diagrams on the sheet for question 1 as a guide to drawing force diagrams for questions 2, 3 and 4. The sheet is suitable for pupils using the red book. It adds the idea of unbalanced forces changing the direction of a moving object.

Extension: Pupils draw force diagrams, and also calculate the resultant force to work out in which direction the object will move.

Expected outcomes

Pupils gain confidence in drawing force diagrams, and appreciate the effects of unbalanced forces.

Answers

Core: **1** **A** unbalanced force, change in shape, caused by force of hand on can crusher

B no unbalanced force (no change of movement or change of shape)

C unbalanced force, change in direction, caused by force from the engine/the wheels turning/the uneven friction of the tyres on the road

D unbalanced force, change in shape and direction, caused by force of hand on racket

E no unbalanced force (no change of movement or change of shape)

F unbalanced force, moving slower, caused by force of brake blocks on wheels/rider's hands on brake levers

2

3 **4**, –

Extension: **1** orange team, 100 N

2 The cart moves forwards.

3 500 N, in the direction of the elephant's pull

4 500 N, the tug pulls the ship

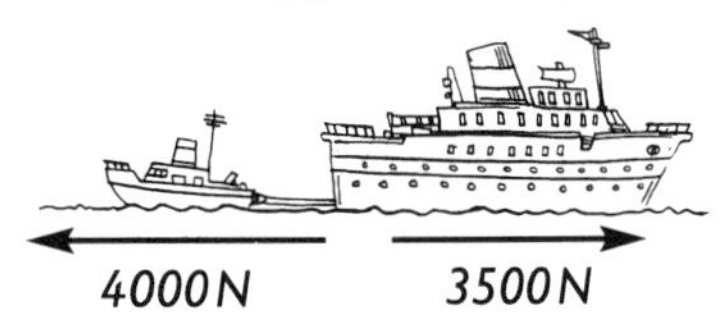

Balanced forces

Key ideas	*Science PoS*
If two forces are the same size and act in opposite directions, they are called balanced forces.	1.2ikmp
The reaction force stops something falling through a solid object. The reaction force balances the weight.	4.2c
When an object floats, the forces of weight and upthrust are equal.	

Activity	*Description*	*Differentiation*
	A: Making bridges – Pupils design, make and test a bridge using straws, paper and sticky tape.	Core
	B: Stretching – Pupils look at the results of an experiment to investigate the effect of a stretching force on a spring, and consider the relationship between weight and extension.	Core
	C: Balanced forces – Pupils practise drawing force diagrams, to reinforce learning of the effects of balanced forces on an object.	Help

Answers to book questions

Red book

a **B, D** show balanced forces.

b **A** will move upwards, **B** will stay still, **C** will move to the right, **D** will stay still.

c The forces are weight and the upwards force of the chair. Diagrams should show up and down force arrows of equal lengths.

d The diagram of the boat should show an upthrust arrow (upwards) and a weight arrow (downwards), of equal length.

1 **a** a car travelling at steady speed on a motorway – balanced

b a car speeding up to overtake a slow lorry – unbalanced

c a car slowing down to stop at traffic lights – unbalanced

2 50N

3 The diagram should show four arrows, upwards (for lift), downwards (for weight), forwards (for thrust of engine), backwards (for air resistance), the sizes of the opposite forces are equal.

Green book

a **B, D** show balanced forces.

b A will go up; B will stay still; C will go backwards; D will stay still

c The forces are weight and the upwards force of the chair. Diagrams should show up and down force arrows of equal lengths.

d upthrust

e weight

1 When two forces are equal and in opposite directions, they are called *balanced* forces.
If a man pulls a dog with a force of 10N, and the dog pulls the man with a force of *10N*, the forces are balanced.
The forces of *upthrust* and *weight* are balanced when a hot-air balloon floats.

2 The diagram should show equal sized arrows, in opposite directions.

3 The boat floats because the upthrust is equal to the weight. The forces are balanced.

Activity 8.5A Making bridges

Core

Purpose

To design, make and test a bridge using straws, paper and sticky tape.

Running the activity

Pupils work in groups to draw their designs, build the bridge, test it to see how many masses it can support and then compare the results with the rest of the class. You may want to limit the number of straws and the length of sticky tape given to each group.

There are several separate tasks to cover and it may be useful to set a time for each one. Pupils could design and make the bridge in one lesson, and then test it as a whole-class activity in the next lesson.

ICT opportunities

The design of the bridge can be carried out using drawing or design software such as Microsoft® *Word* and *Design View*.

Expected outcomes

Pupils design a bridge, make the bridge from the materials supplied, and obtain results as to how many masses the bridge can hold.

Pitfalls

Pupils must ensure that the bridge platform is big enough to hold a reasonable number (4–5) of 100 g masses so that the bridge can be tested.

Answers

1, 2, 3 –

4 Diagrams should show equal sized force arrows for the weight of the masses downwards, and for the force of the bridge upwards.

5 –

Stretching

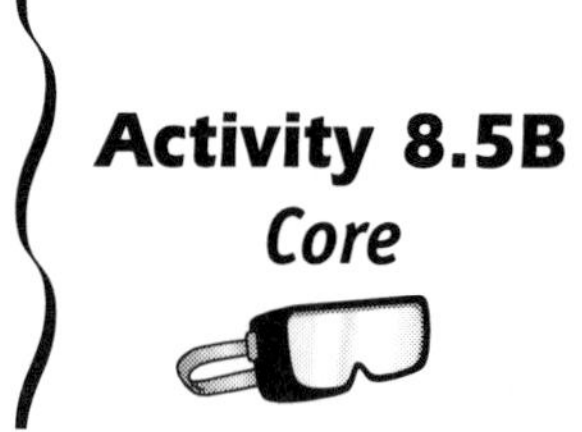

Purpose

To compare the extension of a spring and a rubber band.

Running the activity

Pupils work in pairs. They hang weights on a spring and record the extension, and then do the same for a rubber band. They are given a format for a results table, and are asked to plot separate graphs for the spring and the rubber band. They analyse their results and evaluate the experiment.

The sheet mentions weights, not masses. The masses provided could be labelled in newtons to avoid confusion if this is thought necessary. Alternatively, the teacher may prefer to ask the pupils to add a column to their tables and record first the mass, and then convert this to weight.

Other relevant material

Skill sheet 5: Drawing charts and graphs

Expected outcomes

Pupils plot a graph of extension against weight for a spring and an elastic band, and use it to infer that there is a relationship between extension and weight. Once the elastic limit of the spring or elastic band is reached, the relationship breaks down.

Pitfalls

A set of weights 100–600 N has been selected for this experiment, but suitable weights depend on the spring and elastic band chosen. Test the spring and elastic band in advance to find their elastic limit, and choose weights accordingly, changing the weights on the sheet.

Safety notes

Wear eye protection. Warn pupils to be careful when bending down near clamp stands. They should take care not to drop weights on their feet.

Answers

1. The elastic band stretches more than the spring for a given weight. It breaks more easily.
2. yes, the greater the weight, the longer the extension, up to a certain weight (the elastic limit)
3. yes, the greater the weight, the longer the extension, up to a certain weight (the elastic limit).
4. e.g. take another set of results for each or take a set of results when unloading
5. e.g. test springs made of different materials and of different lengths

Activity 8.5C Help — Balanced forces

Purpose

To reinforce learning of the effects of balanced forces on an object, and to practise drawing force diagrams.

Running the activity

Help: Pupils work individually or in pairs. They complete the force diagrams on the sheet by drawing force arrows.

Expected outcomes

Pupils complete the force diagrams on the sheet.

Answers

1

2

upthrust

weight

3

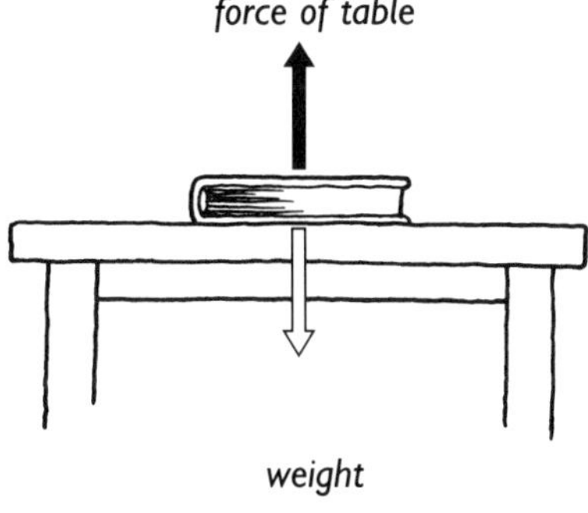

4

5

8.6 Speed

Key ideas	*Science PoS*
Speed is the distance an object travels in a certain time. Speed = distance travelled (in metres)/time taken (in seconds) The units used for speed are metres per second, m/s, or kilometres per hour, km/h.	1.2gikp 4.2a

Activity	*Description*	*Differentiation*
	A: Speeding trolleys – Pupils carry out a datalogging activity to compare the speed of a trolley travelling down ramps of different slopes. Light gates are used to measure the speed of the trolley.	Core
	B: Speed freak – Pupils practise using the equation for speed, to reinforce learning of the concept of speed	Core

Answers to book questions

Red book

a i 5 km/h
ii 5 m/s
iii 100 km/h
iv 400 km/h
v 4 m/s
b 0.05 km/h

1

Distance travelled	Time taken	Speed
100 km	2 hours	*50 km/h*
40 m	*8seconds*	5 m/s
200 km	4 hours	*50 km/h*
200 km	*10 hours*	20 km/h
50 km	30 minutes	*100 km/h*

2 –

Green book

a 100 m ÷ 20 s = 5 m/s
b cheetah
c 96 km/h

1 The speed of an object is usually measured in metres per *second* or *kilometres* per hour. To find the speed of an object, you must find the *distance* the object travels and the time taken for it to travel that *distance*.

2

Distance travelled	Time taken	Speed
100 km	2 hours	*50 km/h*
40 m	8 seconds	*5 m/s*
200 km	4 hours	*50 km/h*
150 km	3 hours	*50 km/h*

Activity 8.6A *Core*

Speeding trolleys

Activity notes

Purpose

To carry out a datalogging activity to compare the speed of a trolley travelling down ramps of different slopes. Light gates are used to measure the speed of the trolley.

Running the activity

This is an ICT activity that requires the use of datalogging equipment. If pupils are familiar with using datalogging equipment, the activity can be run quickly, otherwise they may need a demonstration of the kit before they start.

Pupils work in groups. They draw up their own results table, carry out the experiment and plot a bar chart. They answer questions to analyse the results and evaluate the experiment.

Instead of using datalogging equipment and light gates, the activity can be run using ticker tape, or alternatively pupils can measure the distance the trolley travels after being released from the ramp at different heights.

ICT opportunities

ICT PoS 2b Datalogging

A spreadsheet program such as Microsoft® *Excel* can be used to graph the results.

Expected outcomes

Pupils carry out the speeding trolleys experiment. They obtain a set of results and suggest a basic conclusion (the higher the ramp, the faster the trolley) and evaluation.

Pitfalls

The results from datalogging are very accurate, perhaps down to several decimal places. Pupils need to round to a suitable number of decimal places.

The experiment must be set up so that the card passes through the light gates and breaks the beam. Light gates should not be too close to windows as the sunlight may affect the results.

Safety notes

Use a catch box at the bottom of the ramp to stop the trolleys.

Make sure the ramps cannot fall off the tables.

Answers

1 –

2 As the height of the slope increases, the speed of the trolley increases.

3 e.g. repeat the experiment at least once and obtain an average to improve the accuracy

Speed freak

Activity 8.6B
Core

Purpose

To reinforce learning of the concept of speed, and practise using the equation for speed.

Running the activity

Pupils work individually or in pairs to answer the questions.

Expected outcomes

Pupils answer the questions and gain experience in calculating speed.

Answers

1 cat 10 m/s, dog 5 m/s, kangaroo 80 m/s

2 Mark is quicker at 10 m/s while James runs at a speed of 8 m/s.

3 **A** 80 km/h, **B** 100 km/h, **C** 40 km/h, train **B**

4 640 km/h

Forces and relationships

Developing thinking skills

A class discussion led by the teacher can be used to introduce the context of the spread. Pupils can then work in small groups, ideally in pairs. The questions in the text are intended to prompt either whole class discussion or small group discussion, as appropriate. The teacher will have the opportunity to intervene and challenge individual pupils. It is advisable not to tell the pupils the answers, but to ask them another question which takes them forward in their thinking. This will help them to develop higher thinking skills. Many of the questions are very open and do not have a simple answer. It is useful to allow some time for pupils to feedback ideas to the class after the group work.

Think about: relationships

The idea of a relationship linking the input variable and outcome variable is taken further in the context of forces. Pupils are asked to predict the outcome of changing the slope of the ramp down which a toy car is running. They also consider the relationship between the weight in a shoe and the force needed to pull it against the force of friction.

Key ideas	*Science PoS*
Relationships and variables	1.2j
How to determine the speed of a moving object	4.2a
The quantitative relationship between speed, distance and time.	

KS2 precursor concepts	*Science PoS*
Pupils should be able to identify patterns in the data, draw conclusions and explain them scientifically.	KS2 1.2kln

Other relevant material

Skill sheet 6: Interpreting graphs

Answers to book questions

Red book

a car will go faster (speed increases)

b car will go slower (speed decreases)

c input variable – height of slope; outcome variable – speed

d yes, the higher the slope the faster the car moves

e input variable – weight; outcome variable – extension

f yes, the greater the weight, the greater the extension of the spring. Also possible to say that for every 1 newton put on the spring, the extension is 10 mm.

g input variable

h a straight line – as the weight increases by 1 N, the extension increases by about 10 mm

i about 25 mm

1 a the thing that we change or that is changed in an experiment

b A relationship links two or more variables together.

2 a input variable – force; outcome variable – distance

b –

c Yes, the greater the force, the longer the distance the go-kart travels. Also possible to say that for every force of 10 newtons, the distance travelled is 5 cm.

Green book

a – e see Red book **a – e**

f yes, the more weight in the shoe, the *greater* the extension of the spring in the newtonmeter.

1 We link variables together in *relationships.* When you throw a ball, the more *force* you use to throw the ball, the *higher/further* it will go.

2 a input variable – force; outcome variable – distance

b Yes. The more force you use to push a go-kart, the *further* the go-kart will travel.

Book notes

A day at the zoo

Setting the scene

This spread gets pupils thinking about different animals and their babies, and introduces ideas about the roles of zoos. The **unit map** can be used to help brainstorm key words about the unit topics.

KS2 precursor concepts	*Science PoS*
Pupils should know the main stages of the human life cycle, and that reproduction is one of the life processes common to animals and humans.	KS2 2.1a, 2.2f

Activity	*Description*	*Differentiation*
	Life cycles – The first part supports the question about the human life cycle in the book. Pupils then draw a time line showing the four main stages in the human life cycle, and compare it to that of an Emperor penguin.	Core

ICT opportunities

Many zoos have web sites which can be used for research into their role in protecting different species. Try:
www.weboflife.co.uk/londonzoo, or
www.zooweb.net

Answers to book questions

Red book

a 9 months

b Human babies are protected by their parents. They are carried/pushed around.

c warmth, food, protection

1 elephant, human, kangaroo, hamster

2 Zebras need to be able to move away from predators otherwise they will get eaten. Lions are not at risk from predators.

3 baby → child → adolescent → adult

4 –

Green book

a elephant, human, hamster

b so that it does not get eaten by predators

c gives it food and protection

1 Very small animals, such as the hamster, have *short* pregnancies. Big animals, such as the elephant, have very *long pregnancies*. The amount of time that an animal is pregnant is called its *gestation period.*

2 baby → child → adolescent → adult

3 –

Activity 9.1
Core

Life cycles

Purpose

To support the question in the pupil books about the human life cycle, and then to compare different life cycles.

Running the activity

Pupils are given the four stages of the human life cycle, which they have to put in the correct order then produce a flow diagram. You may use this to help pupils with question 2 (red book)/3 (green book) if necessary.

Pupils compare the life cycles of humans and Emperor penguins by comparing time lines. They are required to estimate the length of time each stage lasts in humans. The last part of the activity, asking how the differences help the human and the penguin, could be done as a group discussion.

Answers

1. A flow diagram of the four stages: baby, child, adolescent, adult.
2. A time line showing *length* of each stage: baby (2 years), child (4 years), adolescent (12 years), adult (approx. 60 years)
3. An X close to adolescent
4. - Similarities: humans and Emperor penguins both have four similar stages in their life cycles. (Penguins go through adolescence.)
   - Differences: each stage lasts longer in humans compared with penguins.
   - For penguins, having only a short time as a helpless baby is advantageous as penguins are at risk of predation. For humans having a longer time of dependence on parents is not a problem as humans tend to live as families and are not at risk of predation.

Spot the difference

Key ideas	*Science PoS*
Sperm are made in the testes. They pass down the sperm tube and out of the penis. Eggs are made in the ovaries. They pass down the oviduct to the uterus.	2.2g

Activity	*Description*	*Differentiation*
	A: Male parts – Pupils label the parts and functions of the human male reproductive system.	Core, Help
	B: Female parts – Pupils label the parts and functions of the human female reproductive system.	Core, Help

Answers to book questions

Red book

1 a Sperm are made in the *testes*. When the sperm leave the testes they pass down the *sperm tube*. Glands add a special liquid to make *semen*. The sperm then leave through the *penis*.

b Eggs are made in the *ovaries*. Every month an egg is released and passes down the *oviduct* to the *uterus*.

2 The fetus develops.

3 The muscles open and close the uterus.

4 a Sperm will not be able to leave the testes.

b Sperm will not be able to get to the eggs.

Green book

a in the testes

b testes, sperm tube, penis

c in the ovaries

1 a Sperm are made in the *testes*. When the sperm leave the testes they pass down the *sperm tube*. Glands add a special liquid to make *semen*. The sperm then leave through the *penis*.

b Eggs are made in the *ovaries*. Every month an egg is released and passes down the *oviduct* to the *uterus*.

2 The fetus develops.

3 a Sperm will not be able to leave the testes.

b Sperm will not be able to get to the eggs.

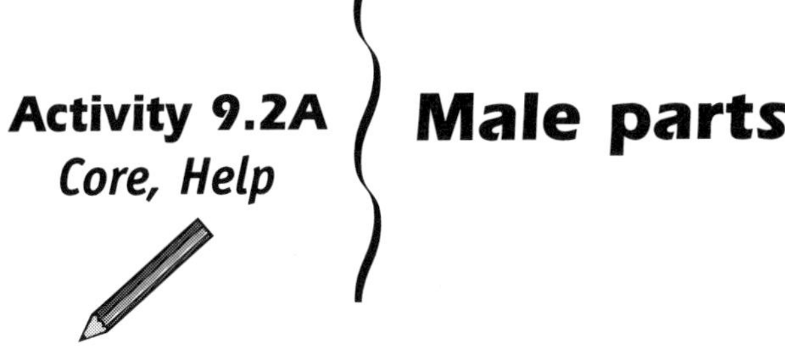

Activity 9.2A *Core, Help* — Male parts

Purpose

To reinforce details in the book spread about the male reproductive system.

Running the activity

Core: Pupils copy a diagram of the reproductive system and label it with the name and what each part does. You may choose to give some pupils a photocopy to label.

Help: Pupils write the name of each part on the diagram (from a given list), then cut out, sort and stick down boxes giving the job for each part. (You will to provide need scissors and glue.)

Expected outcomes

Pupils revise the parts of the male reproductive system.

Answers

Diagram labelled clockwise from top right:

glands – add fluids to sperm to make semen
sperm tube – carries sperm to the penis
testis – where the sperm are made
scrotum – a bag of skin which holds the testes
penis – carries sperm out of the body

Activity 9.2B *Core, Help* — Female parts

Purpose

To reinforce details in the book spread about the female reproductive system.

Running the activity

Core: Pupils copy a diagram of the reproductive system and label it with the name and what each part does. You may choose to give some pupils a photocopy to label.

Help: Pupils write the name of each part on the diagram (from a given list), then cut out, sort and stick down boxes giving the job for each part. (You will need to provide scissors and glue.)

Expected outcomes

Pupils revise the parts of the female reproductive system.

Answers

Diagram labelled clockwise from top right:

oviduct – carries the egg to the uterus
ovary – where the eggs are made
vagina – receives the sperm
cervix – the opening of the uterus
uterus – where the baby grows

A new generation

Key ideas	*Science PoS*
In sexual intercourse, millions of sperm are released into the woman's vagina. Most will die, but one may make it to the egg. Fertilisation happens when the nucleus of a sperm joins up with the nucleus of an egg.	1.2jm 2.1e, 2.2g

Activity	*Description*	*Differentiation*
	A: Fertilisation – Pupils put the sequence of events in order, and consider some causes of infertility.	Core (Help)
	B: Sperm meets egg – Pupils compare internal and external fertilisation.	Core
	C: The sperm's story – This sheet supports question 2 in the green book/3 in the red book. Pupils write a story about a sperm's journey from testis to egg.	Core

Other relevant material

Knowledge of cells and the cell nucleus from unit 6 is needed here.

Answers to book questions

Red book

a The sperm will die.

b No, because they all came from different eggs fertilised by different sperm.

1 Because most of the sperm will die, this increases the chances of one sperm making it to the egg.

2 The nucleus of a sperm joins with the nucleus of an egg.

3 –

4 Identical twins come from the same egg and sperm – the fertilised egg splits into two. Non-identical twins come from two different eggs and sperm.

Green book

a an egg and a sperm

b The man puts his penis into the woman's vagina and sperm are released *or* through sexual intercourse

c The nucleus of a sperm joins with the nucleus of an egg.

d The sperm will die.

1 Because most of the sperm will die, this increases the chances of one sperm making it to the egg.

2 –

3 Identical twins come from the same egg and sperm. Non-identical twins come from different eggs and sperm.

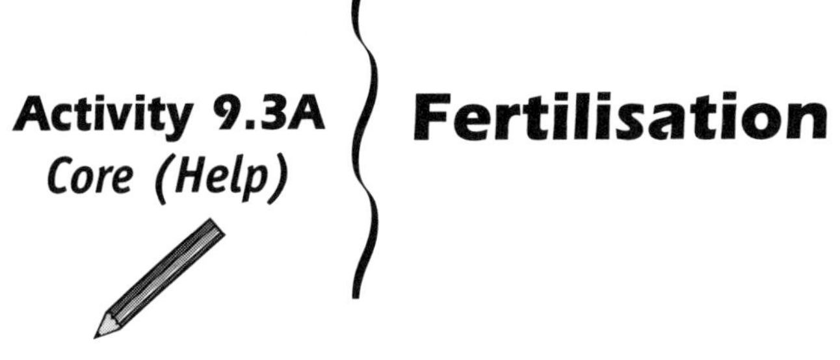

Activity 9.3A Core (Help) — Fertilisation

Purpose

To reinforce the book spread section 'How the sperm and egg meet', and to apply this knowledge to explain infertility.

Running the activity

Core/Help: This is a simple sequencing activity. Pupils write out the statements in the correct order, then answer the question about infertility. For less able pupils, you may photocopy the Core sheet to allow them to cut out the boxes and arrange them in the correct order. These can then be stuck into their books. (You will need to provide scissors and glue.)

Answers

1 The correct order is: c, e, a, d, b

2 Not many sperm – less chance of a sperm reaching the egg; oviducts blocked – sperm cannot get to the egg; not making an egg – no egg for sperm to fertilise.

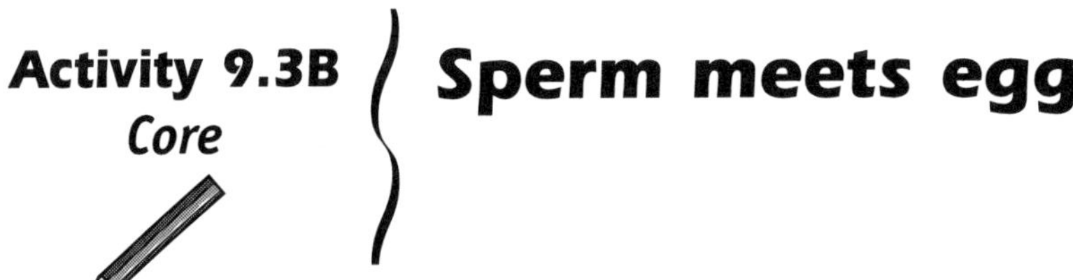

Activity 9.3B Core — Sperm meets egg

Purpose

To compare internal and external fertilisation, in terms of the numbers of eggs produced by different animals.

Running the activity

Pupils study a table and answer questions based on it.

Expected outcomes

Pupils should see from the table a clear relationship between type of fertilisation and number of eggs produced, and relate this to the care given to offspring.

Answers

1 Animals with external fertilisation produce large numbers of eggs. Animals with internal fertilisation produce only a small number of eggs.

2 There is a good chance of the egg being fertilised. Because the human looks after its offspring for many years, it is better to have just one baby at a time to care for.

3 The chances of sperm fertilising eggs externally are much smaller, so the more eggs that are produced, the greater chance there is of some being fertilised. Also, many of the eggs may die as the trout does not look after its young.

4 human, cat, dog, eagle; fewer eggs, easier to care for a small number of offspring

5 because the babies are left to fend for themselves and many die; it has a lot of eggs to make sure that some might survive

The sperm's story

Activity 9.3C
Core

Purpose

To support question 3 in the red book/2 in the green book.

Running the activity

The sheet can be used to give prompts for answering the question in the pupil book. Some pupils may choose to present the information as a strip cartoon.

Expected outcomes

Pupils complete their story about a sperm's journey from testes to egg.

Pregnancy

Key ideas	Science PoS
It takes nine months for a human baby to develop fully inside its mother. This is called pregnancy.	2.2h

Activity	Description	Differentiation
	The fetus – Core and Help pupils label a diagram of a fetus in the uterus and consider the job of each part. Extension pupils consider the parts in terms of a life support machine.	Core, Help, Extension

Answers to book questions

Red book

a The fertilised cell embeds in the uterus wall and grows into a tiny ball of cells, known as the embryo.

b At 4 weeks it has just a few features (head and legs), but at 39 weeks it is bigger and fully developed.

c They need to be kept warm because they may not have much fat

d The placenta gets food and oxygen to the embryo/fetus and gets rid of waste products such as carbon dioxide.

e Once the baby is born, it feeds by mouth and gets rid of waste as urine and faeces. It does not need the placenta.

1 amnion – protects the baby from bumps
cord – joins the placenta to the fetus
placenta – supplies the fetus with food and oxygen
afterbirth – pushed out of the uterus after the baby is born

2 The breasts grow; the mother often eats more food; the placenta, amnion and cord are made; more blood is pumped to the fetus; often there are emotional changes.

3 The baby is pushed out of the uterus by strong muscles of the uterus wall and some other of the mother's muscles. The baby is still attached to the mother by the cord, so the cord has to be cut and tied. The placenta is no longer needed and leaves the uterus a few minutes later as the afterbirth.

4 –

Green book

a a tiny ball of cells

b when the egg is fertilised

c At 4 weeks it has just a few features (head and legs), but at 39 weeks it is bigger and fully developed.

d the cord

e to get food and oxygen to the embryo/fetus and to get rid of waste products such as carbon dioxide

f about 9 months

g the placenta that is pushed out of the uterus after the baby is born

h the baby can feed and get rid of waste by itself

1 amnion – protects the baby from bumps
cord – joins the placenta to the fetus
placenta – supplies the fetus with food and oxygen
afterbirth – pushed out of the uterus after the baby is born

2 Pregnancy lasts about 9 months. The baby is pushed out by the strong *muscles* of the uterus. The *cord* that joins the baby to the placenta is cut and tied when the baby is born. The *placenta* also comes out of the uterus a few minutes later. This is known as the *afterbirth*.

3 –

The fetus

Activity 9.4
Core, Help, Extension

Purpose

To reinforce the book spread.

Running the activity

Core: Pupils label a diagram of a pregnant woman showing the fetus. The names of the parts and what they do are not given on the sheet.

Help: Pupils label the same diagram with the name of each part (chosen from a given list). They then complete a table about the job of each part in the diagram.

Extension: Pupils consider the mother's body as like a life support machine. They describe the parts of the mother's body that give support to the fetus, then consider the needs of premature babies.

Expected outcomes

Pupils reinforce their knowledge of the different parts that enable a fetus to develop.

Answers

Core: **1** labels clockwise from top right:
fetus – the developing baby
uterus – the place that feeds and shelters the fetus
vagina – the baby is pushed out here
cervix – a ring of muscle at the entrance of the uterus which widens to let the baby out
amnion – protects the fetus from bumps
cord – joins the placenta to the fetus
placenta – supplies the fetus with food and oxygen

Help: **1** labels clockwise from top right: spine, fetus, uterus, vagina, cervix, amnion, cord, placenta

2 Left-hand column: amnion, cord, placenta, uterus, fetus, vagina, cervix, spine

Extension: **1** Description of the parts (see Core above).

2 Can provide: warmth, protection from bumps
Cannot provide: food, water, waste removal

Adolescence

Key ideas	*Science PoS*
Adolescence is a time when physical and emotional changes happen.	1.2jm
Puberty is the first part of adolescence when most of the physical changes happen.	2.2fg

Activity	*Description*	*Differentiation*
	Growth spurts – pupils analyse data to show height changes as children get older.	Core

Answers to book questions

Red book

a various physical and emotional changes take place

b substances that cause the physical and emotional changes in the body

c when dead cells and blood leave the body after the uterus lining breaks down

d normally between 45–55 years

1 adolescence – a time in everyone's life when physical and emotional changes take place
puberty – the first part of adolescence in which most of these changes takes place
hormones – substances that cause the changes in boys and girls
period – dead cells and blood leave the body through the vagina
menopause – time when women stop having periods

2 a Any three from: hair starts to grow on body, including pubic hair; voice deepens; testes start to make sperm and hormones; shoulders broaden; sexual organs get bigger.

b Any three from: hair starts to grow on body, including pubic hair; breasts grow; ovaries start to release eggs and make hormones; hips widen; periods start.

3 testosterone in boys, oestrogen in girls

4 a period

b ovulation

c uterus lining start to thicken

Green book

a various physical and emotional changes take place

b puberty

c substances that cause the physical and emotional changes in the body

d to make sperm and hormones

e they start to release eggs and produce hormones

f about 28 days

g when dead cells and blood leave the body after the uterus lining breaks down

1 adolescence – a time in everyone's life when physical and emotional changes take place
puberty – the first part of adolescence in which most of these changes take place
period – dead cells and blood leave the body through the vagina

2 a Any three from: hair starts to grow on body, including pubic hair; voice deepens; testes start to make sperm and hormones; shoulders broaden; sexual organs get bigger.

b Any three from: hair starts to grow on body, including pubic hair; breasts grow; ovaries start to release eggs and make hormones; hips widen; periods start.

3 a period/the uterus lining breaks down and blood and dead cells are lost through the vagina

Growth spurts

Activity 9.5
Core

Purpose

To reinforce the book spread and to give pupils an opportunity to analyse graphs.

Running the activity

Pupils are given a graph showing how height changes as girls and boys grow up and develop. They then analyse the graph and answer the questions.

Expected outcomes

Pupils have an understanding of growth spurts at puberty.

Answers

1 10–12 years
2 13–14 years
3 1 or 2 cm
4 15–16 cm
5 2 or 3 cm
6 4–5 cm
7 boys
8 girls
9 boys
10 between 0–4 years
11 better diet, healthier lifestyle, etc.

Pregnant pause

Developing thinking skills

A class discussion led by the teacher can be used to introduce the context of the spread. Pupils can then work in small groups, ideally in pairs. The questions in the text are intended to prompt either whole class discussion or small group discussion, as appropriate. The teacher will have the opportunity to intervene and challenge individual pupils. It is advisable not to tell the pupils the answers, but to ask them another question which takes them forward in their thinking. This will help them to develop higher thinking skills. Many of the questions are very open and do not have a simple answer. It is useful to allow some time for pupils to feedback ideas to the class after the group work.

Think about: analysing graphs

Pupils are required to draw a bar chart and a line graph to investigate the differences between the gestation periods of a number of animals.

They are required to look at patterns in their chart and graph and relate this to the knowledge they have acquired during this unit. It may be worthwhile referring pupils back to the 'setting the scene' spread at the start of the unit to refresh their memories about some of the animals mentioned in this spread.

Key ideas	*Science PoS*
Animals that are predators have shorter gestation periods than animals who are prey.	2.2h

ICT opportunities

A spreadsheet can be used to produce the graphs for these activities.

Answers to book questions

Red book

a (bar chart)
b The bigger the animal, the longer it is pregnant.
c Bigger animals take longer to develop because they are made of more cells/they are more complex.
d kangaroo
e Its baby is born early, but continues to develop in its mother's pouch.
f between 30 and 62 days
g (graph)
h (graph)
i All prey have longer gestation periods than predators.
j prey
k Babies that are more developed when born stand a better chance of escaping from predators. Predators are at less risk of being attacked – a mother can defend her baby better, so having helpless babies is less of a problem.

Green book

a (bar chart)
b elephant
c mouse
d elephant
e mouse
f the bigger the animal is, the longer it is pregnant
g kangaroo
h Its baby is born early, but continues to develop in its mother's pouch.
i (graph)
j (graph)
k prey
l longer gestation period/pregnant for longer
m The baby zebra will have a better chance of surviving because it will be more developed, so will be more able to escape from the predators.

Energy circus

Activity	Description	Differentiation
	A circus of four activities. **A: Energy from food** – A selection of foods for pupils to divide into 'high energy' and 'low energy' foods. **B: Energy in fuel** – Heating water in a boiling tube for 1 minute with a candle. **C: Energy to run** – One pupil runs on the spot while another saunters on the spot for 1 minute. **D: Energy to lift** – One pupil lifts as many sandbags as possible from floor to bench, while another lifts one sandbag every 5 seconds for the same time.	Core

Equipment needed

Two lots of each of the following set-ups:

A: Energy from food

A selection of foods that will fit into one of two categories: high energy and low energy. Both types should be mixed together. Suggestions include:

- bottle of higher energy fizzy drink (e.g. Lucozade)
- bottle of low calorie fizzy drink
- butter/margarine
- bar of chocolate
- 4 pieces of fruit/vegetables
- skimmed milk
- full cream milk
- bread
- cake
- sausages
- notice: **DO NOT EAT THE FOOD**

Tips: Use as many empty packets as possible. Pack the packets so they look full.

B: Energy in fuel

Set up the apparatus before the activity starts, otherwise the group starting here will fall behind.

- boiling tube
- candle
- clamp stand
- thermometer
- stopclock
- measuring cylinder ($25cm^3$)
- notice: **BEWARE – THE APPARATUS MAY BE HOT**

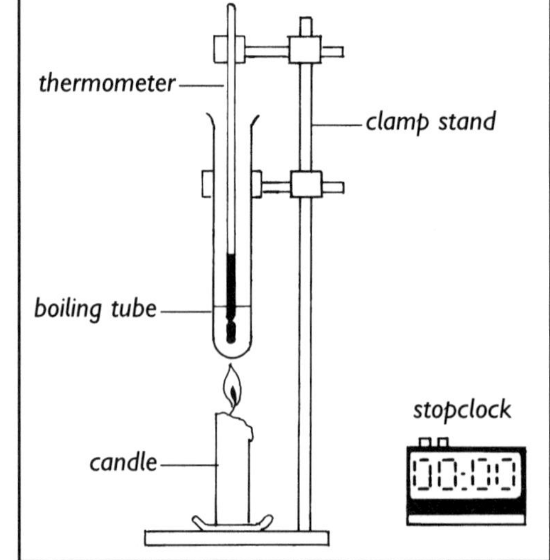

C: Energy to run

- 2 stopclocks

D: Energy to lift

- 2 stopclocks
- as many 10N sandbags as possible (at least 20)

continued

Energy circus ⊳⊳⊳ continued

For your information

Running the activities

Divide the class into eight groups. Have two stations for each activity. Rotate every 5 minutes. This is only an elicitation activity; it should not take more than 20–25 minutes. The activities relate to the first four sections of the book spread.

Alternatively, elect a group to do each activity and then report back to the class.

Expected outcomes

Pupils start thinking about energy.

Pitfalls

Make sure pupils muddle the different foods before the next group arrives. **(1.1A)**

Safety notes

Warn pupils that no food should be consumed in a laboratory. **(1.1A)**

Remind pupils doing **1.1B** to wear eye protection and beware of the hot apparatus, particularly as the apparatus may be hot when they arrive at that station.

Asthmatics may have to take care when taking strenuous exercise. **(1.1C, 1.1D)**

Energy out!

Activity	Description	Differentiation
	A display of objects about the room. Pupils decide if the objects are giving out light energy, sound energy or heat energy, or whether they are moving.	Core

Equipment needed

A large number of objects about the room that give out light, sound or heat energy, or which move. Each object needs a notice, for example:

- ball **DROP THE BALL**
- wind-up toy **WIND UP THE TOY**
- spinning top **SPIN THE TOP**
- torch **SWITCH ON THE TORCH – SWITCH IT OFF AS YOU LEAVE**
- box of matches **STRIKE ONE MATCH**
- lit candle **LOOK AT THE CANDLE**
- room lights switched on **LOOK AT THE LIGHTS IN THE ROOM**
- notice by the window **LOOK AT THE SUN**
- lit Bunsen burner **LOOK AT THE BUNSEN BURNER**
- filled hot water bottle **FEEL THE HOT WATER BOTTLE**
- filled electric kettle **BOIL SOME WATER IN THE KETTLE**
- whistle **BLOW THE WHISTLE – THEN DISINFECT IT**
- hand bell **RING THE BELL**
- different musical instruments **PLUCK THE STRING** (or similar instruction)
- a tray of marbles **TIP THE TRAY**

For your information

Running the activities

Pupils make a table as shown on the activity sheet.

Expected outcomes

Pupils develop an appreciation that energy is given off by a large range of devices.

Safety notes

Anything blown into should be disinfected after use.
Beware of hot objects like Bunsen burners and matches.

Energy in, energy out

Activity	Description	Differentiation
	Identifying energy being transferred out of electrical devices.	Core

Equipment needed

As many safe, mains electrical devices as possible, with an emphasis on those that obviously give out light energy, sound energy, heat energy or move. For example:

- desk lamp
- fan
- iron/soldering iron
- room heater
- radio or cassette player
- curling tongs/hair styling brush

Do not use a food processor, tumble dryer, television or electric kettle as these are used in the next activity.

For your information

Running the activities

Objects should be spread about the room. Pupils observe energy transfers and fill in a table as given on the activity sheet.

Expected outcomes

Pupils complete the table and prepare to begin writing energy transfers.

Safety notes

All hot objects require a warning notice: **WARNING – HOT**
Do not use any electrical device which could trap fingers or cut.

Stored energy

Activity	Description	Differentiation
	Deciding how energy is stored in different objects.	Core

Equipment needed

Set up the following mini-demonstrations around the room:

- candle burning
- wind-up toy
- lit Bunsen burner
- 'battery' in a circuit causing a lamp to light
- cotton reel racer (see **1.4B**)
- mini pinball machine or any other toy where a spring 'shoots' a ball
- pop-up greetings card
- model of a bungee jumper (clamp stand, rubber string and small doll)
- water dripping from a tap
- sandbag to lift up and drop, with notice: **LIFT UP AND DROP**

Tips

Try to avoid catapults, bows and arrows, etc.

For your information

Running the activity

The objects could be placed around the room and pairs of pupils tour them, guided by their activity sheets. Alternatively, the teacher could demonstrate from the front of the class, whereupon larger demonstrations may be desirable.

Expected outcomes

Pupils complete a table, as shown on their activity sheet.

Safety notes

Pupils should wear eye protection for demonstrations with stretched elastic bands (cotton reel racer).

Cotton reel racers

Activity	Description	Differentiation
	Finding out how much energy can be stored in an elastic band.	Core, Help

Equipment needed

For each group:

- cotton reel
- long match to act as a paddle
- short match to act as an anchor
- wax washer made from a candle by cutting with a wire and slipping off the wick
- 3 rubber bands of suitable length
- stopclock
- 1 metre rule

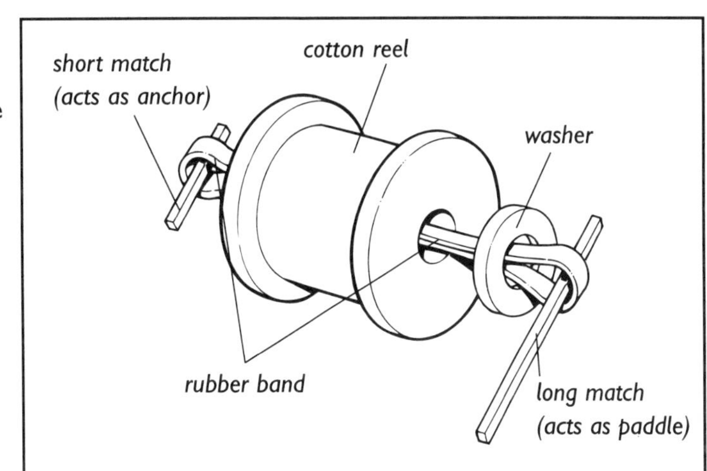

Tips

Try it out until there is an in-house version that works with the apparatus available.

For your information

Running the activity

Pupils work in small groups to develop and test a cotton reel racer, as shown on their activity sheets. Then as a class they race their cotton reel racers in a Derby, where the distance covered and movement time are measured and recorded.

Core: Pupils are given some guidance at each stage.

Help: Pupils are told what to do, and record their results on the sheet.

Expected outcomes

Pupils record the characteristics of their cotton reel racer and its 'race results'. They then suggest improvements.

Pitfalls

It is essential to check that a working cotton reel racer can be built out of the components being supplied. A working model would help struggling groups, who may find it difficult to interpret the diagram.

Safety notes

Pupils should wear eye protection as the rubber bands may be over-wound.

Energy in food

Activity	*Description*	*Differentiation*
	Burning foods to heat water with the energy released.	Core

Other relevant material

Skill sheet 2: Lighting a Bunsen burner

Skill sheet 4: Energy transfer diagrams

Equipment needed

For each group:

- boiling tube
- clamp stand
- thermometer
- heatproof mat
- lit Bunsen burner
- 25 cm^3 measuring cylinder
- mounted needle
- dried pea with small hole
- dried raisin.

Tips

Do not use peanuts – some pupils may be allergic to them.

Before the activity, make a small hole in each dried pea using a heated needle (to avoid pupils stabbing themselves when trying to get the needle into the pea).

For your information

Running the activity

This could be done as a demonstration, if time is short. Alternatively, one group could do the pea and the other the raisin, and they could swap results. Some pupils could do **1.5A** while others did **1.5B**.

Expected outcomes

One raisin has more energy than one pea, if the raisin and the pea are average sized.

Pitfalls

It is worth checking that temperature rise is reasonable for one pea and one raisin of the size given. If not, it may be necessary to increase or decrease the volume of water accordingly.

Safety notes

Pupils should wear eye protection while burning the pea/raisin and heating water.
Make sure the peas are 'pre-drilled' to avoid pupils stabbing themselves with a needle.

Bell in a vacuum demonstration

Activity	*Description*	*Differentiation*
(goggles icon)	A teacher demonstration to show that sound does not travel through a vacuum.	Core (no pupil sheets)

Equipment needed

For the teacher demonstration:

- bell jar
- electric bell with battery connection
- battery/power pack
- 2 thick rubber bands
- bung with hole for tubing
- tubing to vacuum pump
- vacuum pump
- glass sheet
- foam cushion

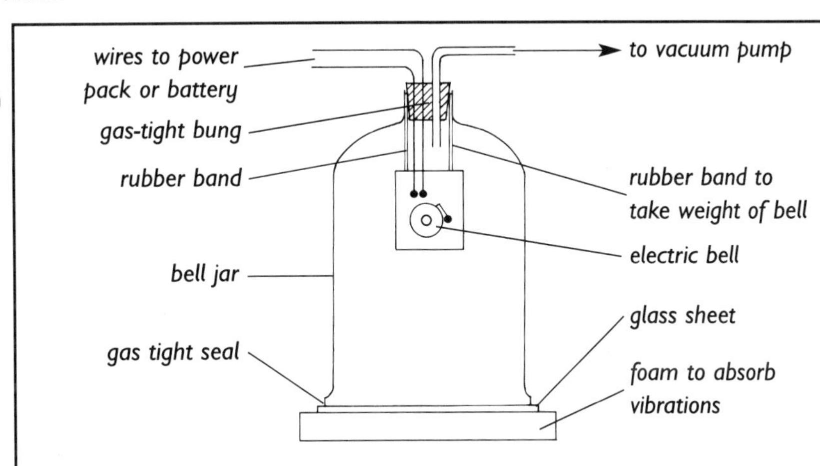

For your information

Running the activity

This is intended as a teacher demonstration. There are no activity sheets.

Practise using the vacuum pump in advance. Pump out as much air as possible. If the vacuum is good the sound will fade to almost nothing. Then allow air to re-enter, and the volume of sound will increase.

Expected outcomes

Pupils realise that air is needed in the bell jar for sound to travel.

Pitfalls

Make sure the bell is suspended in the jar, not sitting on a surface (otherwise sound will be transferred from the jar by the vibrations).

Safety notes

Used only a glass bell jar designed to be evacuated. Check the bell jar before use for any chips, cracks or nicks – discard if any are found. A safety screen is needed between the class and the demonstration. All present need to wear eye protection.

CRO demonstrations

Activity	*Description*	*Differentiation*
	Teacher demonstrations using a CRO to show the effects of changing first the amplitude and then the frequency of a vibration.	Core (no pupil sheets)

Equipment needed

For the teacher:

- signal generator
- loudspeaker
- CRO

For your information

Running the activity

These are intended as teacher demonstrations. There are no activity sheets. First turn the volume of the signal up and down to show that the amplitude of the vibrations alters. Then increase and decrease the pitch to show that the frequency is altered.

To demonstrate the audible range in humans, turn the frequency of the signal generator up and down and point out the change in frequency. Get pupils to all raise their hands and ask them to lower their hands when they no longer hear the sound. Get as many adults as possible to join in. Turn up the frequency of sound until inaudible.

Expected outcomes

Audible range for humans is about 20 Hz to 20 kHz.

Pitfalls

Practise with the CRO and signal generator in advance.

Safety notes

Keep the volume of sound low.

The best fuel?

Activity	Description	Differentiation
	A teacher demonstration of the experiment described in the pupils' book (heating water with lighter fuel).	Core (no pupil sheets)

Equipment needed

For the teacher:

- balance
- teat pipette
- 100 cm^3 measuring cylinder
- metal crucible with mineral wool
- clamp stand with two clamps
- thermometer
- heatproof mat
- lighter fuel
- container for water (e.g. empty fizzy drinks can)

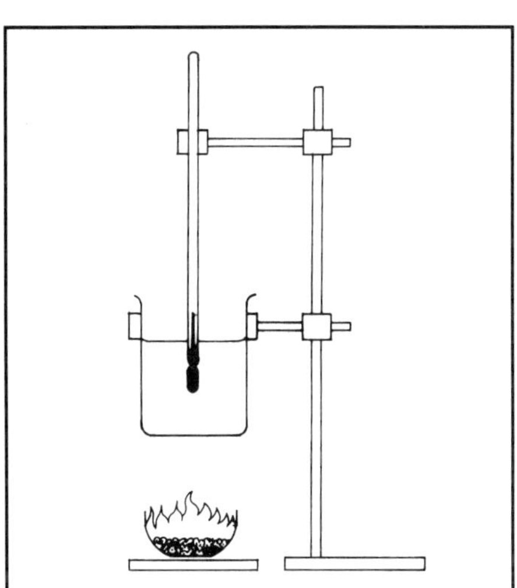

Tips

Mineral is needed for the lighter fuel, to act as a wick.

For your information

Safety notes

Eye protection will be needed for the teacher and those pupils close to the demonstration.

A tight squeeze

Type	Description	Differentiation
[goggles icon]	Using sand, water and air to investigate whether solids, liquids and gases can be squashed.	Core, Help

Equipment needed

For each group:

- plastic syringe (any size)
- sand
- water

For your information

Running the activity

Pupils investigate how easy it is to squash a solid, liquid and gas.

Core: Pupils make a prediction then are given the experimental method. They have to devise a way of recording their results (a table), analyse their results and explain them in terms of particles.

Help: The teacher can either show pupils what to do or give them the full instructions on the Core sheet. This Help sheet is for pupils to record their predictions, results and conclusions.

Pitfalls

Test the sand before the water, otherwise any water left in the syringe will make the sand damp.

Expected outcomes

Pupils discover that air can be squashed but sand and water cannot.

Safety notes

Pupils need to keep their fingers firmly over the ends of the syringes to prevent water from squirting. Wet floors can be slippery.

Moving particles

Type	*Description*	*Differentiation*
	Using peas in a box to model particles and changes of state.	Core

Equipment needed

For each group:

- clear plastic box with lid (e.g. a lunch box)
- enough dried peas to fill the base of the box

For your information

Running the activity

Pupils make a model of a solid using peas to represent particles. This is then shaken to represent heating the solid until it turns into a liquid, then into steam.

If using a totally clear box, this activity could be demonstrated to the whole class by placing the box on the overhead projector.

Safety notes

Be careful not to let peas fall on the floor, otherwise people may slip.

Investigating dissolving

Type	*Description*	*Differentiation*
	Guiding pupils through an investigation into the dissolving of sugar.	Core, Help, Extension

Equipment needed

For each group:

- a 250 cm^3 beaker
- a spatula
- sugar lumps
- caster sugar
- supply of hot water
- a stirring rod
- a thermometer
- a stopclock
- granulated sugar
- supply of cold water
- access to a digital balance

For your information

Running the activity

This is an investigation into the variables which affect the rate that sugar dissolves.

Core: Pupils have to find out which dissolves fastest – lump, granulated or caster sugar. They have to think about the variables that will affect the rate of dissolving, then plan and carry out an experiment to test their prediction. The sheet gives some guidance through each stage of the investigation.

Help: For less able pupils, photocopy the top half of the Core sheet showing the introduction and equipment available but use the Help sheet for more guided predictions, plans, etc. Pupils can write their answers and record their results on this sheet.

Extension: Pupils have to think about all the variables that affect the rate of sugar dissolving, then chose one variable to investigate. They plan their own investigations with some guidance.

Tip: Weigh a sugar lump first, then get the pupils to use the same weight of granulated or caster sugar.

Expected outcomes

Pupils should discover that caster sugar dissolves the fastest, and that the rate of dissolving increases with temperature. Extension pupils may also find that stirring increases the rate of dissolving.

Pitfalls

Pupils may have trouble determining the exact end point when all the sugar has dissolved. This may lead to errors in their results.

They may have some difficulty in understanding the theory behind why a sugar lump dissolves slower than a powder.

Safety notes

Hot water can scald – remind pupils to take care.
Pupils should also be reminded not to eat or taste the sugar.

Distillation

Type	Description	Differentiation
(goggles)	A teacher demonstration of the distillation of salt water, then completing a flow diagram.	Help

Equipment needed

For the teacher:

- Bunsen burner
- 2 clamp stands with clamps
- flask with bung and thermometer
- beaker
- tripod, gauze and heatproof mat
- salty water
- condenser

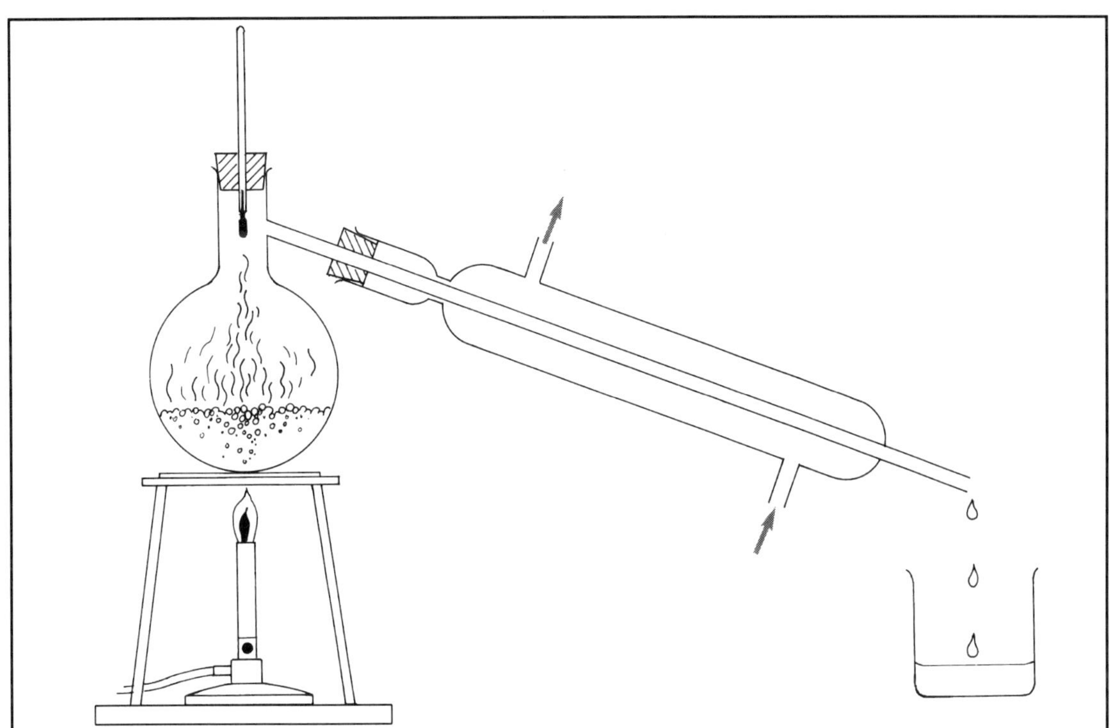

For your information

Running the activity

This is a demonstration of distillation. Pupils should write down their observations and the results.

Help: Pupils can fill in this sheet either during or after the process has been demonstrated.

Expected outcomes

Pupils should observe the distillation process and understand the different stages and changes of state that occur.

Safety notes

All present should wear eye protection.

Use anti-bumping granules or a couple of bits of pot in the flask. Ensure the whole apparatus is stable. Do not let the flask boil dry.

Technician's notes

Pond survey

Type	*Description*	*Differentiation*
	Pupils visit a pond, make observations and collect samples of pond water for microscopic analysis and classification back in the laboratory.	Core, Help

Other relevant material

Activity 3.2 Resource sheets 1 and 2

Skill sheet 8: Using a microscope

Equipment needed

For each group:

- microscope
- cavity slides
- coverslips
- specimen tubes
- dropping pipettes
- plastic gloves
- containers with string for pond dipping
- reference books and keys to identify organisms

Tips

Plastic drinks bottles may be cut down and string tied round for pond dipping.

For your information

Running the activity

Core: Pupils visit a pond and observe the living things they can see. They bring back samples of the pond water to make observations in the laboratory. They then classify the organisms they have observed into the major taxonomic groups.

Help: Pupils carry out the Core activity but use their Help sheets to record their observations.

Expected outcomes

Hopefully the results will reveal more invertebrates than vertebrates, so pupils can begin to appreciate that there is a pyramid of numbers.

Pitfalls

If you do not have a school pond, advance planning is necessary.

Safety notes

Refer to school and LEA policy and ensure parental consent, adequate supervision, etc. if the pond is away from the school site.

Remind pupils not to pick plants and to take care of living specimens which will be returned to the pond after the activity.

Disposable plastic gloves should be worn if plants are sampled by hand. Broken skin should be covered by waterproof plasters. Hands need to be washed afterwards.

Remind pupils to take care of microscopes. Never use a microscope where the sun's rays reflect off the mirror into it.

Spot the species!

Type	Description	Differentiation
	Pupils observe and list similarities and differences between a frog and a toad.	Core, Help

Equipment needed

For each group (optional):

- colour photographs of frog and toad, or
- access to live frog and toad

For your information

Running the activity

Core: Pupils are prompted to design their own table for recording their observations.

Help: Pupils write down their observations in the table provided.

Expected outcomes

Pupils should realise that there are sufficient differences for toads and frogs to belong to different species.

Safety notes

Live specimens (if used) should be handled with care.

Hands should be washed with soap and hot water both before and after handling.

A winter coat

Type	Description	Differentiation
	This is a datalogging practical. Pupils use temperature sensors to test whether a layer of cotton wool helps to keep water in a flask hot.	Core, Help, Extension

Equipment needed

For each group:

- computer
- 2 temperature sensors
- printer (optional)
- cotton wool
- elastic bands to hold the cotton wool around the flask
- interface
- datalogging software
- 2 flasks
- 2 clamp stands with clamps
- 2 bored corks or cotton wool to stopper the flasks

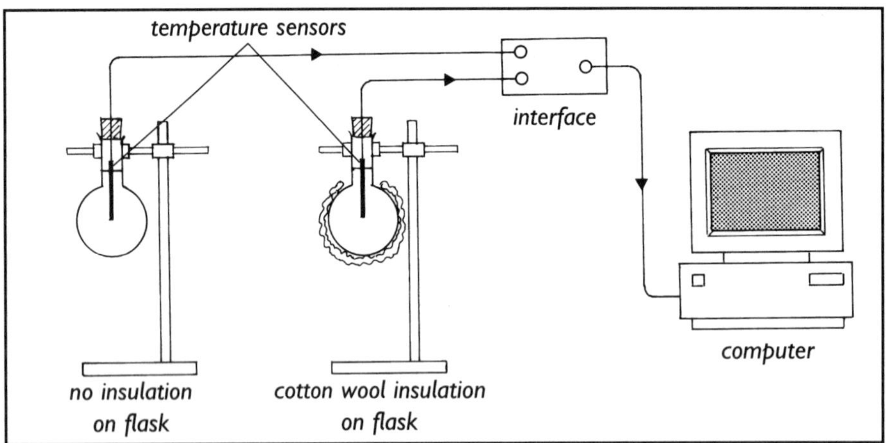

For your information

Running the activity

This activity tests whether a layer of cotton wool helps to keep the water in a flask hot. This relates to animals in winter growing a thicker layer of fur. The activity should be carried out in small groups.

Core: Pupils are given equipment but have to decide how to set it up. The sheet leads them through a full investigation.

Help: The teacher carries out the experiment as a demonstration. Pupils draw a graph and analyse the results.

Extension: Pupils are told what they need to investigate, and given some suggestions for things to think about. They then have to devise an experiment and write up their results as a report.

ICT opportunities

ICT PoS 2b: Datalogging

Expected outcomes

Pupils should realise from the model that a thicker layer of fur keeps the heat in.

Pitfalls

Make sure the water is at the same temperature in both flasks to within 2–3 °C at the start, otherwise analysis of results is difficult.

Safety notes

Remind pupils of the dangers of hot water. In cases of scalding, cool the skin at once with plenty of running water, and keep it in the cold water for 10 minutes. Pupils should wear eye protection. The teacher or technician should dispense the hot water from the kettles.

Putting fires out

Type	Description	Differentiation
	Pupils compare how quickly sand, water and foam put out a fire.	Core, Help

Equipment needed

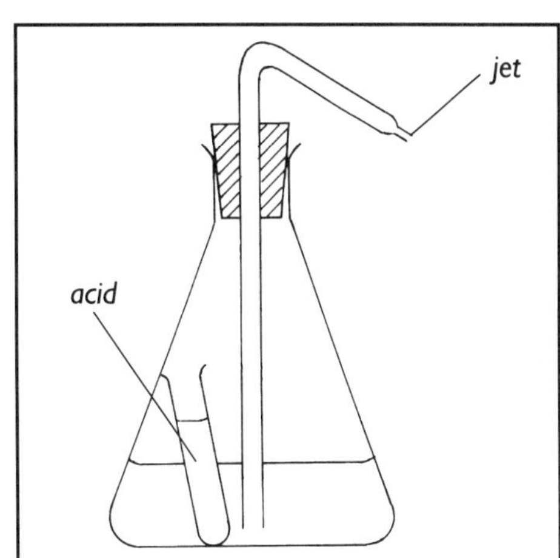

For each group:

- approximately 20 wooden splints (these could be provided ready broken in half for the pupils)
- 3 pieces of newspaper, approximately A4 size
- 3 heatproof mats and/or tin lids
- stopclock
- beaker (250 cm^3) containing approximately 100 cm^3 of sand
- wash bottle of water
- measuring cylinder (to measure 50 cm^3)
- delivery tube with jet inserted in rubber bung to fit the flask, as shown in the diagram
- spatula
- sodium hydrogencarbonate
- dilute hydrochloric acid
- ignition tube
- washing-up liquid

Tips

It is useful to collect tin lids or clean, small food cans (e.g. catfood tins) to light the fires in.

For your information

Running the activity

Pupils set up mini fires and use sand, water and foam to put them out. They time how long each fire takes to go out.

Core: The method is given for the experiment, and there are structured questions for analysis and evaluation.

Help: This gives a framework for recording, analysing and evaluating. Diagrams only are provided for the method, so the pupils will need help to carry out the experiment, or it could be carried out as a demonstration.

Expected outcomes

Pupils should compare how quickly each method puts the fire out, and also compare their ease of use. They should realise how each method breaks the fire triangle.

Pitfalls

The activity can be messy. Pupils should dry the bench and use a fresh heatproof mat or tin lid, if sufficient are available, for each of the three fires.

Safety notes

Wear eye protection. Ensure pupils keep their fires small and remind them about the risks of using acids. The foam may be acid and its use should be carefully controlled.

Burning metals

Type	Description	Differentiation
	Pupils burn magnesium, iron and copper and see that they produce new substances (oxides) and release energy.	Core (with Extension questions), Help

Other relevant material

Skill sheet 2: Lighting a Bunsen burner
Skill sheet 7: Word equations (for Extension)

Equipment needed

For each group:
- Bunsen burner
- heatproof mat
- pair of tongs
- blue glass (for each pupil)
- magnesium ribbon (1–2 cm)
- steel wool (a walnut-sized piece)
- copper foil (1–2 cm^2)

For your information

Running the activity

Pupils work in small groups, or alternatively, the teacher might choose to demonstrate this experiment. The three metals are heated in a Bunsen burner flame and the pupils record their observations.

Core: Instructions are given for the experiment. Pupils draw up their own table to record the observations, and questions prompt them to draw conclusions.

Extension: There are optional Extension questions at the foot of the Core sheet, which can be cut off if not required. The questions ask pupils to write word equations.

Help: A table is provided for recording, and structured questions lead to conclusions. The method is not described on this sheet, so pupils will need help to carry out the experiment, or the sheet could be used to accompany a teacher demonstration.

Expected outcomes

Pupils see that when magnesium, iron and copper burn, they produce new substances (oxides) and release energy.

Safety notes

Wear eye protection. Only small pieces of the metals should be provided. Warn pupils to take care heating the metals. Copper compounds are harmful. Burning magnesium should be viewed through blue glass or pupils told to look away when they have seen how bright it is.

How much energy?

Type	Description	Differentiation
	This is a teacher demonstration using a temperature sensor to illustrate how energy can be transferred by burning a fuel.	Core

Other relevant material

Skill sheet 6: Interpreting graphs

Equipment needed

For the class:

- computer
- temperature sensor
- crucible
- heatproof mat
- water (20 cm^3)
- clampstand to hold the boiling tube, and also the temperature sensor if necessary
- interface
- printer (optional)
- methylated spirits (1 cm^3)
- boiling tube
- splint to light the methylated spirits

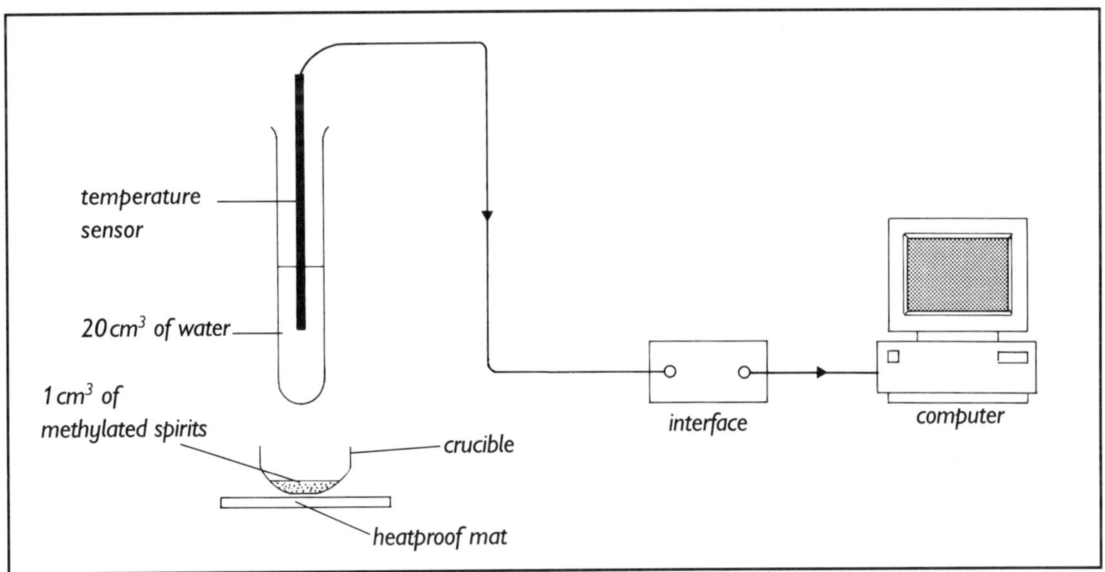

For your information

Running the activity

Pupils see how heat energy can be transferred to water by burning a fuel. A temperature sensor and datalogging software are used to monitor the energy transfer. This activity should be carried out as a teacher demonstration because of the potential hazards involved in burning a fuel close to electrical equipment.

The Core sheet gives a format for recording and analysing for pupils to copy and complete. If preferred, it could be used as a write-on Help sheet.

ICT opportunities

ICT PoS 2b: Datalogging

Expected outcomes

A measurable temperature rise should be observed. This should help pupils appreciate that energy is transferred from the burning fuel to the water.

Safety notes

Wear eye protection. Methylated spirits is highly flammable – use only the stated amount. Ensure that the electrical wiring is kept well away from the flame.

A good fuel?

Type	*Description*	*Differentiation*
	Pupils burn different fuels and evaluate them against a set of criteria.	Core, Help

Other relevant material

Skill sheet 2: Lighting a Bunsen burner

Equipment needed

For each group:

- Bunsen burner
- heatproof mat
- tripod and gauze
- splints
- tin lids or milk-bottle tops
- stopclock
- selection of fuels, e.g. coal, coke, paper, wood, barbecue firelighters, methylated spirits, lubricating oil – four fuels for Core, three for Help, each selection to include both solid and liquid fuels

Tips

It is useful to collect tin lids or milk-bottle tops to test the fuels on.

For your information

Running the activity

Pupils work in small groups. They burn samples of different fuels and make observations. They are prompted to score the fuels according to four given criteria, and to rank the fuels.

Core: Pupils plan their own results table. Instructions are given to carry out the experiment with four fuels, and questions lead them to evaluate the experiment and plan further experiments.

Help: A table is provided for recording, for three fuels. The questions provide a more structured format for the evaluation of the fuels. The method is not described on this sheet, so pupils will need help to carry out the experiment, or the sheet could be used to accompany a teacher demonstration.

Expected outcomes

Pupils gain an awareness of factors other than energy content that affect the quality of a fuel.

Pitfalls

Some fuels such as coal are difficult to light, and may need to be demonstrated by the teacher. The liquid fuels should be tested by the teacher if pupils cannot be trusted to use only two drops.

Safety notes

Wear eye protection. Only two drops of liquid fuels should be used, and small amounts of solid fuels. Warn pupils to take care heating the fuels and to wash their hands after the experiment.

What happens when a fuel burns?

Type	Description	Differentiation
	Pupils collect the gas from a burning candle and bubble it through limewater to show that carbon dioxide gas is released when the wax burns.	Core, Help

Equipment needed

For each group:

- filter pump
- 2 clamp stands and clamps
- candle in holder (or nightlight), supported under the funnel
- funnel, delivery tubes and bung set up as shown in the diagram
- boiling tube
- limewater
- splints

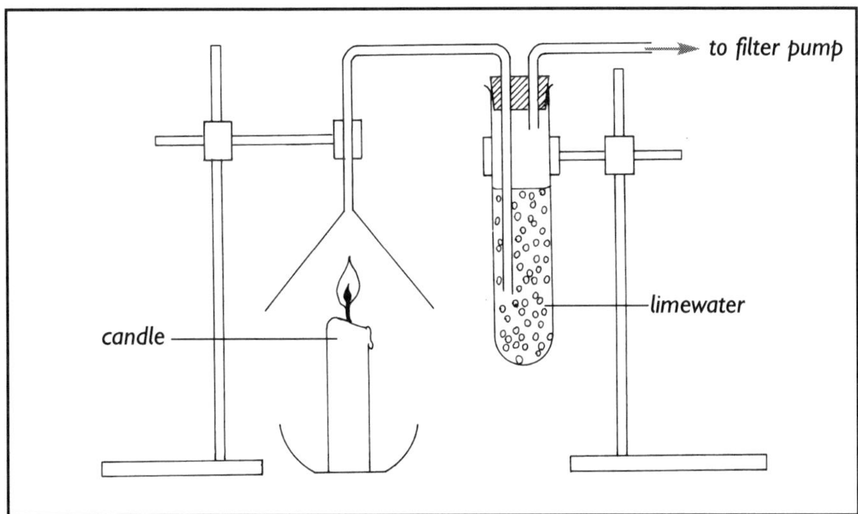

For your information

Running the activity

Pupils may carry out the experiment in small groups, or the teacher might choose to demonstrate.

Core: Pupils are given a method for the experiment, and questions prompt them to draw conclusions.

Help: The method is not given, and the teacher may prefer to use this sheet to accompany a demonstration. The questions are more structured to help pupils draw conclusions.

Expected outcomes

The gas from the burning candle turns the limewater milky, showing that carbon dioxide gas is released when the wax burns.

Safety notes

Wear eye protection. Warn pupils to take care with the burning candle, and not to touch the hot wax.

Grow your own greenhouse effect

Type	*Description*	*Differentiation*
	A temperature sensor is used to compare the temperatures inside and outside a glass jar, which represents a greenhouse. This is a datalogging activity which starts with a prediction and leads pupils through the stages of a full investigation.	Core, Help

Other relevant material

Skill sheet 6: Interpreting graphs

Equipment needed

For the class:

- computer
- interface
- 2 temperature sensors
- printer (optional)
- clampstand and clamps to hold the temperature sensors
- glass jar

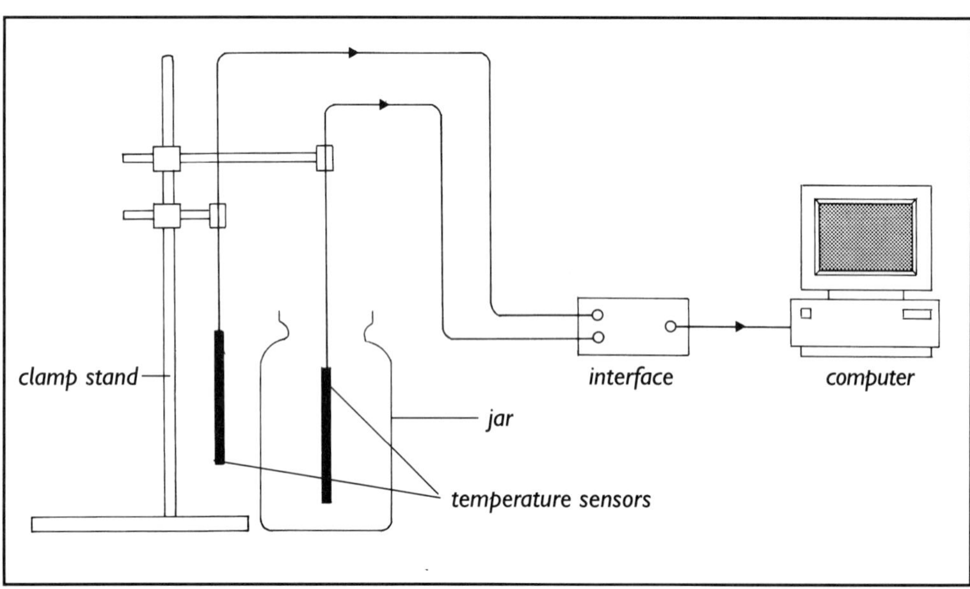

For your information

Running the activity

The activity is intended as a teacher demonstration. The equipment should be set up to record while pupils are working on the book spread.

Core: Pupils are asked to make a prediction, and plan a results table. They go on to obtain, analyse and evaluate the results.

Help: The sheet gives a more structured format for analysis and conclusion only.

ICT opportunities

ICT PoS 2b: Datalogging

Expected outcomes

The temperature difference obtained will depend on the ambient conditions. On a hot sunny day, a significant temperature difference can be obtained after half an hour, but you may wish to set the experiment up to record over a day and discuss how and why both graphs follow the same pattern.

Pitfalls

A sunny day is essential.

Find the fault

Type	*Description*	*Differentiation*
	Pupils visit circuits set up around the room that do not work, and decide what is wrong with them, to check their understanding that a complete circuit is needed for a transfer of energy.	Core (no pupil sheets)

Other relevant material

Skill sheet 4: Energy transfer diagrams

ICT opportunities

A useful piece of software for making circuits is available on the CD-ROM *Crocodile Clips* (Crocodile Clips Ltd). *Crocodile Clips 3 Elementary* can be downloaded from the internet: www.crocodile-clip.com/education/.

Equipment needed

For the class: four sets of the following four experiments, preferably set up in advance and labelled 1, 2, 3 and 4:

- Circuit 1: a series circuit with 1 lamp and 1 battery, but the filament of the lamp is broken
- Circuit 2: a series circuit with 1 lamp and 1 battery, but the leads are both attached to the same side of the lamp
- Circuit 3: a series circuit with 1 lamp and 2 batteries, but one of the batteries is the wrong way round
- Circuit 4: a complicated circuit with, say, 5 lamps and 2 batteries, but one of the leads is not connected. The circuit should be set up so that the leads look muddled.
- 4 spare bulbs ready to replace the faulty one in each circuit 1

For your information

Running the activity

This is a short activity. It is suggested that the class be divided into pairs, and the pairs grouped (four pairs in a group). The pairs visit each of four circuits and write down what is wrong with each one. At their last circuit, they put the circuit right and prepare to report back to the class.

Expected outcomes

Circuit 1: the filament lamp has no filament.
Circuit 2: both connections to the lamp are on the same side of the holder.
Circuit 3: the two batteries are different ways around.
Circuit 4: in the spaghetti of wires, one is not connected.

Pitfalls

Make sure that circuits 2, 3 and 4 are not 'mended' by pairs 1, 2 or 3.

Demonstration: the current either side of a lamp

Type	*Description*	*Differentiation*
	Teacher demonstration that the current is the same on either side of the lamp in a series circuit.	Core (no pupil sheets)

Equipment needed

For the demonstration:

- lamp
- battery
- 4 leads
- 2 ammeters, preferably analogue and large enough to be seen from a distance

For your information

Running the activity

This is a teacher demonstration. The circuit should be set up with an ammeter on each side of the lamp.

Expected outcomes

The current shown on both ammeters should be the same.

Pitfalls

It is important that pupils are not distracted by the inaccuracy of the ammeters. Digital ammeters can show readings that vary by ±0.02 A, and therefore the second decimal place is likely to differ between the ammeters. This distracts pupils, who do not realise that such a difference is within the limits of accuracy of the measuring device. One possible solution is to use digital ammeters that measure only to 0.1 A or to use analogue meters, which pupils will not read to a hundredth of an amp. The large, old-fashioned display ammeters are ideal.

Investigating current

Type	Description	Differentiation
	Pupils see how varying the number of batteries affects the current (Core), and how varying the number of lamps affects the current (Extension).	Core, Extension

Other relevant material

Skill sheet 5: Drawing graphs
Skill sheet 6: Interpreting graphs

Equipment needed

For each pair or group (Core):
- 5 batteries
- lamp (12 V)
- ammeter
- 7 leads

For each pair or group (Extension):
- 2 batteries
- 5 lamps (3 V)
- ammeter
- 8 leads

For your information

Running the activity

Pupils work in pairs or small groups.

Core: Pupils make a prediction about what effect changing the number of batteries will have on the current. They build a circuit from a realistic diagram, and are given a table format for recording their results. They draw a line graph and analyse their results.

Extension: This activity has a similar format to the Core one, except that pupils are looking at the effect of the number of lamps on the current. Circuit diagrams are provided from which to build their circuits, rather than realistic diagrams. Pupils are asked to use their graph to predict the outcome of a further experiment.

More able pupils could do both experiments, or could go straight to the Extension activity and pick up on the Core experiment when groups report back at the end of the lesson.

Expected outcomes

Core: The current should be proportional to the number of batteries in the circuit.

Extension: The current is inversely proportional to the number of lamps. The graph will be a curve with a negative gradient.

Pitfalls

Core: Ensure that pupils do not use too many batteries, or they will 'blow' the lamp. For five 1.5 V batteries, the lamp used needs to be >7.5 V, probably 12 V. The lamp will not glow when one battery is used, but the current will show on the ammeter. If the Core and Extension activities are being run together, pupils will have to be warned which lamp to use.

Extension: The sheet assumes a voltage of 3 V (two 1.5 V batteries). A lamp should be chosen that glows brightly with 3 V. Adding more lamps will make each dimmer, but the ammeter will measure the current. Make sure that the lamps for Core and Extension, which are likely to be different, are kept separately.

Demonstration: the voltage across different parts of a circuit

Type	*Description*	*Differentiation*
	Teacher demonstration to show that there is a voltage across those parts of a circuit where energy is put in (the batteries) or leaves (in this case, a lamp).	Core (no pupil sheets)

Equipment needed

For the demonstration:

- lamp (3 V)
- battery
- 2 black leads
- 8 red leads
- 4 voltmeters

Make a simple series circuit with a lamp and a battery. Use black leads to connect the series circuit. Connect two red leads to each voltmeter for the teacher to connect across the battery, the lamp, the first lead and the second lead.

For your information

Running the activity

The activity is a teacher demonstration. Voltmeters are connected into a simple series circuit across the battery, the lamp, and the leads.

Expected outcomes

The voltage across the battery and the lamp should be the same. There should be no voltage across the leads, as an insignificant amount of energy is lost from the circuit in the leads.

Tips

Use the largest voltmeters available. Use four voltmeters so that pupils can see them simultaneously.

Investigating voltage: batteries

Type	*Description*	*Differentiation*
	Pupils find out how the voltage changes when the number of batteries in a circuit is increased: more batteries means more energy being sent out, which means more voltage.	Core, Extension

Equipment needed

For each pair or group:

- 5 batteries
- lamp (12 V)
- voltmeter
- 8 leads

For your information

Running the activity

Pupils work in small pairs or groups.

Core: Pupils make a prediction about how the voltage will change as they add more batteries to a circuit. They build a circuit from a realistic diagram, and are given a table format for recording their results. They draw a line graph and analyse their results.

Extension: This activity has a similar format to the Core one. Circuit diagrams are provided from which to build their circuits, rather than realistic diagrams. Pupils are asked to use their graph to predict the outcome of a further experiment.

Pitfalls

Ensure that pupils do not use too many batteries, or they will 'blow' the lamp. For five 1.5 V batteries, the lamp used needs to be >7.5 V, probably 12 V. The lamp will not glow when one battery is used, but the voltage will register on the voltmeter.

Demonstration: 'class and matches' model

Type	Description	Differentiation
	Class demonstration to give pupils experience of using models.	Core (no pupil sheets)

Equipment needed

For the class:

- chalk or tape to mark a circle on the ground
- large box of very long household matches

For your information

Running the activity

A 'circuit' is marked on the floor with chalk or tape. The circle must be big enough for all members of the class to walk around at once (the pupils should be quite close together).

One teacher, or a trusted pupil, stands at one side of the circle. He or she is the battery and he or she will put energy into the circuit by giving out matches. Another teacher stands opposite, again on the 'circuit'. He or she is the lamp, and he or she will take energy out of the circuit by taking in the matches and striking them.

The pupils stand on the circle. They walk slowly around the circle and collect a match from the 'battery' as they go by, and deliver the match to the 'lamp'. The pupils themselves actually represent the charge carriers, but as charge carriers have not been introduced, the moving pupils are considered to represent the current. Pupils can be asked to speed up a little to represent an increase in current, or slow down to represent a decrease in current.

Pitfalls

Use the largest type of household matches, so they are easily seen.

Safety notes

If only one teacher is available, he or she should be the 'lamp' (who strikes the matches).

Series and parallel circuits: current

Type	*Description*	*Differentiation*
	Pupils set up their own series and parallel circuits and measure the current at three points.	Core, Extension

ICT opportunities

An explanation of series and parallel circuits is read out in the CD-ROM *Eyewitness Encyclopedia of Science 2.0* (Dorling Kindersley) under 'Physics', 'Electric circuits'.

A useful piece of software for making circuits is available on the CD-ROM *Crocodile Clips 3* (Crocodile Clips Ltd). *Crocodile Clips 3 Elementary* can be downloaded from the internet: www.crocodile-clip.com/education/.

Equipment needed

For each pair or group:

- battery
- 2 lamps
- ammeter
- 5 leads

For your information

Running the activity

Pupils work in pairs or small groups. Some groups could do this activity while others do Activity 5.6B, with all groups reporting back at the end.

Core: The circuit diagrams are given in the table. The table can be photocopied for less able students, who will find it difficult to draw so many circuit diagrams.

Extension: Pupils build their circuits from circuit diagrams. They need to construct their own table for recording their results. A final question hints at the mathematical relationship between the currents in different loops of a parallel circuit.

Expected outcomes

The current should be the same at all points in a series circuit.
The current varies at different points in a parallel circuit, dividing at branches.

Series and parallel circuits: voltage

Type	*Description*	*Differentiation*
	Pupils set up their own series and parallel circuits and measure the voltage across each lamp and across the 'battery'.	Core

ICT opportunities

An explanation of series and parallel circuits is read out in the CD-ROM *Eyewitness Encyclopedia of Science 2.0* (Dorling Kindersley) under 'Physics', 'Electric circuits'.

A useful piece of software for making circuits is available on the CD-ROM *Crocodile Clips* (Crocodile Clips Ltd). *Crocodile Clips 3 Elementary* can be downloaded from the internet: www.crocodile-clip.com/education/.

Equipment needed

For each pair or group:

- battery
- 2 lamps
- voltmeter
- 6 leads

For your information

Running the activity

Pupils work in pairs or small groups. Some groups could do this activity while others do Activity 5.6A, with all groups reporting back at the end. The Core sheet expects pupils to be able to build circuits from circuit diagrams by this point.

Expected outcomes

The voltage is different across the components in a series circuit, and adds to the voltage across the battery.

The voltage should be the same across the different components in a parallel circuit.

What do magnets do?

Type	*Description*	*Differentiation*
	Pupils can carry out simple experiments with magnets, if they seem unfamiliar with magnets.	Core (Help)

Equipment needed

For each pair:

- 2 bar magnets
- small samples of iron, copper, nickel and aluminium
- compass

For your information

Running the activity

Pupils work in pairs. They test different metals with a bar magnet, see the effect of a magnetic field on a compass, and experiment with pushing magnets together. They look at some statements about magnets and write out the correct ones.

If preferred, the Core sheet could be used as a write-on disposable Help sheet, with answer lines drawn on beside questions 1–4. For question 5, they could tick or colour the correct statements, or cut them out and stick them in their books.

Instead of making detailed notes, pupils could feed back their observations at the beginning of the demonstrations (Activities 5.7B and 5.7C).

Expected outcomes

Pupils find out that iron and nickel are magnetic, but copper and aluminium are not. The compass needle shows the magnetic field. Same poles repel, opposite poles attract.

Pitfalls

Give pupils a time limit for this activity.

Demonstration: the magnetic field around a bar magnet and a coil

Type	*Description*	*Differentiation*
	Teacher demonstration to familiarise pupils with magnetic fields and magnetic field lines. These are visualised using iron filings, and the direction of the field lines is found using a compass. The shape of the magnetic field around a bar magnet and a coil is shown to pupils.	Core (no pupil sheets)

Equipment needed

For the demonstration:

- overhead projector
- bar magnet
- 2 acetate sheets (overhead transparencies)
- 4 small cubes with sides the depth of the bar magnet (to prop up the corners of the acetate sheet)
- iron filings in a pepper shaker
- 10 see-through plotting compasses
- copper solenoid in a Perspex platform (commercially available)
- 2 leads
- power pack

For your information

Running the activity

This teacher demonstration is best done on an overhead projector.

The pattern of the field using iron filings: Put the bar magnet under an overhead transparency and prop up the corners of the transparency so that it is flat. Sprinkle the iron filings thinly onto the overhead transparency and tap gently until they form lines. Focus the overhead projector on the magnetic field lines.

For the coil, best results are obtained using a commercial apparatus produced for the purpose, which has a solenoid in a Perspex platform. Again, it can be used on the overhead projector. Put an overhead transparency under the apparatus to catch the iron filings. Connect the coil to a power supply following the manufacturer's recommendation. Sprinkle the filings on the Perspex platform and tap gently.

The direction of the field using plotting compasses: If see-through compasses are used, this can also be done on the overhead projector. The compasses along the bar magnet will not be projected due to the shadow of the magnet and their direction should be confirmed by a pupil. Compasses should be placed inside as well as around the coil. The electricity should be turned off when the direction of the magnetic field has been seen.

Expected outcomes

The fields around the bar magnet and the coil are similar. (See Activity notes 5.7B.)

Safety notes

Wear eye protection. Iron filings are dangerous if they get into the eyes. They may also irritate the skin, especially if skin problems are present. Wash hands after use.

Demonstration: how a coil behaves like a magnet

Type	*Description*	*Differentiation*
	Teacher demonstration to show pupils that a coil with a current through it behaves like a bar magnet.	Core (no pupil sheets)

Equipment needed

For the demonstration:

- 2 powerful permanent magnets
- overhead projector
- power pack
- coil made from 32–30 SWG enamel-coated wire and a minimum of 50 turns with long straight ends for connecting to power pack
- wooden stool

For your information

Tips

The coil must be as light as possible, yet have 50 or more turns. It must be hung from a power pack with no connections because connections and leads introduce extra mass. Powerful permanent magnets give a more pronounced effect.

Running the activity

This activity is a teacher demonstration.

First run through what happens when two bar magnets are brought together. They either repel (like poles) or attract (unlike poles). Demonstrate this with large magnets or small but powerful magnets on the overhead projector.

Set up a lightweight coil with a current through it, hanging by the wires from a battery or power pack (see diagram). Bring up one pole of a powerful magnet and the coil will be repelled. Bring up the other pole of the powerful magnet and the coil will be attracted. Do the same for the other side of the coil and show that the two ends of the coil are two different poles. Turn off the electricity and show that the effect is lost.

Expected outcomes

Like poles of the magnet repel; unlike poles attract. One end of the coil behaves like a north pole and the other like a south pole. The effect is lost when the electricity is turned off.

Pitfalls

The coil has to be very light, so 30–32 SWG wire is suitable. Plastic-coated wire is too rigid. Enamel-coated wire is ideal. If only bare wire is available, then the coil must be elongated to prevent short circuits. A 1 cm diameter, 50 turn coil of 30 SWG copper wire with 1 V across it needs a strong permanent magnet to push it. 50 turns is the maximum number with bare wire, as otherwise the coil is too long and will become very floppy. More than 50 turns is possible with enamel-coated wire as the coil can be more compact. However, care must be taken not to make the coil too heavy, or the movement will be too slight to see from a distance.

Safety notes

Increased voltage across the coil gives a more obvious movement, but care must be taken not to allow the coil to overheat.

Electromagnets

Type	Description	Differentiation
	Pupils carry out a class investigation to establish the three main facts about electromagnets: they need a core of magnetic material, and the magnetic field strength increases with increased number of turns in the coil and with increased current.	Core, Help, Extension

Other relevant material

Skill sheet 5: Drawing charts and graphs
Skill sheet 6: Interpreting graphs

ICT opportunities

There is a video clip of an electromagnet being used in the CD-ROM *Eyewitness Encyclopedia of Science 2.0* (DK Multimedia) under 'Physics', 'Electromagnets'.

Equipment needed

For each group (changing the core):

- rods of copper, aluminium, soft iron, steel and nickel (if available)
- 1 m length plastic coated wire, stripped at both ends
- 2 crocodile clips
- 3 leads
- ammeter
- variable power pack set at 5 V maximum
- 30 paperclips

For each group (changing the current or changing the number of turns):

- soft iron core
- 1 m length plastic-coated wire, stripped at both ends
- 2 crocodile clips
- 3 leads
- ammeter
- variable power pack set at 5 V maximum
- 30 paperclips

Tips

Metal rods make the best cores. These should be at least 1 cm in diameter and at least 10 cm long. Rods of copper, aluminium, soft iron and steel can be bought at metal merchants. Nickel 'rods' could be made by rolling nickel sheets into suitably sized cylinders.T

Confirm the maximum voltage to be used using the wire chosen for the experiment. For example, if 25 SWG copper wire is used, a 0.5 A current should give about 4.5 V.

For your information

Running the activity

This class investigation should be started by drawing the diagram for the experiment on the board (see right), and giving a demonstration of a simple electromagnet picking up paperclips. Follow with a class discussion as to what could change the strength of an electromagnet. List the variables the pupils suggest. The teacher can then pick out the three variables that are going to be investigated, and establish that the variable being measured is number of paperclips being lifted. Safety precautions should be established (maximum current/voltage).

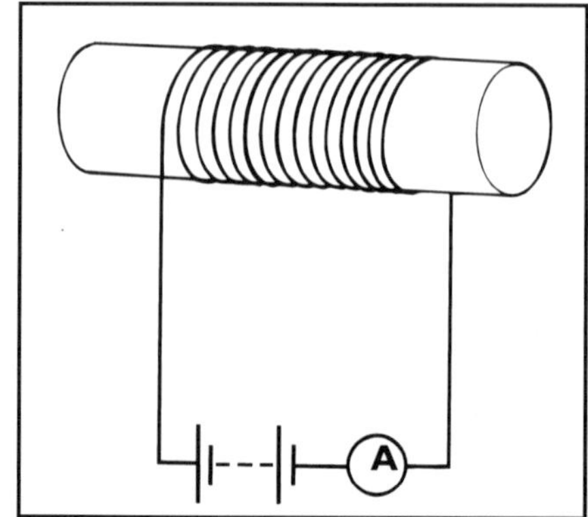

continued

Electromagnets ⊳⊳⊳ continued

The discussion should then be developed to introduce the idea of a class investigation. Pupils must understand that, if different groups are going to compare their results, then the 'variables you are keeping the same' must be kept the same across different groups. The teacher should write up the values for the 'variables to be kept the same'. Suggested values are:

- If you are keeping the core the same, it should be **iron**.
- If you are keeping the current the same, it should be **0.5 A**.
- If you are keeping the number of turns the same, it should be **20 turns**.

Pupils should be arranged in ability pairs/groups.

The activity sheets have been written assuming that 'changing the material of the core' is the Help activity for less able pupils. 'Changing the number of turns' and 'changing the current' are addressed by variable-independent sheets at Core and Extension level. If the pupils were in mixed ability groups, the Core sheets could be used and the less able pupils given an additional writing frame for 'Planning and predicting'.

The sheets guide pupils through the investigation and ask them to prepare feedback to the class as a whole. This feedback from different groups should establish the relationship between the three variables and the strength of the electromagnet.

Core: Pupils plan their investigation and make a prediction. They draw a graph and analyse their results. Skill sheets 9 and 10 (writing frames) may be helpful for some pupils.

Help: This covers the investigation into the material of the core. The sheet provides a framework for planning and predicting, and a table for recording.

Extension: This is similar to the Core sheet, but the questions are less directed.

Expected outcomes

A 0.5 A current through a 1 m 25 SWG copper wire should give a voltage of 4.5 V. Success is determined by picking up paperclips.

Changing the core: Iron, steel and (if available) nickel will make electromagnets. Aluminium and copper will not.

Changing the number of turns: Increasing the number of turns will increase the strength of the electromagnet.

Changing the current: 0.1 A, 0.2 A, 0.3 A, 0.4 A and 0.5 A currents are realistic. Increasing the current will increase the strength of the electromagnet.

Pitfalls

Too high a current will cause the plastic insulation on the wire to melt. It is best to use power packs with the maximum voltage set to 5 V, or batteries.

Safety notes

Coils can become hot. Electromagnets should be kept on a heatproof mat. Warn pupils not to go higher than the maximum voltage that has been set by the teacher.

Looking at plant cells

Type	*Description*	*Differentiation*
	Pupils prepare and observe slides of onion cells, using a microscope.	Core

Other relevant material

Skill sheet 8: Using a microscope

Equipment needed

For the class:

- large Spanish onion
- a video camera, e.g. Flexicam (optional)

For each pair:

- craft knife or scalpel
- white tile
- forceps
- microscope slide
- iodine drop bottle
- coverslip
- mounted needle
- microscope

For your information

Running the activity

Pupils work in pairs. The activity sheet gives a method for carrying out the practical, along with analysis questions at the end. A microscope could be linked to a video camera (e.g. Flexicam) to display slides to the whole class.

Expected outcomes

Pupils produce a labelled drawing of plant cells as seen under the microscope.

Pitfalls

Some pupils may need help with peeling a thin layer of onion skin.

Pupils should take care to avoid introducing air bubbles under the coverslip.

Safety notes

Iodine is harmful. Warn pupils to take care if they are cutting the onion. If in doubt, the pieces of onion could be cut ready for them. Pupils should take care with microscopes and slides.

Looking at animal cells

Type	*Description*	*Differentiation*
	Pupils look at pre-prepared animal cell slides, using a microscope.	Core

Other relevant material

Skill sheet 8: Using a microscope

Equipment needed

For the class:

- a video camera e.g. Flexicam (optional)

For each pair:

- pre-prepared slides – the practice of using cheek cell scrapes is discouraged due to the risk of infection, but check with local guidelines. It is possible to use the epithelial cells from the trachea of a pig or sheep, obtained from a local butcher. Alternatively, place a piece of Sellotape onto a wrist, pull off and stick onto a slide.
- microscope

For your information

Running the activity

Pupils work in pairs. The activity sheet gives a method for carrying out the experiment, along with analysis questions at the end. A microscope could be linked to a video camera (e.g. Flexicam) to display slides to the whole class.

Expected outcomes

Pupils produce a labelled drawing of animal cells as seen under the microscope.

Safety notes

Pupils should take care with microscopes and slides.

Making a model cell

Type	Description	Differentiation
	Pupils make models of plant and animal cells.	Core, Extension

Other relevant material

A range of textbooks, Microsoft® *Encarta* or the Internet could be used to find pictures of cells.

Equipment needed

For each group:

- 2 clear plastic bags (cell membrane)
- green Plasticine (chloroplasts)
- shoe box (cell wall)
- 2 tennis balls (nucleus)
- smaller plastic bag (vacuole)
- liquid or wallpaper paste (cytoplasm)
- water (sap)

For your information

Running the activity

Pupils work in groups. Each group can choose to produce an animal cell, a plant cell or both cell types. You may decide to direct groups to make certain models. Their finished models can be displayed in the classroom.

Core: Pupils are told what each part of the model represents in the cell. They follow the instructions to build the model, and then draw a labelled diagram and answer questions to reinforce their understanding and evaluate the models.

Extension: Pupils are given the apparatus and have to select the best material to represent each part of the cell.

Expected outcomes

Each group should produce large models of cells which can be used for display purposes. This should enable pupils to view the cell as a three-dimensional object rather than just a two-dimensional drawing.

Pitfalls

The activity can be messy. Have plenty of paper towels ready in case of wallpaper paste being spilled.

Some pupils may have difficulty in visualising the cell as a three-dimensional object and may need help in building their models.

Safety notes

Warn pupils to clear up any liquid spilled on the floor to avoid accidents. Wallpaper paste contains fungicide – wash hands thoroughly after use.

What do plants need for photosynthesis?

Type	Description	Differentiation
	Pupils test leaves for starch in order to find out whether a plant needs light and carbon dioxide for photosynthesis.	Core, Help

Other relevant material

Skill sheet 2: Lighting a Bunsen burner

ICT opportunities

Simulation software could be used to change the variables, to see their effect on photosynthesis.

Equipment needed

For the class:

- hotplates for heating waterbaths

For each group:

- destarched plant, e.g. geranium
- black tape
- conical flask containing soda lime
- split bung to fit around leaf stalk
- clampstand and clamp
- forceps
- scalpel and cutting tile (optional)
- Bunsen burner
- heatproof mat
- tripod and gauze
- beaker (250 cm^3)
- boiling tube
- tube holder
- ethanol
- white tile
- iodine dropper bottle
- paper towel

continued

What do plants need for photosynthesis?

continued

Tips

The leaves must be completely decolourised in ethanol for pupils to see the colour change with iodine.

For your information

Running the activity

Pupils work in small groups, or the activity could be carried out as a teacher demonstration. Plants must first be left in the dark for 24 hours to destarch them. After the destarched plants have been set up as shown, they must be left in a light place for a further 24 hours. The pupils then test the leaves for starch, which should take about 30 minutes. Pupils test three leaves at the same time, cutting a shape in the side of each to identify which are leaves 1, 2 and 3. Alternatively, pupils should test one leaf at a time to ensure that they don't get them mixed up. A preheated water bath will be needed for heating the ethanol (see Safety notes below).

Core: The method is given for the activity, and pupils come up with their own format for recording results. Questions ask them to draw conclusions about what the plant needs for photosynthesis. Question 4 could be used as an extension question.

Help: This sheet provides a table for pupils to record their results, and more structured questions lead them to their conclusions. Instructions for the experiment are not given on this sheet, so pupils will need help with the activity, or the sheet could be used to accompany a teacher demonstration.

Expected outcomes

Iodine will change from orange to black when starch is present in the leaf. The presence of starch indicates that the plant has been photosynthesising. Areas of leaves covered with black tape will not turn iodine black, indicating that the leaf needs light for photosynthesis. Leaves kept in the presence of sodium hydroxide will not turn iodine black, indicating that carbon dioxide is needed for photosynthesis. Leaves that have been kept in the light with carbon dioxide will turn iodine black, indicating that starch has been produced by photosynthesis.

Pitfalls

The plants must be thoroughly destarched before use otherwise false results will be obtained. Old leaves should be avoided. Put soda lime in the conical flasks before the start of this activity.

Safety notes

Ethanol is flammable. Use a hotplate for the waterbath to heat the ethanol. Do not use a naked flame to heat it. Warn pupils to take care with boiling water. If they scald themselves, cool the skin with plenty of cold running water.

What gas is made in photosynthesis?

Type	*Description*	*Differentiation*
	Pupils observe that plants make a gas during photosynthesis, and test the gas to find out whether it is oxygen.	Core

Equipment needed

For each group (or teacher demonstration):

- water plant, e.g. pondweed
- glass funnel
- Plasticine to support funnel in beaker
- beaker (250 cm^3)
- test tube
- splint
- Bunsen burner
- heatproof mat
- lamp (optional)

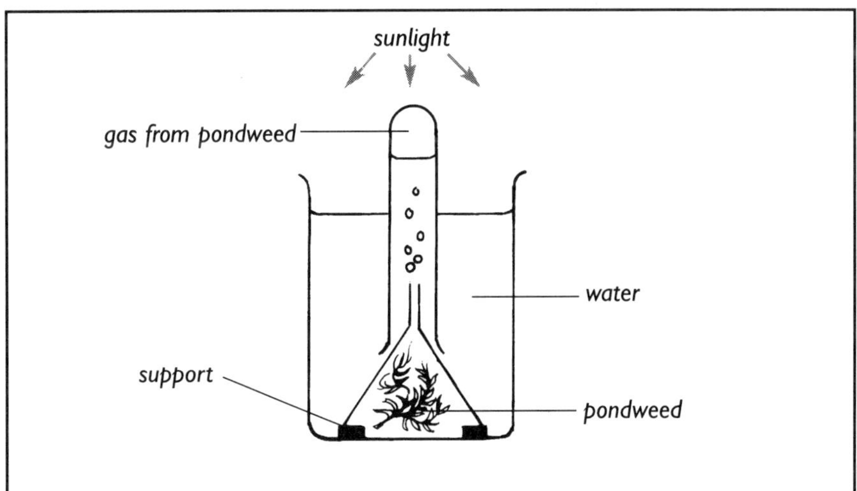

For your information

Running the activity

The pupils work in groups, or the activity can be run as a teacher demonstration to save time. Pupils are instructed to set up the experiment and leave it for 24 hours on a window sill. The gas that has collected the next day is tested with a glowing splint, or the gas can be produced more quickly by shining a lamp on the plant.

Questions lead pupils to draw conclusions and analyse the experiment.

Expected outcomes

The glowing splint will be relit, showing that the gas that is produced by the photosynthesising plant is oxygen.

When do plants grow the fastest?

Type	Description	Differentiation
	A datalogging activity to compare the growth of seedlings during daylight and at night. A position sensor is used to monitor the growth.	Core

Other relevant material

Skill sheet 6: Interpreting graphs

Equipment needed

For the class:

- computer
- interface
- position sensor
- printer (optional)
- wire or arm with counterweight
- clampstand
- cotton thread
- seedlings, e.g. of wheat growing on growth medium, e.g. cotton wool (see Tips below)

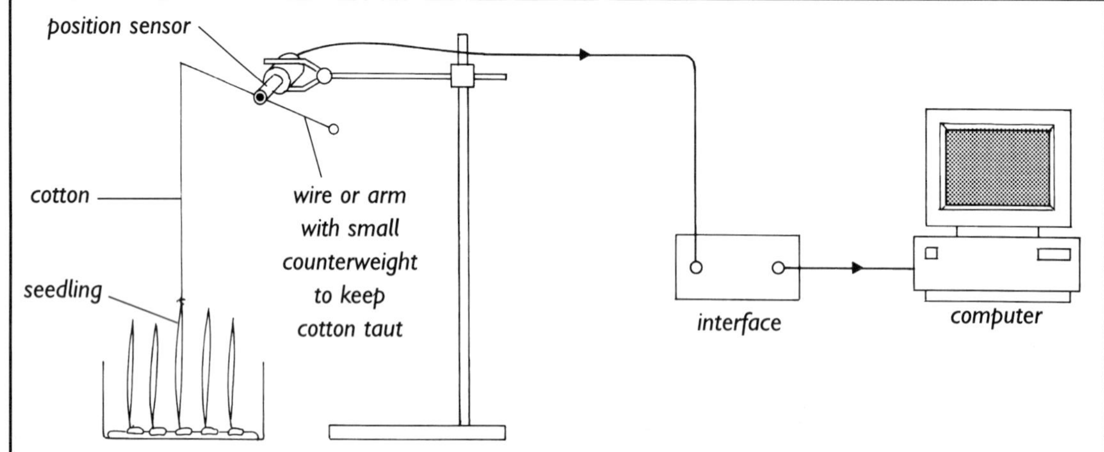

Tips

Plant the seeds in a crystallising basin on moist cotton wool 3–4 days in advance.
Use a small piece of Plasticine to counterbalance the wire or arm.

For your information

Running the activity

This activity will probably be run as a teacher demonstration unless there are enough position sensors available for each group of pupils. The growing seedlings are set up and left by a window for three days. The results are more convincing if the experiment can be left longer. A spreadsheet for entering data and plotting a graph are available on the CD–ROM that accompanies this pack.

Pupils are asked questions leading them to a conclusion, and also to evaluate the experiment.

Pitfalls

Do not forget to water the seedlings.

Expected outcomes

The position sensor will indicate a general increase in size. There will be a marked increase in the growth of plants during the day, that may be less obvious with younger plants.

Safety notes

Warn pupils not to eat the plants. Pupils must use electrical equipment in an appropriate manner.

Looking at leaves

Type	Description	Differentiation
	Pupils look at pre-prepared leaf slides, using a microscope.	Core

Other relevant material

Skill sheet 8: Using a microscope

Equipment needed

For the class:
- video camera, e.g. Flexicam (optional)
- microscope

For each pair:
- pre-prepared (bought) slide of TS of a leaf, stained
- microscope

For your information

Running the activity

Pupils work in pairs. The activity sheet gives a method for carrying out the practical, and directs pupils to record a labelled diagram of the slide. Question 6 could be used as an optional extension question. A microscope could be linked to a video camera (e.g. Flexicam) to display slides to the whole class.

Expected outcomes

Pupils produce a labelled drawing of a section through the leaf as seen under the microscope.

Safety notes

Pupils should take care with microscopes and slides.

Looking at root hairs

Type	*Description*	*Differentiation*
	Pupils look at pre-prepared slides of roots showing root hairs, using a microscope.	Core

Other relevant material

Skill sheet 8: Using a microscope

Equipment needed

For the class:

- video camera, e.g. Flexicam (optional)
- microscope

For each pair:

- pre-prepared (bought) slide of TS of a leaf, stained
- microscope

For your information

Running the activity

Pupils work in pairs. The activity sheet gives a method for carrying out the practical, and directs pupils to record a labelled diagram of the slide. A microscope could be linked to a video camera (e.g. Flexicam) to display slides to the whole class.

Expected outcomes

Pupils produce a labelled drawing of a root as seen under the microscope.

Safety notes

Pupils should take care with microscopes and slides.

Water transport in celery

Plant power
6.5 B

Type	*Description*	*Differentiation*
	Pupils observe coloured water travelling up the veins in a celery stalk, and observe a dyed vein using a microscope.	Core

Other relevant material

Skill sheet 8: Using a microscope

Equipment needed

For the class (optional):

- hair dryer
- white carnation
- beaker
- red food dye

For each group:

- celery stalk
- beaker (a large one can be used to stand all the celery stalks in for the class)
- red food dye
- craft knife or scalpel
- white tile
- microscope slide
- coverslip
- mounted needle
- distilled water
- dropper
- microscope

For your information

Running the activity

Pupils work in groups. They are instructed to leave celery stalks in dyed water overnight and observe them the next day. To carry out the activity in the same day, the celery stalks need to be left for at least a few hours before they are used. Alternatively, a cool hair dryer blowing over the leaves will speed up the movement of dye up the stalk.

Pupils then make a slide of a thin cross-section and observe it under a microscope. Structured questions lead them to analyse the structure and function of the veins.

As a demonstration in parallel with this activity, a white carnation can be left in dyed water overnight to show pupils that the dye travels up the veins and colours the flower.

Expected outcomes

The celery stalk will become stained in the veins that carry water (xylem). With a very thin cross-section of the stalk, the structure of the stained veins should become clearly visible under a light microscope.

Pitfalls

Make sure pupils cut a very thin cross-sections. Some pupils may need help with this.

Safety notes

Pupils must use knives carefully, and take care with microscopes and slides. Remind pupils not to eat the celery.

Growing pollen tubes

Type	*Description*	*Differentiation*
	Pupils use a microscope to observe the growth of a pollen tube.	Core (with Extension questions)

Other relevant material

Skill sheet 8: Using a microscope

Equipment needed

For each pair:

- flower (e.g. lily or buttercup)
- sucrose solution (10%) and dropper
- mounted needle
- warm area for incubating pollen (25–30 °C)
- cavity slide
- coverslip
- microscope
- fine art brush (optional)

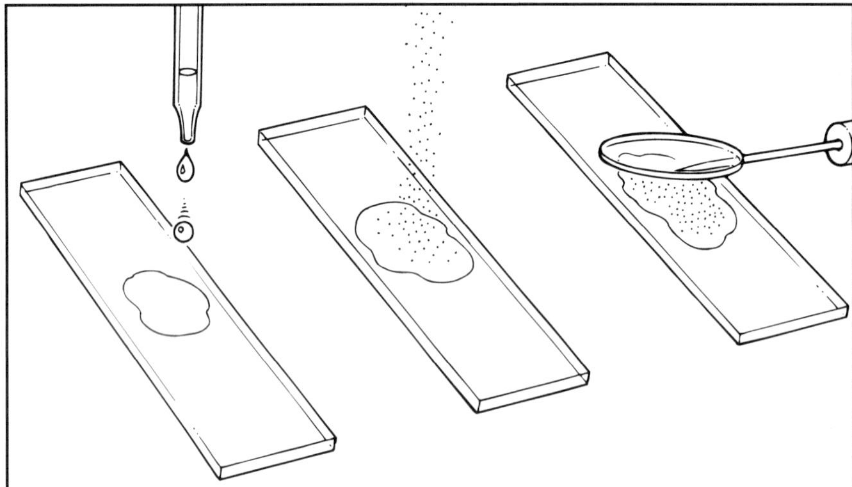

For your information

Running the activity

Pupils work in pairs.

Core: Pupils prepare a slide of pollen grains in sucrose solution. These must be left in a warm place for 30 minutes before being observed under the microscope. The pollen grains could be incubated ready before the lesson if time is short. Pupils observe and record the growth of the pollen tube during the lesson.

Extension: There are optional Extension questions at the foot of the Core sheet, which can be cut off if not required. These ask more detailed questions about the process of fertilisation.

Expected outcomes

The pupils will observe the growth of the pollen tube over 10-minute periods using a microscope, and draw a flow diagram to record their observations.

Safety notes

Pupils should take care with microscopes and slides. Remind them not to eat any plant material and to wash their hands afterwards. Plant pollens may cause allergic reactions in asthmatics and those who suffer from hayfever.

Properties of metals

Type	Description	Differentiation
	A short experiment testing samples of different metals, followed by a demonstration of thermal conductivity (with the same metals if possible).	Core

Equipment needed

For each group:

- small (2 cm × 2 cm) samples of the metals: iron, copper, aluminium, zinc and nickel
- 2 crocodile clips
- a cell in a cell holder
- 3 leads
- lamp
- magnet

For the teacher:

- apparatus to demonstrate thermal conductivity

Traditional apparatus is a metal box that holds water which is heated over a Bunsen burner. In one side are holes for rods which are provided with the apparatus. Drawing pins are attached to the ends of the rods using wax. The water is heated, the rods conduct and the wax melts. Obviously, the range of metals tested will depend on the rods provided with the apparatus.

An alternative is strips of metal with temperature-sensitive indicators stuck to their surface. These are commercially available in sets. The bottom of the strips are placed in hot water. Again, the range of metals will be restricted by those present in the purchased set.

For your information

Running the activity

Pupils carry out simple experiments to investigate the appearance and magnetic properties of a range of metals, and whether or not they conduct electricity.

Experiments on the thermal conductivity of metals involve using large and/or expensive pieces of apparatus, so it is assumed that this experiment will be a demonstration. This may be shown using the classic demonstration, with rods of metal leading from a box filled with hot water to a drawing pin held with wax, or the commercially available samples of metal with in-built temperature-sensitive strips.

Every effort should be made to use the same metals for each experiment, but this is unlikely to be entirely successful as nickel should be included as another example of a magnetic metal, yet is unlikely to be included in a commercial apparatus for comparing thermal conductivity.

Expected outcomes

Pupils record their results in a table of properties then answer questions based on their results.

Pitfalls

Samples of metals should be cleaned with a commercial cleaner, e.g. Brasso.
Get the pupils to test their circuit first to show that battery and lamp are functioning.
Make sure that the joints between the rods and the box of water are water-tight.

Safety notes

Most safety problems are avoided if the thermal conductivity experiment is a demonstration.

Pupils should wash their hands after handling metals.

Check for sharp edges to metal samples.

Display of metallic elements

Type	Description	Differentiation
	Pupils learn about the appearance of various metallic elements, including the hazardous ones they need to know about.	Core (no pupil sheets)

Equipment needed

Samples of the following metals:

- lithium
- potassium
- magnesium
- calcium
- nickel
- zinc
- sodium
- mercury
- aluminium
- iron
- copper

All the samples should be placed in small bottles or jars with the symbol for the element on the outside. Each lid should be sealed, whether the contents are dangerous or not.

See specific safety notes below.

Tips

Label bottles of metals with a yellow dot so they can be easily separated from the non-metal sample used in activity 7.4A.

For your information

Running the activity

Pupils are shown samples of lithium, sodium, potassium and mercury. They are not allowed to handle these samples.

The other samples (magnesium, aluminium, calcium, iron, nickel, copper and zinc) may be passed around the class in sealed bottles for pupils to examine.

This activity could be run in conjunction with 7.3B, by dividing the class into two groups and swapping over.

Expected outcomes

Pupils learn about the appearance of elements and the hazards involved with handling them.

Pitfalls

Teachers must ensure that pupils do not open the sample bottles.

Safety notes

All elements should have the appropriate hazard warning symbols (see Hazcards).

The samples of potassium, lithium and sodium should be under oil, the containers sealed and each placed within another, unbreakable, container which is also sealed.

The sample of mercury should be very carefully sealed and the container placed within a second container which is also sealed.

Metallic elements

Type	*Description*	*Differentiation*
	Pupils use a database of elements to answer questions about metals.	Core

Other relevant material

The database for this activity is on the CD-ROM that accompanies this pack.

ICT opportunities

Most CD-ROM encyclopedias have an interactive periodic table. However, the majority are far too complicated for Year 7 pupils. One of the best is in the *Encyclopedia of Science 2.0 Eyewitness* (Dorling Kindersley), but this still includes complicated terms.

The version of the periodic table shown in the book is based on that given at: www.webelements.com

For your information

Running the activity

The database is meant for pupils at all stages in KS3. It contains information not needed at this stage, nor for this activity. The teacher may wish to 'hide' the columns *Appearance, Position in periodic table* and *Density* to make what appears on the screen less intimidating.

If the number of computers is limited, this activity could be run in conjunction with 7.3A by dividing the class into two groups and swapping over.

Expected outcomes

Pupils learn about the properties of metals. They realise that metallic elements vary in their properties, despite sharing many basic characteristics. Pupils gain experience of handling large amounts of information using a database.

Display of non-metallic elements

Type	*Description*	*Differentiation*
	Pupils learn about the appearance of various non-metallic elements, including the hazardous ones they need to know about.	Core (no pupil sheets)

Equipment needed

Samples of the following non-metals:

- hydrogen*
- nitrogen*
- sulphur
- bromine
- helium*
- oxygen*
- chlorine
- iodine

All the samples should be placed in small bottles or jars with the symbol for the element on the outside. Each lid should be sealed, whether the contents are dangerous or not.

See specific safety notes and tips below.

Tips

Label bottles of non-metals with a red dot so they can be easily separated from the metal samples used in activity 7.3A.

* The bottles containing hydrogen, helium, oxygen and nitrogen could be left empty but sealed and the labelled with the symbol.

For your information

Running the activity

Pupils are shown samples of chlorine and bromine. They are not allowed to handle these samples.

The other samples (hydrogen, helium, carbon, nitrogen, oxygen, sulphur and iodine) may be passed around the class in sealed bottles for pupils to examine.

This activity could be run in conjunction with 7.4B, by dividing the class into two groups and swapping over.

Expected outcomes

Pupils learn about the appearance of elements and the hazards involved with handling them.

Pitfalls

Teachers must ensure that pupils do not open the sample bottles.

Safety notes

All elements should have the appropriate hazard warning symbols (see Hazcards).

The samples of chlorine gas and bromine should be in sealed containers and each placed within another sealed container. An unopened vial of bromine can be used, but this should be placed inside another container and packed so that it is visible from one side but will not rattle around.

Non-metallic elements

Type	*Description*	*Differentiation*
	Pupils use a database of elements to answer questions about non-metals.	Core

Other relevant material

The database for this activity is on the CD-ROM that accompanies this pack.

ICT opportunities

Most CD-ROM encyclopedias have an interactive periodic table. However, the majority are far too complicated for Year 7 pupils. One of the best is in the *Encyclopedia of Science 2.0 Eyewitness* (Dorling Kindersley), but this still includes complicated terms.

The version of the periodic table shown in the book is based on that given at: www.webelements.com

For your information

Running the activity

The database is meant for pupils at all stages in KS3. It contains information not needed at this stage, nor for this activity. The teacher may wish to 'hide' the columns *Position in periodic table*, *Is it a magnetic material?* and *Density* to make what appears on the screen less intimidating.

If the number of computers is limited, this activity could be run in conjunction with 7.4A by dividing the class into two groups and swapping over.

Expected outcomes

Pupils learn about the properties of metals. They realise that metallic elements vary in their properties, despite sharing many basic characteristics. Pupils gain experience of handling large amounts of information using a database.

Technician's notes

Optional demonstration

Burning magnesium in air

This should be a swift demonstration to remind pupils about chemical reactions. The magnesium burns with a bright white flame, and a white powder is made.

The word equation could be put on the board.

Equipment needed

For the teacher:

- magnesium
- tongs
- Bunsen burner
- heatproof mat
- goggles

For each pupil:

- a piece of cobalt glass

Safety notes

Pupils must observe the bright magnesium flame through blue glass to avoid damaging their eyes, or be told to look away immediately when they see how bright the flame is.

Making iron sulphide

Type	Description	Differentiation
	Pupils react iron and sulphur, and consider the properties before and after heating.	Core

Other relevant material

Skill sheet 7: Word equations

Equipment needed

For the class:

- 4 samples of powdered sulphur in sealed, transparent jars
- 4 samples of iron filings in sealed, transparent jars
- 4 samples of purchased iron(II) sulphide in sealed, transparent jars
- 4 magnets

For the teacher:

- wooden mallet
- newspaper
- forceps

For each group:

- disposable test tube (a combustion tube) containing 0.5 cm^3 of the iron/sulphur mixture
- test tube holder
- Bunsen burner
- heatproof mat

Tips

Make up a mixture of iron filings and powdered sulphur in the ratio of 5 g iron filings to 3 g powdered sulphur. This ensures that the sulphur is present in slight excess. Make sure the mixture is well mixed, because the iron filings settle to the bottom of the bottle. Place 0.5 cm^3 of the mixture in each test tube before the lesson.

For your information

Running the activity

A well-ventilated room is required for this experiment. Sets of one sealed jar of sulphur, one sealed jar iron filings, one sealed jar iron(II) sulphide and one magnet should be placed about the room for student groups to share. Each group of pupils heats the iron/sulphur until it starts and then stops glowing. They then place the test tube on the heatproof mat to cool. Once cool, they try to tap the iron(II) sulphide out of the test tube. If this fails, they should take the test tube to the teacher, who will break the test tube and pick out the iron(II) sulphide.

Expected outcomes

The mixture in the test tube will start to glow, indicating that a chemical reaction is happening. The glow will stop when the reaction is complete. If the mixture was well mixed and there was a slight excess of sulphur, the lump of iron(II) sulphide made should not stick to a magnet.

Pitfalls

The mixture of iron and sulphur must be carefully prepared. Only a small amount of the mixture should be placed in each combustion tube.

The iron(II) sulphide often becomes stuck in the bottom of the test tube. The teacher should ensure that the test tube is wrapped in newspaper before breaking it using a mallet.

Safety notes

Iron filings are a hazard. They cause skin irritation and are very dangerous if they get into the eyes. Placing the mixture into the test tubes reduces the risk.

The room must be well ventilated for the iron and sulphur reaction.

Pupils should wear eye protection, both for observing the demonstration and for carrying out the experiment.

The test tubes become extremely hot. They should be left for 10 minutes to cool. If necessary, the teacher should remove the iron(II) sulphide from the test tube by breaking the test tube. This creates a hazard and the broken glass should be disposed of carefully.

Will it rust?

Type	Description	Differentiation
	An investigation into the conditions required for rusting to occur	Core, Help

Equipment needed

(Pupils are expected to plan their own experiments, so the numbers of nails, test tubes, racks, etc. per group may vary.)

Available to the whole class:

- container of deoxygenated water, with tap
- paraffin or cooking oil
- grease
- bungs that fit test tubes
- 10 cm^3 measuring cylinders
- clean iron nails
- anhydrous calcium chloride
- enamel paint, paintbrush and newspaper
- test tubes
- test tube racks
- pipettes

Tips

The water must be deoxygenated. Simmer the water for 15–20 minutes, pour carefully into a container (the container should have a tap). Add oil to exclude air from the upper surface. This should be done, if possible, on the day the experiment will be set up.

New iron nails should be used. The nails should be soaked in ethanol/methylated spirits to cut any grease on the surface (which is added to prevent rusting while stored), then dried on the day of the experiment.

For your information

Running the activity

This activity takes place over two lessons. Planning and carrying out the experiment takes place in the first lesson. Observing, recording and analysing the results takes place in a later lesson (3–7 days), when the nails have had time to rust.

Core: Pupils are expected to plan their own investigation, so the number of test tubes per group may vary. The actual experiment is limited, with only plus/minus values for the variables, so the planning exercise is left rather open.

Help: This version is much more structured, guiding pupils at each stage.

Expected outcomes

The iron nail exposed to air and water will rust in 3–7 days. Nails from which oxygen and/or water have been successfully excluded will not rust.

Pitfalls

Purchased iron nails often have grease on the surface to prevent rusting.

Failure to deoxygenate the water often causes this experiment to give anomalous results.

Safety notes

Calcium chloride is classified as an irritant.

The paint used is likely to contain a hazardous solvent.

Measuring forces

Type	Description	Differentiation
	Pupils practise reading newtonmeter scales, and use newtonmeters and newton scales to measure forces.	Core

Equipment needed

For each pair/group:

- newtonmeter
- newton scales
- string
- objects to weigh, e.g. textbook, pencil case, shoe

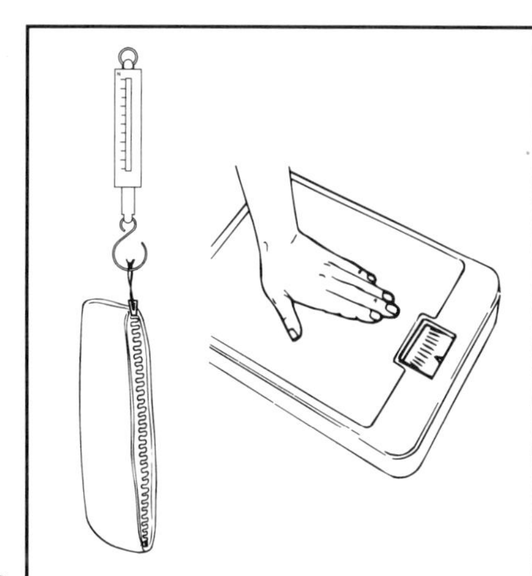

For your information

Running the activity

Pupils work individually at first to answer question 1, which asks them to read the newtonmeter scales pictured on the sheet. This helps ensure they will read the newtonmeters correctly for the practical that follows. They continue in pairs to measure forces using the newtonmeter and newton scales, recording their results in a table that they draw for themselves. The practicals are quite short and the teacher may add other objects for the pupils to weigh.

Expected outcomes

Pupils gain experience in reading newtonmeter scales, and in using newtonmeters and newton scales correctly. They begin to appreciate the relationship between mass and weight, and compare forces of different sizes.

Shoe soles

Type	*Description*	*Differentiation*
	Pupils carry out an investigation to find the relationship between the mass of a shoe and the force needed to pull it against friction.	Core

Other relevant material

Skill sheet 5: Drawing charts and graphs

ICT opportunities

The results can be graphed using a spreadsheet such as Microsoft® *Excel*.

Equipment needed

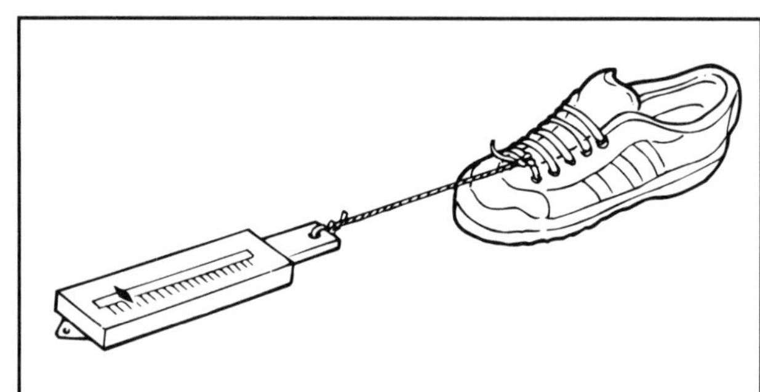

For each pair/group:

- set of masses, 100–600 g
- shoe
- newtonmeter
- string
- suitable surface to pull the shoe over, e.g. carpet

For your information

Running the activity

Core: Pupils work in groups towards a full investigation. They write their plans before they start, then carry out the experiment and draw a graph of their results. They analyse their results and evaluate the experiment.

To make the experiment a fair test, the surface, shoe and masses should be the same in each experiment.

Pupils should carry out each reading at least twice to obtain average results. The experiment will not take long to complete so this will not be too time-consuming. Pupils should record their results in a table which has columns for 'Force needed in newtons' and 'Mass in grams'.

Extension: There is an optional Extension question at the foot of the Core sheet, which can be cut off if not required. It asks pupils to suggest a modification to relate the experiment to a real-life problem.

Expected outcomes

Pupils carry out an investigation, and see that the heavier the shoe, the greater the friction.

Pitfalls

Care should be taken to make accurate readings when looking at newtonmeters side-on. It is difficult to read the newtonmeter at the same time as pulling it along – one pupil should pull while the other takes the reading.

Making bridges

Type	*Description*	*Differentiation*
	Pupils design, make and test a bridge using straws, paper and sticky tape.	Core

ICT opportunities

The design of the bridge can be carried out using drawing or design software such as Microsoft® *Word* and *Design View*.

Equipment needed

For each group:

- 20 straws
- 2 pieces of A4 paper
- 50 cm length of sticky tape
- about 4–5 100 g masses to test bridges

For your information

Running the activity

Pupils work in groups to draw their designs, build the bridge, test it to see how many masses it can support and then compare the results with the rest of the class. You may want to limit the number of straws and the length of sticky tape given to each group.

There are a lot of activities to cover and it may be useful to set a time for each one. Pupils could design and make the bridge in one lesson, and then test it as a whole-class activity in the next lesson.

Expected outcomes

Pupils design a bridge, make the bridge from the materials supplied, and obtain results as to how many masses the bridge can hold.

Pitfalls

Pupils must ensure that the bridge platform is big enough to hold a reasonable number (4–5) of 100 g masses so that the bridge can be tested.

Stretching

Type	Description	Differentiation
	Pupils compare the effect of a stretching force on a spring and an elastic band, and consider the relationship between weight and extension.	Core

Other relevant material

Skill sheet 5: Drawing charts and graphs

Equipment needed

For each pair:

- spring
- elastic band, about the same length as the spring
- clamp stand with 2 bosses and clamps
- metre rule
- mass holder
- masses from 100 g to 600 g, possibly labelled with their weights in newtons

For your information

Running the activity

Pupils work in pairs. They hang weights on a spring and record the extension, and then do the same for a rubber band. They are given a format for a results table, and are asked to plot separate graphs for the spring and the rubber band. They analyse their results and evaluate the experiment.

The sheet mentions weights, not masses. The masses provided could be labelled in newtons to avoid confusion if this is thought necessary. Alternatively, the teacher may prefer to ask the pupils to add a column to their tables and record first the mass, and then convert this to weight.

Expected outcomes

Pupils plot a graph of extension against weight for a spring and an elastic band, and use it to infer that there is a relationship between extension and weight. Once the elastic limit of the spring or elastic band is reached, the relationship breaks down.

Pitfalls

A set of weights 100–600 N has been selected for this experiment, but suitable weights depend on the spring and elastic band chosen. Test the spring and elastic band in advance to find their elastic limit, and choose weights accordingly, changing the weights on the sheet.

Safety notes

Wear eye protection. Warn pupils to be careful when bending down near clamp stands. They should take care not to drop weights on their feet.

Speeding trolleys

Type	Description	Differentiation
	Pupils carry out a datalogging activity to compare the speed of a trolley travelling down ramps of different slopes. Light gates are used to measure the speed of the trolley.	Core

ICT opportunities

A spreadsheet program such as Microsoft® *Excel* can be used to graph the results.

Equipment needed

For each group:

- computer
- 2 light gates
- spreadsheet software
- trolley or toy car
- card (10 cm depth, positioned to pass through light gates)
- metre rule
- interface
- datalogging software
- printer (optional)
- ramp e.g. PVC guttering
- Plasticine (to attach card to car)
- books (to support ramp)
- clampstands (to hold light gates)

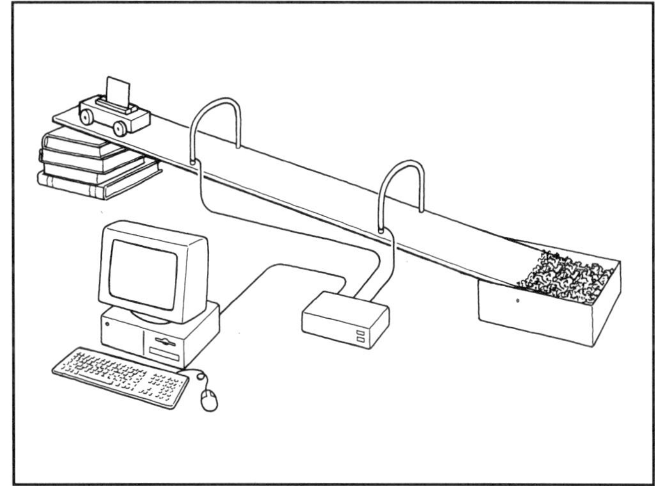

Tips

Instead of using datalogging equipment and light gates, the activity can be run using ticker tape, or alternatively pupils can measure the distance the trolley reaches after being released from the ramp at different heights.

For your information

Running the activity

This is an ICT activity that requires the use of datalogging equipment. If pupils are familiar with using datalogging equipment, the activity can be run quickly, otherwise they may need a demonstration of the kit before they start.

Pupils work in groups. They draw up their own results table, carry out the experiment and plot a bar chart. They answer questions to analyse the results and evaluate the experiment.

Expected outcomes

Pupils carry out the speeding trolleys experiment. They obtain a set of results and suggest a basic conclusion (the higher the ramp, the faster the trolley) and evaluation.

Pitfalls

The results from datalogging are very accurate, perhaps down to several decimal places. Pupils need to round to a suitable number of decimal places.

The experiment must be set up so that the card passes through the light gates and breaks the beam. Light gates should not be too close to windows as the sunlight may affect the results.

Safety notes

Use a catch box at the bottom of the ramp to stop the trolleys.
Make sure the ramps don't fall off the tables.

Water transport in celery

Type	Description	Differentiation
	Pupils observe coloured water travelling up the veins in a celery stalk, and observe a dyed vein using a microscope.	Core

Other relevant material

Skill sheet 8: Using a microscope

Equipment needed

For the class (optional):

- hair dryer
- white carnation
- beaker
- red food dye

For each group:

- celery stalk
- beaker (a large one can be used to stand all the celery stalks in for the class)
- red food dye
- craft knife or scalpel
- white tile
- microscope slide
- coverslip
- mounted needle
- distilled water
- dropper
- microscope

For your information

Running the activity

Pupils work in groups. They are instructed to leave celery stalks in dyed water overnight and observe them the next day. To carry out the activity in the same day, the celery stalks need to be left for at least a few hours before they are used. Alternatively, a cool hair dryer blowing over the leaves will speed up the movement of dye up the stalk.

Pupils then make a slide of a thin cross-section and observe it under a microscope. Structured questions lead them to analyse the structure and function of the veins.

As a demonstration in parallel with this activity, a white carnation can be left in dyed water overnight to show pupils that the dye travels up the veins and colours the flower.

Expected outcomes

The celery stalk will become stained in the veins that carry water (xylem). With a very thin cross-section of the stalk, the structure of the stained veins should become clearly visible under a light microscope.

Pitfalls

Make sure pupils cut a very thin cross-sections. Some pupils may need help with this.

Safety notes

Pupils must use knives carefully, and take care with microscopes and slides. Remind pupils not to eat the celery.

Growing pollen tubes

Type	*Description*	*Differentiation*
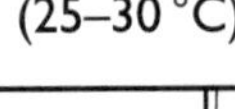	Pupils use a microscope to observe the growth of a pollen tube.	Core (with Extension questions)

Other relevant material

Skill sheet 8: Using a microscope

Equipment needed

For each pair:

- flower (e.g. lily or buttercup)
- sucrose solution (10%) and dropper
- mounted needle
- warm area for incubating pollen (25–30 °C)
- cavity slide
- coverslip
- microscope
- fine art brush (optional)

For your information

Running the activity

Pupils work in pairs.

Core: Pupils prepare a slide of pollen grains in sucrose solution. These must be left in a warm place for 30 minutes before being observed under the microscope. The pollen grains could be incubated ready before the lesson if time is short. Pupils observe and record the growth of the pollen tube during the lesson.

Extension: There are optional Extension questions at the foot of the Core sheet, which can be cut off if not required. These ask more detailed questions about the process of fertilisation.

Expected outcomes

The pupils will observe the growth of the pollen tube over 10-minute periods using a microscope, and draw a flow diagram to record their observations.

Safety notes

Pupils should take care with microscopes and slides. Remind them not to eat any plant material and to wash their hands afterwards. Plant pollens may cause allergic reactions in asthmatics and those who suffer from hayfever.

Properties of metals

Type	Description	Differentiation
	A short experiment testing samples of different metals, followed by a demonstration of thermal conductivity (with the same metals if possible).	Core

Equipment needed

For each group:

- small (2 cm × 2 cm) samples of the metals: iron, copper, aluminium, zinc and nickel
- 2 crocodile clips
- a cell in a cell holder
- 3 leads
- lamp
- magnet

For the teacher:

- apparatus to demonstrate thermal conductivity

Traditional apparatus is a metal box that holds water which is heated over a Bunsen burner. In one side are holes for rods which are provided with the apparatus. Drawing pins are attached to the ends of the rods using wax. The water is heated, the rods conduct and the wax melts. Obviously, the range of metals tested will depend on the rods provided with the apparatus.

An alternative is strips of metal with temperature-sensitive indicators stuck to their surface. These are commercially available in sets. The bottom of the strips are placed in hot water. Again, the range of metals will be restricted by those present in the purchased set.

For your information

Running the activity

Pupils carry out simple experiments to investigate the appearance and magnetic properties of a range of metals, and whether or not they conduct electricity.

Experiments on the thermal conductivity of metals involve using large and/or expensive pieces of apparatus, so it is assumed that this experiment will be a demonstration. This may be shown using the classic demonstration, with rods of metal leading from a box filled with hot water to a drawing pin held with wax, or the commercially available samples of metal with in-built temperature-sensitive strips.

Every effort should be made to use the same metals for each experiment, but this is unlikely to be entirely successful as nickel should be included as another example of a magnetic metal, yet is unlikely to be included in a commercial apparatus for comparing thermal conductivity.

Expected outcomes

Pupils record their results in a table of properties then answer questions based on their results.

Pitfalls

Samples of metals should be cleaned with a commercial cleaner, e.g. Brasso.
Get the pupils to test their circuit first to show that battery and lamp are functioning.
Make sure that the joints between the rods and the box of water are water-tight.

Safety notes

Most safety problems are avoided if the thermal conductivity experiment is a demonstration.

Pupils should wash their hands after handling metals.

Check for sharp edges to metal samples.

Display of metallic elements

Type	Description	Differentiation
	Pupils learn about the appearance of various metallic elements, including the hazardous ones they need to know about.	Core (no pupil sheets)

Equipment needed

Samples of the following metals:

- lithium
- potassium
- magnesium
- calcium
- nickel
- zinc
- sodium
- mercury
- aluminium
- iron
- copper

All the samples should be placed in small bottles or jars with the symbol for the element on the outside. Each lid should be sealed, whether the contents are dangerous or not.

See specific safety notes below.

Tips

Label bottles of metals with a yellow dot so they can be easily separated from the non-metal sample used in activity 7.4A.

For your information

Running the activity

Pupils are shown samples of lithium, sodium, potassium and mercury. They are not allowed to handle these samples.

The other samples (magnesium, aluminium, calcium, iron, nickel, copper and zinc) may be passed around the class in sealed bottles for pupils to examine.

This activity could be run in conjunction with 7.3B, by dividing the class into two groups and swapping over.

Expected outcomes

Pupils learn about the appearance of elements and the hazards involved with handling them.

Pitfalls

Teachers must ensure that pupils do not open the sample bottles.

Safety notes

All elements should have the appropriate hazard warning symbols (see Hazcards).

The samples of potassium, lithium and sodium should be under oil, the containers sealed and each placed within another, unbreakable, container which is also sealed.

The sample of mercury should be very carefully sealed and the container placed within a second container which is also sealed.

Metallic elements

Type	Description	Differentiation
	Pupils use a database of elements to answer questions about metals.	Core

Other relevant material

The database for this activity is on the CD-ROM that accompanies this pack.

ICT opportunities

Most CD-ROM encyclopedias have an interactive periodic table. However, the majority are far too complicated for Year 7 pupils. One of the best is in the *Encyclopedia of Science 2.0 Eyewitness* (Dorling Kindersley), but this still includes complicated terms.

The version of the periodic table shown in the book is based on that given at:
www.webelements.com

For your information

Running the activity

The database is meant for pupils at all stages in KS3. It contains information not needed at this stage, nor for this activity. The teacher may wish to 'hide' the columns *Appearance, Position in periodic table* and *Density* to make what appears on the screen less intimidating.

If the number of computers is limited, this activity could be run in conjunction with 7.3A by dividing the class into two groups and swapping over.

Expected outcomes

Pupils learn about the properties of metals. They realise that metallic elements vary in their properties, despite sharing many basic characteristics. Pupils gain experience of handling large amounts of information using a database.

Display of non-metallic elements

Type	Description	Differentiation
	Pupils learn about the appearance of various non-metallic elements, including the hazardous ones they need to know about.	Core (no pupil sheets)

Equipment needed

Samples of the following non-metals:

- hydrogen*
- nitrogen*
- sulphur
- bromine
- helium*
- oxygen*
- chlorine
- iodine

All the samples should be placed in small bottles or jars with the symbol for the element on the outside. Each lid should be sealed, whether the contents are dangerous or not.

See specific safety notes and tips below.

Tips

Label bottles of non-metals with a red dot so they can be easily separated from the metal samples used in activity 7.3A.

*The bottles containing hydrogen, helium, oxygen and nitrogen could be left empty but sealed and the labelled with the symbol.

For your information

Running the activity

Pupils are shown samples of chlorine and bromine. They are not allowed to handle these samples.

The other samples (hydrogen, helium, carbon, nitrogen, oxygen, sulphur and iodine) may be passed around the class in sealed bottles for pupils to examine.

This activity could be run in conjunction with 7.4B, by dividing the class into two groups and swapping over.

Expected outcomes

Pupils learn about the appearance of elements and the hazards involved with handling them.

Pitfalls

Teachers must ensure that pupils do not open the sample bottles.

Safety notes

All elements should have the appropriate hazard warning symbols (see Hazcards).

The samples of chlorine gas and bromine should be in sealed containers and each placed within another sealed container. An unopened vial of bromine can be used, but this should be placed inside another container and packed so that it is visible from one side but will not rattle around.

Non-metallic elements

Type	*Description*	*Differentiation*
	Pupils use a database of elements to answer questions about non-metals.	Core

Other relevant material

The database for this activity is on the CD-ROM that accompanies this pack.

ICT opportunities

Most CD-ROM encyclopedias have an interactive periodic table. However, the majority are far too complicated for Year 7 pupils. One of the best is in the *Encyclopedia of Science 2.0 Eyewitness* (Dorling Kindersley), but this still includes complicated terms.

The version of the periodic table shown in the book is based on that given at: www.webelements.com

For your information

Running the activity

The database is meant for pupils at all stages in KS3. It contains information not needed at this stage, nor for this activity. The teacher may wish to 'hide' the columns *Position in periodic table*, *Is it a magnetic material?* and *Density* to make what appears on the screen less intimidating.

If the number of computers is limited, this activity could be run in conjunction with 7.4A by dividing the class into two groups and swapping over.

Expected outcomes

Pupils learn about the properties of metals. They realise that metallic elements vary in their properties, despite sharing many basic characteristics. Pupils gain experience of handling large amounts of information using a database.

7.6 Optional demonstration

Burning magnesium in air

This should be a swift demonstration to remind pupils about chemical reactions. The magnesium burns with a bright white flame, and a white powder is made.

The word equation could be put on the board.

Equipment needed

For the teacher:

- magnesium
- tongs
- Bunsen burner
- heatproof mat
- goggles

For each pupil:

- a piece of cobalt glass

Safety notes

Pupils must observe the bright magnesium flame through blue glass to avoid damaging their eyes, or be told to look away immediately when they see how bright the flame is.

Making iron sulphide

Type	Description	Differentiation
	Pupils react iron and sulphur, and consider the properties before and after heating.	Core

Other relevant material

Skill sheet 7: Word equations

Equipment needed

For the class:

- 4 samples of powdered sulphur in sealed, transparent jars
- 4 samples of iron filings in sealed, transparent jars
- 4 samples of purchased iron(II) sulphide in sealed, transparent jars
- 4 magnets

For the teacher:

- wooden mallet
- newspaper
- forceps

For each group:

- disposable test tube (a combustion tube) containing 0.5 cm^3 of the iron/sulphur mixture
- test tube holder
- Bunsen burner
- heatproof mat

Tips

Make up a mixture of iron filings and powdered sulphur in the ratio of 5 g iron filings to 3 g powdered sulphur. This ensures that the sulphur is present in slight excess. Make sure the mixture is well mixed, because the iron filings settle to the bottom of the bottle. Place 0.5 cm^3 of the mixture in each test tube before the lesson.

For your information

Running the activity

A well-ventilated room is required for this experiment. Sets of one sealed jar of sulphur, one sealed jar iron filings, one sealed jar iron(II) sulphide and one magnet should be placed about the room for student groups to share. Each group of pupils heats the iron/sulphur until it starts and then stops glowing. They then place the test tube on the heatproof mat to cool. Once cool, they try to tap the iron(II) sulphide out of the test tube. If this fails, they should take the test tube to the teacher, who will break the test tube and pick out the iron(II) sulphide.

Expected outcomes

The mixture in the test tube will start to glow, indicating that a chemical reaction is happening. The glow will stop when the reaction is complete. If the mixture was well mixed and there was a slight excess of sulphur, the lump of iron(II) sulphide made should not stick to a magnet.

Pitfalls

The mixture of iron and sulphur must be carefully prepared. Only a small amount of the mixture should be placed in each combustion tube.

The iron(II) sulphide often becomes stuck in the bottom of the test tube. The teacher should ensure that the test tube is wrapped in newspaper before breaking it using a mallet.

Safety notes

Iron filings are a hazard. They cause skin irritation and are very dangerous if they get into the eyes. Placing the mixture into the test tubes reduces the risk.

The room must be well ventilated for the iron and sulphur reaction.

Pupils should wear eye protection, both for observing the demonstration and for carrying out the experiment.

The test tubes become extremely hot. They should be left for 10 minutes to cool. If necessary, the teacher should remove the iron(II) sulphide from the test tube by breaking the test tube. This creates a hazard and the broken glass should be disposed of carefully.

7.7 A Will it rust?

Type	Description	Differentiation
	An investigation into the conditions required for rusting to occur	Core, Help

Equipment needed

(Pupils are expected to plan their own experiments, so the numbers of nails, test tubes, racks, etc. per group may vary.)

Available to the whole class:

- container of deoxygenated water, with tap
- paraffin or cooking oil
- grease
- bungs that fit test tubes
- 10 cm^3 measuring cylinders
- clean iron nails
- anhydrous calcium chloride
- enamel paint, paintbrush and newspaper
- test tubes
- test tube racks
- pipettes

Tips

The water must be deoxygenated. Simmer the water for 15–20 minutes, pour carefully into a container (the container should have a tap). Add oil to exclude air from the upper surface. This should be done, if possible, on the day the experiment will be set up.

New iron nails should be used. The nails should be soaked in ethanol/methylated spirits to cut any grease on the surface (which is added to prevent rusting while stored), then dried on the day of the experiment.

For your information

Running the activity

This activity takes place over two lessons. Planning and carrying out the experiment takes place in the first lesson. Observing, recording and analysing the results takes place in a later lesson (3–7 days), when the nails have had time to rust.

Core: Pupils are expected to plan their own investigation, so the number of test tubes per group may vary. The actual experiment is limited, with only plus/minus values for the variables, so the planning exercise is left rather open.

Help: This version is much more structured, guiding pupils at each stage.

Expected outcomes

The iron nail exposed to air and water will rust in 3–7 days. Nails from which oxygen and/or water have been successfully excluded will not rust.

Pitfalls

Purchased iron nails often have grease on the surface to prevent rusting.

Failure to deoxygenate the water often causes this experiment to give anomalous results.

Safety notes

Calcium chloride is classified as an irritant.

The paint used is likely to contain a hazardous solvent.

Measuring forces

Type	Description	Differentiation
	Pupils practise reading newtonmeter scales, and use newtonmeters and newton scales to measure forces.	Core

Equipment needed

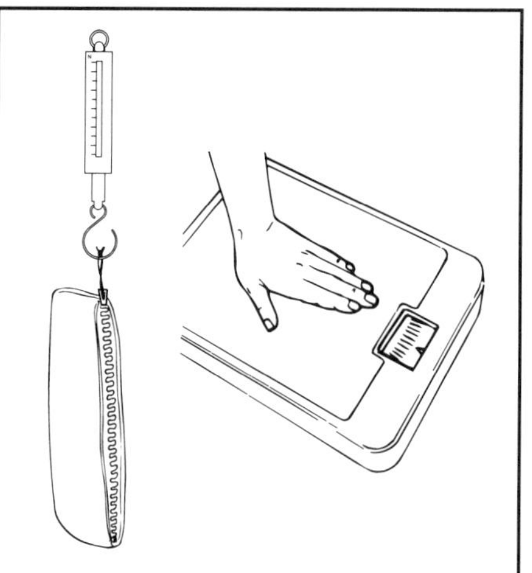

For each pair/group:

- newtonmeter
- newton scales
- string
- objects to weigh, e.g. textbook, pencil case, shoe

For your information

Running the activity

Pupils work individually at first to answer question 1, which asks them to read the newtonmeter scales pictured on the sheet. This helps ensure they will read the newtonmeters correctly for the practical that follows. They continue in pairs to measure forces using the newtonmeter and newton scales, recording their results in a table that they draw for themselves. The practicals are quite short and the teacher may add other objects for the pupils to weigh.

Expected outcomes

Pupils gain experience in reading newtonmeter scales, and in using newtonmeters and newton scales correctly. They begin to appreciate the relationship between mass and weight, and compare forces of different sizes.

Shoe soles

Type	Description	Differentiation
	Pupils carry out an investigation to find the relationship between the mass of a shoe and the force needed to pull it against friction.	Core

Other relevant material

Skill sheet 5: Drawing charts and graphs

ICT opportunities

The results can be graphed using a spreadsheet such as Microsoft® *Excel*.

Equipment needed

For each pair/group:

- set of masses, 100–600 g
- shoe
- newtonmeter
- string
- suitable surface to pull the shoe over, e.g. carpet

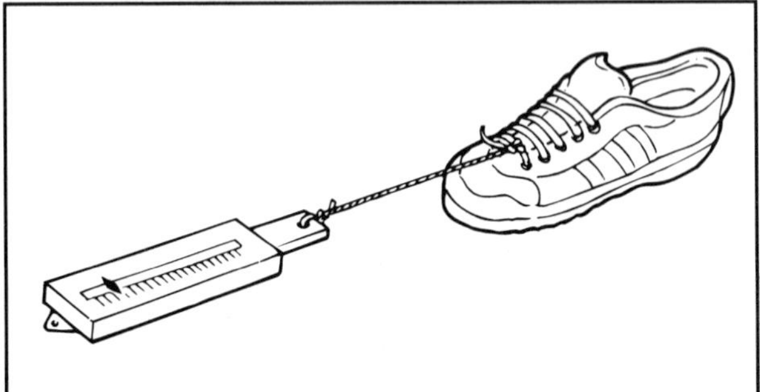

For your information

Running the activity

Core: Pupils work in groups towards a full investigation. They write their plans before they start, then carry out the experiment and draw a graph of their results. They analyse their results and evaluate the experiment.

To make the experiment a fair test, the surface, shoe and masses should be the same in each experiment.

Pupils should carry out each reading at least twice to obtain average results. The experiment will not take long to complete so this will not be too time-consuming. Pupils should record their results in a table which has columns for 'Force needed in newtons' and 'Mass in grams'.

Extension: There is an optional Extension question at the foot of the Core sheet, which can be cut off if not required. It asks pupils to suggest a modification to relate the experiment to a real-life problem.

Expected outcomes

Pupils carry out an investigation, and see that the heavier the shoe, the greater the friction.

Pitfalls

Care should be taken to make accurate readings when looking at newtonmeters side-on. It is difficult to read the newtonmeter at the same time as pulling it along – one pupil should pull while the other takes the reading.

Making bridges

Type	Description	Differentiation
	Pupils design, make and test a bridge using straws, paper and sticky tape.	Core

ICT opportunities

The design of the bridge can be carried out using drawing or design software such as Microsoft® *Word* and *Design View*.

Equipment needed

For each group:

- 20 straws
- 2 pieces of A4 paper
- 50 cm length of sticky tape
- about 4–5 100 g masses to test bridges

For your information

Running the activity

Pupils work in groups to draw their designs, build the bridge, test it to see how many masses it can support and then compare the results with the rest of the class. You may want to limit the number of straws and the length of sticky tape given to each group.

There are a lot of activities to cover and it may be useful to set a time for each one. Pupils could design and make the bridge in one lesson, and then test it as a whole-class activity in the next lesson.

Expected outcomes

Pupils design a bridge, make the bridge from the materials supplied, and obtain results as to how many masses the bridge can hold.

Pitfalls

Pupils must ensure that the bridge platform is big enough to hold a reasonable number (4–5) of 100 g masses so that the bridge can be tested.

8.5 B

Stretching

Type	*Description*	*Differentiation*
	Pupils compare the effect of a stretching force on a spring and an elastic band, and consider the relationship between weight and extension.	Core

Other relevant material

Skill sheet 5: Drawing charts and graphs

Equipment needed

For each pair:

- spring
- elastic band, about the same length as the spring
- clamp stand with 2 bosses and clamps
- metre rule
- mass holder
- masses from 100 g to 600 g, possibly labelled with their weights in newtons

For your information

Running the activity

Pupils work in pairs. They hang weights on a spring and record the extension, and then do the same for a rubber band. They are given a format for a results table, and are asked to plot separate graphs for the spring and the rubber band. They analyse their results and evaluate the experiment.

The sheet mentions weights, not masses. The masses provided could be labelled in newtons to avoid confusion if this is thought necessary. Alternatively, the teacher may prefer to ask the pupils to add a column to their tables and record first the mass, and then convert this to weight.

Expected outcomes

Pupils plot a graph of extension against weight for a spring and an elastic band, and use it to infer that there is a relationship between extension and weight. Once the elastic limit of the spring or elastic band is reached, the relationship breaks down.

Pitfalls

A set of weights 100–600 N has been selected for this experiment, but suitable weights depend on the spring and elastic band chosen. Test the spring and elastic band in advance to find their elastic limit, and choose weights accordingly, changing the weights on the sheet.

Safety notes

Wear eye protection. Warn pupils to be careful when bending down near clamp stands. They should take care not to drop weights on their feet.

Speeding trolleys

Type	Description	Differentiation
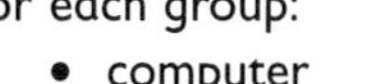	Pupils carry out a datalogging activity to compare the speed of a trolley travelling down ramps of different slopes. Light gates are used to measure the speed of the trolley.	Core

ICT opportunities

A spreadsheet program such as Microsoft® *Excel* can be used to graph the results.

Equipment needed

For each group:

- computer
- 2 light gates
- spreadsheet software
- trolley or toy car
- card (10 cm depth, positioned to pass through light gates)
- metre rule
- interface
- datalogging software
- printer (optional)
- ramp e.g. PVC guttering
- Plasticine (to attach card to car)
- books (to support ramp)
- clampstands (to hold light gates)

Tips

Instead of using datalogging equipment and light gates, the activity can be run using ticker tape, or alternatively pupils can measure the distance the trolley reaches after being released from the ramp at different heights.

For your information

Running the activity

This is an ICT activity that requires the use of datalogging equipment. If pupils are familiar with using datalogging equipment, the activity can be run quickly, otherwise they may need a demonstration of the kit before they start.

Pupils work in groups. They draw up their own results table, carry out the experiment and plot a bar chart. They answer questions to analyse the results and evaluate the experiment.

Expected outcomes

Pupils carry out the speeding trolleys experiment. They obtain a set of results and suggest a basic conclusion (the higher the ramp, the faster the trolley) and evaluation.

Pitfalls

The results from datalogging are very accurate, perhaps down to several decimal places. Pupils need to round to a suitable number of decimal places.

The experiment must be set up so that the card passes through the light gates and breaks the beam. Light gates should not be too close to windows as the sunlight may affect the results.

Safety notes

Use a catch box at the bottom of the ramp to stop the trolleys.
Make sure the ramps don't fall off the tables.